Change No. 1

FM 5-0, C1
Headquarters
Department of the Army
Washington, DC, 18 March 2011

The Operations Process

1. Change 1 to FM 5-0, 26 March 2010, is updated to align with Change 1 to FM 3-0.

2. This change modifies the Army operational concept to emphasize mission command.

3. This change replaces the command and control element of combat power and warfighting function with mission command.

4. Significant changes are marked with a plus-minus sign at the beginning of the discussion (±).

Remove Old Pages	Insert New Pages
Foreword	n/a
pages i through ix	pages i through viii
pages 1-1 through 1-13	pages 1-1 through 1-11
pages 2-1 through 2-10	pages 2-1 through 2-10
pages 3-1 through 3-6	pages 3-1 through 3-6
pages 3-11 through 3-13	pages 3-11 through 3-13
pages 4-1 through 4-10	pages 4-1 through 4-10
pages 5-1 through 5-4	pages 5-1 through 5-4
pages 5-9 through 5-14	pages 5-9 through 5-14
pages 6-1 through 6-2	pages 6-1 through 6-2
pages 6-5 through 6-8	pages 6-5 through 6-8
pages A-1through A-10	pages A-1through A-10
pages B-1 through B-39	pages B-1 through B-40
pages C-7 through C-10	pages C-7 through C-10
pages D-1 through D-4	pages D-1 through D-4
pages E-1 through E-6	pages E-1 through E-6
pages E-11 through E-27	pages E-11 through E-24
pages F-1 through F-2	pages F-1 through F-2
pages F-5 through F-8	pages F-5 through F-8
pages G-1 through G-2	pages G-1 through G-2
pages Glossary-1 through Glossary-9	pages Glossary-1 through Glossary-9
pages References-1 thru References-4	pages References-1 thru References-4
pages Index-1 through Index-10	pages Index-1 through Index-10

Published by Books Express Publishing
Books Express Publishing, 2011
ISBN 978-1-78039-945-4

Books Express publications are available from all good retail and online booksellers. For
publishing proposals and direct ordering please contact us at: info@books-express.com

5.   File this transmittal sheet in front of the publication for reference purposes.

DISTRUBUTION RESTRICTION: Approved for public release; distribution is unlimited.

By order of the Secretary of the Army:

GEORGE W. CASEY, JR.
General, United States Army
Chief of Staff

Official:

Joyce E. Morrow

JOYCE E. MORROW
Administrative Assistant to the
Secretary of the Army
1104903

DISTRIBUTION:
Active Army, Army National Guard, and United States Army Reserve: Not to be distributed. Electronic media only.

Field Manual
No. 5-0

Headquarters
Department of the Army
Washington, DC, 26 March 2010

The Operations Process

Contents

Distribution Restriction: Approved for public release; distribution is unlimited.

*This publication supersedes FM 5-0, 20 January 2005, and FMI 5-0.1, 31 March 2006.

Figures

Tables

Preface

FM 5-0 (C1), The Operations Process, constitutes the Army's view on planning, preparing, executing, and assessing operations. It describes how commanders—supported by their staffs, subordinate commanders, and other military and civilian partners—exercise mission command during the conduct of full spectrum operations. It describes how design assists commanders with understanding complex problems and developing an operational approach to solve or manage those problems throughout the conduct of operations.

This manual applies to all Army forces. The principal audience for this manual is Army commanders and unit staffs (officers, noncommissioned officers, and Soldiers). Commanders and staffs of Army headquarters serving as a joint task force or a multinational headquarters should also refer to applicable joint or multinational doctrine for the exercise of command and control. Trainers and educators throughout the Army also use this manual.

Terms that have joint or Army definitions are identified in both the glossary and the text. *Glossary references*: The glossary lists most terms used in field manual (FM) 5-0 that have joint or Army definitions. Terms for which FM 5-0 is the proponent field manual (the authority) are indicated with an asterisk in the glossary. *Text references*: Definitions for which FM 5-0 is the proponent field manual are printed in boldface in the text. These terms and their definitions will be incorporated into the next revision of FM 1-02, *Operational Terms and Graphics*. For other definitions in the text, the term is italicized and the number of the proponent manual follows the definition.

FM 5-0 applies to the Active Army, the Army National Guard (ARNG)/Army National Guard of the United States (ARNGUS), and the United States Army Reserve (USAR) unless otherwise stated.

The proponent of this publication is the United .States Army Training and Doctrine Command (TRADOC). The preparing agency is the Combined Arms Doctrine Directorate, U.S. Army Combined Arms Center. Send written comments and recommendations on DA Form 2028 (Recommended Changes to Publications and Blank Forms) to Commander, U.S. Army Combined Arms Center and Fort Leavenworth, ATTN: ATZL-MCK-D (FM 5-0), 300 McPherson Avenue, Fort Leavenworth, KS 66027-2337; by e-mail to: leav-cadd-web-cadd@conus.army.mil; or submit an electronic DA Form 2028.

Introduction

This change to FM 5-0 updates the operations process to account for new doctrine established in change 1 to FM 3-0 (2008). While the major activities of the operations process have not changed, changes in FM 3-0 that significantly impact FM 5-0 include—

- Replacement of the term and definition of **command and control** with the term and definition of **mission command.** The revised definition of mission command now accounts for both the Army's philosophy of command (formerly known as mission command) as well as the exercise of authority and direction to accomplish missions (formerly known as command and control). (**Note**: Joint, other Service, and some allied doctrine retain the term command and control).
- Replacement of the term, definition, and tasks of the **command and control warfighting function** with the term, definition, and tasks of the **mission command warfighting function.**
- Rescindment of the term **battle command.** While the term is rescinded, the commander's activities of understand, visualize, describe, direct, lead, and assess remain the primary activities commanders use to drive the operations process.
- Replacement of the five **Army information tasks** (information engagement, command and control warfare, information protection, operations security, and military deception) with the mission command warfighting task **Conduct inform and influence and cyber/electro-magnetic activities.** As part of this change, the terms **information engagement, command and control warfare,** and **information protection** are rescinded. In addition, the term and definition of **psychological operations** is replaced with the term and definition of **military information support operations**.

FM 5-0, Change 1, provides doctrine on the operations process as a whole, a chapter on design, and a chapter for each activity of the operations process. The appendixes describe the tactics, techniques, and procedures for conducting the military decisionmaking process, conducting troop leading procedures, and writing operation plans and orders.

Chapter 1 provides an overview of the operations process. It describes the general nature of operations in which commanders, supported by their staffs, exercise mission command. Next, this chapter describes the operations process and highlights the commander's role in its execution. Discussions of integrating processes, continuing activities, and running estimates follow. The chapter concludes by discussing fundamentals commanders and staffs consider for the effective execution of the operations process. *Change 1 updates the chapter with the new mission command taxonomy and modifies the fundamentals of the operations process.*

Chapter 2 addresses the planning. It describes planning as an essential element of mission command and a continuous activity of the operations process. This chapter defines planning, describes planning at the different levels of war, and lists the value of effective planning. This chapter concludes offering fundamentals for effective planning and describes the key components of a plan or order. *Change 1 updates the chapter with the new mission command taxonomy.*

Chapter 3 describes design. It describes a methodology that assists commanders, staffs, and others in understanding the operational environment, framing problems, and developing an operational approach to solve those problems. This chapter addresses requirements to reframe the problem when changes in the operational environment render the operational approach and its associated logic no longer applicable. *Change 1 updates the chapter with the new mission command taxonomy.*

Chapter 4 is about preparation—the activity that helps transition the force from planning to execution. The chapter discusses activities within the headquarters and across the force that improve a unit's ability to execute operations. *Change 1 updates the chapter with the new mission command taxonomy and updates the discussion on building partnerships and teams.*

Chapter 5 provides doctrine on execution. It lists fundamentals to guide execution and describes the roles of the commander and staff when directing and synchronizing the current operation. It describes assessment and decisionmaking in execution and concludes with a discussion of the rapid decisionmaking and synchronization process. *Change 1 updates the chapter with the new mission command taxonomy and adds a discussion of operational adaptability.*

Chapter 6 provides the fundamentals of assessment, including its definition and purpose. It describes the assessment process and offers guidelines for effective assessment. *Change 1 updates the chapter with the new mission command taxonomy.*

Ten appendixes complement the body of this manual. Appendix A discusses command post organization and operations. The steps of the military decisionmaking process are in appendix B. Troop leading procedures are addressed in appendix C. Commanders planning guidance and formats for operation plans and orders are addressed in appendixes D and E respectively. Appendix F provides formats for developing task organization. Running estimates are described in appendix G. Guidelines for developing a formal assessment plan are addressed in appendix H. Techniques for conducting rehearsals and developing military briefings are addressed in appendixes I and J respectively. *The updated appendixes account for the new mission command taxonomy to include the mission command warfighting task, "Conduct inform and influence and cyber/electrometric activities." The modified operation order format accounts for these changes.*

This page intentionally left blank.

Chapter 1

±Fundamentals of the Operations Process

This chapter describes the general nature of operations in which commanders, supported by their staffs, exercise mission command. Next, this chapter describes the operations process and highlights the commander's role in its execution. Discussions of the integrating processes, continuing activities, and running estimates follow. The chapter concludes with the fundamentals commanders and staffs consider for the effective execution of the operations process.

±THE NATURE OF OPERATIONS

1-1.   To understand doctrine regarding the operations process, Soldiers first must appreciate the general nature of operations. Military operations are characterized by the continuous, mutual adaptation of give and take, moves and countermoves among all participants. In operations, Army forces face thinking and adaptive enemies, changing civilian perceptions and differing agendas of various actors (organizations and individuals) in an operational area. Leaders can never predict with certainty how enemies or civilians will act and react or how events may develop.

1-2.   The enemy is not an inanimate object to be acted upon but an independent and active force with its own objectives. While friendly forces try to impose their will on the enemy, the enemy resists and seeks to impose its will on friendly forces. This dynamic also occurs among civilian groups whose own desires influence and are influenced by operations. Appreciating these relationships among opposing human wills is essential to understanding the fundamental nature of operations. As all sides take action, each side reacts, learns, and adapts.

1-3.   Whether operations are designed to relieve suffering from a natural disaster or to defeat a large enemy force, operations are conducted in complex, ever-changing, and uncertain operational environments. An *operational environment* is a composite of the conditions, circumstances, and influences that affect the employment of capabilities and bear on the decisions of the commander (JP 3-0). An operational environment includes physical areas (air, land, maritime, and space domains) and cyberspace. It also includes the information that shapes conditions in those areas as well as enemy, adversary, friendly, and neutral aspects relevant to operations. An operational environment is not isolated or independent but interconnected by various influences (for example, information and economics) from around the globe.

COMPLEX AND EVER CHANGING

1-4.   An operational environment is both complex and continuously changing. Complexity describes situations with many parts and subparts (structural complexity) as well as the behaviors and resulting relationships among those parts and subparts (interactive complexity). How the many entities behave and interact with each other within an operational environment is difficult to discern and always results in differing circumstances. No two operational environments are the same. While aspects of an operational environment may be less complex than other aspects, an operational environment as a whole is both structurally and interactively complex.

1-5.   In addition, an operational environment is not static but continually evolves. This evolution results in part, from humans interacting within an operational environment as well as from their ability to learn and adapt. As people take action within an operational environment, the operational environment changes. Some of these changes are anticipated while others are not. Some changes are immediate and apparent while other changes are delayed or hidden. The complex and dynamic nature of an operational environment makes determining the relationship between cause and effect difficult and contributes to the uncertainty of military operations.

UNCERTAINTY

1-6.   Uncertainty is what is not known about a given situation or a lack of understanding of how a situation may evolve. Effective leaders accept that they conduct operations in operational environments that are inherently uncertain. They realize that concrete answers or perfect solutions to operational problems are rarely apparent. For example, the commander and staff may be uncertain about the exact location and strength of an enemy force. Even if the staff feels confident about the enemies location and strength, the commander still questions what to infer from those facts—the enemy's intentions, for example. And even if the commander makes a reasonable inference, the many options available to the enemy make predicting the enemy's exact behavior quite difficult.

1-7.   Similarly, clearly discerning the motivations and reactions of various population groups with respect to the friendly force or the enemy often proves difficult. American ideas of what is normal or rational are not universal. Members of other societies often have different world views, notions of rationality, appropriate behavior, levels of religious devotion, and cultural norms. These differences in perspectives add to the uncertain nature of operations.

1-8.   Chance and friction also contribute to the uncertain nature of operations. Chance is the lack of order or clear predictability of operations. A major sand storm that delays offensive operations or the death of a key local leader that leads to an eruption of violence illustrates chance. Friction is the combination of countless factors that impinge on the conduct of operations. Friction may range from broken equipment that slows movement to unclear and complicated plans that leads to confusion.

1-9.   During operations, leaders make decisions, develop plans, and direct actions under varying degrees of complexity and uncertainty. Predictability in operations is rare, making centralized decisionmaking and orderly processes ineffective. Commanders seek to counter the uncertainty of operations by empowering subordinates at the scene to make decisions, act, and quickly adapt to changing circumstances. As such, commanders exercise mission command throughout the conduct of operations.

±MISSION COMMAND

1-10.   *Mission command* is the exercise of authority and direction by the commander using mission orders to enable disciplined initiative within the commander's intent to empower agile and adaptive leaders in the conduct of full spectrum operations. It is commander-led and blends the art of command and the science of control to integrate the warfighting functions to accomplish the mission (FM 3-0).

1-11.   Effective mission command requires an environment of mutual trust and understanding among commanders and subordinates. It requires a command climate in which commanders encourage subordinates to exercise disciplined initiative to seize opportunities and counter threats within the commander's intent. Through mission orders, commanders focus their orders on the purpose of the operation rather than on the details of how to perform assigned tasks. Doing this minimizes detailed control and allows subordinates the greatest possible freedom of action. Finally, when delegating authority to subordinates, commanders set the necessary conditions for success by allocating appropriate resources to subordinates based on assigned tasks.

1-12.   The commander is the central figure in mission command. Commanders combine the art of command and the science of control to understand situations, make decisions, and direct actions. However, commanders cannot exercise mission command alone except in the smallest organizations. Thus, commanders perform these functions through *mission command networks and systems*—the coordinated application of personnel, networks, procedures, equipment and facilities, knowledge management, and information management systems essential for the commander to conduct operations (FM 3-0).

1-13.   A commander's mission command networks and systems begins with people. No amount of technology can reduce the importance of the human dimension. Therefore, commanders base their mission command networks and systems on human characteristics more than on equipment and procedures. The staff is a key component of the mission command system. Staff members assist commanders and exercise control on their behalf to include—

- Providing relevant information and analyses.
- Maintaining running estimates and making recommendations.

- Preparing plans and orders.
- Monitoring operations.
- Controlling operations.
- Assessing the progress of operations.

See appendix A for a detailed discussion of how commanders organize their headquarters into command posts during the conduct of operations.

±THE OPERATIONS PROCESS

1-14. Throughout operations, commanders, assisted by their staffs, integrate numerous process and activities within the headquarters and across the force as they exercise mission command. The Army's overarching framework to do this is the operations process. The *operations process* consists of the major mission command activities performed during operations: planning, preparing, executing, and continuously assessing the operation. The commander drives the operations process through leadership (FM 3-0). The activities of the operations process are not discrete; they overlap and recur as circumstances demand as shown in figure 1-1.

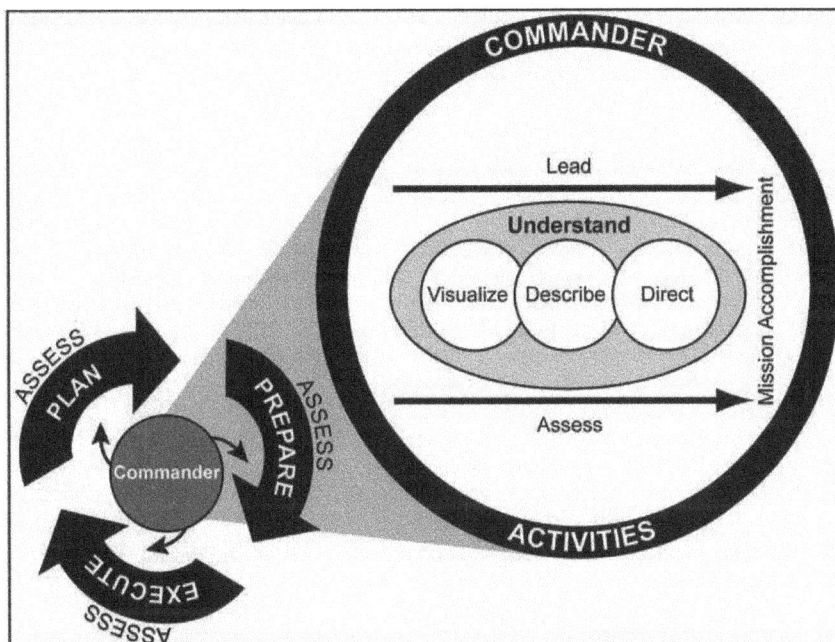

Figure 1-1. The operations process

THE COMMANDER'S ROLE

1-15. At the center of the operations process is the commander. Commanders drive the operations process by combining the art of command with the science of control to understand, visualize, describe, direct, lead, and assess operations. The commander's role in the operations process takes on different emphasis during planning, preparing, executing, and assessing. For example, during planning commanders focus their activities on understanding, visualizing, and describing while directing, leading, and assessing. During execution, commanders often focus on directing, leading, and assessing while improving their understanding and modifying their visualization.

Understand

1-16. Throughout the operations process, commanders seek to build and maintain their understanding of the operational environment and the problem. To understand something is to grasp its nature and significance. Understanding includes establishing context—the set of circumstances that surround a particular event or situation. Commanders lead design activities (see chapter 3) and collaborate and dialog with superior, subordinate, and adjacent commanders, and other military and civilian partners to gain a greater understanding of the operational environment and the problem. Commanders continuously update their understanding throughout the conduct of operations based on inputs from others and their personal observations. Based on their updated understanding to include an assessment of progress, commanders adjust operations as required. (See paragraphs 1-41 to 1-50 for a detailed discussion of situational understanding).

Visualize

1-17. As commanders begin to understand the situation to include the problem, they start envisioning potential solutions. Collectively, this is known as the commander's visualization—the mental process of developing situational understanding, determining a desired end state, and envisioning the broad sequence of events by which the force may achieve the end state. The commander's visualization provides the basis for developing plans and orders. During execution, it helps commanders determine if, when, and what to decide as they adapt to changing conditions.

Describe

1-18. As commanders visualize an operation during planning, they describe it to their staffs and subordinates to facilitate shared understanding of the situation, the mission, and their commander's intent. During planning, commanders ensure subordinates understand the visualization well enough to begin course of action development and preparation activities. Commanders describe their visualization in their initial commander's intent and planning guidance to include an operational approach—the broad general actions that will guide the force toward the desired end state. They describe gaps in their visualization by identifying commander's critical information requirements (CCIRs). During execution, commanders describe their updated visualization as planning guidance that results in fragmentary orders.

Direct

1-19. Commanders direct all aspects of operations. Commanders make decisions and direct actions based on their situational understanding during planning, preparation, execution, and assessment. They use control measures to focus the operation on the desired end state. Commanders direct operations by—

- Preparing and approving plans and orders.
- Assigning and adjusting tasks, task organization, and control measures based on changing conditions.
- Positioning units to maximize combat power, anticipate actions, or create or preserve options.
- Positioning key leaders to ensure observation and supervision at critical times and places.
- Allocating resources based on opportunities and threats.
- Accepting risk to create opportunities to seize, retain, and exploit the initiative.
- Committing the reserve.
- Changing priorities of support.

Lead

1-20. *Leadership* is the process of influencing people by providing purpose, direction, and motivation, while operating to accomplish the mission and improving the organization (FM 6-22). Leadership inspires Soldiers to accomplish things that they otherwise might not. Through leadership, commanders provide purpose, direction, and motivation to subordinate commanders, their staff, and Soldiers throughout the conduct of operations. In turn, Soldiers respond to the leadership of the commander, and may seek to emulate the style of leadership the commander exhibits. (See FM 6-22 for a detailed discussion on leadership).

1-21. Commanders are ultimately responsible for what their forces do or fail to do. As such, where the commander locates within the area of operations is an important consideration. Commanders balance their time between leading the staff through the operations process and providing purpose, direction, and motivation to subordinate commanders and Soldiers away from the command post. No standard pattern or simple prescription exists for command presence; different commanders lead differently.

1-22. By spending time with the staff, the commander learns from the staff while providing knowledge and expertise to ensure directives from the headquarters reflect their intent. By circulating among subordinate units, commanders assess subordinates' preparation and execution, get to know new units in the task organization, and personally motivate Soldiers. Commanders also visit with civilian organization to build teams and partnerships and promote unity of effort.

Assess

1-23. Commanders assess continuously to better understand current conditions and determine how the operation is progressing. Commanders incorporate the assessments of the staff, subordinate commanders, and other partners to form their personal assessment of the situation. (See chapter 6 for doctrine on assessment.) Based on their assessment, commanders modify plans and orders to better accomplish the mission. If their assessment reveals a significant variance from their original commander's visualization, commanders reframe the problem.

ACTIVITIES OF THE OPERATIONS PROCESS

1-24. The activities of the operations process (plan, prepare, execute, and assess) may be sequential at the start of an operation. However, once operations have begun, a headquarters often conducts parts of each activity simultaneously. Planning is continuous. After the completion of the initial order, the commander and staff continuously revise the plan based on changing circumstances. Preparing begins when a unit receives a mission. It always overlaps with planning and continues through execution for some subordinate units. Execution puts a plan into action. As the unit is executing the current operation, the commander and staff are planning future operations based on the assessment of progress. Assessing is continuous and influences the other three activities. Subordinate units of the same command may be in different stages of the operations process. At any time during the operations process, commanders may reframe based on a shift in understanding or significant changes in the operational environment. This may lead to a new perspective on the problem resulting in an entirely new plan.

Planning

1-25. Planning is the art and science of understanding a situation, envisioning a desired future, and laying out effective ways of bringing that future about. Planning is both conceptual and detailed. Conceptual planning includes developing an understanding of the operational environment, framing the problem, defining a desired end state, and developing an operational approach to achieve the desired end state. Conceptual planning generally corresponds to the art of operations and is commander led. Both design (see chapter 3) and the military decisionmaking process (see appendix B) assist commanders and staffs with the conceptual aspects of planning. Detailed planning translates the operational approach into a complete and practical plan. Detailed planning generally corresponds to the science of operations and encompasses the specifics of implementation. Detailed planning works out the scheduling, coordination, or technical issues involved with moving, sustaining, administering, and directing forces.

1-26. Planning results in a plan or order that communicates the commander visualization and directs actions of subordinates focusing on the desired end state. Planning is continuous. While planning may start an iteration of the operations process, commanders and staffs revise plans and develop branches and sequels during execution (see chapter 2 for the fundamentals of planning).

Preparation

1-27. Preparation consists of activities that units perform to improve their ability to execute an operation. Activities of preparation help the force and Soldiers improve their ability to execute an operation. Preparation creates conditions that improve friendly forces' opportunities for success. It requires staff, unit, and Soldier actions to transition the force from planning to execution. It includes building effective teams among modular formation and with joint, interagency, intergovernmental, and multinational partners.

1-28. Activities of preparation help develop a shared understanding of the situation and what is required for execution. These activities—such as backbriefs, rehearsals, and inspections—help units, staffs, and Soldiers better understand their roles in upcoming operations, practice complicated tasks, and ensure equipment and weapons function properly. (Chapter 4 addresses preparation in detail.)

Execution

1-29. Planning and preparation accomplish nothing if the commander does not execute effectively. Execution is putting a plan into action while using situational understanding to assess progress and adjust operations as the situation changes. Execution focuses on concerted action to seize and retain the initiative, build and maintain momentum, and exploit success. Commanders create conditions for seizing the initiative by acting while encouraging operational adaptability across the force. (Chapter 5 discusses execution.)

Assessment

1-30. Assessment is continuously monitoring and evaluating the current situation and the progress of an operation. Assessment involves continuously analyzing the operational environment to help commanders and their staffs understand the current situation and its evolution during operations. Based on this understanding, commanders and staffs evaluate relevant information to help them judge how operations are progressing toward achieving objectives and the desired end state.

1-31. Assessment precedes and guides the other activities of the operations process and concludes each operation or phase of an operation. However, the focus of assessment differs during planning, preparation, and execution. During planning, assessment focuses on gathering information about the operational environment to assist the commander and staff with understanding the current situation. Assessment activities during planning also include developing an assessment plan that describes measurable tasks, objectives, end state conditions, and associated criterion to assist with assessing progress. During preparation and execution, assessment focuses on monitoring the current situation and evaluating the operation's progress toward stated objectives and end state conditions.

±INTEGRATING PROCESSES AND CONTINUING ACTIVITIES

1-32. Throughout the operations process, commanders and staffs synchronize the warfighting functions in accordance with the commander's intent and concept of operations. Commanders and staffs use several integrating processes and continuing activities to do this.

1-33. Integrating processes combine efforts of the commander and staff to synchronize specific functions throughout the operations process. The integrating process includes—
- Intelligence preparation of the battlefield. (See FM 2-01.3.)
- Targeting. (See FM 3-60.)
- Intelligence, surveillance, and reconnaissance synchronization. (See TC 2-01.)
- Composite risk management. (See FM 5-19.)
- Knowledge management. (See FM 6-01.1.)

1-34. The commander and staff also ensure several activities are continuously planned for and coordinated. The following continuing activities require particular concern of the commander and staff throughout the operations process:
- Intelligence, surveillance, and reconnaissance. (See TC 2-01.)
- Security operations. (See FM 3-90.)
- Protection. (See FM 3-37.)
- Liaison and coordination. (See FM 6-0.)
- Terrain management. (See FM 3-90.)
- Information management. (See FM 6-0.)
- Airspace command and control. (See FM 3-52.)

±RUNNING ESTIMATES

1-35. The running estimate is a principle knowledge management tool used by the commander and staff throughout the operations process. A running estimate assesses the current situation to determine if the current operation is proceeding according to the commander's intent and if future operations are supportable.

1-36. Effective plans and successful execution hinge on current running estimates. Running estimates always include recommendations for anticipated decisions. During planning, commanders use these recommendations to select feasible courses of action for further analysis. During preparation and execution, commanders use recommendations from running estimates in decisionmaking. Failure to maintain running estimates may lead to errors or omissions that result in flawed plans or bad decisions.

1-37. The commander's running estimate includes a summary of the problem, the operational approach, and all variables that affect the mission. Commanders integrate personal knowledge of the situation, analysis of the operational and mission variables, assessments by subordinate commanders and other organizations, and relevant details gained from running estimates. Commanders use their personal estimates to cross-check and supplement the running estimates of the staff. (See appendix G for more detailed discussion on running estimates.)

±FUNDAMENTALS

1-38. The operations process, while simple in concept (plan, prepare, execute, and assess), is dynamic in execution. Commanders and staffs use the operations process to integrate numerous processes and activities executed throughout the headquarters and subordinate units. Commanders organize and train their staff to plan, prepare, and execute operations simultaneously while continually assessing. Commanders are responsible for training their staffs as integrated teams to do this. They use the following fundamentals to guide the effective execution of the operations process:

- Commanders drive the operations process.
- Situational understanding is fundamental to effective decisionmaking throughout the operations process.
- Design pervades the operations process.
- Commanders continually consider and combine tasks focused on the population as well as those tasks focused on enemy forces.
- Continuous assessment enables organizational learning and operational adaptability.

COMMANDER CENTRIC

Commanders drive the operations process.

1-39. Commanders are the most important participant in the operations process. While staffs perform essential functions that amplify the effectiveness of operations, commanders play the central role in the operations process by applying the art of command and science of control to understand, visualize, describe, direct, lead, and assess operations. Through leadership—the process of influencing people by providing purpose, direction, and motivation—commanders drive the operations process. Commanders rely on their education, experience, knowledge, and judgment as they make decisions and lead subordinates throughout the conduct of operations.

1-40. Mission command requires commanders to take prudent risks, exercise initiative, and act decisively. Because uncertainty exists in all military operations, commanders incur risk when making decisions during the conduct of operations. Faced with an uncertain situation, there is a natural tendency to hesitate and gather more information to reduce the uncertainty. However, waiting and gathering information might reduce uncertainty but will not eliminate it. Waiting may even increase uncertainty by providing the enemy with time to seize the initiative or it may allow events to deteriorate. It is far better to manage uncertainty by acting and developing the situation.

SITUATIONAL UNDERSTANDING

Situational understanding is fundamental to effective decisionmaking throughout the operations process.

1-41. *Situational understanding* is the product of applying analysis and judgment to relevant information to determine the relationships among the mission variables to facilitate decisionmaking (FM 3-0). Success in operations demands timely and effective decisions based on applying judgment to available information and knowledge. Building and maintaining situational understanding is essential for commanders when establishing the situation's context, developing effective plans, assessing operations, and making quality decisions during execution.

1-42. Commanders and staffs continually work to maintain their situational understanding and work through periods of reduced understanding as the situation evolves. As commanders develop their situational understanding, they see patterns emerge, dissipate, and reappear in their operational environment. These patterns help them direct their own forces' actions with respect to other friendly forces, civilian organizations, the enemy, the terrain, and the population. While complete understanding is the ideal for planning and decisionmaking, commanders accept they will often have to act despite significant gaps in their understanding.

Operational and Misson Variables

1-43. Commanders and staffs use the operational and mission variables to help build their situational understanding. They analyze and describe an operational environment in terms of eight interrelated operational variables: political, military, economic, social, information, infrastructure, physical environment, and time (known as PMESII-PT). (See FM 3-0.) Upon receipt of a mission, commanders filter information categorized by the operational variables into relevant information with respect to the mission. They use the mission variables, in combination with the operational variables, to refine their understanding of the situation and to visualize, describe, and direct operations. The mission variables are mission, enemy, terrain and weather, troops and support available, time available, and civil considerations. As a set, the mission variables are abbreviated METT-TC. (See FM 3-0.)

Cultural Understanding

1-44. As part of building their situational understanding, commanders consider how culture (both their own and others' within an operational area) affects operations. Culture is the shared beliefs, values, customs, behaviors, and artifacts members of a society use to cope with the world and each other. Culture influences how people make judgments about what is right and wrong and how they assess what is important and unimportant. Culture provides a framework for rational thought and decisions. What one culture considers rational another culture may consider irrational.

1-45. Understanding the culture of a particular society or group within a society can significantly improve the force's ability to accomplish the mission. Leaders are mindful of cultural factors in three contexts:

- Awareness of the cultures within a region that the organization operates.
- Sensitivity to the different backgrounds, traditions, and operational methods of the various military (joint and multinational), civilian (intergovernmental, nongovernmental, and private), and host-nation organizations.
- Awareness of how one's own culture affects how one perceives a situation.

1-46. Understanding other cultures applies to all operations, not just those dominated by stability. For example, some enemies consider surrender a dishonor worse than death whereas others consider surrender an honorable option. Commanders use different tactics with the enemy depending on the culture.

1-47. Understanding the culture of joint and multinational forces and civilian organizations within an operational area is crucial to successful operations. Army leaders learn the customs as well as the doctrine and procedures of their partners. These leaders consider how culture influences how their military and civilian partners understand situations and arrive at decisions. This understanding helps build unity of effort.

1-48. Effective Army leaders understand and appreciate their own culture (individual, military, and national) in relation to the various cultures of others in the operational area. Just as culture shapes how other groups view themselves and the world around them, culture shapes how commanders, leaders, and Soldiers perceive the world. Individuals tend to interpret events according to the principles and values intrinsic to their culture. Effective commanders acknowledge that their individual perceptions greatly influence how they understand situations and make decisions. Through reflection, collaboration, and analysis of differences between their culture and that of the cultures in the operational area, commanders expose and question their assumptions about the situation. (See FM 3-24 and FM 2-01.3 for details to analyze socio-cultural data.)

Red Teaming

1-49. Red teams also assist the commander and staff in building and maintaining their understanding. Red teaming is a function that provides commanders an independent ability to fully explore alternative plans and operations in the context of the operational environment and from the perspective of partners, adversaries, and others. Red teams assist the commander and staff with critical and creative thinking and help them avoid groupthink, mirror imaging, cultural missteps, and tunnel vision throughout the conduct of operations.

1-50. Throughout the operations process, red team members help identify relevant actors, clarify the problem, and explain how others may view the problem from their perspectives. They challenge assumptions and the analysis used to build the plan. In essence, red teams provide the commander and staff with an independent capability to challenge the organization's thinking.

DESIGN

Design pervades the operations process.

1-51. Design underpins the commander's role in leading innovative, adaptive efforts throughout the operations process. Design—an approach to critical and creative thinking—assists commanders with understanding, visualizing, and describing problems and developing approaches to solve them. Commanders use design to gain a greater understanding of the operational environment and an appreciation of the problem. They visualize and describe an operational approach that serves as the main idea. This idea informs detailed planning and guides the force through preparation and execution. While continuously assessing changes in the operational environment and the progress of operations, design helps commanders determine if they need to reframe the problem, which may lead to a new operational approach. (Chapter 3 discusses design in detail). Key aspects of design continuously applied throughout the operations process include—

- Critical and creative thinking.
- Collaboration and dialog.

Critical and Creative Thinking

1-52. To assist commanders in understanding and decisionmaking, commanders and staffs apply critical and creative thinking throughout the operations process. Critical thinking is a deliberate process of thought used to discern truth in situations where direct observation is insufficient, impossible, or impractical. Critical thinkers are purposeful and reflective thinkers that apply self-regulating judgment about what to believe or what to do in response to observations, experience, verbal or written expressions, or arguments. Critical thinking involves determining the meaning and significance of what is observed or expressed. It also involves determining whether adequate justification exists to accept conclusions as true based on a given inference or argument. Critical thinking is key to understanding situations, identifying problems, finding causes, arriving at justifiable conclusions, making quality plans, and assessing the progress of operations.

1-53. Creative thinking involves creating something new or original. Often leaders face unfamiliar problems or old problems requiring new solutions. Creative thinking leads to new insights, novel approaches, fresh perspectives, and new ways of understanding and conceiving things. Leaders look at different options to solve problems by using adaptive approaches (drawing from previous similar circumstances) or innovative approaches (coming up with completely new ideas). In both instances, leaders use creative thinking to apply imagination and depart from the old way of doing things. (See FM 6-22 for a detailed discussion on critical and creative thinking.)

Collaboration and Dialog

1-54. Commanders encourage active collaboration and dialog throughout the operations process. Collaboration and dialog aids in developing shared situational understanding throughout the force. Throughout the operations process, commanders, subordinate commanders, staffs, and other partners collaborate and dialog actively, sharing and questioning information, perceptions, and ideas to better understand situations and make decisions. Collaboration is two or more people or organizations working together toward common goals by sharing knowledge and building consensus. Dialog is a way to collaborate that involves the candid exchange of ideas or opinions among participants that encourages frank discussions in areas of disagreement.

1-55. Effective collaboration includes continuous dialog that leads to increased understanding of the situation across the force, including the current problems. In addition to the organizations within their command, commanders also collaborate with civilian and other military organizations in the operational area to better understand their perspectives and build unity of effort. This leads to a shared understanding of the situation and improves coordination and cooperation among all participants toward common objectives.

1-56. Through collaboration and dialog, the commander creates a learning environment by allowing participants to think critically and creatively and share their ideas, opinions, and recommendations without fear of retribution. Groupthink—a characteristic exhibited by members of a group who seek to reach consensus on issues while minimizing conflict within the group—is the antithesis of healthy collaboration. Effective collaboration and dialog requires candor and a free, yet mutually respectful, competition of ideas. Participants must feel free to make viewpoints based on their expertise, experience, and insight; this includes sharing ideas that contradict the opinions held by those of higher rank. Successful commanders willingly listen to novel ideas and counter arguments concerning any problem.

1-57. Disciplined questioning helps commanders, staffs, subordinate commanders, and other partners probe their own and others' thinking as they collaborate and dialog. Disciplined questioning helps to explore ideas, understand problems, and uncover assumptions. These questions help challenge claims or premises by revealing a contradiction or internal inconsistency in logic. Examples of disciplined questions that probe reasons and evidence include the following:

- Could you give me an example?
- How does X relate to Y?
- When you say X, are you implying Y?
- All your reasoning depends on the idea that X exists. Why have you based your reasoning on X instead of Y?
- Why do you think that is true? What is your evidence?

1-58. Collaboration occurs during planning and continues through execution regardless of the physical location of participants. Today's information systems and collaborative planning tools enable commanders and staffs worldwide to collaborate in real time. During planning, commanders, subordinates, and other partners share their understanding of the situation, participate in course of action development and decisionmaking, and resolve conflicts before the higher headquarters issues the operation order. This collaboration results in an improved understanding of the situation, commander's intent, concept of operations, and tasks to subordinate units throughout the force. Since all echelons develop their plans nearly simultaneously, collaborative planning shortens planning time.

1-59. Similar benefits of collaboration apply during preparation and execution. Commanders, subordinates, and partners compare assessments of the situation and exchange ideas on how to act during execution. Coupled with firm decisionmaking by the commander, collaboration and dialog enable the force to adapt more quickly in changing conditions. Assessment, which occurs continuously, is also enhanced when commanders and subordinates collaborate in assessing the progress of the operation, to include sharing ideas on what is or is not working and how to modify plans to better accomplish the mission. Knowledge management facilitates collaboration and the transfer of knowledge among the commander, staff, subordinate commanders, and other partners throughout the operations process. (See FM 6-01.1.)

FULL SPECTRUM OPERATIONS

Commanders continually consider and combine tasks focused on the population as well as those tasks focused on enemy forces.

1-60. Military operations involve more than combat between armed opponents. Winning battle and engagements while shaping the civilian situation is critical to long-term success. Because of this, commanders conduct full spectrum operations—offense, defense, stability or civil support operations—to balance actions taken to protect the population with actions taken against the enemy. Commanders continually consider and combine stability tasks focused on the population with offensive and defensive tasks forces on the enemy throughout the operations process. For homeland security, commanders focus tasks on civil support with defensive and offensive tasks. No single element is always more important than the others. Rather, combinations of the elements, which commanders constantly adapt to changing conditions, are the key to successful full spectrum operations.

ASSESS, LEARN, AND ADAPT

Continuous assessment enables organizational learning and operational adaptability.

1-61. Army organizations must learn throughout the conduct of operations to effectively adapt to changing circumstances. Assessment is a continuous activity of the operations process and a primary feedback mechanism that enables the command as a whole to learn and adapt (see chapter 6).

1-62. Plans are based on imperfect understanding and assumptions on how the commander expects a situation to evolve. Continuous assessment helps commanders recognize shortcomings in the plan and changes in the operational environment. During execution, commanders and their staffs principally learn by assessing the results of action. In those instances when assessment reveals minor variances from the commander's visualization, commanders adjust plans as required. In those instances when assessment reveals a significant variance from the commander's original visualization, commanders reframe the problem and develop an entirely new plan as required.

1-63. The learning that occurs through assessment enables operational adaptability—a quality that Army leaders and forces exhibit based on critical and creative thinking, comfort with ambiguity and uncertainty, a willingness to accept prudent risk, and their ability to rapidly adjust to changing circumstances. Operational adaptability requires a mindset based on flexibility of thought calling for leaders at all levels who are comfortable with collaborative planning and decentralized execution, have a tolerance for ambiguity, and possess the ability and willingness to make rapid adjustments according to the situation.

This page intentionally left blank.

Chapter 2
Planning

This chapter provides an overview of planning. It describes planning as an essential element of mission command and a continuous activity of the operations process. It defines planning, describes planning at the different levels of war, and lists the value of effective planning. This chapter concludes by offering fundamentals for effective planning and describing how to develop key components of a plan or order.

PLANNING AND PLANS

2-1.   *Planning* is the process by which commanders (and the staff, if available) translate the commander's visualization into a specific course of action for preparation and execution, focusing on the expected results (FM 3-0). Put another way, planning is the art and science of understanding a situation, envisioning a desired future, and laying out an operational approach to achieve that future. Based on this understanding and operational approach, planning continues with the development of a fully synchronized operation plan or order that arranges potential actions in time, space, and purpose to guide the force during execution.

2-2.   Planning is both a continuous and a cyclical activity of the operations process. While planning may start an iteration of the operations process, planning does not stop with production of an order. During preparation and execution, the plan is continuously refined as situational understanding improves. Through assessment, subordinates and others provide feedback as to what is working, what is not working, and how the force can do things better. In some circumstances, commanders may determine that the current order (to include associated branches and sequels) is no longer relevant to the situation. In these instances, commanders reframe the problem and initiate planning activities to develop a new plan.

2-3.   Planning may be highly structured involving commanders, staff, subordinate commanders, and others to develop a fully synchronized plan. Planning is also less structured, such as platoon leaders and squad leaders rapidly determining a scheme of maneuver for a hasty attack. Planning is conducted for different planning horizons, from long-range to short-range. Depending on the echelon and circumstances, units may plan in years, months, or weeks, or in days, hours, and minutes.

2-4.   A product of planning is a plan or order—a directive for future action. Commanders issue plans and orders to subordinates to communicate their understanding of the situation and their visualization of an operation. A plan is a continuous, evolving framework of anticipated actions that maximizes opportunities. It guides subordinates as they progress through each phase of the operation. Any plan is a framework from which to adapt, not a script to be followed to the letter. The measure of a good plan is not whether execution transpires as planned, but whether the plan facilitates effective action in the face of unforeseen events. Good plans and orders foster initiative.

2-5.   Plans and orders come in many forms and vary in scope, complexity, and length of time addressed. Generally, a plan is developed well in advance of execution and is not executed until directed. A plan becomes an order when directed for execution based on a specific time or an event. Some planning results in written orders complete with attachments. Other planning produces brief fragmentary orders issued verbally and followed in writing. See appendix E for instructions and formats for writing plans and orders.

PLANNING AND THE LEVELS OF WAR

2-6.   The levels of war help clarify the links between strategic objectives and tactical actions. The three levels are strategic, operational, and tactical, although no distinct limits or boundaries exist between them.

2-7.   The levels of war correspond to specific levels of responsibility and planning with decisions at one level affecting other levels. Among the levels of war, the planning horizons differ greatly.

2-8.   Joint strategic planning provides strategic guidance and direction to friendly forces for security cooperation planning, joint operations planning, and force planning. Joint strategic planning occurs primarily at the national and theater strategic levels. This planning helps the President, the Secretary of Defense, and other members of the National Security Council—

- Formulate political-military assessments.
- Define political and military objectives and end states.
- Develop strategic concepts and options.
- Allocate resources.

2-9.   Combatant commanders prepare strategic estimates, strategies, and plans to accomplish their mission. Commanders base these estimates, strategies, and plans on strategic guidance and direction from the President, Secretary of Defense, and Chairman of the Joint Chiefs of Staff. (See JP 5-0 for more information on joint strategic planning.)

2-10. Typically, operational-level planning focuses on developing plans for campaigns and major operations. Joint force commanders (combatant commanders and their subordinate joint task force commanders) and their component commanders (Service and functional) conduct operational-level planning. Planning at the operational level focuses on *operational art*, the application of creative imagination by commanders and staffs—supported by their skill, knowledge, and experience—to design strategies, campaigns, and major operations and organize and employ military forces. Operational art integrates ends, ways, and means across the levels of war (JP 3-0). Operational-level planners use the Joint Operation Planning and Execution System (known as JOPES), the joint operation planning process (known as JOPP), and elements of operational design to develop campaign plans, joint operation plans and orders, and supporting plans. (JP 5-0 discusses joint operation planning. JP 3-31 discusses operational level planning from a land component perspective.)

2-11. While components of a joint force assist joint force commanders in developing a campaign plan, Army forces do not develop independent campaign plans. A *campaign plan* is a joint operation plan for a series of related major operations aimed at achieving strategic or operational objectives within a given time and space (JP 5-0). Army forces develop supporting plans (operation plans and orders) nested with the joint force commander's campaign plan.

2-12. Operational- and tactical-level planning complement each other but have different aims. Operational-level planning involves broader dimensions of time, space, and purpose than tactical-level planning involves. It is often more complex and less defined. Operational-level planners need to define an operational area, estimate forces required, and evaluate operation requirements. In contrast, tactical-level planning proceeds from an existing operational design. Normally, areas of operations are prescribed, objectives and available forces are identified, and sequences of activities are specified for tactical-level commanders.

2-13. Tactical-level planning revolves around how best to achieve objectives and accomplish tasks assigned by higher headquarters. Planning horizons for tactical-level planning are relatively shorter than planning horizons for operational-level planning. While tactical-level planning works within the framework of an operational-level plan, tactical planning includes developing long-range plans for solving complex problems. These plans combine offensive, defensive, and stability or civil support operations to achieve objectives and accomplish the mission over extended periods.

THE VALUE OF PLANNING

2-14. All planning is based on imperfect knowledge and assumptions about the future. Planning cannot predict exactly what the effects of the operation will be, how enemies will behave with precision, or how civilians will respond to the friendly force or the enemy. Nonetheless, the understanding and learning that occurs during planning have great value. Even if units do not execute the plan precisely as envisioned—and few ever do—the process of planning results in improved situational understanding that facilitates future decisionmaking. General of the Army Dwight D. Eisenhower referred to this quality of planning when saying, "Plans are worthless, but planning is everything."

2-15. All military activities benefit from some kind of planning. If commanders had no way to influence the future, if they believed that the natural course of events would lead to a satisfactory outcome, or if they could achieve the desired results purely by reacting, they would have no reason to plan. While there may be instances where these conditions apply, they are rare. Planning and plans help leaders—

- Understand and develop solutions to problems.
- Anticipate events and adapt to changing circumstances.
- Task-organize the force and prioritize efforts.
- Direct, coordinate, and synchronize action.

PLANNING HELPS LEADERS UNDERSTAND AND DEVELOP SOLUTIONS TO PROBLEMS

2-16. A problem is an issue or obstacle that makes it difficult to achieve a desired goal or objective. In a broad sense, a problem exists when an individual becomes aware of a significant difference between what actually is and what is desired. In the context of operations, an operational problem is the issue or set of issues that impede commanders from achieving their desired end state.

2-17. Throughout operations, Army leaders face various problems, often requiring unique and creative solutions. Planning helps commanders and staffs understand problems and develop solutions. Not all problems require the same level of planning. For simple problems, leaders often identify them and quickly decide on a solution—sometimes on the spot. Planning is critical, however, when a problem is actually a set of interrelated issues, and the solution to each affects the others. For complex situations, planning offers ways to deal with the complete set of problems as a whole. Some situations require extensive planning, some very little. In general, the more complex a situation, the more important and involved the planning effort.

2-18. Just as planning is only part of the operations process, planning is only part of problem solving. In addition to planning, problem solving includes implementing the planned solution (execution), learning from the implementation of the solution (assessment), and modifying or developing a new solution as required. The object of problem solving is not just to solve near-term problems but to do so in a way that forms the basis for long-term success.

2-19. The Army problem solving model appears in figure 2-1. Army problem solving applies to all Army activities, not just operations. The Army problem solving model establishes the base logic for the military decisionmaking process and troop leading procedures.

```
• Identify the problem.
• Gather information.
• Determine evaluation criteria.
• Generate potential solutions.
• Analyze potential solutions.
• Select the best solution.
• Make and implement the decision. .
```

±Figure 2-1. The Army problem solving model

2-20. Depending on the structure of the problem, leaders may take different approaches to both understanding problems and developing solutions. (See table 2-1.) The degree of interactive complexity of a given situation (see chapter 1) is the primary factor that determines the problem's structure. In terms of structure, there are three types of problems: well-structured, medium-structured, and ill-structured. Perception of the individual as to whether a problem is well, medium, or ill structured depends, in part, on the knowledge, skills, and ability of that individual.

Table 2-1. Types of problems and solution strategies

	Well-structured	Medium-structured	Ill-structured
Problem Structuring	The problem is self-evident.	Professionals easily agree on its structure.	Professionals have difficulty agreeing on problem structure and will have to agree on a shared hypothesis.
Solution Development	Solution techniques are available and there are verifiable solutions.	There may be more than one "right" answer. Professionals may disagree on the best solution. A desired end state can be agreed on.	Professionals will disagree on— • How the problem can be solved. • The most desirable end state. • Whether the end state can be attained.
Execution of Solution	Success requires learning to perfect technique.	Success requires learning to perfect techniques and to adjust the solution.	Success requires learning to perfect technique, adjust the solution, and continuously refine understanding of the problem.
Adaptive Iteration	No adaptive iteration required.	Adaptive iteration is required to find the best solution.	Adaptive iteration is required both to refine the problem and to find the best solution.

Well-Structured Problems

2-21. Well-structured problems are easy to identify, required information is available, and methods to solve them are fairly obvious. While often difficult to solve, well-structured problems have verifiable solutions. Problems of mathematics and time and space relationships, as in the case with detailed logistics planning and engineering projects, illustrate well-structured problems.

Medium-Structured Problems

2-22. Medium-structured problems are more interactively complex than well-structured problems. For example, a field manual describes how a battalion task force conducts a defense, but it offers no single solution that applies to all circumstances. Leaders can agree on the problem ("how best to conduct a defense"), appropriate tasks, and the end state for the operation. However, they may disagree about how to apply the doctrinal principles to a specific piece of terrain against a specific enemy. Furthermore, a defense can succeed against one enemy yet fail against another under precisely the same circumstances. Success and failure may differ as a function of interactive complexity rather than a structure or technical difference between the two enemy forces. Success during execution requires not only learning to perfect a technique but also adjusting the solution based on changing conditions. Army problem solving, the military decisionmaking process (MDMP) (see appendix B), and troop leading procedures (TLP) (see appendix C) are methods to help leaders understand and develop solutions for medium-structured problems.

Ill-Structured Problems

2-23. Ill-structured problems are the most interactive. They are also complex, nonlinear, and dynamic— and therefore the most challenging to solve. Unlike well- or medium-structured problems, leaders disagree about how to solve ill-structured problems, what the end state should be, and whether the desired end state is even achievable. At the root of this lack of consensus is the difficulty in agreeing on what is the problem. Unlike medium-structured problems, there is no clear action to take because the nature of the problem itself is not clear. This is often the case in operations involving multiple military (joint and multinational) and civilian organizations over extended periods. Leaders use design to help them understand complex, ill-structured problems and to develop a broad operational approach to manage or solve them. (See chapter 3.) Based on this understanding and operational approach, Army leaders continue more detailed planning using the MDMP to develop a fully synchronized plan or order that serves as the practical scheme for solving the problem.

PLANNING HELPS ANTICIPATE EVENTS AND ADAPT TO CHANGING CIRCUMSTANCES

2-24. The defining challenges to effective planning are uncertainty and time. Uncertainty increases with the length of the planning horizon and the rate of change in the operational environment. Planning horizon refers to how far into the future commanders try to shape events. The farther into the future the commander plans, the wider the range of possibilities and the more uncertain the forecast.

2-25. A fundamental tension exists between the desire to plan far into the future to facilitate preparation and coordination and the fact that the farther into the future the commander plans, the less certain the plan will remain relevant. Given the fundamentally uncertain nature of operations, the object of planning is not to eliminate uncertainty but to develop a framework for action in the midst of such uncertainty. Planning provides an informed forecast of how future events may unfold. It entails identifying and evaluating potential decisions and actions in advance to include thinking through consequences of certain actions. Planning involves thinking about ways to influence the future as well as how to respond to potential events. Put simply, planning is thinking critically and creatively about what to do, how to do it, and what can go wrong along the way.

2-26. Planning keeps the force oriented on future objectives despite the requirements of current operations. By anticipating events beforehand, planning helps the force seize or retain the initiative. To seize the initiative, the force anticipates events and acts purposefully and effectively before the enemy can act or before situations deteriorate. (For example, the force identifies the possibility of and implements controls to prevent large-scale looting by the populace.)

2-27. Planning entails identifying and evaluating potential decisions and actions in advance rather than responding to events as they unfold. Planning involves visualizing consequences of possible courses of action to determine whether they will contribute to achieving the desired end state.

2-28. Effective planning also anticipates the inherent delay between decision and action, especially between the levels of war and echelons. Sound plans draw on fundamentals of mission command to overcome this effect, fostering initiative within the commander's intent to act appropriately and decisively when orders no longer address the changing situation sufficiently. This ensures commanders act promptly as they encounter opportunities or accept risk to create opportunities and counter threats when they lack clear direction. Identifying decision points and developing branch plans and sequels are keys to anticipating events and are inherent in effective planning.

2-29. A *branch* describes the contingency options built into the base plan. A branch is used for changing the mission, orientation, or direction of movement of a force to aid success of the operation based on anticipated events, opportunities, or disruptions caused by enemy actions and reactions (JP 5-0). Branches are also used in stability operations to address how civilians potentially act and react.

2-30. In a campaign, a *sequel* is a major operation that follows the current major operation. In a single major operation, a sequel is the next phase. Plans for a sequel are based on the possible outcomes (success, stalemate, or defeat) associated with the current operation (JP 5-0). A counteroffensive, for example, logically follows a defense; exploitation and pursuit follow successful attacks. Building partner capacity is a logical sequence to restoring essential services, and security force assistance is a logical sequel to restoring minimum civil security. Normally, executing a sequel begins another phase of an operation if not a new operation. Branches and sequels are tied to execution criteria. Commanders carefully review them before execution and update them based on assessment of current operations.

PLANS TASK-ORGANIZE THE FORCE AND PRIORITIZE EFFORTS

2-31. When developing their concept of operations, commanders first visualize the decisive operation and develop shaping and sustaining operations to support the decisive operation. The decisive operation is the focal point around which commanders develop the entire operation and prioritize effort. When developing their concept of operations and associated tasks to subordinate units, commanders ensure subordinates have the means to accomplish them. They do this by task-organizing the force and establishing priorities of support.

2-32. Task-organizing is the act of configuring an operating force, support staff, or sustainment package of specific size and composition to meet a unique task or mission. It includes allocating available assets to subordinate commanders and establishing their command and support relationships. Through task organization, commanders establish relationships and allocate resources to weight the decisive operation. Task-organizing results in task organization—a temporary grouping of forces designed to accomplish a particular mission. Appendix F contains guidelines and formats for developing task organizations.

2-33. In addition to task-organizing, commanders establish priorities of support. ***Priority of support* is a priority set by the commander to ensure a subordinate unit has support in accordance with its relative importance to accomplish the mission**. Priorities of movements, fires, sustainment, and protection all illustrate priorities of support that commanders use to weight the decisive operation.

2-34. The concept of operations may also identify a main effort if required; otherwise, the priorities of support go to the unit conducting the decisive operation. The *main effort* is the designated subordinate unit whose mission at a given point in time is most critical to overall mission success. It is usually weighted with the preponderance of combat power (FM 3-0). Designating a main effort temporarily gives that unit priority of support. Commanders shift resources and priorities to the main effort as circumstances and the commander's intent require. Commanders may shift the main effort several times during an operation. A unit conducting a shaping operation may be designated as the main effort until the decisive operation commences. However, the unit with primary responsibility for the decisive operation becomes the main effort upon execution of the decisive operation.

PLANS DIRECT, COORDINATE, AND SYNCHRONIZE ACTION

2-35. Plans and orders direct, coordinate, and synchronize subordinate actions and inform those outside the unit how to cooperate and provide support. Effective plans clearly stipulate end state conditions and objectives that help coordinate the activities of the force. Good plans direct subordinate actions by stating who, what (the task), where, when, and why (the purpose to perform the task). They leave much of the how (the method to perform the task) to subordinates. Directing and coordinating actions synchronize the force as a whole to accomplish the mission. A key aspect of planning is synchronization—arranging actions in time, space, and purpose to generate maximum effort or combat power at the decisive point and time.

2-36. Synchronization is a way, not an end. Commanders balance it with agility and initiative. However, overemphasizing the directing and coordinating functions of planning can result in detailed and rigid plans that stifle initiative. Mission command encourages the use of mission orders to avoid creating overly restrictive instructions to subordinates. Mission orders direct, coordinate, and synchronize action while allowing subordinates the maximum freedom of action to accomplish missions within the commander's intent.

CONCEPTUAL AND DETAILED PLANNING

2-37. Planning activities occupy a continuum ranging from conceptual to detailed. (See figure 2-2.) On one end of the continuum is conceptual planning. Developing tactical and operational concepts for the overall conduct of military operations is conceptual planning. Understanding the operational environment and the problem, determining the operation's end state, establishing objectives, and sequencing the operation in broad terms all illustrate conceptual planning. Conceptual planning helps answer questions of what to do and why. In general, conceptual planning focuses heavily on synthesis supported by analysis. Conceptual planning generally corresponds to the art of operations and is the focus of the commander with staff support. The commander's activities of understanding and visualization are key aspects of conceptual planning.

2-38. At the other end of the continuum is detailed planning. Detailed planning translates the broad operational approach into a complete and practical plan. Generally, detailed planning is associated with the science of war and falls under the purview of the staff, focusing on specifics of execution. Detailed planning works out the scheduling, coordination, or technical problems involved with moving, sustaining, synchronizing, and directing the force. Unlike conceptual planning, detailed planning does not involve establishing end state conditions and objectives; instead, it works out actions to accomplish the commander's intent and concept of operations.

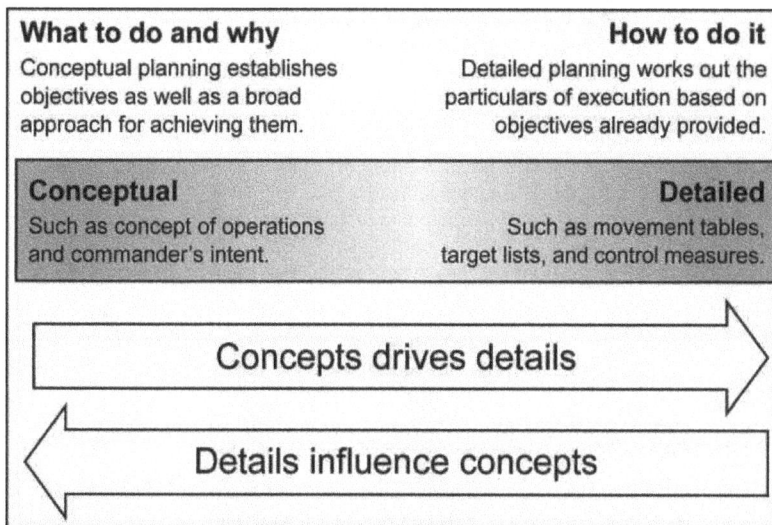

What to do and why

Conceptual planning establishes objectives as well as a broad approach for achieving them.

How to do it

Detailed planning works out the particulars of execution based on objectives already provided.

Conceptual

Such as concept of operations and commander's intent.

Detailed

Such as movement tables, target lists, and control measures.

Concepts drives details

Details influence concepts

Figure 2-2. The planning construct

2-39. The commander personally leads the conceptual component of planning. While commanders are also engaged in parts of detailed planning, they often leave the specifics to the staff. Conceptual planning provides the basis for all subsequent planning. Planning normally progresses from general to specific. For example, the commander's intent and concept of operations form the framework for the entire plan. This framework leads to schemes of support, such as schemes of intelligence, movement and maneuver, fires, protection, sustainment, and mission command. In turn, the schemes of support lead to the specifics of execution, including tasks to subordinate units. However, the dynamic does not operate in only one direction, as shown in figure 2-2. Conceptual planning must respond to detailed constraints. For example, the realities of deployment schedule (a detailed concern) influence the concept of operations (a conceptual concern).

2-40. Full spectrum operations demand a flexible and adaptive approach to planning. Based on the situation, Army leaders use and combine several methods to help them understand the situation and make decisions. Methodologies that assist commanders and staffs with planning include—

- Design. (See chapter 3.)
- The MDMP. (See appendix B.)
- TLP. (See appendix C.)

±DESIGN

2-41. Commanders conduct design to help them with the conceptual aspects of planning to include understanding, visualizing, and describing operations. After receipt of or in anticipation of a mission, commanders use design to understand the operational environment, frame the problem, and develop an operational approach to solve the problem.

2-42. Design emphasizes developing a holistic understanding of the operational environment and problem through collaboration and dialog. From this understanding, commanders continue to use design as they consider an operational approach for problem resolution. The operational approach serves as the foundation for more detailed planning and orders production using the MDMP.

THE MILITARY DECISIONMAKING PROCESS

2-43. The MDMP combines the conceptual and detailed aspects of planning. Commanders use it to build plans and orders for extended operations as well to develop orders for short-term operations within the framework of a long-range plan. The MDMP can be conducted based on a design concept or based on a higher order or directive without the benefits of formal design activities preceding the MDMP.

2-44. The MDMP helps commanders understand situations, develop courses of action, and decide on a course of action to accomplish missions. This methodology includes identifying and understanding the problem and determining a desired outcome. From this understanding, commanders develop several options for achieving that outcome. Commanders study and test these options in detail and then evaluate them against a set of criteria. Such actions help commanders determine the best option. This comparative analysis may result in a choice that modifies one of the options by incorporating features of others. The MDMP proceeds with the production of a fully synchronized plan or order for execution.

2-45. The MDMP integrates activities of the commander, staff, subordinate commanders, and other military and civilian partners when developing an operation plan or order. Not only does the MDMP integrate people into the planning process, it also integrates several processes and continuing activities as described in appendix B.

DESIGN AND THE MILITARY DECISIONMAKING PROCESS INTERFACE

2-46. Depending on the situation—to include the complexity of the problem—commanders conduct design before, in parallel with, or after the MDMP. When faced with an ill-structured problem or when developing initial plans for extended operations, commanders often initiate design before the MDMP. This sequence helps them better understand the operational environment, frame the problem, and develop an operational approach to guide more detailed planning.

2-47. Commanders may also elect to conduct design in parallel with the MDMP. In this instance, members of the staff conduct mission analysis as the commander and other staff members engage in design activities. Knowledge products—such as results from intelligence preparation of the battlefield and running estimates—help inform the design team about the operational environment. Commanders may direct some staff members to focus their mission analysis on certain areas. This focus helps commanders better understand aspects of the operational environment while examining the environmental and problem frames as part of design. The results of mission analysis (to include intelligence preparation of the battlefield and running estimates) inform commanders as they develop their design concept that, in turn, facilitate course of action development during the MDMP.

2-48. In time-constrained conditions requiring immediate action or if the problem is well structured, commanders may conduct the MDMP and publish an operation order without formally conducting design. As time becomes available during execution, commanders may then initiate design to help refine their commander's visualization and the initial plan developed using the MDMP.

TROOP LEADING PROCEDURES

2-49. TLP extend the MDMP to the small-unit level. TLP are a dynamic process used to analyze a mission, develop a plan, and prepare for an operation. These procedures enable leaders to maximize available planning time while developing effective plans and adequately preparing their unit for an operation. TLP consist of eight steps as addressed in appendix C. The sequence of the steps of TLP is not rigid. The sequence is modified to meet conditions of METT-TC. Some steps are done concurrently while others continue throughout the operation.

FUNDAMENTALS OF PLANNING

2-50. Effective planning requires dedication, study, and practice. Planners must be technically and tactically competent, be disciplined to use doctrinally correct terms and symbols, and understand fundamentals of planning. Fundamentals of planning that aid in effective planning include the following:

- Commanders focus planning.
- Commanders plan for full spectrum operations.

- Commanders continuously test the validity of assumptions.
- Planning is continuous.
- Planning is time sensitive.
- Simple, flexible plans work best.
- Commanders avoid planning pitfalls.

COMMANDERS FOCUS PLANNING

2-51. ±The responsibility for planning is inherent in command. Commanders are planners—the most important participants in effective planning. Often they have the most experience and are ultimately responsible for the execution of the plan. As such, the plan must reflect how commanders intend to conduct operations. Commanders use plans and orders to describe their understanding and visualization and to direct action during execution.

2-52. Commanders ensure the approaches to planning meet requirements of time, simplicity, and level of detail. They ensure that all plans comply with domestic and international law. Commanders also ensure the product is relevant and suitable for subordinates. Generally, the more involved commanders are in planning, the faster the commander and staff can plan. Through personal involvement, commanders learn from the staff and others about the situation while ensuring that the plan reflects the commander's intent. During planning, commanders focus on developing and describing their commander's visualization.

2-53. *Commander's visualization* is the mental process of developing situational understanding, determining a desired end state, and envisioning the broad sequence of events by which the force will achieve that end state (FM 3-0). Figure 2-3 depicts the general sequence involved in developing the commander's visualization. First, commanders understand the conditions that make up the current situation. From this understanding, commanders next visualize desired conditions that represent a desired end state. After envisioning a desired end state, commanders then conceptualize an operational approach of how to change current conditions to the desired future conditions.

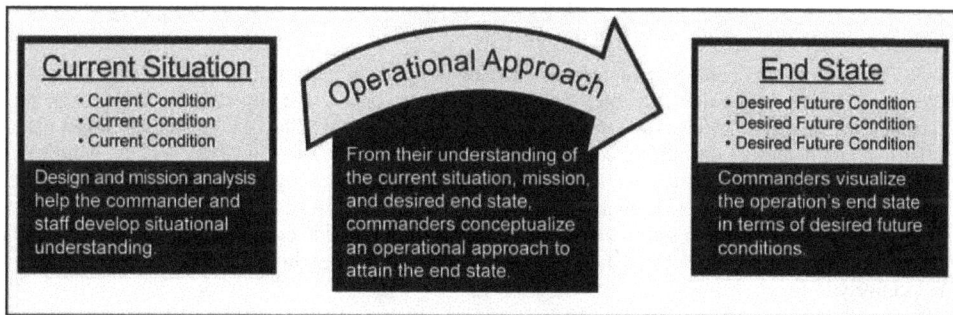

Figure 2-3. Commander's visualization

2-54. A condition is an existing state of affairs in the operational environment. Some desired future conditions may be prescribed by higher authority. For example, the higher headquarters may establish a desired future condition that an enemy force has withdrawn across the international border. Other future conditions are envisioned by the commander based on their understanding of the current situation and the mission. The operational approach represents the envisioned broad general actions designed to achieve the desired end state. The commander's visualization of the end state and operational approach of how to achieve that end state serve as the framework for more detailed planning.

2-55. ±To develop their commander's visualization, commanders draw on several sources of knowledge and relevant information. These include—

- The elements of operational art. (See FM 3-0.)
- Input from the staff, other commanders, and partners.
- Principles of war. (See FM 3-0.)
- Operational themes (see FM 3-0) and related doctrine.
- Running estimates.
- The common operational picture.
- Their experience and judgment.
- Subject matter experts.

2-56. Commanders describe their visualization in doctrinal terms, refining and clarifying it as circumstances require. Commanders express their initial visualization as—

- Initial commander's intent.
- Planning guidance, including an initial operational approach.
- Commander's critical information requirements (CCIRs).
- Essential elements of friendly information that must be protected.

COMMANDERS PLAN FOR FULL SPECTRUM OPERATIONS

2-57. Full spectrum operations requires continuous, simultaneous combinations of offense, defense, and stability for operations conducted overseas or civil support for operations conducted in the United States and its territories. (See FM 3-0.) Operations conducted outside the United States and its territories often involve more than combat between armed opponents. Winning battles and engagements is important but alone is not sufficient. Shaping the civil situation is just as important to long-term success. Hence, when developing their concept of operations, commanders equally consider stability tasks focused on the population with offensive and defensive tasks focused on the enemy. These stability operations shape the broader situation and restore security and normalcy.

2-58. The concept of operations provides the unifying direction for the entire operation. Within the concept of operations, the proportion and role of offensive, defensive, and stability tasks vary based on several factors. Commanders, however, always develop plans to account for follow-on operations. When planning offensive and defensive operations, commanders anticipate what will follow. They seek to avoid creating conditions that may lead to greater instability. They plan for and assign tasks to forces to establish or maintain civil security and civil control, restore essential services, and provide support to governments. Doing this helps to improve stability among the civilians and avoids creating conditions for insurgency. (See FM 3-07 and JP 3-28 for details concerning planning for stability and civil support operations respectively.)

COMMANDERS CONTINUOUSLY SEEK TO VERIFY ASSUMPTIONS

2-59. Commanders and staffs gather facts, develop assumptions, and consider opinions as they build their plan. A fact is something known to exist or have happened. Facts concerning the operational and mission variables serve as the basis for developing situational understanding during planning. An assumption is a supposition on the current situation or a presupposition on the future course of events, either or both assumed to be true in the absence of positive proof. An assumption may also be an explanation of past behavior. An assumption is accepted as true in the absence of actions or information contradicting it. Assumptions are probably correct but cannot be verified. Appropriate assumptions used during planning have two characteristics:

- They are likely to be true.
- They are necessary, that is essential, to continue planning.

2-60. In the absence of facts, the commander and staff consider assumptions from their higher headquarters and develop their own assumptions necessary for continued planning. Assumptions could relate to any mission variable, such as the strength and disposition of an enemy force or postconflict conditions.

2-61. Assumptions must be logical and reflect the reality of the situation. Commanders and staffs use care with assumptions to ensure they are not based on preconceptions; bias; false historical analogies; or simple, wishful thinking. Additionally, planners must be aware of any unstated assumptions.

2-62. Accepting a broad assumption without understanding its sublevel components often leads to other faulty assumptions. For example, a division commander might assume a combined arms battalion from the continental United States is available in 30 days. This commander must also understand the sublevel components—adequate preparation, load and travel time, viable ports and airfields, favorable weather, and enemy encumbrance. The commander considers how the sublevel components hinder or aid the battalion's ability to be available.

2-63. Commanders and staffs continuously question whether their assumptions are valid throughout planning and the operations process. Key points concerning the use of assumptions include—

- Assumptions must be logical, realistic, and considered likely to be true.
- Too many assumptions result in a higher probability that the plan or proposed solution may be invalid.
- The use of assumptions requires the staff to develop branches and sequels to execute if one or more key assumptions prove false.
- Often, an unstated assumption may prove more dangerous than a stated assumption proven wrong.

PLANNING IS CONTINUOUS

2-64. Even after the operation order is issued, planning continues throughout the operations process. Since situations (or the information available about them) continuously change, plans are revised as time allows and variations (options or branches) continue to be developed. Accurately predicting an operation's outcome is difficult, as is anticipating the possible contingencies. As planners develop a solution to a problem, the problem changes. Continuous planning enables organizations to adjust from an existing concept of operations based on a common understanding of the situation and the expected result. Based on their assessment, the commander and staff refine and revise the plan during preparation and execution.

PLANNING IS TIME SENSITIVE

2-65. Time is a critical factor in operations. Time management is, therefore, important in planning. Whether done deliberately or rapidly, all planning requires skillfully using available time to optimize planning and preparation throughout the unit. Understanding how time affects conducting operations helps commanders determine how fast and how far ahead to plan. Taking more time to plan often results in greater synchronization; however, any delay in execution risks yielding the initiative—with more time to prepare and act—to the enemy. When allocating planning time, commanders must ensure subordinates have enough time to plan and prepare their own actions.

One-Third–Two-Thirds Rule

2-66. Effective execution requires issuing timely plans and orders to subordinates. Timely plans are those issued soon enough to allow subordinates enough time to plan, issue their orders, and prepare for operations. At a minimum, commanders follow the "one-third–two-thirds rule" to allocate time available. They use one-third of the time available before execution for their planning and allocate the remaining two-thirds to their subordinates for planning and preparation.

2-67. When time is short, commanders develop the best possible products. In time-constrained environments, best products contain just enough information for commanders to make a reasoned decision and subordinates to assess the situation quickly and plan, prepare, and execute the necessary actions. To optimize available time and ensure the best possible synchronization, commanders encourage collaborative and parallel planning between their headquarters and higher and lower headquarters.

Collaborative and Parallel Planning

2-68. *Collaborative planning* **is commanders, subordinate commanders, staffs, and other partners sharing information, knowledge, perceptions, ideas, and concepts regardless of physical location throughout the planning process.** Collaboration occurs during all operations process activities, not just planning. (See chapter 1.) During planning, commanders, subordinate commanders, and others in the area of operations share assessments, statuses, and ideas. Commanders, subordinate commanders, and staffs share their understanding of the situation, participate in course of action (COA) development and decisionmaking, and resolve conflicts before the higher headquarters' order is issued. This collaboration can improve understanding of the situation, commander's intent, concept of operations, and tasks to subordinate units throughout the force. Since several echelons develop their plans simultaneously, collaborative planning can significantly shorten the time required for synchronization.

2-69. *Parallel planning* **is two or more echelons planning for the same operation nearly simultaneously.** Since several echelons develop their plans simultaneously, parallel planning can significantly shorten planning time. The higher headquarters continuously shares information concerning future operations with subordinate units through warning orders and other means. Frequent communication between commanders and staffs and sharing of information, such as intelligence preparation of the battlefield products, helps subordinate headquarters plan. Parallel planning requires significant interaction among echelons. With parallel planning, subordinate units do not wait for their higher headquarters to publish an order to begin developing their own plans and orders.

2-70. Higher commanders are sensitive not to overload subordinates with planning requirements. Generally, the higher the headquarters, the more time and staff resources are available to plan and explore options. Higher headquarters involve subordinates with developing those plans and concepts that have the highest likelihood of being adopted or fully developed.

Planning in Time

2-71. Tension exists between planning too far ahead and not planning enough. Planning too far into the future may overwhelm planning staffs' capabilities, especially those of subordinate organizations. It also risks preparations and coordination becoming irrelevant. However, not planning far enough ahead may result in losing the initiative and being unprepared for unforeseen opportunities and threats. Commanders should plan to the foreseeable end of the operation, even if that future condition is somewhat unclear. They can and should extend and add detail to their basic plan as their operation develops and their visualization becomes clearer, including anticipated sequels to the current operation.

2-72. Planning horizons help commanders think about operations and divide planning responsibilities among integrating cells (current operations integration, future operations, and plans). Planning horizons are measured from weeks or months to hours or days. Organizations often plan within several different planning horizons simultaneously. As commanders think in terms of planning horizons, they can better organize their planning efforts and allocate resources. As a rule, the higher the echelon, the more distant the planning horizon with which it is concerned. (See appendix A for a discussion of organizing responsibilities within the command post by planning horizons.)

SIMPLE, FLEXIBLE PLANS WORK BEST

2-73. Simplicity is a principle of war. It is vital to effective planning. Effective plans and orders are simple and direct. Staffs prepare clear, concise orders to ensure thorough understanding. They use doctrinally correct operational terms and graphics. Doing this minimizes chances of misunderstanding. Shorter rather than longer plans aid in simplicity. Shorter plans are easier to disseminate, read, and remember.

2-74. Complex plans often rely on intricate coordination that has a greater potential to fail in execution. Operations are always subject to the fog of war and friction. The more detailed the plan, the greater the chances it will no longer be applicable. Sometimes the situations change in response to friendly and enemy actions. Sometimes outside factors occur beyond the control of either side (such as the weather).

2-75. Simple plans require an easily understood concept of operations. Planners also promote simplicity by minimizing details where possible and by limiting the actions or tasks to what the situation requires. Subordinates can then develop specifics within the commander's intent. For example, instead of assigning a direction of attack, planners can designate an axis of advance.

2-76. Simple plans are not simplistic plans. Simplistic refers to something made overly simple by ignoring the situation's complexity. Good plans simplify complicated situations. However, some situations require more complex plans than others do. Commanders at all levels weigh the apparent benefits of a complex concept of operations against the risk that subordinates will be unable to understand or follow it. Commanders prefer simple plans because they can understand and execute them more easily.

2-77. Flexible plans help units adapt quickly to changing circumstances. Commanders and planners build opportunities for initiative into plans by anticipating events that allow them to operate inside of the enemy's decision cycle or react promptly to deteriorating situations. Identifying decision points and designing branches ahead of time—combined with a clear commander's intent—help create flexible plans. Incorporating control measures to reduce risk also makes plans more flexible. For example, a commander may hold a large, mobile reserve to compensate for the lack of information concerning an anticipated enemy attack.

2-78. Commanders stress the importance of mission orders as a way of building simple, flexible plans. *Mission orders* is a technique for developing orders that emphasizes to subordinates the results to be attained, not how they are to achieve them. It provides maximum freedom of action in determining how to best accomplish assigned missions (FM 3-0). Mission orders focus on what to do and the purpose of doing it without prescribing exactly how to do it. Control measures are established to aid cooperation among forces without imposing needless restrictions on freedom of action. Mission orders contribute to flexibility by allowing subordinates freedom to seize opportunities or react effectively to unforeseen enemy actions and capabilities.

2-79. Mission orders follow the five-paragraph format and are as brief and simple as possible. Mission orders clearly convey the unit's mission and commander's intent. They summarize the situation (current or anticipated starting conditions), describe the operation's objectives and end state (desired conditions), and provide a simple concept of operations to accomplish the unit's mission. When assigning tasks to subordinate units, mission orders include all components of a task statement: who, what, when, where, and why. However, commanders particularly emphasize the purpose (why) of the tasks to guide (along with the commander's intent) individual initiative. Effective plans and orders foster mission command by—

- Describing the situation to create a common situational understanding.
- Conveying the commander's intent and concept of operations.
- Assigning tasks to subordinate units and stating the purpose for conducting the task.
- Providing the control measures necessary to synchronize the operation while retaining the maximum freedom of action for subordinates.
- Task organizing forces and allocating resources.
- Directing preparation activities and establishing times or conditions for execution.

2-80. Mission orders contain the proper level of detail; they are neither so detailed that they stifle initiative nor so general that they provide insufficient direction. The proper level depends on each situation and is not easy to determine. Some phases of operations require tighter control over subordinate elements than others require. An air assault's air movement and landing phases, for example, require precise synchronization. Its ground maneuver plan requires less detail. As a rule, the base plan or order contains only the specific information required to provide the guidance to synchronize combat power at the decisive time and place while allowing subordinates as much freedom of action as possible. Commanders rely on individual initiative and coordination to act within the commander's intent and concept of operations. The attachments to the plan or order contain details regarding the situation and instructions necessary for synchronization.

COMMANDERS AVOID PLANNING PITFALLS

2-81. Commanders recognize the value of planning and avoid common planning pitfalls. These pitfalls generally stem from a common cause: the failure to appreciate the unpredictability and uncertainty of military operations. Pointing these out is not a criticism of planning but of improper planning. The four pitfalls consist of—

- Attempting to forecast and dictate events too far into the future.
- Trying to plan in too much detail.
- Using planning as a scripting process.
- Institutionalizing rigid planning methods.

2-82. The first pitfall is *attempting to forecast and dictate events too far into the future*. This may result from believing a plan can control the future. People tend to plan based on assumptions that the future will be a linear continuation of the present. Their plans often underestimate the scope of changes in directions that may occur and the results of second- and third-order effects. Even the most effective plans cannot anticipate all the unexpected events. Often, events overcome plans much sooner than anticipated. Effective plans include sufficient branches and sequels to account for the nonlinear nature of events.

2-83. The second pitfall consists of *trying to plan in too much detail*. Sound plans include necessary details; however, planning in unnecessary detail consumes limited time and resources that subordinates need. This pitfall often stems from the desire to leave as little as possible to chance. In general, the less certain the situation, the fewer details a plan should include. However, people often respond to uncertainty by planning in more detail to try to account for every possibility. This attempt to prepare detailed plans under uncertain conditions generates even more anxiety, which leads to even more detailed planning. Often this over planning results in an extremely detailed plan that does not survive the friction of the situation and that constricts effective action.

2-84. The third pitfall consists of *using planning as a scripting process* that tries to prescribe the course of events with precision. When planners fail to recognize the limits of foresight and control, the plan can become a coercive and overly regulatory mechanism. Commanders, staffs, and subordinates mistakenly focus on meeting the requirements of the plan rather than deciding and acting effectively.

2-85. The fourth pitfall is the danger of *institutionalizing rigid planning methods* that lead to inflexible or overly structured thinking. This tends to make planning rigidly focused on the process and produces plans that overly emphasize detailed procedures. Effective planning provides a disciplined framework for approaching and solving complex problems. The danger is in taking that discipline to the extreme.

2-86. Using a prescribed planning methodology does not guarantee that a command will improve its situation. Planning takes on value when done properly, using methods appropriate to the conditions and activities being planned. Done appropriately and well, planning proves to be a valuable activity that greatly improves performance and is a wise investment of time and effort. Done poorly, planning can be worse than irrelevant and a waste of valuable time and energy. Planning keeps the force oriented on future objectives despite the problems and requirements of current operations.

KEY COMPONENTS OF A PLAN

2-87. While each plan is unique, all plans seek a balance for combining ends, ways, and means against risk. Ends are the desired conditions of a given operation. Ways are actions to achieve the end state. Means are the resources required to execute the way. The major components of a plan are based on the answers to the following questions:

- What is the force trying to accomplish and why (ends)? This is articulated in the unit's mission statement and the commander's intent.
- What conditions, when established, constitute the desired end state (ends)? The desired conditions are described as part of the commander's intent.
- How will the force achieve these desired conditions (ways)? The way the force will accomplish the mission is described in the concept of operations.

- What sequence of actions is most likely to attain these conditions (ways)? The sequence of actions, to include phasing, is described in the concept of operations.
- What resources are required, and how can they be applied to accomplish that sequence of actions (means)? The application of resources throughout the operation is addressed in the concept of operations, the warfighting function schemes of support (for example, the scheme of protection and scheme of sustainment), tasks to subordinate units, and task organization.
- What risks are associated with that sequence of actions, and how can they be mitigated (risks)? The concept of operations incorporates risk mitigation as does coordinating instructions.

2-88. The unit's mission statement, commander's intent, concept of operations, tasks to subordinate units, coordinating instructions, and control measures are key components of a plan. Commanders ensure their mission and end state are nested with those of their higher headquarters. Whereas the commander's intent focuses on the end state, the concept of operations focuses on the way or sequence of actions by which the force will achieve the end state. The concept of operations expands on the mission statement and commander's intent. It describes how and in what sequence the commander wants the force to accomplish the mission. Within the concept of operations, commanders may establish objectives as intermediate goals toward achieving the operation's end state. When developing tasks for subordinate units, commanders ensure that the purpose of each task nests with the accomplishment of another task, with the achievement of an objective, or directly to the attainment of an end state condition.

MISSION STATEMENT

2-89. The *mission* is the task, together with the purpose, that clearly indicates the action to be taken and the reason therefore (JP 1-02). Commanders analyze a mission in terms of the commander's intent two echelons up, specified tasks, and implied tasks. They also consider the mission of adjacent units to understand how they contribute to the decisive operation of their higher headquarters. Results of that analysis yield the essential tasks that—with the purpose of the operation—clearly specify the action required. This analysis produces the unit's mission statement—a clear statement of the action to be taken and the reason for doing so. The mission statement contains the elements of who, what, when, where, and why, but seldom specifies how. The format for writing a task to subordinate units also follows this format. See appendix B for detailed instructions for writing mission and task statements as part of the MDMP.

COMMANDER'S INTENT

2-90. The *commander's intent* is a clear, concise statement of what the force must do and the conditions the force must establish with respect to the enemy, terrain, and civil considerations that represent the desired end state (FM 3-0). The commander's intent succinctly describes what constitutes success for the operation. It includes the operation's purpose and the conditions that define the end state. It links the mission, concept of operations, and tasks to subordinate units. A clear commander's intent facilitates a shared understanding and focuses on the overall conditions that represent mission accomplishment. During planning, the initial commander's intent summarizes the commander's visualization and is used to develop and refine courses of action. During execution, the commander's intent spurs individual initiative.

2-91. The commander's intent must be easy to remember and clearly understandable two echelons down. The shorter the commander's intent, the better it serves these purposes. Typically, the commander's intent statement is three to five sentences long.

CONCEPT OF OPERATIONS

2-92. The *concept of operations* is a statement that directs the manner in which subordinate units cooperate to accomplish the mission and establishes the sequence of actions the force will use to achieve the end state. It is normally expressed in terms of decisive, shaping, and sustaining operations (FM 3-0). The concept of operations expands on the mission statement and commander's intent by describing how and in what sequence the commander wants the force to accomplish the mission.

2-93. Commanders ensure they identify the decisive operation and units responsible for conducting the decisive operation. From this focal point, commanders articulate shaping operations and the principal task of the units assigned each shaping operation. Commanders complete their concept of operations with sustaining actions essential to the success of decisive and shaping operations. Individual schemes of support by warfighting function are addressed in subparagraphs of paragraph 3 (execution) in the base plan, after the concept of operations. The concept of sustainment is addressed in paragraph 4 (sustainment).

2-94. When writing the concept of operations, commanders consider nested concepts, the sequence of actions and phasing, decisive points and objectives, and lines of operations and lines of effort.

Nested Concepts

2-95. *Nested concepts* **is a planning technique to achieve unity of purpose whereby each succeeding echelon's concept of operations is aligned by purpose with the higher echelons' concept of operations.** An effective concept of operations describes how the forces will support the mission of the higher headquarters and how the actions of subordinate units fit together to accomplish the mission. Commanders do this by organizing their forces by purpose. Commanders ensure the primary tasks for each subordinate unit include a purpose that links the completion of that task to achievement of another task, an objective, or an end state condition.

Sequence of Actions and Phasing

2-96. The concept of operations is described in sequence from the start of the operation to the projected status of the force at the operation's end. If the situation dictates a significant change in tasks during the operation, the commander may phase the operation. Within this sequence, the commander designates a main effort by phase.

2-97. Part of the art of planning is determining the sequence of actions that best accomplishes the mission. Commanders consider many factors when deciding how to sequence actions. The most important factor is resources. Commanders synchronize subordinate unit actions to link the higher headquarters' concept of operations with their own concept of operations.

2-98. Ideally, commanders plan to accomplish the mission with simultaneous actions throughout the area of operations. However, resource constraints and the friendly force's size may limit commanders' ability to do this. In these cases, commanders phase the operation. A *phase* is a planning and execution tool used to divide an operation in duration or activity. A change in phase usually involves a change of mission, task organization, or rules of engagement. Phasing helps in planning and controlling and may be indicated by time, distance, terrain, or an event (FM 3-0). Well designed phases—

- Focus effort.
- Concentrate combat power in time and space at a decisive point.
- Achieve their objectives deliberately and logically.

Note: In joint operation planning, a phase is a definitive stage of an operation or campaign during which a large portion of the forces and capabilities are involved in similar or mutually supporting activities for a common purpose.

2-99. Phasing assists in planning and controlling operations. Individual phases gain significance only in the overall operation's context. Links between phases and the requirement to transition between phases are critically important. Commanders establish clear conditions for how and when these transitions occur. Although phases are distinguishable to friendly forces, an effective plan conceals these distinctions from adversaries through concurrent and complementary actions during transitions.

Decisive Points and Objectives

2-100. Commanders can base a concept of operations on a single objective, lines of operations, or lines of effort. Identifying decisive points and determining objectives are central to creating the concept of operations in all cases. A *decisive point* is a geographic place, specific key event, critical factor, or function that, when acted upon, allows commanders to gain a marked advantage over an adversary or contribute materially to achieving success (JP 3-0). Examples of potential geographic decisive points include port facilities, distribution networks and nodes, and bases of operations. Specific events and elements of an enemy force may also be decisive points. Decisive points have a different character during operations dominated by stability or civil support. These decisive points may be less tangible and more closely associated with important events and conditions. Examples include—

- Participation in elections by a certain group.
- Electric power restored in a certain area.
- Police and emergency services reestablished.

2-101. Often, a situation presents more decisive points than the force can act upon. The art of planning includes selecting decisive points that best lead to mission accomplishment and acting on them in a sequence that most quickly and efficiently leads to mission success. Once identified for action, decisive points become objectives. Objectives provide the basis for determining tasks to subordinate units. The most important objective forms the basis for developing the decisive operation.

> *Note:* An objective can be physical (an enemy force or terrain feature) or conceptual in the form of a goal (rule of law established). As a graphic control measure, an *objective* is a location on the ground used to orient operations, phase operations, facilitate changes of direction, and provide for unity of effort (FM 3-90).

Lines of Operations and Lines of Effort

2-102. Lines of operations and lines of effort are two key elements of operational design that assist in developing a concept of operations. Major combat operations are typically designed using lines of operations. These lines tie tasks to the geographic and positional references in the area of operations. Commanders synchronize activities along complementary lines of operations to achieve the desired end state. Lines of operations may be either interior or exterior. (See FM 3-0.)

2-103. The line of effort is a useful tool for framing the concept of operations when stability or civil support operations dominate. Lines of effort link multiple tasks with goal-oriented objectives that focus efforts toward establishing end state conditions. Using lines of effort is essential in planning when positional references to an enemy or adversary have little relevance. In operations involving many nonmilitary factors, lines of effort may be the only way to link subordinate unit tasks with objectives and desired end state conditions. Lines of effort are often essential to helping commanders visualize how military capabilities can support the other instruments of national power. They are a particularly valuable tool when used to achieve unity of effort in operations involving multinational forces or civilian organizations, where unity of command is elusive if not impractical. (See appendix B and FM 3-07 for a detailed discussion on describing the concept of operations by lines of effort.)

TASKS TO SUBORDINATE UNITS

2-104. The commander's intent describes the desired end state while the concept of operations broadly describes how to get there. In contrast, tasks to subordinate units direct individual units to perform specific tasks. A *task* is a clearly defined and measurable activity accomplished by individuals and organizations (FM 7-0). Tasks are specific activities that contribute to accomplishing missions or other requirements. Tasks direct friendly action. The purpose of each task should nest with completing another task, achieving an objective, or attaining an end state condition.

2-105. When developing tasks for subordinate units, commanders and staffs use the same who, what (task), when, where, and why (purpose) construct as they did to develop the unit's mission statement. Sometimes commanders may want to specify the type or form of operation to use to accomplish a task. For example, the commander may direct an infiltration to avoid tipping off the enemy and synchronize the timing of the unit's tasks with other units' tasks.

COORDINATING INSTRUCTIONS

2-106.   Coordinating instructions apply to two or more units. They are located in the coordinating instructions subparagraph of paragraph 3 (execution) of plans and orders. Examples include CCIRs, fire support coordination and airspace coordinating measures, rules of engagement, risk mitigation measures, and the time or condition when the operation order becomes effective.

CONTROL MEASURES

2-107.   Planners develop and recommend control measures to the commander for each considered COA. A *control measure* is a means of regulating forces or warfighting functions (FM 3-0). Control measures assign responsibilities, coordinate actions between forces, impose restrictions, or establish guidelines to regulate freedom of action. Control measures are essential to coordinating subordinates' actions and are located throughout the plan.

2-108.   Control measures can free up subordinate commanders to conduct operations within their assigned area of operations without having to conduct additional coordination. Such control measures reduce the need for subordinates to ask higher headquarters for permission to act or not to act. Commanders establish only the minimum control measures needed to provide essential coordination and deconfliction among units. The fewer restrictions, the more latitude subordinates have to exercise individual initiative.

2-109.   Control measures can be permissive or restrictive. Permissive control measures allow specific actions to occur; restrictive control measures limit the conduct of certain actions. For example, a coordinated fire line—a line beyond which conventional and indirect surface fire support means may fire at any time within the boundaries of the establishing headquarters without additional coordination—illustrates a permissive control measure. A route—the prescribed course to be traveled from a specific point of origin to a specific destination—illustrates a restrictive control measure. (FM 1-02 contains definitions of control measures and how to depict them. FM 3-90 discusses control measures commonly used in offensive and defensive operations.)

Chapter 3
Design

This chapter establishes the fundamentals that guide the application of design. It defines and explains the goals of design. It discusses design in context and describes how leaders drive design. Next, it describes the design methodology that includes framing the operational environment, framing the problem, and developing a design concept. The chapter concludes with a discussion of reframing.

DESIGN DEFINED

3-1. ±*Design* **is a methodology for applying critical and creative thinking to understand, visualize, and describe complex, ill-structured problems and develop approaches to solve them**. Critical thinking captures the reflective and continuous learning essential to design. Creative thinking involves thinking in new, innovative ways while capitalizing on imagination, insight, and novel ideas. Design is a way of organizing the activities of understanding, visualizing, and describing within an organization. Design occurs throughout the operations process before and during detailed planning, through preparation, and during execution and assessment.

3-2. ±Planning consists of two separate, but closely related components: a conceptual component and a detailed component. The conceptual component is represented by the cognitive application of design. The detailed component translates broad concepts into a complete and practical plan. During planning, these components overlap with no clear delineation between them. As commanders conceptualize the operation, their vision guides the staff through design and into detailed planning. Design is continuous throughout planning and evolves with increased understanding throughout the operations process. Design underpins the role of the commander in the operations process, guiding the iterative and often cyclic application of understanding, visualizing, and describing. As these iterations occur, the design concept—the tangible link to detailed planning—is forged.

3-3. Design enables commanders to view a situation from multiple perspectives, draw on varied sources of situational knowledge, and leverage subject matter experts while formulating their own understanding. Design enables commanders to develop a thorough understanding of the operational environment and formulate effective solutions to complex, ill-structured problems. The commander's visualization and description of the actions required to achieve the desired conditions must flow logically from what commanders understand and how they have framed the problem. Design provides an approach for how to generate change from an existing situation to a desired objective or condition.

3-4. Moreover, design requires effective and decisive leadership that engages subordinate commanders, coordinating authorities, representatives of various staff disciplines, and the higher commander in continuing collaboration and dialog that leads to enhanced decisionmaking. (Paragraphs 1-54 through 1-59 discuss collaboration and dialog.) This facilitates collaborative and parallel planning while supporting shared understanding and visualization across the echelons and among diverse organizations. It is the key to leveraging the cognitive potential of a learning organization, converting the raw intellectual power of the commander and staff into effective combat power.

3-5. Innovation, adaptation, and continuous learning are central tenets of design. Innovation involves taking a new approach to a familiar or known situation, whereas adaptation involves taking a known solution and modifying it to a particular situation or responding effectively to changes in the operational environment. Design helps the commander lead innovative, adaptive work and guides planning, preparing, executing, and assessing operations. Design requires agile, versatile leaders who foster continuous organizational learning while actively engaging in iterative collaboration and dialog to enhance decisionmaking across the echelons.

3-6.   A continuous, iterative, and cognitive methodology, design is used to develop understanding of the operational environment, make sense of complex, ill-structured problems, and develop approaches to solving them. In contrast to detailed planning, design is not process-oriented. The practice of design challenges conventional wisdom and offers new insights for solving complex, ill-structured problems. While plans and orders flow down the echelons of command, new understanding may flow up from subordinate echelons where change often appears first. By enhancing and improving commanders' understanding, design improves a higher authority's understanding of the operational environment and the problems commanders are tasked to solve.

DESIGN GOALS

3-7.   Successfully applying design seeks four concrete goals that, once achieved, provide the reasoning and logic that guide detailed planning processes. Each goal is an essential component to reshaping the conditions of the operational environment that constitute the desired end state. Collectively, they are fundamental to overcoming the complexities that characterize persistent conflict. The goals of design are—

- Understanding ill-structured problems.
- Anticipating change.
- Creating opportunities.
- Recognizing and managing transitions.

UNDERSTANDING ILL-STRUCTURED PROBLEMS

3-8.   Persistent conflict presents a broad array of complex, ill-structured problems best solved by applying design. Design offers a model for innovative and adaptive problem framing that provides leaders with the cognitive tools to understand a problem and appreciate its complexities before seeking to solve it. This understanding is fundamental to design. Without thoroughly understanding the nature of the problem, commanders cannot establish the situation's context or devise approaches to effect change in the operational environment. Analyzing the situation and the operational variables provides the critical information necessary to understand and frame these problems. (FM 3-0 discusses the operational variables. See chapter 2 for a discussion on the structure of problems.)

3-9.   A commander's experience, knowledge, judgment, and intuition assume a crucial role in understanding complex, ill-structured problems. Together, they enhance the cognitive components of design, enhancing commanders' intuition while further enabling commanders to identify threats or opportunities long before others might. This deepens and focuses commanders' understanding. It allows them to anticipate change, identify information gaps, and recognize capability shortfalls. This understanding also forms the basis of the commander's visualization. Commanders project their understanding beyond the realm of physical combat. They must anticipate the operational environment's evolving military and nonmilitary conditions. Therefore, design encompasses visualizing the synchronized arrangement and use of military and nonmilitary forces and capabilities to achieve the desired end state. This requires the ability to discern the conditions required for success before committing forces to action.

3-10. Ultimately, understanding complex, ill-structured problems is essential to reducing the effects of complexity on full spectrum operations. This understanding allows commanders to better appreciate how numerous factors influence and interact with planned and ongoing operations. Assessing the complex interaction among these factors and their influences on operations is fundamental to understanding and effectively allows the commander to make qualitatively better decisions under the most dynamic and stressful circumstances.

ANTICIPATING CHANGE

3-11. Applying design involves anticipating changes in the operational environment, projecting decisionmaking forward in time and space to influence events before they occur. Rather than responding to events as they unfold, design helps the commander to anticipate these events and recognize and manage transitions. Through the iterative and continuous application of design, commanders contemplate and evaluate potential decisions and actions in advance, visualizing consequences of possible operational approaches to determine whether they will contribute to achieving the desired end state. A thorough design effort reduces the effects of complexity during execution and is essential to anticipating the most likely reactions to friendly action. During detailed planning, these actions and sequences are often linked along lines of effort, which focus the outcomes toward objectives that help to shape conditions of the operational environment.

3-12. Design alone does not guarantee success in anticipating change—it also does not ensure that friendly actions will quantifiably improve the situation. However, applied effectively and focused toward a common goal, design provides an invaluable cognitive tool to help commanders anticipate change as well as innovate and adapt approaches appropriately. Performed haphazardly and without proper focus and effort, it may become time-consuming, ineffective, process-focused, and irrelevant. Iterative, collaborative, and focused design offers the means to anticipate change effectively in the current situation and operational environment as well as achieve lasting success and positive change.

CREATING OPPORTUNITIES

3-13. The ability to seize, retain, and exploit the initiative is rooted in effective design. Applying design helps commanders anticipate events and set in motion the actions that allow forces to act purposefully and effectively. Exercising initiative in this manner shapes the situation as events unfold. Design is inherently proactive, intended to create opportunities for success while instilling the spirit of the offense in all elements of full spectrum operations. Effective design facilitates mission command, ensuring that forces are postured to retain the initiative and, through detailed planning, consistently able to seek opportunities to exploit that initiative.

3-14. The goals of design account for the interdependent relationships among initiative, opportunity, and risk. Effective design postures the commander to combine the three goals to reduce or counter the effects of complexity using the initial commander's intent to foster individual initiative and freedom of action. Design is essential to recognizing and managing the inherent delay between decision and action, especially between the levels of war and echelons. The iterative nature of design helps the commander to overcome this effect, fostering initiative within the initial commander's intent to act appropriately and decisively when orders no longer sufficiently address the changing situation. This ensures commanders act promptly as they encounter opportunities or accept prudent risk to create opportunities when they lack clear direction. In such situations, prompt action requires detailed foresight and preparation.

RECOGNIZING AND MANAGING TRANSITIONS

3-15. A campaign quality Army requires versatile leaders—critical and creative thinkers who recognize and manage not just friendly transitions but those of adversaries as well as the operational environment. Commanders must possess the versatility to operate along the spectrum of conflict and the vision to anticipate and adapt to transitions that will occur over the course of a campaign. Design provides the cognitive tools to recognize and manage transitions by educating and training the commander. Educated and trained commanders can identify and employ adaptive, innovative solutions, create and exploit opportunities, and leverage risk to their advantage during these transitions.

DESIGN IN CONTEXT

3-16. The introduction of design into Army doctrine seeks to secure the lessons of eight years of war and provide a cognitive tool to commanders who will encounter complex, ill-structured problems in future operational environments like in March 2003. Division commanders of the 101st Airborne (Air Assault), 4th Infantry Division, and 1st Armored Division were ordered to maneuver their units from Kuwait and into Iraq to defeat the Iraqi Army and to seize key cities and infrastructure. This was a task familiar to each of them—a structured problem—and they communicated their intent and began to build orders through the military decisionmaking process. Soon after accomplishing their mission, they were issued further instructions to "establish a safe and secure environment" in Ninewa Province, Diyala Province, and Baghdad. This was a task unfamiliar to them—an ill-structured problem—and each of them realized that they had to first understand the problem and frame the task before seeking to solve it. These commanders used design intuitively and adapted their existing processes to gain this understanding.

3-17. As learned in recent conflicts, challenges facing the commander in operations often can be understood only in the context of other factors influencing the population. These other factors often include but are not limited to economic development, governance, information, tribal influence, religion, history, and culture. Full spectrum operations conducted among the population are effective only when commanders understand the issues in the context of the complex issues facing the population. Understanding context and then deciding how, if, and when to act is both a product of design and integral to the art of command.

PERSISTENT CONFLICT

3-18. In the 21st century, several global trends shape the emerging strategic environment and exacerbate the ideological nature of current struggles. These trends present dilemmas as well as opportunities. Such trends include—

- Globalization.
- Technological diffusion.
- Demographic shifts.
- Resource scarcity.
- Climate changes and natural disasters.
- Proliferation of weapons of mass destruction.
- Failed or failing states.

3-19. The collective impact of these trends makes it likely that persistent conflict will characterize the next century. *Persistent conflict* is the protracted confrontation among state, nonstate, and individual actors that are increasingly willing to use violence to achieve their political and ideological ends. (FM 3-0) Conflicts will erupt unpredictably, vary in intensity and scope, and endure for extended periods. In a dynamic and multidimensional operational environment, design offers tools vital to solving the complex, ill-structured problems presented by persistent conflict.

±EVOLVING CHARACTER OF CONFLICT

3-20. Although the essential nature of conflict is timeless, its character reflects the unique conditions of each era. Conflict is invariably complex because it is fundamentally human in character. . Design provides additional tools necessary to understand this environment and to mitigate the adverse effects of complexity on full spectrum operations. As modern conflict evolves, it is characterized by several key factors:

- Conducted between and among *diverse actors*, both state and nonstate, with the former frequently acting covertly, and the latter sometimes acting through state sponsorship or as a proxy for a state.
- Unavoidably waged *among the people*.
- Increasingly *unpredictable* and sudden, with the potential to expand rapidly into unanticipated locations and continue for unexpected durations.
- Increasing *potential for spillover*, creating regionally and globally destabilizing effects.
- Waged in *transparency*.
- Increasingly likely to include *hybrid threats*, the diverse and dynamic combination of regular forces, irregular forces, and/or criminal elements all unified to achieve mutually benefitting effects.

FUNDAMENTALS OF DESIGN

3-21. Today's operational environment presents situations so complex that understanding them—let alone attempting to change them—is beyond the ability of a single individual. Moreover, significant risk occurs when assuming that commanders in the same campaign understand an implicit design concept or that their design concepts mutually support each other. The risks multiply, especially when a problem involves multiple units, Services, multinational forces, or other instruments of national power. Commanders mitigate these risks with collaboration and by applying the design fundamentals:

- Apply critical thinking.
- Understand the operational environment.
- Solve the right problem.
- Adapt to dynamic conditions.
- Achieve the designated goals.

Apply Critical Thinking

3-22. Commanders ensure that superiors and subordinates share a common understanding of the purpose behind intended actions. Initial guidance provided by a higher political or military authority may prove insufficient to create clearly stated, decisive, and attainable objectives in complex situations that involve political, social, economic, and other factors. After commanders conduct a detailed study of the situation, they may conclude that some desired goals are unrealistic or not feasible within the limitations. These limitations stem from the inherent tension that often exists among different goals, historical tensions in the local population, interactions of different actors seeking to improve their own survivability and position, and limited resources and time available to achieve the mission. One can never fully understand the dynamics of a conflict in advance. Well-intentioned guidance without detailed study may lead to an untenable or counterproductive solution.

3-23. Design helps mitigate the risk associated with guidance that does not fully account for the complexities of the operational environment by using a critical and creative approach for learning, innovation, and adaptation. Design helps to clarify objectives in the context of the operational environment and within the limits imposed by policy, strategy, orders, or directives. This does not imply that commanders can arbitrarily disregard instructions. If, however, they receive unclear guidance or consider the desired conditions unachievable, commanders engage in active dialog. Dialog clarifies guidance and enables commanders to offer recommendations to achieve a mutual understanding of the current situation and the desired end state. Design can assist commanders in leading the top-down/bottom-up approach at all echelons.

Understand the Operational Environment

3-24. Design challenges leaders to understand the impact of their decisions and actions on the operational environment. (See chapter 1.) Gaining a deeper and more thorough understanding of the operational environment enables more effective decisionmaking and helps to integrate military operations with the other instruments of national power. In an environment characterized by the presence of joint, interagency, intergovernmental, and multinational partners, such understanding is essential to success. In this context, human variables, interactions, and relationships are frequently decisive. Military force may be necessary to achieve national policy aims, but, by itself, force proves insufficient to achieve victory in these situations. More importantly, leaders and Soldiers must recognize the relationship between the character of conflict and the approach one takes to effect changes in the operational environment.

3-25. Developing a thorough understanding of the operational environment is a continuous process. Even though this understanding will never be perfect, attempting to comprehend its complex nature helps identify unintended consequences that may undermine well-intentioned efforts. Deep understanding reveals the dynamic nature of the human interactions and the importance of identifying contributing factors. Leaders can gain this understanding by capitalizing on multiple perspectives and varied sources of knowledge. For example, intelligence knowledge generated as part of the intelligence process contributes to contextual understanding of the operational environment. (See FM 2-0.) Design encourages the commander and staff to seek and address complexity before attempting to impose simplicity.

Solve the Right Problem

3-26. Commanders use design to ensure they are solving the right problem. When commanders use design, they closely examine the symptoms, the underlying tensions, and the root causes of conflict in the operational environment. From this perspective, they can identify the fundamental problem with greater clarity and consider more accurately how to solve it. Design is essential to ensuring commanders identify the right problem to solve. Effective application of design is the difference between solving a problem right and solving the right problem.

Adapt to Dynamic Conditions

3-27. Innovation and adaptation lead to capitalizing on opportunities by quickly recognizing and exploiting actions that work well while dismissing those that do not. Adaptation does not rely on being able to anticipate every challenge. Instead, it uses continuous assessment to determine what works and what does not. Adaptation occurs through the crucial process of assessment and subsequent changes in how one approaches problems. In the military domain, adaptation demands clearly articulated measures of effectiveness. These measures define success and failure along with after action reviews that capture and implement lessons at all echelons.

3-28. Effective use of design improves the ability to adapt. Adaptation in this sense involves reframing the situation to align with new information and experiences that challenge existing understanding. Through framing and reframing achieved through iterative collaboration and dialog, design provides a foundation for organizational learning and contributes to the necessary clarity of vision required by successful commanders.

Achieve the Designated Goals

3-29. If the link between strategy and tactics is clear, the likelihood that tactical actions will translate into strategic success increases significantly. For complex, ill-structured problems, integrating and synchronizing operations to link sequences of tactical actions to achieve a strategic aim may prove elusive. Through design, commanders employ operational art to cement the link between strategic objectives and tactical action ensuring that all tactical actions will produce conditions that ultimately define the desired end state. As understanding of the operational environment and problem improves, design adapts to strengthen the link between strategy and tactics, promoting operational coherence, unity of effort, and strategic success.

LEADING DESIGN

3-30. ±Commanders are the central figure in design. Generally, the more complex a situation is, the more important the commander's role is in design. Commanders draw on design to overcome the challenges of complexity. They foster iterative collaboration and dialog while leveraging their collective knowledge, experience, judgment, and intuition to generate a clearer understanding of the conditions needed to achieve success. Design supports the commander's ability to understand and visualize the operational environment.

3-31. The practice of design is not exclusive to a particular level of command. Design can apply to all levels, depending on the context and circumstances. However, given the complexity of the operational environment, the need for design at lower echelons often increases as brigades and battalions contend with the challenges of shaping environments and conducting operations over extended periods.

3-32. In leading design, commanders typically draw from a select group within the planning staff, red team members, and subject matter experts internal and external to the headquarters. The commander selects these individuals based on their expertise relative to the problem. The commander expects these individuals to gain insights and inputs from areas beyond their particular expertise—either in person or through reachback—to frame the problem more fully. Design serves to establish the context for guidance and orders. By using members of the planning staff to participate in the design effort, commanders ensure continuity between design and detailed planning as well as throughout the operations process. These are purpose-built, problem-centric teams, and the commander may choose to dissolve them once they complete the design effort.

3-33. Commanders compare similarities of their current situations with their own experiences or history and the design team's experiences or history to distinguish unique features that require novel, innovative, or adaptive solutions. They understand that each situation requires a solution tailored to the context of the problem. Design provides an approach for leading innovative, adaptive efforts from which to effectively act on and efficiently solve a complex, ill-structured problem. It fosters thinking and interacting as commanders develop approaches to resolve the differences between the current conditions and desired conditions of the environment through the conduct of full spectrum operations.

3-34. Commanders leverage design to create and exploit opportunity, not just to ward off the risk of failure. Design provides the means to convert intellectual power into combat power. A creative design tailored to a unique operational environment promises—

- Economy of effort.
- Greater coherence across rotations among units and between successive operations.
- Better integration and coordination among the instruments of national power.
- Fewer unintended consequences.
- Effective adaptation once the situation changes.

3-35. Design requires the commander to lead adaptive, innovative efforts to leverage collaboration and dialog to identify and solve complex, ill-structured problems. To that end, the commander must lead organizational learning and develop methods to determine if reframing is necessary during the course of an operation. This requires continuous assessment, evaluation, and reflection that challenge understanding of the existing problem and the relevance of actions addressing that problem.

DESIGN METHODOLOGY

3-36. Three distinct elements collectively produce a design concept as depicted in figure 3-1. Together, they constitute an organizational learning methodology that corresponds to three basic questions that must be answered to produce an actionable design concept to guide detailed planning:

- Framing the operational environment—what is the context in which design will be applied?
- Framing the problem—what problem is the design intended to solve?
- Considering operational approaches—what broad, general approach will solve the problem?

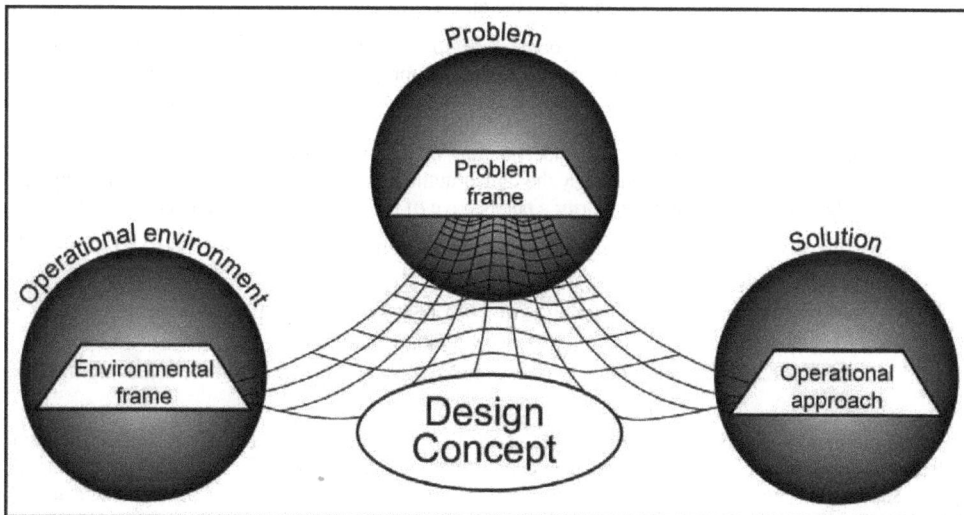

Figure 3-1. The design methodology

3-37. During design, the commander and staff consider the conditions, circumstances, and factors that affect the use of capabilities and resources as well as bear on decisionmaking. As an organizational learning methodology, design fosters collaboration and dialog as commanders and staffs formulate conditions that define a desired end state and develop approaches that aim to achieve those conditions. When initial efforts do not achieve a thorough enough understanding of behaviors or events, commanders reframe their understanding of the operational environment and problem. This cycle of inquiry, contextual understanding, and synthesis relies on continuous collaboration and dialog. Collaboration—especially with joint, interagency, intergovernmental, and multinational partners—is fundamental to success. Collaboration affords commanders opportunities to revise their understanding or approaches so they can execute feasible, acceptable, and suitable approaches to achieve desired conditions or objectives.

3-38. Design is essentially nonlinear. It flows back and forth between environmental framing and problem framing while considering several operational approaches. No hard lines separate the efforts of each design element. When an idea or issue is raised, the commander can address it in the appropriate element, even if the idea or issue is outside the current focus. The change in emphasis shifts from focusing on understanding the tendencies and potentials of actors in the operational environment, to understanding how they relate to and affect the problem, to understanding their likely contributions toward transforming existing conditions to a desired end state. As commanders and staffs gain new knowledge or begin a new line of questioning, they often shift their focus among elements of design while building understanding and refining potential operational approaches to solve the problem.

FRAMING THE OPERATIONAL ENVIRONMENT

3-39. Framing involves selecting, organizing, interpreting, and making sense of a complex reality to provide guideposts for analyzing, understanding, and acting. Framing facilitates hypothesizing, or modeling, that scopes the part of the operational environment or problem under consideration. Framing provides a perspective from which commanders can understand and act on a complex, ill-structured problem.

3-40. In understanding the operational environment, the commander and staff focus on defining, analyzing, and synthesizing the characteristics of the operational variables. They do so in the context of the dynamic interactions and relationships among and between relevant operational variables and actors in the operational environment. Often, learning about the nature of the situation helps them to understand the groupings, relationships, or interactions among relevant actors and operational variables. This learning typically involves analysis of the operational variables while examining the dynamic interaction and relationships among the myriad other factors in the operational environment.

3-41. Understanding the operational environment begins with analyzing the context of the situation in accordance with guidance and direction from a higher authority. This fosters learning while generating an increased understanding of the operational environment. Commanders and their staffs review relevant directives, documents, data, previous guidance, and missions. Commanders inform their higher authority of new information or differences in initial understanding of the operational environment. Commanders also confirm the desired end state if provided by the higher authority, or propose their own. For the commander, this knowledge clarifies the higher authority's perspective of the operational environment.

3-42. To achieve a shared understanding of higher directives and policy, the commander and staff—

- Clarify the reasons and expectations to change existing conditions.
- Compare current or new instructions with other standing guidance or policies.
- Identify and resolve conflicting guidance with known facts.
- Assess feasibility, acceptability, and suitability of any directed action for achieving the desired end state.

3-43. Commanders apply critical thinking to every aspect of this analysis. Critical thinking leads to a deeper appreciation of the higher commander's intent and helps to refine the higher commander's understanding of the operational environment. This is an essential step to gain a shared understanding of the situation. The environmental frame depicts the current state of the operational environment. Based on higher guidance, it also defines the desired conditions that constitute a desired end state by examining the tendencies and potentials of relevant actors and operational variables.

Environmental Frame

3-44. The commander and staff develop a contextual understanding of the situation by framing the operational environment. The environmental frame is a narrative and graphic description that captures the history, culture, current state, and future goals of relevant actors in the operational environment. The environmental frame describes the context of the operational environment—how the context developed (historical and cultural perspective), how the context currently exists (current conditions), and how the context could trend in the future (future conditions or desired end state). The environmental frame enables commanders to forecast future events and the effects of potential actions in the operational environment. The environmental frame explains the actors and relationships within a system and surfaces assumptions to allow for more rapid adaptation. The environmental frame evolves through continuous learning, but scopes aspects of the operational environment relevant to higher guidance and situations.

3-45. Within the environmental frame, commanders review existing guidance, articulate existing conditions, determine the desired end state and supporting conditions, and identify relationships and interactions among relevant operational variables and actors. They analyze groupings of actors that exert significant influence in the operational environment knowing that individual actors rarely share common goals. By identifying and evaluating tendencies and potentials of relevant actor interactions and relationships, commanders and their staffs formulate a desired end state that accounts for the context of the operational environment and higher directives.

End State and Conditions

3-46. The desired end state consists of those desired conditions that, if achieved, meet the objectives of policy, orders, guidance, and directives issued to the commander. A condition is a reflection of the existing state of the operational environment. Thus, a desired condition is a sought-after future state of the operational environment. Commanders explicitly describe the desired conditions and end state for every operation. This description provides the necessary integration between tactical tasks and the conditions that define the end state.

3-47. Time is a significant consideration when developing the desired end state. How time relates to the desired end state heavily influences not only the expectations of higher authorities but also how commanders use forces and capabilities to achieve desired conditions. Staffs exercise diligence throughout design to account for the expected time required to achieve the desired conditions. They also qualify whether the desired conditions are intended to be lasting or transient in nature. This temporal dimension is essential to developing effective operational approaches. It impacts the feasibility, acceptability, suitability, and completeness of any resulting plan.

3-48. The characteristics and factors of conditions vary. Conditions may be tangible or intangible. They may be military or nonmilitary. They may focus on physical or psychological factors. They may describe or relate to perceptions, levels of comprehension, cohesion among groups, or relationships between organizations or individuals. When describing conditions that constitute a desired end state, the commander considers their relevance to higher policy, orders, guidance, or directives. Since every operation focuses on a clearly defined, decisive, and attainable end state, success hinges on accurately describing those conditions. These conditions form the basis for decisions that ensure operations progress consistently toward the desired end state.

Relevant Actors

3-49. Commanders use the environmental frame to understand and explain behaviors of relevant actors in the operational environment. An actor is an individual or group within a social network who acts to advance personal interests. Relevant actors may include states and governments; multinational actors such as coalitions; and regional groupings, alliances, terrorist networks, criminal organizations, and cartels. They may also include multinational and international corporations, nongovernmental organizations, and other actors able to influence the situation either through, or in spite of, the appropriate civil, religious, or military authority.

3-50. A diagram illustrating relevant actor relationships is a valuable tool for understanding and visualizing the operational environment. However, such diagrams may become so complicated for more complex situations that they impart only limited insight and inhibit critical and creative thought when viewed in isolation. The environmental frame's narrative captures a more detailed understanding of the relevant actors and their interactions and relationships. Often relationships among actors are multifaceted and differ depending on the scale of interaction and their temporal aspects (history, duration, type, and frequency). Clarifying the relationships among actors requires intense effort since relationships must be examined from multiple perspectives. Commanders can also depict relationships by identifying and categorizing their unique characteristics.

Tendencies and Potentials

3-51. In developing understanding of the interactions and relationships of relevant actors in the operational environment, commanders and staffs consider natural tendencies and potentials in their analyses. Tendencies reflect the inclination to think or behave in a certain manner. Tendencies are not considered deterministic but as models describing the thoughts or behaviors of relevant actors. Tendencies identify the likely pattern of relationships between the actors without external influence. Once identified, commanders and staffs evaluate the potential of these tendencies to manifest within the operational environment. Potential is the inherent ability or capacity for the growth or development of a specific interaction or relationship. Not all interactions and relationships support achieving the desired end state. The desired end state accounts for tendencies and potentials that exist among the relevant actors or other aspects of the operational variables in the environmental frame.

FRAMING THE PROBLEM

3-52. Problem framing involves understanding and isolating the root causes of conflict—defining the essence of a complex, ill-structured problem. Problem framing begins with refining the evaluation of tendencies and potentials and identifying tensions among the existing conditions and the desired end state. It articulates how the operational variables can be expected to resist or facilitate transformation and how environmental inertia can be leveraged to ensure the desired conditions are achieved. The staff relies on text and graphics to articulate the problem frame.

The Problem Frame

3-53. The problem frame is a refinement of the environmental frame that defines, in text and graphics, the areas for action that will transform existing conditions toward the desired end state. The problem frame extends beyond analyzing interactions and relationships in the operational environment. It identifies areas of tension and competition—as well as opportunities and challenges—that commanders must address so to transform current conditions to achieve the desired end state. Tension is the resistance or friction among and between actors. The commander and staff identify the tension by analyzing the relevant actors' tendencies and potentials within the context of the operational environment.

3-54. The commander and staff challenge their hypotheses and models to identify motivations and agendas among the relevant actors. They identify factors that influence these motivations and agendas. The commander and staff evaluate tendencies, potentials, trends, and tensions that influence the interactions among social, cultural, and ideological forces. These may include political, social, or cultural dispositions in one group that may hinder collaboration with another group.

3-55. In the problem frame, analysis identifies the positive, neutral, and negative implications of tensions in the operational environment given the differences between existing and desired conditions. When the commander and staff take action within the operational environment, they may exacerbate latent tensions. Tensions can be exploited to drive change, so they are vital to transforming existing conditions. If left unchecked, other tensions may undermine transformation and must be addressed appropriately. Because tensions arise from differences in perceptions, goals, and capabilities among relevant actors, they are inherently problematic and can both foster and impede transformation. By deciding how to address these tensions, the commander identifies the problem that the design will ultimately solve.

Identifying the Problem

3-56. A concise problem statement clearly defines the problem or problem set to solve. It considers how tension and competition affect the operational environment by identifying how to transform the current conditions to the desired end state—before adversaries begin to transform current conditions to their desired end state. The statement broadly describes the requirements for transformation, anticipating changes in the operational environment while identifying critical transitions. The problem statement accounts for the time and space relationships inherent in the problem frame.

CONSIDERING OPERATIONAL APPROACHES

3-57. Considering operational approaches to the problem provides focus and sets boundaries for the selection of possible actions that together lead to achieving the desired end state. The staff synthesizes and reduces much of the information and products created during the design to create the design concept and a shared understanding of a rationale behind it. The staff converges on the types and patterns of actions determining how they will achieve the desired conditions by creating a conceptual framework linking desired conditions to potential actions. The entire staff considers how to orchestrate actions to solve the problem in accordance with an operational approach.

The Operational Approach

3-58. **The *operational approach* is a broad conceptualization of the general actions that will produce the conditions that define the desired end state**. In developing the operational approach, commanders consider the direct or indirect nature of interaction with relevant actors and operational variables in the operational environment. As commanders consider various approaches, they evaluate the types of defeat or stability mechanisms that may lead to conditions that define the desired end state. Thus, the operational approach enables commanders to begin visualizing and describing possible combinations of actions to reach the desired end state given the tensions identified in the environmental and problem frames. As courses of action are developed during detailed planning, the operational approach provides the logic that underpins the unique combinations of tasks required to achieve the desired end state.

3-59. One method to depict the operational approach is by using lines of effort that provide a graphic to articulate the link among tasks, objectives, conditions, and the desired end state. (See appendix B for more detailed guidance on developing lines of effort.) Design offers the latitude to portray the operational approach in a manner that best communicates its vision and structure. Ultimately, the commander determines the optimal method to articulate the operational approach. However, it is important that narratives accompany lines of effort to ensure Soldiers understand the operational approach.

Operational Initiative

3-60. In developing an operational approach, the commander and staff consider how potential actions will enable the force to maintain the operational initiative. The *operational initiative* is the setting or dictating the terms of action throughout an operation (FM 3-0). The staff evaluates what combination of actions might derail opposing actors from achieving their goals while reinforcing their own desired end state. This entails evaluating an action's potential risks and the relevant actors' freedom of action. By identifying the possible emergence of unintended consequences or threats, commanders consider exploitable opportunities to create effects that reinforce the desired end state. The staff explores the risks and opportunities of action by considering exploitable tensions. This includes identifying capabilities and vulnerabilities of the actors who oppose the desired end state. The commander and staff can then formulate methods to neutralize those capabilities and exploit such vulnerabilities.

Resources and Risks

3-61. When creating the broad recommendations for action, the commander and staff consider resources and risks. The staff provides an initial estimate of the resources required for each recommended action in the design concept. Rarely does one organization directly control all the necessary resources. However, to create lasting changes in conditions, the effort may require substantial resources. Creative and efficient approaches can greatly amplify the limited resources directly controlled by the commander. Detailed planning determines the exact resources required.

3-62. The initial planning guidance addresses risk. It explains the acceptable level of risk to seize, retain, or exploit the initiative and broadly outlines risk mitigation measures. Planners identify and consider risks throughout the iterative application of design. Collaboration, coordination, and cooperation among multinational military and civilian partners are essential to mitigating risk, conserving resources, and achieving unity of effort. These are easier to achieve if military and civilian partners participate in design from the outset to build trust and confidence in the effort and one another.

FORGING THE DESIGN CONCEPT

3-63. The design concept is the link between design and detailed planning. It reflects understanding of the operational environment and the problem while describing the commander's visualization of a broad approach for achieving the desired end state. The design concept is the proper output of design, conveyed in text and graphics, which informs detailed planning. It is articulated to the planning staff through the—

- Problem statement.
- Initial commander's intent.
- Commander's initial planning guidance.
- Mission narrative.
- Other products created during design.

3-64. Products created during design include the text and graphics of the operational environment and problem. Diagrams representing relationships between relevant actors convey understanding to the planning staff. The problem statement generated during problem framing communicates the commander's understanding of the problem or problem set upon which the organization will act.

3-65. The initial commander's intent and planning guidance visualize and describe the desired end state along with implications for further planning. The design concept organizes desired conditions and the combinations of potential actions in time, space, and purpose that link the desired end state to the conduct of full spectrum operations. The planning guidance orients the focus of operations, linking desired conditions to potential combinations of actions the force may employ to achieve them. Other information provided in the initial planning guidance includes—

- Information integration.
- Resources.
- Risk.

3-66. The *mission narrative* is the expression of the operational approach for a specified mission. It describes the intended effects for the mission, including the conditions that define the desired end state. The mission narrative represents the articulation, or description, of the commander's visualization for a specified mission and forms the basis for the concept of operations developed during detailed planning. An explicit reflection of the commander's logic, it is used to inform and educate the various relevant partners whose perceptions, attitudes, beliefs, and behaviors are pertinent to the operation. It also informs development of supporting information themes and messages for the mission and serves as a vital tool for integrating information engagement tasks with other activities during execution.

3-67. In applying design, the commander and staff may draw on the elements of operational design relevant to the situation. (See FM 3-0.) The design concept promotes mutual understanding and unity of effort throughout the echelons and partner organizations. Thus, the design concept is the rationale linking design to detailed planning. From the design concept, planners determine how to apply forces and capabilities to achieve the desired end state.

REFRAMING

3-68. ±Reframing is a shift in understanding that leads to a new perspective on the problems or their resolution. Reframing involves significantly refining or discarding the hypotheses or models that form the basis of the design concept. At any time during the operations process, the decision to reframe can stem from significant changes to understanding, the conditions of the operational environment, or the end state. Reframing allows the commander and staff to make adjustments throughout the operations process, ensuring that tactical actions remain fundamentally linked to achieving the desired conditions.

3-69. Because the current operational environment is always changing and evolving, the problem frame must also evolve. Recognizing when an operation—or planning—is not progressing as envisioned or must be reconsidered provides the impetus for reframing in design. Reframing criteria should support the commander's ability to understand, learn, and adapt—and cue commanders to rethink their understanding of the operational environment, and hence rethink how to solve the problem. Generally, reframing is triggered in three ways: a major event causes a "catastrophic change" in the operational environment, a scheduled periodic review shows a problem, or an assessment and reflection challenges understanding of the existing problem and the relevance of the operational approach.

3-70. During operations, commanders decide to reframe after realizing the desired conditions have changed, are not achievable, or cannot be attained through the current operational approach. Reframing provides the freedom to operate beyond the limits of any single perspective. Conditions will change during execution, and such change is expected because forces interact within the operational environment. Recognizing and anticipating these changes is fundamental to design and essential to an organization's ability to learn.

3-71. Reframing is equally important in the wake of success. By its very nature, success transforms the operational environment, creating unforeseen opportunities to exploit the initiative. Organizations are strongly motivated to reflect and reframe following failure, but they tend to neglect reflection and reframing following successful actions.

This page intentionally left blank.

Chapter 4

Preparation

This chapter defines preparation and lists its functions. Next, it describes the relationship of preparation to the other operations process activities. The chapter concludes by listing the preparation activities commonly performed within the headquarters and across the force to improve the unit's ability to execute operations.

PREPARATION FUNCTIONS

4-1.   *Preparation* consists of activities performed by units to improve their ability to execute an operation. Preparation includes, but is not limited to, plan refinement; rehearsals; intelligence, surveillance, and reconnaissance; coordination; inspections; and movement (FM 3-0). Preparation creates conditions that improve friendly forces' opportunities for success. It requires commander, staff, unit, and Soldier actions to ensure the force is ready to execute operations.

4-2.   Preparation helps the force transition from planning to execution. Preparation normally begins during planning and continues into execution by uncommitted units. Preparation activities help commanders, staffs, and Soldiers to understand the situation and their roles in the upcoming operations. The primary functions of preparation include—

- Improving situational understanding.
- Developing a common understanding of the plan.
- Practicing and becoming proficient on critical tasks.
- Integrating, organizing, and configuring the force.
- Ensuring forces and resources are ready and positioned.

IMPROVING SITUATIONAL UNDERSTANDING

4-3.   Developing and maintaining situational understanding requires continuous effort throughout the operations process. (See chapter 1.) Commanders realize that their initial understanding developed during planning may be neither complete nor accurate. During preparation, commanders strive to improve their situational understanding. Leader reconnaissance and intelligence, surveillance, and reconnaissance (ISR) operations help improve understanding the enemy, terrain, and civil considerations. Inspections, rehearsals, liaison, and coordination help leaders improve their understanding of the friendly force. Based on their improved situational understanding, commanders refine the plan as required, prior to execution.

DEVELOPING A COMMON UNDERSTANDING OF THE PLAN

4-4.   A successful transition from planning to execution requires those charged with executing the order to understand the plan fully. The transition between planning and execution takes place both internally in the headquarters (among the plans cell, future operations cell, and current operations integration cell) and externally (between the commander and subordinate commanders). Several preparation activities assist the commander, staff, and subordinates in fully understanding the plan. A confirmation briefing, rehearsals, and the plans-to-operations transition briefing help them all develop a common understanding of the plan. Additionally, when possible, commanders personally brief plans to subordinates to ensure understanding.

PRACTICING AND BECOMING PROFICIENT ON CRITICAL TASKS

4-5.   During preparation, units and Soldiers practice to become proficient in those tasks critical to the success of a specific operation. Commanders issue guidance on which tasks to rehearse and train. They base their guidance on time available and unit readiness. Commanders also allocate time during preparation for units and Soldiers to train on unfamiliar tasks prior to execution. For example, a unit unfamiliar with small boat operations requires significant training and familiarization prior to crossing a river by small boat. Units may need to practice crowd control techniques in support of a local election. Leaders also allocate time for maintaining proficiency on individual Soldier skills (such as zeroing individual weapons, combat lifesaving tasks, language familiarization, and cultural awareness) during preparation.

INTEGRATING, ORGANIZING, AND CONFIGURING THE FORCE

4-6.   Task-organizing the force is an important part of planning. During preparation, commanders allocate time to put the new task organization into effect. This includes detaching units, moving forces, and receiving and integrating new units and Soldiers into the force. When units change task organization, they need preparation time to learn the gaining unit's standard operating procedures (SOPs) and the plan the gaining unit will execute. The gaining unit needs preparation time to assess the new unit's capabilities and limitations and to integrate new capabilities. See appendix F for a detailed discussion on task organization.

ENSURING FORCES AND RESOURCES ARE READY AND POSITIONED

4-7.   ±Effective preparation ensures the right forces are in the right place, at the right time, with the right equipment and other resources ready to execute the operation. Concurrent with task organization, commanders use troop movement to position or reposition forces to the correct location prior to execution. This includes positioning sustainment units and supplies. Preoperations checks confirm that the force has the proper equipment and the equipment is functional prior to execution.

PREPARATION AND THE OPERATIONS PROCESS

4-8.   ±Preparation often begins during planning and continues into execution. During planning, the higher headquarters issues a series of warning orders to subordinates alerting them of an upcoming mission and directing preparation activities such as reconnaissance and troop movements. During execution, uncommitted units continue to prepare. Assessment during preparation focuses on identifying changes in the situation that may require plan refinement and determining the readiness of the force to execute operations.

±THE COMMANDER'S ROLE

4-9.   During preparation, commanders continue to understand, visualize, describe, direct, lead, and assess. They gather additional information to improve their situational understanding, revise the plan, coordinate with other units and partners, and supervise preparation activities to ensure their forces are ready to execute missions.

4-10. During preparation, commanders update and improve their commander's visualization as they receive relevant information that helps satisfy their commander's critical information requirements (CCIRs) and verify assumptions made during planning. Preparation activities—particularly subordinate confirmation briefs and rehearsals—help commanders visualize the situation from their subordinates' perspectives. Additionally, information from ISR and liaisons improves the commander's situational understanding. Commanders describe any changes in their visualization to their subordinates resulting in additional planning guidance and fragmentary orders prior to execution.

4-11. During preparation, commanders circulate among subordinate units and with the population in areas under friendly control. This allows commanders to assess subordinates' preparation, get to know new units in the task organization, and personally motivate Soldiers. By personally briefing subordinates, commanders gain firsthand appreciation for the situation as well as ensure Soldiers understand the commander's intent. Commanders also visit with civilian organizations (other government agencies, intergovernmental organizations, nongovernmental organizations, and elements of the private sector) in the operational area to build personal relationships with civilian partners. Knowledge gained during these visits allows the commander to maintain situational understanding and continuously update their commander's visualization prior to execution.

PREPARATION DURING PLANNING

4-12. Planning and preparation often overlap. In operations, subordinate forces begin preparation before the operation order is published. Subordinate headquarters can begin planning prior to or in parallel with their higher headquarters; they begin preparation as information about the upcoming operation becomes available and as preliminary decisions are made, particularly concerning information gaps. Using warning orders or collaborative planning to disseminate new information increases subordinate units' preparation time. Several preparation activities begin during planning. Commanders often direct troop movements, task-organizing, and sustainment preparation in warning orders before they issue the operation order.

4-13. While waiting on the details of an upcoming operation, units train on basic skills, maintain weapons and equipment, and work on tasks identified as needing improvement during recent operations. Sometimes, preparation during lulls may mean giving Soldiers a chance to rest and restore themselves.

PREPARATION DURING EXECUTION

4-14. During execution, some of the force may be still preparing. Uncommitted forces continue preparation for the operation's next phase or branch. Committed forces revert to preparation when they reach their objectives, occupy defensive positions, or pass into reserve. Units in reserve conduct route reconnaissance for counterattacks and rehearse those actions deemed most likely for their commitment.

ASSESSMENT DURING PREPARATION

4-15. Assessment during preparation focuses on determining the force's readiness to execute the mission and identifying any significant changes in the situation requiring a change to the plan. During preparation, staffs continue to build and maintain their running estimates, providing commanders results of their analysis, conclusions, and recommendations. Commanders continue to modify their understanding and visualization based on new information concerning the friendly force and other aspects of the operational environment. This assessment helps the commander and staffs verify assumptions and refine plans as required. Assessment results during preparation may reveal significant changes in the situation requiring commanders to reframe and develop a new plan.

PREPARATION ACTIVITIES

4-16. Mission success depends as much on preparation as on planning. Higher headquarters may develop the best of plans; however, plans serve little purpose if subordinates do not receive them in time. Subordinates need enough time to understand plans well enough to execute them. Subordinates develop their own plans and prepare for the operation. After they fully comprehend the plan, subordinate leaders rehearse key portions of it and ensure Soldiers and equipment are positioned and ready to execute the operation. To help ensure the force is protected and prepared for execution, commanders, units, and Soldiers conduct the following activities:

- Conduct ISR.
- Conduct security operations.
- Conduct protection.
- Manage terrain.
- Coordinate and conduct liaison.
- Continue to build partnerships and teams.
- Conduct confirmation briefs.
- Conduct rehearsals.
- Conduct plans-to-operations transitions.
- Revise and refine the plan.
- Complete task organization.
- Integrate new Soldiers and units.
- Train.
- Initiate troop movements.

- Prepare terrain.
- Conduct sustainment preparation.
- Initiate deception operations.
- Conduct preoperations checks and inspections.

±CONDUCT INTELLIGENCE, SURVEILLANCE, AND RECONNAISSANCE

4-17. During preparation, commanders take every opportunity to improve their situational understanding prior to execution. This requires aggressive and continuous surveillance and reconnaissance during preparation. Commanders often direct ISR operations early in the planning process that continue in preparation and execution. Through ISR, commanders and staffs continuously plan, task, and employ collection assets and forces. These assets and forces collect, process, and disseminate timely and accurate information, combat information, and intelligence to satisfy CCIRs and other information requirements.

4-18. Commanders consider requesting assistance from sources beyond their control, including long-range surveillance teams and joint assets, through ISR synchronization. They synchronize reconnaissance operations with their own organic assets as well as the intelligence collection and analysis effort to continuously update and improve their situational understanding.

4-19. Commanders give the same care to reconnaissance missions as to any other combined arms operation. They ensure all warfighting functions are synchronized to support forces conducting reconnaissance. This includes, but is not limited to, fires, sustainment, and mission command. Relevant information from surveillance and reconnaissance helps commanders fill in information gaps, validate assumptions, and finalize the plan prior to execution.

±CONDUCT SECURITY OPERATIONS

4-20. The force as a whole is often most vulnerable to surprise and enemy attack during preparation. Forces are often concentrated in assembly areas. Leaders are away from their units and concentrated together during rehearsals. Parts of the force could be moving to task-organize. Required supplies may be unavailable or being repositioned. Security operations—screen, guard, cover, area security, and local security—are essential during preparation. (See FM 3-90.) Units assigned security missions execute these missions while the rest of the force prepares for the overall operation.

±CONDUCT PROTECTION

4-21. Protection is both a warfighting function and a continuing activity. The protection warfighting functions consist of twelve tasks (see FM 3-0) for which commanders and staffs continuously plan and execute to preserve the force. Preserving the force includes protecting personnel (combatants and noncombatants), physical assets, and information of the United States and multinational military and civilian partners. (See FM 3-37 for doctrine on protection.)

4-22. Because the force is often most vulnerable to attack and surprise while preparing, emphasis on protection increases during preparation and continues throughout execution. While all protection tasks are important, commanders particularly emphasize the protection tasks of operations security, survivability, and operational area security during preparation.

4-23. Operations security identifies and implements measures to protect essential elements of friendly information. During preparation, forces implement measures that eliminate or reduce the vulnerability of friendly forces to exploitation. These measures include concealing rehearsals, troop movements, positioning of forces, and other indicators of unit intentions that enemy intelligence may exploit.

4-24. Survivability includes protecting the force while deceiving the enemy. It includes developing and constructing protective positions to reduce the effectiveness of enemy weapon systems. Protective positions can include earth berms, dug-in positions, overhead protection, and counter-surveillance. Survivability tactics range from employing camouflage, concealment, and deception to the hardening of facilities, signal nodes, and critical infrastructure.

4-25. Operational area security focuses on protecting areas, routes, or installations. During preparation, operational area security focuses on protecting assembly areas and securing routes required for task organization, sustainment, or positioning units for upcoming operations.

MANAGE TERRAIN

4-26. **Terrain management is the process of allocating terrain by establishing areas of operation, designating assembly areas, and specifying locations for units and activities to deconflict activities that might interfere with each other.** Terrain management is an important activity during preparation as units reposition and stage prior to execution. Commanders assigned an area of operations manage terrain within their boundaries. Through terrain management, commanders identify and locate units in the area. Staffs can then deconflict operations, control movements, and deter fratricide as units get in position to execute planned missions. Commanders also consider the civilians and civilian organizations located in their area of operations.

COORDINATE AND CONDUCT LIAISON

4-27. Coordinating and conducting liaison helps ensure that military leaders internal and external to the headquarters understand their unit's role in the upcoming operation and are prepared to execute it. In addition to military forces, many civilian organizations may operate in the operational area. Their presence can affect and are affected by the commander's operations. Continuous coordination and liaison between the command and civilian organization helps to build *unity of effort*—coordination and cooperation toward common objectives, even if the participants are not necessarily part of the same command or organization—the product of successful unified action (JP 1). (See FM 3-07 and JP 3-08 for detailed discussions on interagency, intergovernmental organization, and nongovernmental organization coordination.)

4-28. During preparation, commanders coordinate with higher, lower, adjacent, supporting, and supported units and civilian organizations. Coordination includes the following:
- Sending and receiving liaison teams.
- Establishing communication links that ensure continuous contact during execution.
- Exchanging SOPs.
- Synchronizing security operations with ISR plans to prevent breaks in coverage.
- Facilitating civil-military coordination among those involved.

4-29. Establishing and maintaining liaison is vital to external coordination. Liaison provides a means of direct communications between the sending and receiving headquarters. It may begin with planning and continue through preparing and executing, or it may start as late as execution. Available resources and the need for direct contact between sending and receiving headquarters determine when to establish liaison. Establishing liaisons with civilian organizations is especially important in stability operations because of the variety of external organizations and the inherent coordination challenges. (See FM 6-0 for doctrine on liaison.)

±CONTINUE TO BUILD PARTNERSHIPS AND TEAMS

4-30. Developing teams among modular formations and joint, interagency, intergovernmental, and multinational partners is a key mission command task that begins early in the operations process. While the Army's modular brigade-based force allows for greater flexibility, the modular construct creates challenges in building cohesive teams. Often, modular units are task-organized to meet specific mission requirements. In addition, they may not have trained with the higher headquarters that employs them.

4-31. To help build teams among modular formations, commanders encourage active collaboration and dialog with subordinates (see chapter 1). Through collaboration and dialog, commanders gain insight into Soldiers' needs while providing their own vision and expectations. Commanders circulate among subordinate units as much as possible to help establish personal relationships and build the team. By circulating, commanders assess subordinates' preparation and execution, get to know new units in the task organization, and personally motivate Soldiers. Commanders appreciate the situation firsthand and ensure subordinates understand their commander's intent. Commanders lead, coach, and mentor subordinate leaders, establishing close relationships that foster trust and confidence.

4-32. Conducting full spectrum operations requires commanders to shape civil conditions in concert with other military and civilian organizations within an operational area. In some circumstances, commanders have an established command or support relationship with these organizations. In other instances, they will not. In those instances where commanders lack a formal command or support relationship with an organization, they seek unity of effort. (See paragraph 4-48.) They try to build partnerships and teams with these organizations to develop common goals, including local political leaders, host-nation police and security forces, and nongovernmental organizations. Capable and cooperative civilian organizations substantially enhance military operations by performing complementary civil functions that inform and assist the population and add legitimacy to the mission.

4-33. Building partnerships and teams with organizations begins early in planning, is a key activity of preparation, and continues throughout execution. Civilian organizations, including those of the host nation, are frequently present before forces arrive and remain after forces depart. As part of mission analysis, commanders identify civilian organizations in the operational area and develop plans to build relationships with them. During preparation, commanders, staffs, and subordinate commanders identify and make contact with those various organizations. A challenge in building partnerships among civilian and military efforts is the differing capabilities and cultures in the civilian and host-nation organizations compared to those of the headquarters. To help build partnerships, commanders strive to have participants—

- Represented, integrated, and actively involved in planning and coordinating activities.
- Share an understanding of the situation and problems to solve.
- Strive for unity of effort toward achieving a common goal.
- Integrate and synchronize capabilities and activities wherever possible.
- Collectively determine the resources, capabilities, and activities necessary to achieve their goal.

Note: Commanders avoid creating a false impression of the headquarters' readiness to make available classified military materiel, technology, or information when coordinating with foreign governments and international originations. See AR 380-10 for guidance on foreign disclosure and contacts with foreign representatives.

4-34. Developing partnerships with civilian organizations requires considerable effort by the commander, staff, and subordinate commanders. Some organizations willingly cooperate with the command. Other organizations may avoid a close affiliation. Sometimes they fear compromising their impartiality with the local populace or have suspicions that the force may intend to take control of, influence, or even prevent operations. Despite different goals among military and civilian agencies and organizations, discovering common ground is essential to unity of effort.

CONDUCT CONFIRMATION BRIEFS

4-35. The confirmation brief is a key part of preparation. Subordinate leaders give a confirmation brief to the commander immediately after receiving the operation order. A confirmation brief ensures the commander that subordinate leaders understand—

- The commander's intent, mission, and concept of operations.
- Their unit's tasks and associated purposes.
- The relationship between their unit's mission and those of other units in the operation.

Ideally, leaders conduct the confirmation brief in person with selected staff members of the higher headquarters present.

CONDUCT REHEARSALS

4-36. **A *rehearsal* is a session in which a staff or unit practices expected actions to improve performance during execution**. Commanders use this tool to ensure staffs and subordinates understand the concept of operations and commander's intent. Rehearsals also allow leaders to practice synchronizing operations at times and places critical to mission accomplishment. Effective rehearsals imprint a mental picture of the sequence of the operation's key actions and improve mutual understanding and coordination of subordinate and supporting leaders and units. The extent of rehearsals depends on available time. In cases of short-notice requirements, rehearsals may not be possible.

4-37. Rehearsals contribute to external and internal coordination. Even if staff members do not attend a rehearsal, they may receive a tasking for internal coordination. Properly executed, they—

- Help commanders visualize conditions associated with decisionmaking before, during, and after the operation.
- Help prepare commanders and staffs to synchronize the operation at key points. Rehearsals do this by identifying actions, times, and locations that require coordination.
- Reveal unidentified external coordination requirements.
- Support internal coordination by identifying tasks needed to accomplish external coordination.
- Help staff sections update internal coordination tools, such as the synchronization matrix and decision support template.

4-38. Uncommitted units rehearse during execution of the overall operation if time allows. These rehearsals help Soldiers prepare for their part of the operation. For example, the reserve might practice their movements to attack or defend positions. Units defending in depth can rehearse their movements and engagements. (See appendix I for more information on rehearsals.)

±CONDUCT PLANS-TO-OPERATIONS TRANSITION

4-39. The plans-to-operations transition is a preparation activity that occurs within the headquarters to ensure that members of the current operations integration cell fully understand the plan before execution. During preparation, the responsibility for developing and maintaining the plan shifts from the plans (or future operations) cell to the current operations integration cell. This transition is the point at which the current operations integration cell becomes responsible for controlling execution of the operation order. This responsibility includes answering requests for information concerning the order and maintaining the order through fragmentary orders. This transition enables the plans cell to focus its planning efforts on sequels, branches, and other planning requirements directed by the commander.

4-40. The timing of the plans-to-operations transition requires careful consideration. It must allow enough time for members of the current operations integration cell to understand the plan well enough to coordinate and synchronize its execution. Ideally, the plans cell briefs the members of the current operations cell on the plans-to-operations transition before the combined arms rehearsal. This briefing enables members of the current operations integration cell to understand the upcoming operation as well as identify friction points and issues to solve prior to execution. The transition briefing is a mission briefing that generally follows the five-paragraph operation order format. Areas addressed include—

- Task organization.
- Situation.
- Higher headquarters' mission (one and two echelons up).
- Mission.
- Commander's intent (one and two echelons up).
- Concept of operations.
- Commander's critical information requirements.
- Decision support template and matrix.
- Branches and sequels.
- Sustainment.
- Command and signal.
- Outstanding requests for information and outstanding issues.

4-41. Following the combined arms rehearsal, planners and members of the current operations integration cell review additional planning guidance issued by the commander and modify the plan as necessary.

Significant changes may require assistance from the plans cell to include moving a lead planner to the current operations integration cell. The plans cell continues planning for branches and sequels.

±REVISE AND REFINE THE PLAN

4-42. Revising and refining the plan is a key activity of preparation. The commander's situational understanding may change over the course of operations, enemy actions may require revision of the plan, or unforeseen opportunities may arise. During preparation, assumptions made during planning may be proven true or false. Intelligence analysis may confirm or deny enemy actions or show changed conditions in the area of operations because of shaping operations. The status of friendly forces may change as the situation changes. In any of these cases, commanders identify the changed conditions and assess how the changes might affect the upcoming operation. Significant new information requires commanders to make one of three assessments regarding the plan:

- The new information validates the plan with no further changes.
- The new information requires adjustments to the plan.
- The new information invalidates the plan requiring the commander to reframe and develop a new plan.

The earlier the commander identifies the need for adjustments, the more easily the staff can incorporate the changes to the plan and modify preparation activities.

4-43. Plans are not static. They should be made as flexible as possible by including on-order adjustments or variations that can be implemented by fragmentary orders. Commanders adjust the plan based on new information and changing circumstances. These new developments may correct or invalidate assumptions made during planning. With such changes, commanders determine whether the new information requires adjustment to the plan or whether to begin a reframing effort (see chapter 3) and develop a completely new plan. Commanders decide by balancing the loss of synchronization caused by the change against the problems created by executing a plan that no longer fits reality. Any adjustments to the plan must fit within the higher commander's intent. Commanders identify adjustments that create a major change in preparation activities early enough to allow the force to react.

±COMPLETE TASK ORGANIZATION

4-44. During preparation, commanders complete task-organizing their organizations to obtain the right mix of forces, capabilities, and expertise to accomplish a specific mission. The receiving commander integrates units that are attached, placed under operational control, or placed in direct support. The commander directing the task organization also makes provisions for sustainment. The commander may direct task organization to occur immediately before the operation order is issued. This task-organizing is done with a warning order. Doing this gives units more time to execute the tasks needed to affect the new task organization. Task-organizing early allows affected units to become better integrated and more familiar with all elements involved.

±INTEGRATE NEW SOLDIERS AND UNITS

4-45. Commanders, command sergeants major, and staffs help new Soldiers assimilate into their units and new units into the force. They also prepare new units and Soldiers to perform their duties in the upcoming operation with smooth integration.

4-46. For new Soldiers, integration includes—

- Training new Soldiers on the unit SOPs and mission-essential tasks for the operation.
- Orienting new Soldiers on their places and roles in the force and operation.
- Confirming that all personal information is present and correct.

4-47. This integration for units includes—

- Receiving and introducing new units to the force and the area of operations.
- Exchanging SOPs.
- Conducting briefings and rehearsals.

- Establishing communications links.
- Exchanging liaison teams (if required).

±TRAIN

4-48. Training prepares forces and Soldiers to conduct operations according to doctrine, SOPs, and the unit's mission. Training develops the teamwork, trust, and mutual understanding that commanders need to exercise mission command and that forces need to achieve unity of effort. Training does not stop when a unit deploys. If the unit is not conducting operations or recovering from operations, it is training. Training while deployed focuses on fundamental skills, current SOPs, and skills for a specific mission. (See FM 7-0 for details on training the force.)

±INITIATE TROOP MOVEMENTS

4-49. The repositioning of forces prior to execution is a significant activity of preparation. *Troop movement* is the movement of troops from one place to another by any available means (FM 3-90). Troop movement is used to position or reposition units to ensure they are in the right starting places before execution. Commanders integrate operations security measures with troop movements to ensure the movements do not reveal any intentions to the enemy. (See FM 3-37.) Troop movements include assembly area reconnaissance by advance parties and route reconnaissance. They also include movements required by changes to the task organization. Commanders can use a warning order to direct troop movements before issuing the operation order.

±PREPARE TERRAIN

4-50. Terrain preparation starts with the situational understanding of terrain through proper terrain analysis. It involves shaping the terrain to gain an advantage, to include improving cover, concealment and observation, fields of fire, new obstacle effects through reinforcing obstacles, or mobility operations for initial positioning of forces. It can make the difference between the operation's success and failure. Commanders must understand the terrain and the infrastructure of their area of operations as early as possible to identify potential for improvement, establish priorities of work, and begin preparing the area as rapidly as possible.

±CONDUCT SUSTAINMENT PREPARATION

4-51. Resupplying, maintaining, and issuing supplies or equipment occurs during preparation. Any repositioning of sustainment assets can also occur. In addition, sustainment elements need to accomplish many other activities.

4-52. During preparation, sustainment planners at all levels take action to optimize means (force structure and resources) for supporting the commander's plan. These actions include but are not limited to identifying and preparing bases, host-nation infrastructure and capabilities, contract support requirements, lines of communications, and endemic health and environmental factors as well as forecasting and building operational stocks.

4-53. Planners focus on identifying the resources currently available in the theater of operations and ensuring access to them. During preparation, sustainment planning continues to support operational planning (branch and sequel development) and the targeting process.

±INITIATE DECEPTION OPERATIONS

4-54. Deception operations commonly begin during preparation. Commanders use some troop positioning and movement to deceive the enemy. Deceptive electronic activities, camouflage and decoys, and circulation of false information also accompany preparation. These operations impose some burdens on a force but may improve the effectiveness of execution. Preparation of the force cannot compromise the commander's deception plan.

±Conduct Preoperations Checks and Inspections

4-55. Unit preparation includes completing preoperations checks and inspections. These checks ensure units, Soldiers, and systems are as fully capable and ready to execute as time and resources permit. The inspections ensure the force has resources necessary to accomplish the mission. Also during preoperations checks and inspections, leaders check Soldiers' ability to perform crew drills that may not be directly related to the mission. Examples of these drills include those that respond to a vehicle rollover or an onboard fire.

Chapter 5

Execution

This chapter provides doctrine for exercising mission command during execution. It provides fundamentals to guide execution and describes the roles of the commander and staff when directing and synchronizing the current operation. Next, this chapter describes assessment and decisionmaking in execution. The chapter concludes with a discussion of the rapid decisionmaking and synchronization process (RDSP).

FUNDAMENTALS OF EXECUTION

5-1. Planning and preparation accomplish nothing if the command does not execute effectively. *Execution* is putting a plan into action by applying combat power to accomplish the mission and using situational understanding to assess progress and make execution and adjustment decisions (FM 3-0). In execution, commanders focus their efforts on translating decisions into actions to accomplish their missions.

5-2. In any operation, the situation may change rapidly. Operations the commander envisioned in the plan may bear little resemblance to actual events in execution. Subordinate commanders need maximum latitude to take advantage of situations and meet the higher commander's intent when the original order no longer applies. Effective execution requires leaders trained in independent decisionmaking, aggressiveness, and risk taking in an environment of mission command. (See FM 6-0.) During execution, leaders must be able and willing to solve problems within the commander's intent without constantly referring to higher headquarters. Subordinates need not wait for top-down synchronization to act.

5-3. Throughout execution, commanders (assisted by their staff) use forces and other resources for both constructive and destructive purposes to mass effects at decisive points and times. To successfully execute operations, commander's consider the following execution fundamentals:

- Seize and retain the initiative.
- Build and maintain momentum.
- Exploit success.

SEIZE AND RETAIN THE INITIATIVE

5-4. Initiative gives all operations the spirit, if not the form, of the offense. Operationally, seizing the initiative requires leaders to anticipate events so their forces can see and exploit opportunities faster than the enemy can or a situation deteriorates. Once they seize the initiative, Army forces exploit created opportunities. Initiative requires constant effort to force an enemy to conform to friendly purposes and tempo while retaining friendly freedom of action. Subordinates make reasoned decisions within the commander's intent. Their decisions and the commander's intent create conditions for exercising disciplined initiative.

Take Action

5-5. Commanders create conditions for seizing the initiative by acting. Without action, seizing the initiative is impossible. Faced with an uncertain situation, there is a natural tendency to hesitate and gather more information to reduce the uncertainty. However, waiting and gathering information might reduce uncertainty but will not eliminate it. Waiting may even increase uncertainty by providing the enemy with time to seize the initiative. It is far better to manage uncertainty by acting and developing the situation.

5-6. In stability operations, commanders act quickly to improve the civil situation while preventing conditions from deteriorating further. Immediate action to stabilize the situation and provide for the immediate humanitarian needs of the people begins the process toward stability. Friendly forces dictate the terms of action and drive positive change to stabilize the situation rapidly. In turn, this improves the security environment, creating earlier opportunities for civilian agencies and organizations to contribute. By acting proactively to influence events, Army forces exploit the initiative to ensure steady progress toward conditions that support stability. Failing to act quickly may create a breeding ground for dissent and possible recruiting opportunities for enemies or adversaries.

5-7.   ±During execution, action must be synchronized with themes and messages. Commanders use inform and influence activities in their area of operations to communicate, build trust and confidence, and influence perceptions and behavior. Failure to synchronize words and actions may result in adverse behavior by groups whose behavior is key to mission accomplishment.

Create and Exploit Opportunities

5-8.   Events that offer better ways to success are opportunities. Commanders recognize opportunities by continuously monitoring and evaluating the situation. Failure to understand the opportunities inherent in an enemy's action surrenders the initiative. Commander's critical information requirements (CCIRs) must include elements that support exploiting opportunities. Commanders encourage subordinates to act within the commander's intent as opportunities occur. Vision, clear communication of commander's intent, and mission command create an atmosphere conducive to subordinates exercising initiative.

Assess and Take Risk

5-9.   Uncertainty and risk are inherent in all military operations. Recognizing and acting on opportunity means taking risks. Reasonably estimating and intentionally accepting risk is not gambling. Carefully determining the risks, analyzing and minimizing as many hazards as possible, and executing a supervised plan that accounts for those hazards contributes to successfully applying military force. Gambling, in contrast, is imprudently staking the success of an entire action on a single, improbable event. Commanders assess risk in ascending orders of magnitude by answering four questions:

- Am I minimizing the risk of civilian casualties and collateral damage?
- Am I minimizing the risk of friendly losses?
- Am I risking the success of the operation?
- Am I risking the destruction of the force itself?

5-10.   When commanders embrace opportunity, they accept risk. It is counterproductive to wait for perfect preparation and synchronization. The time taken to fully synchronize forces and warfighting functions in a detailed order could mean a lost opportunity. It is far better to quickly summarize the essentials, get things moving, and send the details later. Leaders optimize the use of time with warning orders, fragmentary orders, and verbal updates.

BUILD AND MAINTAIN MOMENTUM

5-11. Momentum comes from seizing the initiative and executing decisive, shaping, and sustaining operations at a rapid and sustainable tempo. Momentum allows commanders to create opportunities to engage the enemy from unexpected directions with unanticipated capabilities. Having seized the initiative, commanders continue to control the relative momentum by maintaining focus and pressure and controlling the tempo. They ensure that they maintain momentum by anticipating transitions and moving rapidly between types of operations.

5-12. Speed promotes surprise and can compensate for lack of forces. It magnifies the impact of success in seizing the initiative. By executing at a rapid tempo, Army forces present the enemy with new problems before it can solve current ones. Rapid tempo should not degenerate into haste. Ill-informed and hasty action usually precludes effective combinations of combat power; it may lead to unnecessary casualties. The condition of the enemy force dictates the degree of synchronization necessary. When confronted by a coherent and disciplined enemy, commanders may slow the tempo to deliver synchronized blows. As the enemy force loses cohesion, commanders increase the tempo, seeking to accelerate the enemy's morale and physical collapse.

EXPLOIT SUCCESS

5-13. Ultimately, only successes that achieve the end state count. To determine how to exploit tactical and operational successes, commanders assess them in terms of the higher commander's intent. However, success will likely occur in ways unanticipated in the plan. Commanders may gain an objective in an unexpected way. Success signals a rapid assessment to answer these questions:

- Does the success generate opportunities that more easily accomplish the objectives?
- Does it suggest other lines of operations or lines of effort?
- Does it cause commanders to change their overall intent?
- Should the force transition to a sequel?
- Should the force accelerate the phasing of the operation?

5-14. Exploitation demands assessment and understanding of the impact on sustainment operations. Sustainment provides the means to exploit success and convert it into decisive results. Sustainment preserves the freedom of action necessary to take advantage of opportunity. Commanders remain fully aware of the status of units and anticipate sustainment requirements, recognizing that sustainment often determines the depth to which Army forces exploit success.

RESPONSIBILITIES DURING EXECUTION

5-15. ±During execution, commanders focus their activities on directing, assessing and leading while improving their understanding and modifying their visualization. Initially, commanders *direct* the transition from planning to execution as the order is issued and the responsibility for integration passes from the plans cell to the current operations integration cell. During execution, the staff *directs*, within delegated authority, to keep the operation progressing successfully. *Assessing* allows the commander and staff to determine the existence and significance of variances from the operations as envisioned in the initial plan. The staff makes recommendations to the commander about what action to take concerning variances they identified. During execution, *leading* is as important as decisionmaking as commanders influence subordinates by providing purpose, direction, and motivation.

COMMANDERS, DEPUTIES, CHIEFS OF STAFF, AND COMMAND SERGEANTS MAJOR

5-16. During execution, commanders at all levels locate where they can exercise command and sense the operation. Sometimes this is at the command post. Other times, commanders may use a command group or mobile command post to command from a forward location. Commanders must balance the need to make personal observations, provide command presence, and sense the mood of subordinates from a forward location with the ability to maintain continuity with the entire force. No matter where they are located, commanders are always looking beyond the current operation to anticipate what's next. They must periodically step back and look at how the force is positioning itself for future operations.

5-17. Deputy commanders provide a command resource during execution. First, they can serve as a senior advisor to the commander. Second, deputy commanders may directly supervise a specific warfighting function (for example, sustainment). Finally, deputy commanders can provide command of a specific operation (such as a gap crossing), area, or part of the unit (such as the covering force) for the commander.

5-18. The chief of staff (COS) or executive officer (XO) integrates the efforts of the whole staff during execution. These efforts include the assignment of responsibilities among staff sections and command post cells for conducting analysis and decisionmaking. While the unit standard operating procedures might specify a division of responsibilities among integrating cells for these matters, often the COS (XO) makes specific decisions allocating responsibilities among cells. The COS (XO) considers the situation, expertise, and capabilities of individual cells as requirements arise or are forecast.

5-19. The command sergeant major provides another set of senior eyes to assist the commander. The command sergeant major assists the commander with assessing operations as well as assessing the condition and moral of forces. In addition, the command sergeant major provides leadership and expertise to units and Soldiers.

STAFF

5-20. In execution, the staff—primarily through the current operations integration cell—integrates forces and warfighting functions to accomplish the mission. The staff assesses short-term actions and activities as part of this integration. While the COS (XO) integrates staff activities among all functional and integrating cells and separate sections, the operations officer integrates the operation through the current operations integration cell. Other staff principals integrate within their areas of expertise.

5-21. Formal and informal integration of the warfighting functions by functional and integrating cells is continuous. The integration occurs both within and among command post cells and staff sections and between headquarters. When staffs need a more structured integration, they establish meetings (to include working groups and boards) to share information, coordinate actions, and solve problems. (See command post operations in appendix A.) The COS (XO) also identifies staff members to participate in the higher commander's working groups and boards.

CURRENT OPERATIONS INTEGRATION CELL

5-22. The current operations integration cell is the integrating cell in the command post with primary responsibility for execution. Staff members in the current operations integration cell actively assist the commander and subordinate units in controlling the current operation. They provide information, synchronize staff and subordinate unit or echelon activities, and coordinate subordinate support requests. The current operations integration cell solves problems and acts within the authority delegated by the commander. It also performs some short-range planning using the RDSP. (See paragraphs **Error! Reference source not found.** through 5-49.)

5-23. The current operations integration cell is staffed and equipped to—

- Monitor and assess execution of the operation, to include tracking tasks assigned to subordinate forces.
- Maintain the location and status of friendly forces (higher, lower, and adjacent) and their resources.
- Maintain the location and status of threat forces.
- Maintain the location and status of significant civilian agencies.
- Track CCIRs and decision points.
- Adjust the current order within its authority or recommend adjustments to the commander.
- Conduct short-range planning to take advantage of opportunities or to counter threats. (The future operations cell or plans cell solves complex planning problems and planning beyond the short-range planning horizon.)
- Conduct knowledge management and information management activities, to include—
  - Managing requests for information.
  - Maintaining displays, such as CCIRs, execution matrixes, and significant events.
  - Maintaining the common operational picture.
  - Receiving and sending reports, including operational and commander summaries.
  - Helping to prepare, authenticate, and distribute operation plans and orders, messages, and other directives.
  - Conducting rehearsals.
  - Collecting, processing, storing, displaying, and disseminating relevant information.

5-24. Several decision support tools assist the commander and staff during execution. Among the most important are the decision support template, decision support matrix, and execution matrix. The current operations integration cell uses these tools among others to help control operations and to determine when anticipated decisions are coming up for execution.

5-25. A *decision support template* is a combined intelligence and operations graphic based on the results of wargaming. The decision support template depicts decision points, timelines associated with movement of forces and the flow of the operation, and other key items of information required to execute a specific friendly course of action (JP 2-01.3). Part of the decision support template is the decision support matrix.

A *decision support matrix* **is a written record of a war-gamed course of action that describes decision points and associated actions at those decision points**. The decision support matrix lists decision points, locations of decision points, criteria to be evaluated at decision points, actions that occur at decision points, and the units responsible to act on the decision points. It also lists the units responsible for observing and reporting information affecting the criteria for decisions.

5-26. The current operations integration cell uses the decision support template and the decision support matrix to determine the need and timing for execution decisions. This involves assessing the progress of the operation and evaluating the criteria for upcoming decision points to see if the criteria for the upcoming decision points have been met or not.

5-27. **An *execution matrix* is a visual and sequential representation of the critical tasks and responsible organizations by time**. An execution matrix could be for the entire force, such as an air assault execution matrix, or it may be specific to a warfighting function, such as a fire support execution matrix. The current operations integration cell uses the execution matrix to determine which friendly actions to expect forces to execute in the near term or, in conjunction with the decision support matrix, which execution decisions to make.

DECISIONMAKING DURING EXECUTION

5-28. Decisionmaking is inherent in executing operations. Commanders observe the progress and results of their operations and intervene to ensure success. Because operations never unfold exactly as envisioned and because understanding of the situation changes, a commander's decisions made during execution are critical to an operation's success. During execution, commanders direct their units forcefully and promptly to overcome the difficulties of enemy action, friendly failures, errors, and other changes in the operational environment.

5-29. Executing, adjusting, or abandoning the original operation is part of decisionmaking in execution. Successful commanders balance the tendency to abandon a well-conceived plan too soon against persisting in a failing effort too long. Effective decisionmaking during execution—

- Relates all actions to the commander's intent and concept of operations to ensure they support the decisive operation.
- Is comprehensive, maintaining integration of combined arms rather than dealing with separate functions.
- Relies heavily on intuitive decisionmaking by commanders and staffs to make rapid adjustments.
- Is continuous and responds effectively to any opportunity or threat.

ASSESSMENT AND DECISIONMAKING

5-30. As commanders assess an operation, they determine when decisions are required. Plans usually identify some decision points; however, unexpected enemy actions or other changes often present situations that require unanticipated decisions. Commanders act when these decisions are required rather than waiting for a set time in the battle rhythm. A commander's visualization of the situation allows subordinate, supporting, and adjacent commanders—and in some cases higher headquarters—to adjust their actions rapidly and effectively in adapting to changing situations whether precipitated by the enemy, changes in friendly force status, or new civil considerations. As commanders assess the operation, they describe their impressions to the staff and subordinates and discuss the desirability of choices available. Once commanders make decisions, their staffs transmit the necessary directives.

5-31. Assessment in execution identifies variances, their magnitude and significance, and the need for decisions and what type—whether execution or adjustment. The commander and staff assess the probable outcome of the operation to determine whether changes are necessary to accomplish the mission, take advantage of opportunities, or react to unexpected threats. Figure 5-1 on page 5-6 depicts a basic model of assessing and decisionmaking during execution.

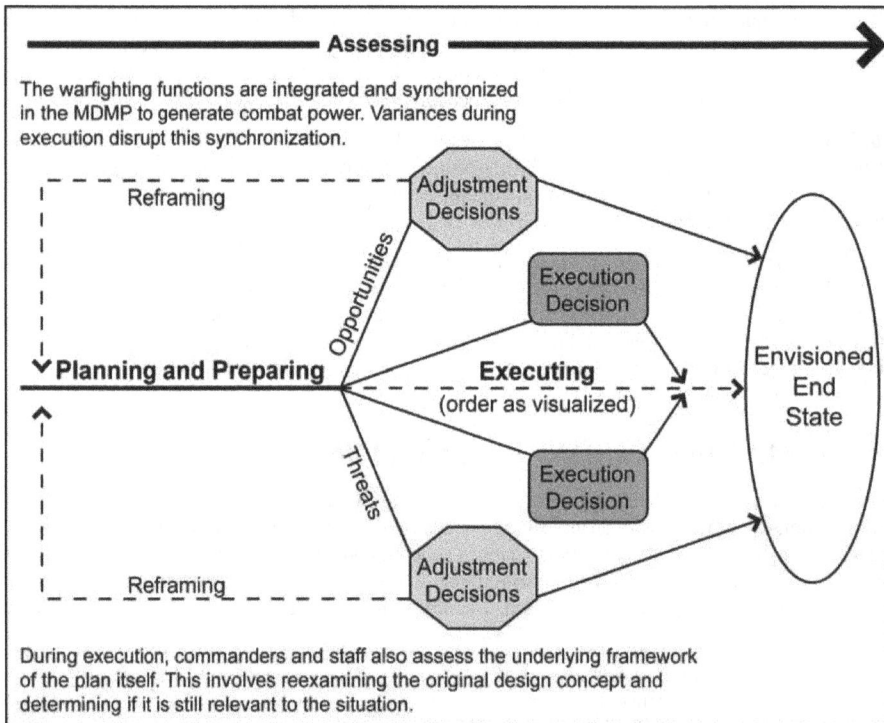

Figure 5-1. Decisions in execution

5-32. A *variance* is a difference between the actual situation during an operation and what the plan forecasted the situation would be at that time or event (FM 6-0). Staffs ensure information systems display relevant information that allows them to identify variances. The commander and staff evaluate emerging variances. If necessary, staffs update the conclusions and recommendations of their running estimates for the commander, who directs the necessary action. Two forms of variances exist: opportunities and threats.

5-33. The first form of variance is an opportunity to accomplish the mission more effectively. Opportunity results from forecasted or unexpected success. When commanders recognize an opportunity, they alter the order to exploit it if the change achieves the end state without incurring unacceptable risk. When exploiting an opportunity, the concept of operations may change but the commander's intent usually remains the same.

5-34. The second form of variance is a threat to mission accomplishment or survival of the force. When a threat is recognized, the commander adjusts the order to eliminate the enemy advantage, restore the friendly advantage, and regain the initiative. Not all threats to the force or mission involve hostile or neutral persons. Disease, toxic hazards, and natural disasters are examples of other threats.

5-35. In some instances, the variance is so extreme that no branch or sequel is available or the current plan lacks enough flexibility to respond to the variance. In this situation, the commander and staff may have to reframe the problem to better understand the operational environment as depicted in figure 5-1. (For more on reframing, see chapter 3.)

TYPES OF DECISIONS

5-36. Decisions made during execution are either execution decisions or adjustment decisions. Execution decisions involve options anticipated in the order. Adjustment decisions involve options that commanders did not anticipate. These decisions may include a decision to reframe the problem and develop an entirely new plan. Commanders may delegate authority for some execution decisions to the staff; however, commanders are always responsible for and involved in decisions during execution. Table 5-1 summarizes the range of possible actions with respect to decisions made during execution.

Table 5-1. Decision types and related actions

Decision Types		Actions
Execution Decisions	**Minor Variances from the Plan** Operation proceeding according to plan. Variances are within acceptable limits.	**Execute Planned Actions** • Commander or designee decides which planned actions best meet situation and directs their execution. • Staff issues fragmentary order. • Staff completes follow-up actions.
	Anticipated Situation Operation encountering variances within the limits for one or more branches or sequels anticipated in the plan.	**Execute a Branch or Sequel** • Commander or staff review branch or sequel plan. • Commander receives assessments and recommendations for modifications to the plan, determines the time available to refine it, and either issues guidance for further actions or directs execution of a branch or sequel. • Staff issues fragmentary order. • Staff completes follow-up actions.
Adjustment Decisions	**Unanticipated Situation— Friendly Success** Significant, unanticipated positive variances result in opportunities to achieve the end state in ways that differ significantly from the plan.	**Make an Adjustment Decision** • Commander recognizes the opportunity or threat and determines time available for decisionmaking. • Based on available planning time, commanders determine if they want to reframe the problem and develop a new design concept or use the military decisionmaking process to develop a new plan. In these instances, the decision initiates planning. Otherwise, the commander directs the staff to refine a single course of action or directs actions by subordinates to exploit the opportunity or counter the threat and exercise initiative within the higher commander's intent.
	Unanticipated Situation— Enemy Threat Significant, unanticipated negative variances impede mission accomplishment.	• Commander normally does not attempt to restore the plan. • Commander issues a verbal warning or fragmentary order to subordinate commanders. • Staff resynchronizes operation, modifies measures of effectiveness, and begins assessing the operation for progress using new measures of effectiveness.

Execution Decisions

5-37. Execution decisions implement a planned action under circumstances anticipated in the order. In their most basic form, execution decisions are decisions the commander foresees and identifies for execution during the operation. They apply resources at times or situations generally established in the order. For example, changing a boundary, altering the task organization, transitioning between phases, and executing a branch are execution decisions. Commanders are responsible for those decisions but may direct the COS (XO) or staff officer to supervise implementation. The current operations integration cell oversees the synchronization of integrating processes needed to implement execution decisions.

Adjustment Decisions

5-38. Adjustment decisions modify the operation to respond to unanticipated opportunities and threats. They often require implementing unanticipated operations and resynchronizing the warfighting functions. Commanders make these decisions, delegating implementing authority only after directing the major change themselves.

5-39. When basic operational assumptions prove inaccurate, the commander may have to change the mission. Commanders do this only as a last resort while still accomplishing the higher commander's intent.

Changing the mission proves most difficult as it may desynchronize the force's operations with those of the overall force.

RAPID DECISIONMAKING AND SYNCHRONIZATION PROCESS

5-40. The RDSP is a decisionmaking and synchronization technique that commanders and staffs commonly use during execution. While identified here with a specific name and method, the approach is not new; its use in the Army is well established. Commanders and staffs develop this capability through training and practice. When using this technique, the following considerations apply:

- *Rapid* is often more important than *process.*
- Much of it may be mental rather than written.
- It should become a battle drill for the current operations integration cells, future operations cells, or both.
- How much of the technique is explicitly performed varies by echelon and the time available.

5-41. While the military decisionmaking process (MDMP) seeks the optimal solution, the RDSP seeks a timely and effective solution within the commander's intent, mission, and concept of operations. Using the RDSP lets leaders avoid the time-consuming requirements of developing decision criteria and comparing courses of action (COAs). Mission variables continually change during execution. This often invalidates or weakens COAs and decision criteria before leaders can make a decision. Under the RDSP, leaders combine their experience and intuition with situational awareness to quickly reach situational understanding. Based on this, they develop and refine workable COAs.

5-42. The RDSP facilitates continuously integrating and synchronizing the warfighting functions to address ever-changing situations. It meets the following criteria for making effective decisions during execution:

- It is comprehensive, integrating all warfighting functions. It is not limited to any one warfighting function.
- It ensures all actions support the decisive operation by relating them to the commander's intent and concept of operations.
- It allows rapid changes to the order or mission.
- It is continuous, allowing commanders to react immediately to opportunities and threats.
- It accommodates, but is not tied to, cyclical processes such as targeting.

5-43. The RDSP focuses on synchronizing actions and understanding relationships within staffs as well as among commanders. Leaders can use it with or without a staff and in interagency and multinational environments.

5-44. The RDSP is based on an existing order and the commander's priorities as expressed in the order. The most important of these control measures are the commander's intent, concept of operations, and CCIRs. Leaders use these priorities as criteria for making decisions.

5-45. The RDSP includes five steps. (See figure 5-2.) The first two may be performed in any order, including concurrently. The last three are performed interactively until commanders identify an acceptable COA.

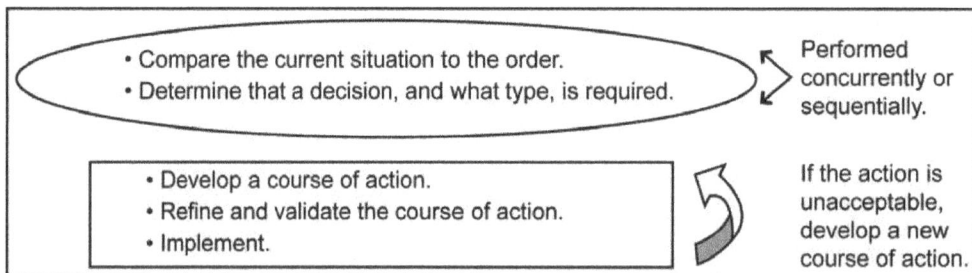

- Compare the current situation to the order.
- Determine that a decision, and what type, is required.

Performed concurrently or sequentially.

- Develop a course of action.
- Refine and validate the course of action.
- Implement.

If the action is unacceptable, develop a new course of action.

Figure 5-2. Rapid decisionmaking and synchronization process

COMPARE THE CURRENT SITUATION TO THE ORDER

5-46. Commanders identify likely variances during planning and identify options that will be present and actions that will be available when each variance occurs. During execution, commanders and staffs monitor the situation to identify changes in conditions. Then they ask if these changes affect the overall conduct of operations or their part of it and if the changes are significant. Finally, they identify if the changed conditions represent variances from the order—especially opportunities and risks. Staff members use running estimates to look for indicators of variances that affect their areas of expertise. (See table 5-2 for examples of indicators.) The commander, COS, and command post cell chiefs look for indicators of variances that affect the overall operation. While these indicators may come from any source, often they come from intelligence, surveillance, and reconnaissance (ISR) efforts or reports from units executing the operation.

±Table 5-2. Examples of change indicators

Types	Indicators	
General	• Answer to a CCIR. • Identification of an IR. • Change in mission. • Change in organization of unit. • Change in leadership of unit. • Signing or implementation of peace treaty or other key political arrangement.	• Change in capabilities of subordinate unit. • Change in role of host-nation military force. • Climate changes or natural disasters impacting on the population, agriculture, industry. • Upcoming local election. • Changes in key civilian leadership.
Intelligence	• Identification of enemy main effort. • Identification of enemy reserves or counterattack. • Indications of unexpected enemy action or preparation. • Increase in enemy solicitation of civilians for intelligence operations. • Identification of an IR. • Insertion of manned surveillance teams. • Disruption of primary and secondary education system. • Unexplained disappearance of key members of intelligence community.	• Enemy electronic attack use. • Indicators of illicit economic activity. • Identification of threats from within the population. • Increased unemployment within the population. • Interference with freedom of religious worship. • Identification of HPT or HVT. • UAS launch. • Answer to a PIR. • Enemy rotary-wing or UAS use.
Movement and Maneuver	• Success or failure in breaching or gap crossing operations. • Capture of significant numbers of EPWs, enemy CPs, supply points, or artillery units. • Establishment of road blocks along major traffic routes. • Unexplained displacement of neighborhoods within a given sector.	• Success or failure of a subordinate unit task. • Modification of an airspace control measure. • Numbers of dislocated civilians sufficient to affect friendly operations. • Damages to civilian infrastructure affecting friendly mobility. • Loss of one or more critical transportation systems.
Fires	• Receipt of an air tasking order. • Battle damage assessment results. • Unplanned repositioning of firing units. • Success or lack thereof in electronic attack. • Identification of HPT or HVT. • Identification of an IR.	• Execution of planned fires. • Modification of a FSCM. • Effective enemy counterfire. • Negative effects of fires on civilians. • Destruction of any place of worship by friendly fire.

±Table 5-2. Examples of change indicators (continued)

Types	Indicators	
Protection	• NBC 1 report or other indicators of enemy CBRN use. • Report or other indicators of enemy improvised explosive device use. • Indicators of coordinated enemy actions against civilians or friendly forces. • Increased criminal activity in a given sector. • Increase in organized protests or riots.	• Identification of threats to communications or computer systems. • Reports of enemy targeting critical host-nation infrastructure. • Identification of threat to base or sustainment facilities. • Escalation of force incidents. • Loss of border security.
Sustainment	• Significant loss of capability in any class of supply. • Opening or closing of civilian businesses within a given area. • Identification of significant incidences of disease and nonbattle injury casualties. • Closing of major financial institutions. • Mass casualties. • Receipt of significant resupply. • Disruption of one or more essential civil services (such as water or electricity). • Contact on a supply route. • Answer to an FFIR. • Mass detainees.	• Degradations to essential civilian infrastructure by threat actions. • Civilian mass casualty event beyond capability of host-nation resources. • Identification of significant shortage in any class of supply. • Outbreak of epidemic or famine within the civilian population. • Medical evacuation launch. • Dislocated civilian event beyond capability of host-nation resources. • Disruption of key logistics lines of communication. • Changes in availability of host-nation support.
Mission Command	• Impending changes in key military leadership. • Interference with freedom of the press or news media. • Receipt of a fragmentary order or warning order from higher headquarters.	• Effective adversary information efforts on civilians. • Loss of civilian communications nodes. • Loss of contact with a CP or commander. • Jamming or interference.

CBRN	chemical, biological, radiological, and nuclear	FFIR	friendly force information requirement	IR NBC	information requirement nuclear, biological, and chemical
CCIR	commander's critical information requirement	FSCM	fire support coordination measure	PIR	priority intelligence requirement
CP	command post	HPT	high-priority target	UAS	unmanned aircraft system
EPW	enemy prisoner of war	HVT	high-value target		

5-47. Staff members are particularly alert for answers to CCIRs that support anticipated decisions. They also watch for exceptional information. *Exceptional information* is information that would have answered one of the commander's critical information requirements if the requirement for it had been foreseen and stated as one of the commander's critical information requirements (FM 6-0). Exceptional information usually reveals a need for an adjustment decision. (See FM 6-0.)

5-48. When performing the RDSP, the current operations integration cell first compares the current situation to the one envisioned in the order. (See chapter 2.) It may obtain assistance from the assessment section or the red team section in this analysis. If the situation requires greater analysis, the COS (XO) may task the future operations cell (where authorized) or the plans cell to perform this analysis. At echelons with no future operations cell, the plans cell or the current operations integration cell performs this function.

DETERMINE THE TYPE OF DECISION REQUIRED

5-49. When a variance is identified, the commander directs action while the chief of operations leads chiefs of the current operations integration cell and selected functional cell in quickly comparing the current situation to the expected situation. This assessment accomplishes the following:

- Describes the variance.
- Determines if the variance provides a significant opportunity or threat and examines the potential of either.
- Determines if a decision is needed by identifying if the variance—
  - Indicates an opportunity that can be exploited to accomplish the mission faster or with fewer resources.
  - Directly threatens the decisive operation's success.
  - Threatens a shaping operation such that it may threaten the decisive operation directly or in the near future.
  - Can be addressed within the commander's intent and concept of operations. (If so, determine what execution decision is needed.)
  - Requires changing the concept of operations substantially. (If so, determine what adjustment decision or new approach will best suit the circumstances.)

5-50. For minor variances, the chief of operations works with other cell chiefs to determine whether changes to control measures are needed. If so, they determine how those changes affect other warfighting functions. They direct changes within their authority (execution decisions) and notify the COS (XO) and the affected command post cells and staff elements.

5-51. Commanders intervene directly in cases that affect the overall direction of the unit. They describe the situation, direct their subordinates to provide any additional information they need, and order either implementation of planned responses or development of an order to redirect the force.

5-52. Staff members constantly compare the current situation to their expectations to identify variances. Likewise, as the time for an anticipated execution decision approaches, staff members assess the situation in their area of expertise. Doing this allows them to confirm that the decision will produce the planned effects. It initiates the RSDP, essentially bypassing recognition and allowing the staff to discover small changes in conditions that might otherwise go unnoticed.

DEVELOP A COURSE OF ACTION

5-53. If the variance requires an adjustment decision, the designated integrating cell and affected command post cell chiefs recommend implementation of a COA or obtain the commander's guidance for developing one. They use the following conditions to screen possible COAs:

- Mission.
- Commander's intent.
- Current dispositions and freedom of action.
- CCIRs.
- Limiting factors, such as supply constraints, boundaries, and combat strength.

5-54. The new options must conform to the commander's intent. Possible COAs may alter the concept of operations and CCIRs if they remain within the commander's intent. However, the commander approves changes to the CCIRs. Functional cell chiefs and other staff section leaders identify areas that may be affected within their areas of expertise by proposed changes to the order or mission. Considerations include but are not limited to those shown in table 5-3 on page 5-12. The commander is as likely as anyone else to detect the need for change and to sketch out the options. Whether the commander, COS, XO, or chief of operations does this, the future operations cell is often directed to flesh out the concept and draft the order. The chief of operations and the current operations integration cell normally lead this effort, especially if the response is needed promptly or the situation is not complex. The commander, COS, or XO is usually the decisionmaking authority, depending on the commander's delegation of authority.

5-55. Commanders may delegate authority for execution decisions to their deputies, COSs (XOs), or their operations officers. They retain personal responsibility for all decisions and normally retain the authority for approving adjustment decisions.

5-56. When reallocating resources or priorities, commanders assign only minimum essential assets to shaping operations. They use all other assets to weight the decisive operation. This applies when allocating resources for the overall operation or within a warfighting function.

±Table 5-3. Considerations for synchronization and decision implementation actions

Types	Actions	
Intelligence	• Modifying priority intelligence requirements and other intelligence requirements. • Updating named areas of interest and target areas of interest. • Updating the intelligence estimate.	• Updating the enemy SITEMP and enemy COA statements. • Modifying the ISR synchronization plan. • Confirming or denying threat COAs. • Updating the ISR synchronization matrix and tools.
Movement and Maneuver	• Assigning new objectives. • Revising or refining the ISR plan. • Assigning new tasks to subordinate units. • Adjusting terrain management. • Employing smoke.	• Modifying airspace control measures. • Making unit boundary changes. • Emplacing obstacles. • Clearing obstacles. • Establishing and enforcing movement priority.
Fires	• Delivering fires against targets or target sets. • Modifying the high-payoff target list and the attack guidance matrix.	• Modifying radar zones. • Modifying the priority of fires. • Modifying fire support coordination measures.
Protection	• Moving air defense weapons systems. • Establishing decontamination sites. • Conducting chemical, biological, radiological, and nuclear reconnaissance. • Establish movement corridors on critical lines of communications.	• Changing air defense weapons control status. • Enhancing survivability through engineer support. • Revising and updating personnel recovery coordination. • Reassigning or repositioning response forces.
Sustainment	• Prioritizing medical evacuation assets. • Repositioning logistics assets. • Positioning and prioritizing internment and resettlement assets.	• Repositioning and prioritizing general engineering assets. • Modifying priorities. • Modifying distribution.
Mission Command	• Moving communications nodes. • Moving command posts. • Modifying information priorities for employing information as combat power. • Synchronizing and adjusting information themes and messages to support the new decision. • Adjusting measures for minimizing civilian interference with operations. • Revising recommended protected targets to the fires cell. • Recommending modifications of stability operations, including employment of civil affairs operations and other units, to perform civil affairs operations tasks.	
COA course of action ISR intelligence, surveillance, and reconnaissance	SITEMP situation template	

5-57. Commanders normally direct the future operations cell to prepare a fragmentary order or the current operations integration cell to issue a fragmentary order setting conditions for executing a new COA. When lacking time to perform the MDMP or quickness of action is desirable, commanders make an immediate adjustment decision—using intuitive decisionmaking—in the form of a focused COA. Developing the focused COA often follows the mental war-gaming by commanders until they reach an acceptable COA. If time is available, commanders may direct the plans cell to develop a new COA using the MDMP, and the considerations for planning become operative.

REFINE AND VALIDATE THE COURSE OF ACTION

5-58. Once commanders describe the new COA, the current operations integration cell conducts an analysis to validate its feasibility, suitability, and acceptability. If acceptable, the COA is refined to resynchronize the warfighting functions enough to generate and apply the needed combat power. Staffs with a future operations cell may assign that cell responsibility for developing the details of the new COA and drafting a fragmentary order to implement it. The commander or COS may direct an "on-call" operations synchronization meeting to perform this task and ensure rapid resynchronization.

5-59. Validation and refinement is done very quickly. Normally, the commander and staff officers conduct a mental war game of the new COA. They consider potential enemy reactions, the unit's counteractions, and secondary effects that might affect the force's synchronization. When time allows, the XO or chief of operations assembles command post cell chiefs and refines and validates the COA in an open forum. Each staff member considers the following:

- Is the new COA feasible in terms of my area of expertise?
- How will this action affect my area of expertise?
- Does it require changing my information requirements?
  - Should any of the information requirements be nominated as a CCIR?
  - What actions within my area of expertise does this change require?
  - Will it require changing objectives or targets nominated by the staff section?
- What other command post cells and elements does this action affect?
- What are potential enemy reactions?
- What are the possible friendly counteractions?
  - Does this counteraction affect my area of expertise?
  - Will it require changing my information requirements?
  - Are any of my information requirements potential CCIRs?
  - What actions within my area of expertise does this counteraction require?
  - Will it require changing objectives or targets nominated by the staff section?
  - What other command post cells and elements does this counteraction affect?

5-60. The validation and refinement show if the COA will acceptably solve the problem. If it does not, the XO or chief of operations modifies it through additional analysis or develops a new COA. The XO informs the commander of any changes made.

IMPLEMENT

5-61. ±When the COA is acceptable, the XO recommends implementation to the commander or implements it directly if the commander has delegated that authority. Implementation normally requires a fragmentary order; in exceptional circumstances, it may require a new operation order. That order changes the concept of operations (in adjustment decisions), resynchronizes the warfighting functions, and disseminates changes to control measures. The staff uses warning orders to alert the unit to a pending change. The staff also establishes sufficient time for the unit to implement the change without losing integration or being exposed to unnecessary tactical risk. Stability operations demand special attention to execution of inform and influence activities. Part of implementing in stability operations includes informing the population of the purpose of an operation and amending the inform and influence plan to account for changes that occur as the operation proceeds.

5-62. Commanders often issue orders to subordinates verbally in situations requiring a quick reaction. At battalion and higher levels, written fragmentary orders confirm verbal orders to ensure synchronization, integration, and notification of all parts of the force. Common revisions to products needed to affect adjustments include the following:

- Updated enemy situation, including the situation template.
- Revised CCIRs.
- Updated ISR plan.
- Updated scheme of maneuver and tasks to maneuver units, including an execution matrix and decision support matrix or template.
- Updated scheme of fires, including the fire support execution matrix, high-payoff target list, and attack guidance matrix.
- Updated information tasks.

5-63. If time permits, leaders verify that subordinates understand critical tasks. Methods for doing this include the confirmation brief and backbrief. These are done both between commanders and within staff elements to ensure mutual understanding.

5-64. After the analysis is complete, the current operations integration cell and command post cell chiefs update decision support templates and synchronization matrixes. When time is available, the operations officer or chief of operations continues this analysis to the operation's end to complete combat power integration. Staff members begin the synchronization needed to implement the decision. This synchronization involves collaboration with other command post cells and subordinate staffs. Staff members determine how actions in their areas of expertise affect others. They coordinate those actions to eliminate undesired effects that might cause friction. The cells provide results of this synchronization to the current operations integration cell and the common operational picture.

5-65. During implementation of the RDSP, the current operations integration cell keeps the warfighting functions synchronized as the situation changes. It considers the following outcomes when making synchronization decisions or allowing others' synchronization in collaboration to proceed:

- Combined arms integration.
- Responsiveness—both anticipatory and reactive.
- Timeliness.

Anticipating certain outcomes lets commanders mass the effects of combat power at decisive times and places.

5-66. Commanders also synchronize collaboratively. Coordination among higher, adjacent, supporting, and subordinate commanders facilitates effective execution by improving interaction between their units as they anticipate and solve problems. Cross talk among subordinate commanders can provide synchronization as well as lead to decisionmaking. Such synchronization occurs without the higher commander becoming involved, except to affirm, either positively or through silence, the decisions or agreements of subordinates.

CAUTIONS

5-67. Validating and refining action is a rapid and largely intuitive activity. It should be done quickly and not be drawn out. Commanders focus on maintaining the tempo and minimizing necessary synchronization. The RDSP is not designed to mass maximum combat power but to make the minimum coordination needed to generate enough combat power to prevail.

5-68. Most decisions during execution are made at a relatively low level by command post cell chiefs. They refine execution of the order without changing it significantly. However, even small changes can affect other staff sections. All changes that affect operations should be coordinated between cells and reported to the staff as a whole. When time does not allow this, the staff element making the change immediately advises all affected elements.

5-69. To work, the RDSP must be done continuously, not tied to the battle rhythm. Commanders can use cyclical events (such as targeting working groups) to review an entire process or evaluate the entire ISR or targeting plan. The key is to be able to act and react in real time as events occur, not at predetermined points. Only in this way can Army forces operate within the enemy's decision cycles at a tempo the enemy cannot match.

Chapter 6

Assessment

This chapter provides the fundamentals of assessment, including its definition, purpose, and process. It discusses how assessment works with the levels of war and offers considerations for effective assessment. This chapter also covers assessment working groups and assessment support with operations research/systems analysis. Guidelines for developing assessment plans are discussed in detail in appendix H.

ASSESSMENT FUNDAMENTALS

6-1. *Assessment* is the continuous monitoring and evaluation of the current situation, particularly the enemy, and progress of an operation (FM 3-0). Commanders, assisted by their staffs and subordinate commanders, continuously assess the operational environment and the progress of the operation. Based on their assessment, commanders direct adjustments thus ensuring the operation remains focused on accomplishing the mission.

6-2. Assessment involves deliberately comparing forecasted outcomes with actual events to determine the overall effectiveness of force employment. More specifically, assessment helps the commander determine progress toward attaining the desired end state, achieving objectives, and performing tasks. It also involves continuously monitoring and evaluating the operational environment to determine what changes might affect the conduct of operations. Assessment helps commanders determine if they need to reframe the problem and develop an entirely new plan. (Chapter 3 addresses reframing.)

6-3. Throughout the operations process, commanders integrate their own assessments with those of the staff, subordinate commanders, and other partners in the area of operations. Primary tools for assessing progress of the operation include the operation order, the common operational picture, personal observations, running estimates, and the assessment plan. The latter includes measures of effectiveness, measures of performance, and reframing criteria. The commander's visualization forms the basis for the commander's personal assessment of progress. Running estimates provide information, conclusions, and recommendations from the perspective of each staff section. They help to refine the common operational picture and supplement it with information not readily displayed.

6-4. Commanders avoid excessive analyses when assessing operations. Committing valuable time and energy to developing excessive and time-consuming assessment schemes squander resources better devoted to other operations process activities. Commanders reject the tendency to measure something just because it is measurable. Effective commanders avoid burdening subordinates and staffs with overly detailed assessment and collection tasks. Generally, the echelon at which a specific operation, task, or action is conducted should be the echelon at which it is assessed. This provides a focus for assessment at each echelon. It enhances the efficiency of the overall operations process.

ASSESSMENT PROCESS

6-5. Assessment is continuous; it precedes and guides every operations process activity and concludes each operation or phase of an operation. Broadly, assessment consists of the following activities:
- Monitoring the current situation to collect relevant information.
- Evaluating progress toward attaining end state conditions, achieving objectives, and performing tasks.
- Recommending or directing action for improvement.

6-6. The three activities that make up the assessment process are also continuous; they are logically sequential while constantly executed throughout the operations process. This process applies to assessments of every type and at every echelon.

MONITORING

6-7. *Monitoring* **is continuous observation of those conditions relevant to the current operation**. Monitoring within the assessment process allows staffs to collect relevant information, specifically that information about the current situation that can be compared to the forecasted situation described in the commander's intent and concept of operations. Progress cannot be judged, nor effective decisions made, without an accurate understanding of the current situation.

6-8. During planning, commanders monitor the situation to develop facts and assumptions that underlie the plan. During preparation and execution, commanders and staffs monitor the situation to determine if the facts are still relevant, if their assumptions remain valid, and if new conditions emerged that affect the operations.

6-9. Commander's critical information requirements and decision points focus the staff's monitoring activities and prioritize the unit's collection efforts. Information requirements concerning the enemy, terrain and weather, and civil considerations are identified and assigned priorities through intelligence, surveillance, and reconnaissance (ISR) synchronization. Operations officers use friendly reports to coordinate other assessment-related information requirements. To prevent duplicated collection efforts, information requirements associated with assessing the operation are integrated into both the ISR plan and friendly force information requirements. (See appendix H for more detail in building an assessment plan.)

6-10. Staffs monitor and collect information from the common operational picture and friendly reports. This information includes operational and intelligence summaries from subordinate, higher, and adjacent headquarters and communications and reports from liaison teams. The staff also identifies information sources outside military channels and monitors their reports. These other channels might include products from civilian, host-nation, and other government agencies. Staffs apply information management and knowledge management principles to facilitate getting this information to the right people at the right time. (See FM 6-0 and FM 6-01.1.)

6-11. Staff sections record relevant information in running estimates. Each staff section maintains a continuous assessment of current operations as a basis to determine if they are proceeding according to the commander's intent, mission, and concept of operations. In their running estimates, staff sections use this new information, updated facts, and assumptions as the basis for evaluation.

EVALUATING

6-12. The staff analyzes relevant information collected through monitoring to evaluate the operation's progress. *Evaluating* **is using criteria to judge progress toward desired conditions and determining why the current degree of progress exists**. Evaluation is the heart of the assessment process where most of the analysis occurs. Evaluation helps commanders determine what is working, determine what is not working, and gain insights into how to better accomplish the mission.

6-13. Criteria in the forms of measures of effectiveness (MOEs) and measures of performance (MOPs) aid in determining progress toward attaining end state conditions, achieving objectives, and performing tasks. MOEs help determine if a task is achieving its intended results. MOPs help determine if a task is completed properly. MOEs and MOPs are simply criteria—they do not represent the assessment itself. MOEs and MOPs require relevant information in the form of indicators for evaluation.

6-14. A *measure of effectiveness* is a criterion used to assess changes in system behavior, capability, or operational environment that is tied to measuring the attainment of an end state, achievement of an objective, or creation of an effect (JP 3-0). MOEs help measure changes in conditions, both positive and negative. MOEs help to answer the question "Are we doing the right things?" MOEs are commonly found and tracked in formal assessment plans. Examples of MOEs for the objective to "Provide a safe and secure environment" may include—

- Decrease in insurgent activity.
- Increase in population trust of host-nation security forces.

6-15. A *measure of performance* is a criterion used to assess friendly actions that is tied to measuring task accomplishment (JP 3-0). MOPs help answer questions such as "Was the action taken?" or "Were the tasks completed to standard?" A MOP confirms or denies that a task has been properly performed. MOPs are commonly found and tracked at all levels in execution matrixes. MOPs are also heavily used to evaluate training. MOPs help to answer the question "Are we doing things right?"

6-16. At the most basic level, every Soldier assigned a task maintains a formal or informal checklist to track task completion. The status of those tasks and subtasks are MOPs. Similarly, operations consist of a series of collective tasks sequenced in time, space, and purpose to accomplish missions. Current operations integration cells use MOPs in execution matrixes and running estimates to track completed tasks. The uses of MOPs are a primary element of battle tracking. MOPs focus on the friendly force. Evaluating task accomplishment using MOPs is relatively straightforward and often results in a *yes* or *no* answer. Examples of MOPs include—

- Route X cleared.
- Generators delivered, are operational, and secured at villages A, B, and C.
- Hill 785 secured.
- $15,000 spent for schoolhouse completion.

6-17. **In the context of assessment, an** *indicator* **is an item of information that provides insight into a measure of effectiveness or measure of performance.** Staffs use indicators to shape their collection effort as part of ISR synchronization. Indicators take the form of reports from subordinates, surveys and polls, and information requirements. Indicators help to answer the question "What is the current status of this MOE or MOP?" A single indicator can inform multiple MOPs and MOEs. Examples of indicators for the MOE "Decrease in insurgent activity" are—

- Number of hostile actions per area each week.
- Number of munitions caches found per area each week.

Appendix H provides a more detailed discussion of developing MOEs, MOPs, and indicators as part of building the assessment plan. Table 6-1 provides additional information concerning MOEs, MOPs, and indicators.

Table 6-1. Assessment measures and indicators

MOE	MOP	Indicator
Answers the question: Are we doing the right things?	Answers the question: Are we doing things right?	Answers the question: What is the status of this MOE or MOP?
Measures purpose accomplishment.	Measures task completion.	Measures raw data inputs to inform MOEs and MOPs.
Measures *why* in the mission statement.	Measures *what* in the mission statement.	Information used to make measuring what or why possible.
No hierarchical relationship to MOPs.	No hierarchical relationship to MOEs.	Subordinate to MOEs and MOPs.
Often formally tracked in formal assessment plans.	Often formally tracked in execution matrixes.	Often formally tracked in formal assessment plans.
Typically challenging to choose the correct ones.	Typically simple to choose the correct ones.	Typically as challenging to select correctly as the supported MOE or MOP.

6-18. Evaluation includes analysis of why progress is or is not being made according to the plan. Commanders and staffs propose and consider possible causes. In particular, the question of whether changes in the situation can be attributed to friendly actions is addressed. Commanders and staffs consult subject matter experts, both internal and external to the staff, on whether staffs have identified the correct underlying causes for specific changes in the situation. Assumptions identified in the planning process are challenged to determine if they are still valid.

6-19. A key aspect of evaluation is determining variances—the difference between the actual situation and what the plan forecasted the situation would be at the time or event. Based on the significance of the variances, the staff makes recommendations to the commander on how to adjust operations to accomplish the mission more effectively. See chapter 5 for a detailed discussion of assessment during execution to include the relationship between the degree of variance from the plan and execution and adjustment decisions.

6-20. Evaluating includes considering whether the desired conditions have changed, are no longer achievable, or are not achievable through the current operational approach. This is done by continually challenging the key assumptions made when framing the problem. When an assumption is invalidated, then reframing may be in order. (Chapter 3 discusses framing and reframing.)

RECOMMENDING OR DIRECTING ACTION

6-21. Monitoring and evaluating are critical activities; however, assessment is incomplete without recommending or directing action. Assessment may diagnose problems, but unless it results in recommended adjustments, its use to the commander is limited.

6-22. Based on the evaluation of progress, the staff brainstorms possible improvements to the plan and makes preliminary judgments about the relative merit of those changes. Staff members identify those changes possessing sufficient merit and provide them as recommendations to the commander or make adjustments within their delegated authority. Recommendations to the commander range from continuing the operation as planned, to executing a branch, or to making adjustments not anticipated. Making adjustments includes assigning new tasks to subordinates, reprioritizing support, adjusting the ISR synchronization plan, and significantly modifying the course of action. Commanders integrate recommendations from the staff, subordinate commanders, and other partners with their personal assessment. From those recommendations, they decide if and how to modify the operation to better accomplish the mission. (See chapter 5 for a detailed discussion of decisions during execution.)

6-23. Assessment diagnoses threats, suggests improvements to effectiveness, and reveals opportunities. The staff presents the results and conclusions of its assessments and recommendations to the commander as an operation develops. Just as the staff devotes time to analysis and evaluation, so too must it make timely, complete, and actionable recommendations. The chief of staff or executive officer ensures the staff completes its analyses and recommendations in time to affect the operation and for information to reach the commander when it is needed.

6-24. When developing recommendations, the staff draws from many sources and considers its recommendations within the larger context of the operations. While several ways to improve a particular aspect of the operation might exist, some recommendations could impact other aspects of the operation. As with all recommendations, the staff should address any future implications.

ASSESSMENT AND THE LEVELS OF WAR

6-25. Assessment occurs at all levels of war and at all echelons. The situation and echelon dictate the focus and methods leaders use to assess. Normally, commanders assess those specific operations or tasks that they were directed to accomplish. This properly focuses collection and assessment at each level, reduces redundancy, and enhances the efficiency of the overall assessment process.

6-26. For units with a staff, assessment becomes more formal at each higher echelon. Assessment resources (to include staff officer expertise and time available) proportionally increase from battalion to brigade, division, corps, and theater army. The analytic resources and level of expertise of staffs available at strategic- and operational-level headquarters include a dedicated core group of analysts. This group specializes in operations research/systems analysis (ORSA), formal assessment plans, and various assessment products. Division, corps, and theater army headquarters, for example, have fully resourced plans, future operations, and current operations integration cells. They have larger intelligence staffs and more staff officers trained in ORSA. Assessment at brigade and below is usually less formal, often relying on direct observations and the judgment of commanders and their staffs.

6-27. Often, time available for detailed analysis and assessment is shorter at the tactical level. Additionally, tactical staffs are progressively smaller and have less analytic capability at each lower echelon. As such, assessment at the tactical level focuses on the near term and relies more on direct observation and judgments than on detailed assessment methods. This is not to say that tactical units cannot use detailed assessment methods.

6-28. For small units (those without a staff), assessment is mostly informal. Small-unit leaders focus on assessing their unit readiness—personnel, equipment, supplies, and morale—and their unit's ability to perform assigned tasks. Leaders also determine whether the unit has completed assigned tasks. If those tasks have not produced the desired results, leaders explore why they have not and consider what smart improvements could be made for unit operations. As they assess and learn, small units change their tactics, techniques, and procedures based on their experiences.

CONSIDERATIONS FOR EFFECTIVE ASSESSMENT

6-29. The following considerations help commanders and staffs develop assessment plans and conduct effective assessments:

- Assessment is continuous.
- Commanders drive assessment through prioritization.
- Assessment incorporates the logic behind the plan.
- Assessment facilitates learning and adapting.
- Commanders and staffs use caution when establishing cause and effect.
- Commanders and staffs combine quantitative and qualitative indicators.
- Assessment incorporates formal and informal methods.

ASSESSMENT IS CONTINUOUS

6-30. Assessment is a continuous activity of the operations process. The focus of assessment, however, changes for each operations process activity. During planning, assessment focuses on understanding current conditions of the operational environment and developing an assessment plan, including what and how to assess progress. Understanding the commander's intent and desired future conditions is key when building the assessment plan. During preparation, assessment focuses on determining the friendly force's readiness to execute the operation and on verifying the assumptions on which the plan is based. During execution, assessment focuses on evaluating progress of the operation. Based on their assessment, commanders direct adjustments to the order, ensuring the operation stays focused on accomplishing the mission. They adjust their assessment plan as required.

6-31. Assessment is continuous, even when the unit is not actively engaged in operations. At a minimum, staffs maintain running estimates of friendly force capabilities and readiness within their areas of expertise. Some running estimates, such as the intelligence estimate, also assess operational environments to which the unit is likely to deploy.

COMMANDERS DRIVE ASSESSMENT THROUGH PRIORITIZATION

6-32. The commander's role is central to the assessment process. Commanders establish priorities for assessment and discipline the staff to meet the requirements of time, simplicity, and level of detail based on the situation. While the staff does the detailed work, to include collecting and analyzing information, commanders ultimately assess the operation. Commanders are also responsible for decisions made based on their assessments.

6-33. ±In assessing operations, commanders consider information and recommendations by the staff, subordinate commanders, and other partners within and outside of their area of operations. Commanders then apply their judgment to assess progress. As commanders monitor the situation, they compare the current situation to their initial commander's visualization and commander's intent. Based on their assessment of progress, commanders direct adjustments to the order—ensuring the operation stays focused on the operation's end state—or reframe the problem and develop an entirely new plan.

6-34. To assist commanders learning throughout the conduct of operations, they establish their commander's critical information requirements, set priorities for assessment in the form of MOEs and reframing criteria, and explicitly state assumptions. When results fail to meet expectations, commanders decide whether this is due to a failure in implementing the plan (execution) or if the plan and its underlying logic are flawed.

ASSESSMENT INCORPORATES THE LOGIC BEHIND THE PLAN

6-35. Effective assessment relies on an accurate understanding of the logic used to build the plan. Each plan is built on assumptions and an operational approach—a broad conceptualization of the general actions that will produce the conditions that define the desire end state. The reasons or logic as to why the commander believes the plan will produce the desired results are important considerations when determining how to assess the operations. Recording and understanding this logic helps the staffs recommend the appropriate MOPs, MOEs and indicators for assessing the operation. It also helps the commander and staff determine if they need to reframe the problem if assumptions prove false or the logic behind the plan appears flawed as operations progress. (See chapter 3 for a discussion of framing and reframing the problem and developing a design concept.)

6-36. When conducting design, the logic used to drive more detailed planning is captured in the design concept that includes the mission narrative and problem statement. As planning continues, staff sections identify and record the logic behind the plan relating to their area of expertise in their running estimates. They also record assumptions and include key assumptions as part of the operation plan or order. An explicit record of this logic used in building the plan proves valuable to the commander and staff as well as to follow-on units and other civilian and military organizations in understanding the plan and assessing the progress of operations.

ASSESSMENT FACILITATES LEARNING AND ADAPTING

6-37. One of the most important questions when assessing the operation is whether the plan is still relevant. Assessment entails measuring progress according to the plan. It also includes periodically reexamining the logic and assumptions of the original plan to determine if the plan is still relevant. Throughout an operation, higher operational objectives may change and conditions may develop that did not exist during planning. These conditions may create a somewhat different situation from the one the commander originally visualized. When this occurs, modifications to the plan may be in order, or it may be necessary to reframe the problem.

6-38. The assessment process prompts the decision to reframe in several ways. Commanders and staffs continuously challenge the key assumptions in the plan. When an assumption is invalidated, reframing may be in order. Another sign of a requirement to reframe is when task completion measured by MOPs is high but purpose accomplishment measured by MOEs is low. That suggests that the wrong tasks have been assigned and reframing is needed.

6-39. As commanders assess and learn throughout the operation, they determine if achieving their original objectives leads to the desired end state. Collaboration and dialog with higher, lower, and adjacent commanders and staffs, backed up by quantitative and qualitative assessments, contribute to this learning. Assessing helps commanders to update their commander's visualization (which may include a revised end state), direct changes to the order, and adapt the force to better accomplish the mission.

COMMANDERS AND STAFFS USE CAUTION WHEN ESTABLISHING CAUSE AND EFFECT

6-40. Establishing cause and effect is sometimes difficult, but it is crucial to effective assessment. Sometimes, establishing causality between actions and their effects can be relatively straightforward, such as in observing a bomb destroy a bridge. In other instances, especially regarding changes in human behavior, attitudes, and perception, establishing links between cause and effect proves difficult. Commanders and staffs must guard against drawing erroneous conclusions in these instances.

6-41. Understanding how cause and effect works requires careful consideration and shrewd judgment. Even when two variables seem to be correlated, commanders must still make assumptions to establish which one is cause and which one is effect. In fact, both may be caused by a third unnoticed variable. Commanders clearly acknowledge all assumptions made in establishing causes and effects. The payoff for correctly identifying the links between causes and effects is effective and smart recommendations. Commanders and staffs are well-advised to devote the time, effort, and energy needed to properly uncover connections between causes and effects. Assumptions made in establishing cause and effect must be recorded explicitly and challenged periodically to ensure they are still valid.

6-42. ±In its simplest form, an effect is a result, outcome, or consequence of an action. Direct effects are the immediate, first-order consequences of a military action unaltered by intervening events. They are usually immediate and easily recognizable. Examples are an enemy command post destroyed by friendly artillery or a terrorist network courier captured by a direct-action mission. Establishing the link between cause and effect in the physical domains is usually straightforward, as is assessing progress.

6-43. ±It is often difficult to establish a link or correlation that clearly identifies actions that produce effects beyond the physical domains. The relationship between action taken (cause) and nonphysical effects may be coincidental. Then the occurrence of an effect is either purely accidental or perhaps caused by the correlation of two or more actions executed to achieve the effect. For example, friendly forces can successfully engage enemy formations with fire and maneuver at the same time as military information support operations. Military information support operations might urge enemy soldiers to surrender. If both these events occur at the same time, then correlating an increase in surrendering soldiers to military information support operations will be difficult. As another example, friendly forces may attempt to decrease population support for an insurgency in a particular city. To accomplish this task, the unit facilitates the reconstruction of the city's power grid, assists the local authorities in establishing a terrorist tips hotline, establishes a civil-military operations center, and conducts lethal operations against high-payoff targets within the insurgency. Identifying the relative impact of each of these activities is extremely challenging but is critical for allocating resources smartly to accomplish the mission. Unrecognized influences completely invisible to assessors can also cause changes unforeseen or attributed inaccurately to actions of the force.

6-44. Furthermore, because commanders synchronize actions across the warfighting functions to achieve an objective or obtain an end state condition, the cumulative effect of these actions may make the impact of any individual task indistinguishable. Careful consideration and judgment are required, particularly when asserting cause-and-effect relationships in stability operations.

COMMANDERS AND STAFFS COMBINE QUANTITATIVE AND QUALITATIVE INDICATORS

6-45. Effective assessment incorporates both quantitative (observation based) and qualitative (opinion based) indicators. Human judgment is integral to assessment. A key aspect of any assessment is the degree to which it relies upon human judgment and the degree to which it relies upon direct observation and mathematical rigor. Rigor offsets the inevitable bias, while human judgment focuses rigor and processes on intangibles that are often key to success. The appropriate balance depends on the situation—particularly the nature of the operation and available resources for assessment—but rarely lies at the ends of the scale.

6-46. A balanced judgment for any assessment identifies the information on which to concentrate. Amassing statistics is easy. Determining which actions imply success proves far more difficult due to dynamic interactions among friendly forces, adaptable enemies, populations, and other aspects of the operational environment such as economics and culture. This is especially true of operations that require assessing the actions intended to change human behavior, such as deception or stability operations. Using quantitative and qualitative indicators reduces the likelihood and impact of the skewed perspective that results from an overreliance on either expert opinion or direct observation.

Quantitative

6-47. In the context of assessment, a quantitative indicator is an observation-based (objective) item of information that provides insight into a MOE or MOP. Little human judgment is involved in collecting a quantitative indicator. Someone observes an event and counts it. For example, the individual tallies the monthly gallons of diesel provided to host-nation security forces by a unit or the monthly number of tips provided to a tips hotline. Then the commander or staff collects that number.

6-48. Some human judgment is inevitably a factor even when dealing with quantitative indicators. Choosing which quantitative indicators to collect requires significant human judgment prior to collection. During collection the choice of sources, methods, and standards for observing and reporting the events require judgment. After collection, the commander or staff decides whether to use the number as an indicator in a formal assessment plan and for which MOEs or MOPs.

6-49. Quantitative indicators prove less biased than qualitative indicators. In general, numbers based on observations are impartial (assuming that the events in question were observed and reported accurately). Often, however, these indicators are less readily available than qualitative indicators and more difficult to select correctly. This is because the judgment aspect of which indicators validly inform the MOE is already factored into qualitative indicators to a degree. Experts factor in all considerations they believe are relevant to answering questions. However, this does not occur inherently with quantitative indicators. The information in quantitative indicators is less refined and requires greater judgment to handle appropriately than information in qualitative indicators.

6-50. Public opinion polling can be easily miscategorized. It often provides an important source of information in prolonged stability operations. Results of a rigorously collected and statistically valid public opinion poll are quantitative, not qualitative. Polls take a mathematically rigorous approach to answering the question of what people really think; they do not offer opinions on whether the people are correct.

6-51. While the results of scientifically conducted polls are quantitative, human judgment is involved in designing a poll. Decisions must be made on what questions to ask, how to word the questions, how to translate the questions, how to select the sample, how to choose interviewers, what training to give interviewers, and what mathematical techniques to use for getting a sample of the population.

Qualitative

6-52. In the context of assessment, a qualitative indicator is an opinion-based (subjective) item of information that provides insight into a MOE or MOP. A high degree of human judgment is involved when collecting qualitative indicators. Qualitative indicators are themselves opinions, not just observed opinions of others such as polls. For example, the division commander estimates the effectiveness of the host-nation forces on a scale of 1 to 5. Sources of qualitative indicators include subject matter experts' opinions and judgments as well as subordinate commanders' summaries of the situation.

6-53. Qualitative indicators can account for real-world complexities that cannot be feasibly measured using quantitative indicators. Qualitative indicators are also more readily available; commanders often have access to staff principals and other subject matter experts from whom to garner opinions. In some cases, the only available indicator for a particular MOE or MOP is an expert opinion. For example, determining changes in the size and number of enemy sanctuaries may prove impossible without asking local commanders. Without large amounts of objective data, subjective indicators can be used to give a relatively informed picture. However, subjective measures have a higher risk of bias. Human opinion is capable of spectacular insight but also vulnerable to hidden assumptions that may prove false.

6-54. Differentiating between quantitative and qualitative indicators is useful but signifies a major tendency rather than a sharp distinction in practice. Quantitative indicators often require a degree of judgment in their collection. For example, determining the number of mortar attacks in a given area over a given period requires judgment in categorizing attacks as mortar attacks. A different delivery system could have been used, or an improvised explosive device could have been mistaken for a mortar attack. The attack could also have landed on a boundary, requiring a decision on whether to count it. Similarly, qualitative indicators always have some basis in observed and counted events. The same indicator may be quantitative or qualitative depending on the collection mechanism. For example, the indicator may measure a change in market activity for village X. If a Soldier observes and tracks the number of exchanges, then the indicator is quantitative. If the battalion commander answers that question in a mandated monthly report based on a gut feel, then the indicator is qualitative.

ASSESSMENT INCORPORATES FORMAL AND INFORMAL METHODS

6-55. Assessment may be formal or informal; the appropriate level of formality depends entirely on the situation. As part of their planning guidance, commanders address the level of detail they desire for assessing an upcoming operation. In protracted stability operations, commanders may desire a formal assessment plan, an assessment working group, and standard reports. Subordinate units use these tools to assess local or provincial governance, economics, essential services, or the state of security. In fast-paced offensive or defensive operations or in an austere theater of operations, a formal assessment may prove impractical. To assess progress in those cases, commanders rely more on reports and assessments from subordinate commanders, the common operational picture, operation updates, assessment briefings from the staff, and their personal observations. The principles in this chapter apply to formal and informal assessment methods. The tools described in table 6-1 on page 6-3 are useful for the assessment process even if not recorded in a formal assessment framework. (Appendix H discusses formal assessment plans.)

6-56. A common informal assessment method is the after action review (AAR). Leaders use the AAR to assess unit performance in training and throughout an operation. Leaders at all echelons conduct AARs to generate candid, professional unit evaluations that include specific recommendations for improving unit performance. (See FM 6-01.1 for tactics, techniques, and procedures on conducting AARs during and after operations.)

6-57. Collecting, assembling, and analyzing information takes time and resources. Commanders balance time and resources for assessment just as they do for planning, preparation, and execution. To help achieve this balance, commanders and staffs ask the following questions:

- What will be assessed and to what detail?
- How will a particular task, objective, end state condition, or assumption be assessed? What MOEs and MOPs will be used?
- What information requirements (indicators) are needed to support a particular assessment?
- Who on the staff has primary responsibility for assessing a particular area? What is the collection plan?

6-58. Commanders must be careful, however, not to over assess. Staffs can easily get bogged down in developing formal assessment procedures for numerous tasks and objectives. Additional numerous reports, questions, and information requirements from higher headquarters can smother subordinate commanders and their staffs. Often standard reports, operational and intelligence summaries, and updates by subordinate commanders suffice. Higher echelons should never ask for something that the lower echelon does not need for its own purposes. The chief of staff or executive officer helps the commander achieve the right balance between formal and informal assessments.

ASSESSMENT WORKING GROUPS

6-59. Assessing progress is the responsibility of all staff sections and not the purview of any one staff section or command post cell. Each staff section assesses the operation from its specific area of expertise. However, these staff sections must coordinate and integrate their individual assessments and associated recommendations across the warfighting functions to produce comprehensive assessments for the commander, particularly in protracted operations. They do this in the assessment working group.

6-60. Assessment working groups are more common at higher echelons (division and above) and are more likely to be required in protracted operations than in fast-paced offensive or defensive operations. Normally, the frequency of meetings is part of a unit's battle rhythm. The staff, however, does not wait for a scheduled working group to inform the commander on issues that require immediate attention. Nor do they wait to take action in those areas within their delegated authority.

6-61. The assessment working group is cross-functional by design and includes membership from across the staff, liaison personnel, and other partners outside the headquarters. Commanders direct the chief of staff, executive officer, or a staff section leader to run the assessment working group. Typically, the operations officer, plans officer, or senior ORSA staff section serves as the staff lead for the assessment working group.

6-62. The assessment working group fuses assessment information to provide a comprehensive assessment of the operation. They consolidate and discuss emerging trends, issues, and impacts relating to events over the various planning horizons. They consider United States government civilian agency tools such as the United States Agency for International Development Tactical Conflict Assessment and Planning

Framework. (See appendix D in FM 3-07.) They examine the assessment plan to ensure MOEs, MOPs, and indicators are still valid and develop new measures and indicators as required. They provide input to ISR synchronization for adjusting collection requirements. The results of the assessment working group support and feed short-, mid-, and long-range planning in the current operations integration, future operations, and plans cells respectively.

6-63. Minority views are heard and dissenters speak up in the assessment working group. Commanders encourage all subject matter experts and relevant staff sections to debate vigorously on the proper understanding of observed trends and their associated causes. Minority views often create critical insights; they also are presented to the commander at the assessment board.

6-64. The frequency with which the assessment working group meets depends on the situation. Additionally, the assessment working group may present its findings and recommendations to the commander for decision. Subordinate commanders may participate and provide their assessments of the operations and recommendations along with the staff. Commanders combine these assessments with their personal assessment, consider recommendations, and then direct changes to improve performance and better accomplish the mission.

ASSESSMENT SUPPORT

6-65. The ORSA staff section supports assessment on many levels. Staff analytical resources and expertise increase at each echelon. Division and corps headquarters, for example, have an assigned ORSA staff section. In addition to managing a formal assessment framework, these staff sections can provide other capabilities to assist the commander. These include—

- Trend analysis.
- Hypothesis testing.
- Forecasting.

6-66. ORSA staff sections can use various mathematical techniques to identify and analyze trends in data. They confirm or rule out suspected trends in a statistically rigorous manner. They can also determine how much a given trend depends on other variables within the information. For example, given sufficient information, the ORSA staff section can determine which essential services trends correlate most to the trend in the number of attacks.

6-67. The ORSA staff section confirms or rules out many theories about given information. For example, the commander may propose a hypothesis that enemy surface-to-air attacks increased because helicopter flight patterns became too predictable. The ORSA cell can analyze the flight patterns and determine a correlation to attacks to confirm or rule out the hypothesis.

6-68. The ORSA staff section can use statistical techniques to predict the next information point in a series. Margins of error for this activity can be significant, but it is one more tool the commander can use to develop estimates in an unknown situation.

Appendix A

Command Post Organization and Operations

This appendix describes how commanders organize their headquarters into command posts (CPs) during the conduct of operations. It describes how commanders further cross-functionally organize the staff within CPs into functional and integrating cells. Next, this chapter provides guidelines for CP operations to include the importance of establishing standard operating procedures and an effective battle rhythm for the headquarters. For specific guidance on CP organization by echelon or type of unit, see the corresponding field manual. For headquarters serving as a joint task force headquarters, see JP 3-33.

±COMMAND POST ORGANIZATION

A-1. Staffs at every echelon are structured differently; however, all staffs are similar. A commander's staff includes a chief of staff (COS) or executive officer (XO) and various staff sections. **A *staff section* is a grouping of staff members by area of expertise under a coordinating, special, or personal staff officer**. The number of coordinating, special, and personal principal staff officers and their corresponding staff sections varies by type of unit and echelon. FM 6-0 details the duties and responsibilities of the coordinating, special, and personal staff.

A-2. In operations, effective mission command requires continuous, and often immediate, close coordination, synchronization, and information sharing across staff sections. To promote this, commanders cross-functionally organize elements of staff sections within CP cells (see A-15 to A-33). Additional staff integration occurs in meetings to include working groups and boards.

COMMAND POSTS

A-3. **±A *command post* is a unit headquarters where the commander and staff perform their activities**. The headquarters' design of the modular force, combined with robust communications, gives commanders a flexible mission command structure consisting of a main CP, a tactical CP, and a command group for brigades, divisions, and corps. Combined arms battalions are also resourced with a combat trains CP and a field trains CP. Theater army headquarters are resourced with a main CP and a contingency CP. See appropriate echelon manuals for doctrine on specific CP and headquarters' organization.

A-4. Each CP performs specific functions by design as well as tasks the commander assigns. Activities common in all CPs include—

- Maintaining running estimates and the common operational picture.
- Controlling operations.
- Assessing operations.
- Developing and disseminating orders.
- Coordinating with higher, lower, and adjacent units.
- Conducting knowledge management and information management. (See FM 6-01.1.)
- Performing CP administration.

Main Command Post

A-5. **±The *main command post* is a facility containing the majority of the staff designed to control current operations, conduct detailed analysis, and plan future operations**. The main CP is the unit's principal CP. It includes representatives of all staff sections and a full suite of information systems to plan, prepare, execute, and assess operations. It is larger in size and staffing and less mobile than the tactical CP. The COS (XO) leads and provides staff supervision of the main CP. Functions of the main CP include—

- Controlling and synchronizing current operations.
- Monitoring and assessing current operations (including higher and adjacent units) for their impact on future operations.
- Planning operations, including branches and sequels.
- Assessing the overall progress of operations.
- Preparing reports required by higher headquarters and receiving reports for subordinate units.
- Providing a facility for the commander to control operations, issue orders, and conduct rehearsals.

Tactical Command Post

A-6. ±The *tactical command post* **is a facility containing a tailored portion of a unit headquarters designed to control portions of an operation for a limited time**. Commanders employ the tactical CP as an extension of the main CP to help control the execution of an operation or a specific task, such as a gap crossing, a passage of lines, or an air assault operation. Commanders may employ the tactical CP to direct the operations of units close to each other. This can occur for a relief in place. The tactical CP may also control a special task force or a complex task, such as reception, staging, onward movement, and integration.

A-7. The tactical CP is fully mobile. As a rule, it includes only the Soldiers and equipment essential to the tasks assigned. The tactical CP relies on the main CP for planning, detailed analysis, and coordination. A deputy commander or the operations officer leads the tactical CP.

A-8. When employed, tactical CP functions include the following:

- Monitor and control current operations.
- Provide information to the common operational picture.
- Assess the progress of operations.
- Monitor and assess the progress of higher and adjacent units.
- Perform short-range planning.
- Provide input to targeting and future operations planning.
- Provide a facility for the commander to control operations, issue orders, and conduct rehearsals.

A-9. When the commander does not employ the tactical CP, the staff assigned to it reinforces the main CP. Unit standard operating procedures (SOPs) should address the specifics for this, including procedures to quickly detach the tactical CP from the main CP.

±Command Group

A-10. A *command group* **consists of the commander and selected staff members who assist the commander in controlling operations away from a command post**. The command group is organized and equipped to suit the commander's decisionmaking and leadership requirements. It does this while enabling the commander to accomplish critical mission command tasks when the commander is away from a command post. The command group consists of critical staff officers necessary to assist the commander in directly influencing the ongoing operation.

A-11. Command group personnel includes staff representation that can immediately affect current operations, such as maneuver, fires (including the air liaison officer), and intelligence. The mission and available staff, however, dictate the command group's makeup. For example, during a deliberate breach, the command group may include an engineer and an air defense officer. When visiting a dislocated civilians' collection point, the commander may take a translator, civil affairs operations officer, a medical officer, and a chaplain.

A-12. Division and corps headquarters are equipped with a mobile command groups. The mobile command group serves as the commander's mobile CP. It consists of ground and air components equipped with information systems. The mobile command group's mobility allows commanders to move to critical locations to personally assess a situation, make decisions, and influence operations. The mobile command group's information systems and small staff allow commanders to do this while retaining communication with the entire force.

Early-Entry Command Post

A-13. ±While not part of the unit's table of organization and equipment, commanders can establish an early-entry command post to assist them in controlling operations during the deployment phase of an operation. **An *early-entry command post* is a lead element of a headquarters designed to control operations until the remaining portions of the headquarters are deployed and operational**. The early-entry command post normally consists of personnel and equipment from the tactical CP with additional intelligence analysis, planners, and other staff officers from the main CP based on the situation.

A-14. The early-entry command post performs the functions of the main and tactical CPs until those CPs are deployed and fully operational. A deputy commander, COS (XO), or operations officer normally leads the early-entry command post.

COMMAND POST CELLS AND STAFF SECTIONS

A-15. ±Within the CP, commanders organize elements of staff sections into CP cells. **A *command post cell* is a grouping of personnel and equipment organized by warfighting function or by planning horizon to facilitate the exercise of mission command**. CP cells are formed from staff elements—personnel and equipment from staff sections. For example, the current operations integration cell contains elements from nearly all staff sections of a headquarters.

A-16. ±While each echelon and type of unit organizes CPs differently, two types of CP cells exist: functional and integrating. (See figure A-1.) Functional cells group personnel and equipment by warfighting function. Integrating cells group personnel and equipment to integrate the warfighting functions by planning horizon.

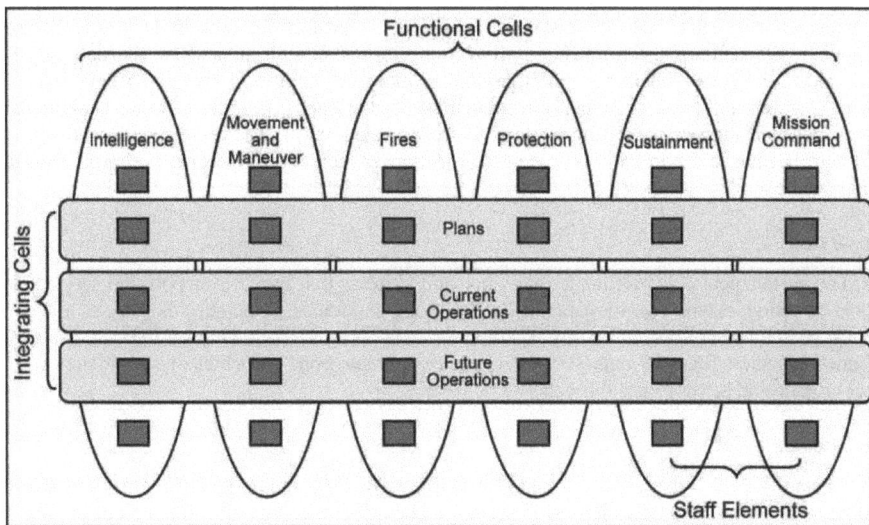

±Figure A-1. Functional and integrating cells

Functional Cells

A-17. ±Functional cells coordinate and synchronize forces and activities by warfighting function. The functional cells within a CP are intelligence, movement and maneuver, fires, protection, sustainment, and mission command. Echelons above brigade are resourced to establish all six functional cells described in paragraphs A-18 through A-23. See appropriate brigade and battalion manuals for specifics on the functional cells at those levels.

Intelligence Cell

A-18. The intelligence cell coordinates activities and systems that help commanders understand the enemy, terrain and weather, and civil considerations. The intelligence cell requests, receives, and analyzes information from all sources to produce and distribute intelligence products. This includes tasks associated with intelligence preparation of the battlefield and intelligence, surveillance, and reconnaissance. Most of the intelligence staff section resides in this cell. The unit's intelligence officer leads this cell.

Movement and Maneuver Cell

A-19. The movement and maneuver cell coordinates activities and systems that move forces to achieve a position of advantage in relation to the enemy. This includes tasks associated with combining forces with direct fire or fire potential (maneuver) and force projection (movement) related to gaining a positional advantage over an enemy. Elements of the operations, airspace command and control, aviation, engineer, geospatial information and service, and space staff sections form this cell. The unit's operations officer leads this cell. Staff elements in the movement and maneuver cell also form the core of the current operations integration cell. (See paragraphs A-30 through A-32.)

±Fires Cell

A-20. The fires cell coordinates activities and systems that provide collective and coordinated use of Army indirect fires, joint fires, and cyber/electromagnetic activities through the targeting process. The fires cell consists of elements of fire support, Air Force (or air component), and electronic warfare staff section. The unit's chief of fires (or fire support officer brigade and below) leads this cell.

±Protection Cell

A-21. The protection cell coordinates the activities and systems that preserve the force through composite risk management. This includes tasks associated with protecting personnel, physical assets, and information. Elements of the following staff sections form this cell: air and missile defense; chemical, biological, radiological, nuclear, and high-yield explosives; engineer; operations security; personnel recovery; force health protection; and provost marshal. Additionally, a safety officer is assigned at theater army and is often augmented as required down to the brigade level. The protection cell coordinates with the signal staff section in the mission command cell to further facilitate the information protection task. The chief of protection leads this cell.

Sustainment Cell

A-22. The sustainment cell coordinates activities and systems that provide support and services to ensure freedom of action, extend operational reach, and prolong endurance. It includes those tasks associated with logistics, personnel services, and Army health system support. The following staff sections form this cell: personnel, logistics, financial management, engineer, and surgeon. The chief of sustainment (or logistics officer brigade and below) leads this cell.

±Mission Command Cell

A-23. The mission command cell is made up of the G-6 (S-6) signal, G-7 (S-7) inform and influence activities, and civil affairs operations staff sections. The mission command cell is unique among the other functional cells in two ways. First, the mission command cell is not responsible for coordinating all the tasks associated with its title. The mission command cell has a narrower focus. Second, the staff sections that reside in the mission command cell report directly to the COS and not through a cell chief.

Integrating Cells

A-24. Whereas functional cells are organized by warfighting functions, integrating cells coordinate and synchronize forces and warfighting functions within a specified planning horizon and include the plans, future operations, and current operations integration cells. **A *planning horizon* is a point in time commanders use to focus the organization's planning efforts to shape future events**. The three planning horizons are long, mid, and short. Generally, they are associated with the plans cell, future operations cell, and current operations integration cell respectively. Planning horizons are situation-dependent; they can range from hours and days to weeks and months. As a rule, the higher the echelon, the more distant the planning horizon with which it is concerned. (See chapter 2 for a discussion of planning in time.)

A-25. Not all echelons and types of units are resourced for all three integrating cells. Battalions, for example, combine their planning and operations responsibilities in one integrating cell. The brigade combat team has a small, dedicated plans cell but is not resourced for a future operations cell. Divisions and above are resourced for all three integrating cells as shown in figure A-2.

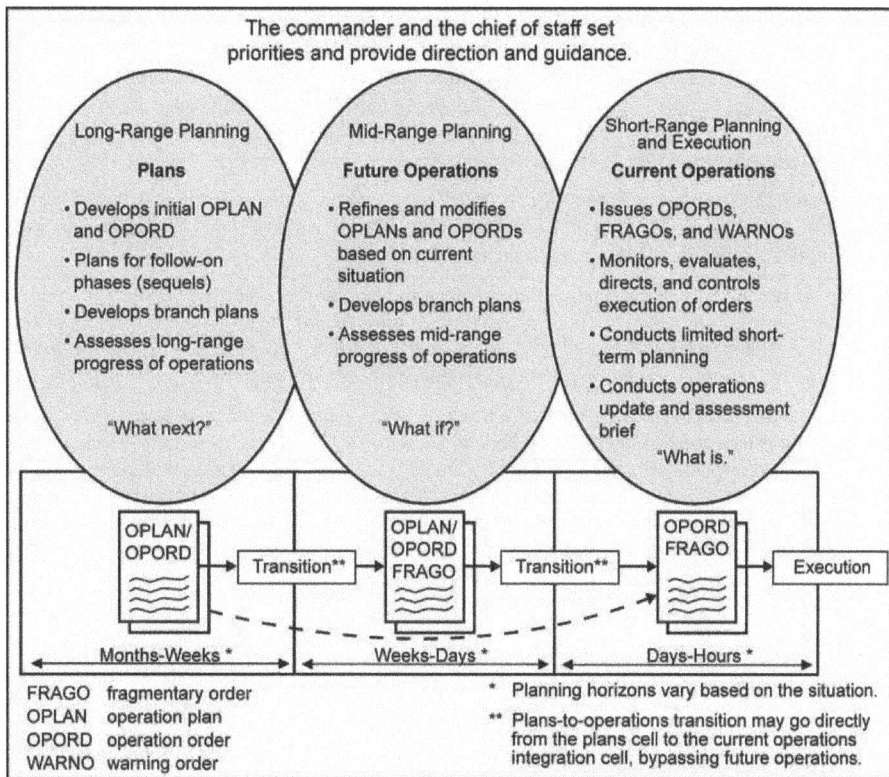

The commander and the chief of staff set priorities and provide direction and guidance.

Long-Range Planning

Plans

- Develops initial OPLAN and OPORD
- Plans for follow-on phases (sequels)
- Develops branch plans
- Assesses long-range progress of operations

"What next?"

Mid-Range Planning

Future Operations

- Refines and modifies OPLANs and OPORDs based on current situation
- Develops branch plans
- Assesses mid-range progress of operations

"What if?"

Short-Range Planning and Execution

Current Operations

- Issues OPORDs, FRAGOs, and WARNOs
- Monitors, evaluates, directs, and controls execution of orders
- Conducts limited short-term planning
- Conducts operations update and assessment brief

"What is."

OPLAN/OPORD → Transition** → OPLAN/OPORD FRAGO → Transition** → OPORD FRAGO → Execution

Months-Weeks * | Weeks-Days * | Days-Hours *

FRAGO   fragmentary order
OPLAN   operation plan
OPORD   operation order
WARNO   warning order

* Planning horizons vary based on the situation.

** Plans-to-operations transition may go directly from the plans cell to the current operations integration cell, bypassing future operations.

Figure A-2. Integration of plans, future operations, and current operations

Plans Cell

A-26. The plans cell is responsible for planning operations for the long-range planning horizons. It prepares for operations beyond the scope of the current order by developing plans and orders, including branch plans and sequels. The plans cell also oversees military deception planning.

A-27. The plans cell consists of a core group of planners and analysts led by the plans officer (or the operations officer at battalion level). All staff sections assist as required. Whereas a brigade has a small, dedicated plans cell, the majority of its staff sections balance their efforts between the current operations integration and plans cells. Battalions are not resourced for a plans cell. Planning in combined arms battalions occurs in the current operations integration cell.

Future Operations Cell

A-28. The future operations cell is responsible for planning operations in the mid-range planning horizon. It focuses on adjustments to the current operation—including the positioning or maneuvering of forces in depth—that facilitates continuation of the current operation. The cell consists of a core group of planners led by an assistant operations officer (the chief of future operations). All staff sections assist as required. Divisions and above headquarters have a future operations cell. Battalion and brigade headquarters do not.

A-29. In many respects, the future operations cell serves as a fusion cell between the plans and current operations integration cells. The future operations cell monitors current operations and determines implications for operations within the mid-range planning horizon. In coordination with the current operations integration cell, the future operations cell assesses whether the ongoing operation must be modified to achieve the current phase's objectives. Normally, the commander directs adjustments to the operation, but the cell may also recommend options to the commander. Once the commander decides to adjust the operation, the cell develops the fragmentary order necessary to implement the change. The future operations cell also participates in the targeting working group since the same planning horizons normally concern them both. The future operations cell updates and adds details to the branch plans foreseen in the current operation and prepares any orders necessary to implement a sequel to the operation.

Current Operations Integration Cell

A-30. The current operations integration cell is the focal point for the execution of the operations. This involves assessing the current situation while regulating forces and warfighting functions in accordance with the mission, commander's intent, and concept of operations.

A-31. The current operations integration cell displays the common operational picture and conducts shift changes, assessments, and other briefings as required. It provides information on the status of operations to all staff members and to higher, subordinate, and adjacent units. The operations synchronization meeting is the most important event in the battle rhythm in support of the current operation.

A-32. The operations officer leads the current operations integration cell and is aided by an assistant operations officer (the chief of operations). The movement and maneuver cell forms the core of the current operations integration cell. Elements or watch officers from each staff section and liaison officers from subordinate and adjacent units form the remainder of the cell. All staff sections are represented in the current operations integration cell, either permanently or on call. (Chapter 5 discusses execution with a focus on the current operations integration cell.)

Staff Sections

A-33. Not all staff sections reside in one of the functional or integrating cells. Personal staff officers and their associated staff sections, such as the inspector general and public affairs staff sections, are examples. Special staff sections such as the operations research/systems analysis, red team, and knowledge management are other examples. These staff sections maintain their distinct organizations. They operate in different CP cells as required and coordinate their activities in the various meetings established in the unit's battle rhythm.

COMMAND POST OPERATIONS

A-34. ±Units must man, equip, and organize command posts to control operations for extended periods. Command post personnel, information systems, and equipment must be able to support 24-hour operations while in continuous communication with all subordinate units and higher and adjacent units. Commanders arrange CP personnel and equipment to facilitate internal coordination, information sharing, and rapid decisionmaking. They also ensure they have procedures to execute the operations process within the headquarters to enhance how they exercise mission command. Commanders use the following to assist them with effective CP operations:

- SOPs.
- Battle rhythm.
- Meetings.

STANDARD OPERATING PROCEDURES

A-35. ±SOPs assist with effective mission command. These SOPs serve two purposes. Internal SOPs standardize each CP's internal operations and administration. External SOPs developed for the entire force standardize interactions among CPs and between subordinate units and CPs. For SOPs to be effective, all Soldiers must know their provisions and train to their standards. (See FM 7-15 for details on the task and subtasks of "Conduct Command Post Operations.")

A-36. Each CP should have SOPs that address the following:
- Organization and setup.
- Staffing and shifts plans.
- Eating and sleeping plans.
- Physical security and defense.
- Priorities of work.
- Equipment and vehicle maintenance.
- Loading plans and equipment checklists.
- Orders production and dissemination procedures.
- Journals and log maintenance.

A-37. In addition to these SOPS, each CP requires—
- CP battle drills.
- Shift-change briefings.
- Reports and returns.
- Operation update and assessment briefings.
- Operations synchronization meeting.
- Transferring control between CPs.

Command Post Battle Drills

A-38. Each CP requires procedures to react to a variety of situations. Specific actions taken by a CP should be defined in its SOPs and rehearsed during training and operations. Typical CP battle drills include—
- React to an air attack.
- React to a ground attack.
- React to a chemical attack.
- React to indirect fire.
- React to jamming or suspected communications compromise.
- Execute time-sensitive targets.
- Execute a close air support or joint fires mission.
- React to a mass casualty incident.
- React to a civil riot or incident.
- React to significant collateral damage.
- React to a misinformation incident.

Shift-Change Briefings

A-39. During continuous operations, CPs operate in shifts. To ensure uninterrupted operations, staffs execute a briefing when shifts change. Depending on the situation, it may be formal or informal and include the entire staff or selected staff members. Normally it is done face-to-face among key CP leaders. The COS (XO) oversees the briefing, with participants briefing their areas of expertise. The briefing's purpose is to inform the incoming shift of—
- Current unit status.
- Significant activities that occurred during the previous shift.
- Significant decisions and events anticipated during the next shift.

The commander may attend and possibly change the focus of the briefing. If the commander issues guidance or makes a decision, issuing a fragmentary order may be necessary.

A-40. The shift-change briefing format and emphasis change based on the situation. For example, the format for a force supporting civil authorities in a disaster area differs from one for a force conducting offensive operations abroad. To facilitate a quick but effective shift-change briefing, unit SOPs should contain tailored formats.

A-41. The shift-change briefing provides a mechanism to formally exchange information periodically among CP staff members. However, CP staff members share information throughout the shift. They coordinate activities and inform each other continuously. Information that answers a commander's critical information requirement and exceptional information is given to the commander immediately. Information that can potentially affect the entire force is disseminated to the commander, higher headquarters, and subordinate units as the situation dictates. Situational understanding for CP staff members includes knowing who needs what relevant information and why they need it. CP staff members exercise initiative when they ensure relevant information gets to people who need it.

Reports and Returns

A-42. A unit's reporting system facilitates timely and effective information exchange among CPs and higher, lower, and adjacent headquarters. An established SOP for reports and returns is key to effective information management. These SOPs include—

- The writer required to submit each report.
- The frequency and time of each report.
- The recipient of each report.

For those reports not standard in a unit SOP, list reports found in annex R of the operation plan and operation order.

Operation Update and Assessment Briefing

A-43. An operation update and assessment briefing may occur daily or anytime the commander calls for one. Its content is similar to the shift-change briefing but has a different audience. The staff presents it to the commander and subordinate commanders. Its purpose is to provide all key personnel with common situational awareness. Often commanders require this briefing shortly before an operation begins to summarize changes made during preparation, including changes resulting from intelligence, surveillance, and reconnaissance efforts.

A-44. During the briefing, staff sections present their running estimates. Subordinate commanders brief their current situation and planned activities. Rarely do all members conduct this briefing face-to-face. Various communications means are used including radio, conference calls, and video teleconference. All CPs and subordinate commanders participate. The briefing follows a sequence and format specified by SOPs. That keeps transmissions short, ensures completeness, and eases note taking. This briefing normally has a format similar to a shift-change briefing. However, it omits CP administrative information and includes presentations by subordinate commanders in an established sequence.

Operations Synchronization Meeting

A-45. The operations synchronization meeting is the key event in the battle rhythm in support of the current operation. Its primary purpose is to synchronize all warfighting functions and other activities in the short-term planning horizon. It is designed to ensure that—

- All staff members have a common understanding of current operation, including upcoming decision points and projected actions at those decision points.
- All warfighting functions are synchronized and appropriate fragmentary orders are issued to subordinates based on the commander's intent for current operations.

A-46. ±The operations synchronization meeting does not replace the shift-change briefing or operation update and assessment briefing. The meeting is chaired by the G-3 (S-3). Representatives of each CP cell and separated staff section attend. Key outputs of the operations synchronization meeting include a fragmentary order addressing any required changes to maintain synchronization of the current operations planning guidance for upcoming working groups and boards.

Transferring Control of Operations Between Command Posts

A-47. The employment and use of CPs are important decisions reflected in the operation order. Often, a particular CP may control a part of the operation or all of the operation for a specific time. Effectively transferring control between CPs requires a well-understood SOP and clear instructions in the operations order.

A-48. ±While all CPs have some ability to exercise control on the move, they lose many capabilities they have when stationary. Therefore, CPs normally control operations from a static location. During moves, control responsibilities are transferred to another CP. Transfer of control requires notifying subordinates since many network operations change to route information to the new controlling CP. SOPs establish these requirements to minimize interruptions when transferring control.

BATTLE RHYTHM

A-49. *Battle rhythm* is a deliberate daily cycle of command, staff, and unit activities intended to synchronize current and future operations (JP 3-33). A headquarters' battle rhythm consists of a series of meetings, briefings, and other activities synchronized by time and purpose. The COS (XO) oversees the battle rhythm. Each meeting, to include working groups and boards, should be logically sequenced so that one meeting's outputs are available as another meeting's inputs (to include higher headquarters meetings). The COS (XO) balances the time required to plan, prepare for, and hold meetings and conduct briefings with other staff duties and responsibilities. The COS (XO) also critically examines attendance requirements. Some staff sections and CP cells may lack the personnel to attend all events. The COS (XO) and staff members constantly look for ways to combine meetings and eliminate unproductive ones.

A-50. The battle rhythm facilitates integration and collaboration. The COS (XO) manages the headquarters' battle rhythm. This battle rhythm serves several important functions, to include—

- Establishing a routine for staff interaction and coordination.
- Facilitating interaction between the commander and staff.
- Synchronizing activities of the staff in time and purpose.
- Facilitating planning by the staff and decisionmaking by the commander.

A-51. The battle rhythm changes during execution as operations progress. For example, early in the operation a commander may require a plans update briefing daily. As the situation changes, the commander may only require a plans update every three days. Many factors help determine a unit's battle rhythm. Some factors include the staff's proficiency, higher headquarters' battle rhythm, and current mission. In developing the unit's battle rhythm, the chief COS (XO) considers—

- Higher headquarters' battle rhythm and report requirements.
- Subordinate headquarters' battle rhythm requirements.
- The duration and intensity of the operation.
- Integrating cells' planning requirements.

MEETINGS

A-52. Meetings are gatherings to present and exchange information, solve problems, coordinate action, and make decisions. They may involve the staff; the commander and staff; or the commander, subordinate commanders, staff, and other partners. Who attends depends on the issue. Commanders establish these meetings to integrate the staff and enhance planning and decisionmaking within the headquarters. Commanders also identify staff members to participate in the higher commander's meeting, including working groups and boards. (See JP 3-33 for a discussion of the various working groups and boards used by joint force commanders.)

A-53. The number of meetings and subjects they address depend on the situation and echelon. While numerous informal meetings occur daily within a headquarters, meetings commonly included in a unit's battle rhythm and the cells responsible for them include—

- A shift-change briefing (current operations integration cell).
- An operation update and assessment briefing (current operations integration cell).
- An operations synchronization meeting (current operations integration cell).
- Planning meetings and briefings (plans or future operations cells).
- Working groups and boards (various functional and integrating cells).

A-54. Often, the commander establishes and maintains only those meetings required by the situation. Commanders—assisted by the COS (XO)—establish, modify, and dissolve meetings as the situation evolves. The COS (XO) manages the timings of these events through the unit's battle rhythm. (See paragraphs A-49 through A-51.)

A-55. For each meeting, the unit's SOPs address—

- Purpose.
- Frequency.
- Composition (chair and participants).
- Inputs and expected outputs.
- Agenda.

A-56. Working groups and boards are types of meetings and are included on the unit's battle rhythm. **A working group is a grouping of predetermined staff representatives who meet to provide analysis, coordinate, and provide recommendations for a particular purpose or function**. Working groups are cross-functional by design to synchronize the contributions of multiple CP cells and staff sections. For example, the targeting working group brings together representatives of all staff elements concerned with targeting. It synchronizes the contributions of all staff elements with the work of the fires cell. It also synchronizes fires with future operations and current operations integration cells.

A-57. Typical working groups and the lead cell or staff section at division and corps headquarters include the—

- Assessment working group (plans or future operations cell).
- Intelligence, surveillance, and reconnaissance working group (intelligence cell).
- Targeting working group (fires cell).
- Protection working group (protection cell).
- Civil affairs operations working group (civil affairs operations staff section).

A-58. The number of subjects that working groups address depends on the situation and echelon. Battalion and brigade headquarters normally have fewer working groups than higher echelons. Working groups may convene daily, weekly, monthly, or on call depending on the subject, situation, and echelon.

A-59. **A board is a grouping of predetermined staff representatives with delegated decision authority for a particular purpose or function**. Boards are similar to working groups. However, commanders appoint boards with the purpose to arrive at a decision. When the process or activity being synchronized requires command approval, a board is the appropriate forum.

Appendix B

The Military Decisionmaking Process

This appendix defines and describes the military decisionmaking process (MDMP). To conduct the MDMP effectively, leaders must first understand the fundamentals of planning and design. (See chapters 2 and 3 respectively.) Additional doctrine on commander's planning guidance, formats for plans and orders, task organization, and running estimates are located in appendixes D, E, F, and G respectively.

OVERVIEW

B-1. The *military decisionmaking process* **is an iterative planning methodology that integrates the activities of the commander, staff, subordinate headquarters, and other partners to understand the situation and mission; develop and compare courses of action; decide on a course of action that best accomplishes the mission; and produce an operation plan or order for execution.** The MDMP helps leaders apply thoroughness, clarity, sound judgment, logic, and professional knowledge to understand situations, develop options to solve problems, and reach decisions. It is a process that helps commanders, staffs, and others think critically and creatively while planning. (See chapter 1.)

Note: Joint force headquarters use the joint operation planning process (known as JOPP), which is similar to the Army's MDMP. (See JP 5-0.) Marine Corps headquarters use the Marine Corps planning process, which is similar to both the MDMP and the joint operation planning process. (See MCWP 5-1.)

B-2. The MDMP facilitates collaborative and parallel planning as the higher headquarters solicits input and continuously shares information concerning future operations with subordinate and adjacent units, supporting and supported units, and other military and civilian partners through planning meetings, warning orders, and other means. Commanders encourage active collaboration among all organizations affected by the pending operations to build a shared understanding of the situation, participate in course of action development and decisionmaking, and resolve conflicts before publication of the plan or order.

B-3. The MDMP also drives preparation. Since time is a factor in all operations, commanders and staffs conduct a time analysis early in the planning process. This analysis helps them determine what actions are required and when those actions must begin to ensure forces are ready and in position before execution. This may require the commander to direct subordinates to start necessary movements; conduct task organization changes; begin intelligence, surveillance, and reconnaissance (ISR) operations; and execute other preparation activities before completing the plan. These tasks are directed in a series of warning orders (WARNOs) as the commander and staff conducts the MDMP.

B-4. During planning, assessment focuses on developing an understanding of the current situation and determining what to assess and how to assess progress using measures of effectiveness and measures of performance. Developing the unit's assessment plan occurs during the MDMP—not after the plan or order is developed. (See chapter 6 for a discussion of the fundamentals of assessment. See appendix H for details in developing an assessment plan.)

B-5. Depending on complexity of the situation, commanders may initiate design activities before or in parallel with the MDMP. Commanders may choose to conduct design to assist them in understanding the operational environment, framing the problem, and considering operational approaches to solve or manage the problem. The products of design, including the operational approach, would guide more detailed planning as part of the MDMP. Commanders may also conduct design in parallel with the MDMP. In this instance, members of the staff conduct mission analysis as the commander and other staff members engage in design activities prior to course of action development. In time-constrained conditions or if the problem is relatively straight forward, commanders may conduct the MDMP without the benefit of a formal design process. During execution, commander may conduct design to help refine their understanding and visualization and adjust the plan as required. (See chapter 2 for a discussion on the interface between design and the MDMP.)

THE STEPS OF THE MILITARY DECISIONMAKING PROCESS

B-6. The MDMP consists of seven steps as shown in figure B-1. Each step of the MDMP has various inputs, a method (step) to conduct it, and outputs. The outputs lead to an increased understanding of the situation facilitating the next step of the MDMP. Commanders and staffs generally perform these steps sequentially; however, they may revisit several steps in an iterative fashion as they learn more about the situation before producing the plan or order.

B-7. Commanders initiate the MDMP upon receipt of or in anticipation of a mission. Commanders and staffs often begin planning in the absence of a complete and approved higher headquarters' operation plan (OPLAN) or operation order (OPORD). In these instances, the headquarters begins a new planning effort based on a WARNO and other directives, such as a planning order or an alert order from their higher headquarters. This requires active collaboration with the higher headquarters and parallel planning among echelons as the plan or order is developed.

THE ROLE OF COMMANDERS AND STAFFS IN THE MDMP

B-8. ±The commander is the most important participant in the MDMP. More than simply decisionmakers in this process, commanders use their experience, knowledge, and judgment to guide staff planning efforts. While unable to devote all their time to the MDMP, commanders remain aware of the current status of the planning effort, participate during critical periods of the process, and make sound decisions based on the detailed work of the staff. During the MDMP, commanders focus their activities on understanding, visualizing, and describing as addressed in chapter 2.

B-9. The MDMP stipulates several formal meetings and briefings between the commander and staff to discuss, assess, and approve or disapprove planning efforts as they progress. However, experience has shown that optimal planning results when the commander meets informally at frequent intervals with the staff throughout the MDMP. Such informal interaction among the commander and staff can improve understanding of the situation and ensure the planning effort adequately reflects the commander's visualization of the operation.

B-10. The chief of staff (COS) or executive officer (XO) is a key participant in the MDMP. The COS (XO) manages and coordinates the staff's work and provides quality control during the MDMP. The COS (XO) must clearly understand the commander's intent and guidance because COSs (XOs) supervise the entire process. They provide timelines to the staff, establish briefing times and locations, and provide any instructions necessary to complete the plan.

B-11. The staff's effort during the MDMP focuses on helping the commander understand the situation, making decisions, and synchronizing those decisions into a fully developed plan or order. Staff activities during planning initially focus mission analysis. The products developed during mission analysis help commanders understand the situation and develop the commander's visualization. During course of action (COA) development and COA comparison, the staff provides recommendations to support the commander in selecting a COA. After the commander makes a decision, the staff prepares the plan or order that reflects the commander's intent, coordinating all necessary details.

MODIFYING THE MDMP

B-12. The MDMP can be as detailed as time, resources, experience, and the situation permit. Conducting all the steps and substeps of the MDMP is detailed, deliberate, and time-consuming. Commanders use the full MDMP when they have enough planning time and staff support to thoroughly examine two or more COAs and develop a fully synchronized plan or order. This typically occurs when planning for an entirely new mission.

Key inputs	Steps	Key outputs
• Higher headquarters' plan or order or a new mission anticipated by the commander	Step 1: **Receipt of Mission**	• Commander's initial guidance • Initial allocation of time
	Warning order	
• Higher headquarters' plan or order • Higher headquarters' knowledge and intelligence products • Knowledge products from other organizations • Design concept (if developed)	Step 2: **Mission Analysis**	• Problem statement • Mission statement • Initial commander's intent • Initial planning guidance • Initial CCIRs and EEFIs • Updated IPB and running estimates • Assumptions
	Warning order	

• Mission statement
• Initial commander's intent, planning guidance, CCIRs, and EEFIs
• Updated IPB and running estimates
• Assumptions
	Step 3: **Course of Action (COA) Development**	• COA statements and sketches
		  - Tentative task organization
		  - Broad concept of operations
		• Revised planning guidance
		• Updated assumptions

• Updated running estimates • Revised planning guidance • COA statements and sketches • Updated assumptions	Step 4: **COA Analysis (War Game)**	• Refined COAs • Potential decision points • War-game results • Initial assessment measures • Updated assumptions
• Updated running estimates • Refined COAs • Evaluation criteria • War-game results • Updated assumptions	Step 5: **COA Comparison**	• Evaluated COAs • Recommended COAs • Updated running estimates • Updated assumptions
• Updated running estimates • Evaluated COAs • Recommended COA • Updated assumptions	Step 6: **COA Approval**	• Commander-selected COA and any modifications • Refined commander's intent, CCIRs, and EEFIs • Updated assumptions
	Warning order	
• Commander-selected COA with any modifications • Refined commander's intent, CCIRs, and EEFIs • Updated assumptions	Step 7: **Orders Production**	• Approved operation plan or order

CCIR	commander's critical information requirement	EEFI	essential element of friendly information
COA	course of action	IPB	intelligence preparation of the battlefield

±Figure B-1. The steps of the military decisionmaking process

B-13. Commanders may alter the steps of the MDMP to fit time-constrained circumstances and produce a satisfactory plan. In time-constrained conditions, commanders assess the situation, update the commander's visualization, and direct the staff to perform the MDMP activities that support the required decisions. (See paragraphs B-186 through B-202.) In extremely compressed situations, commanders rely on more intuitive decisionmaking techniques, such as the rapid decisionmaking and synchronization process described in chapter 5.

PERFORMING THE MILITARY DECISIONMAKING PROCESS

B-14. This section describes the methods and provides techniques for conducting each step of the MDMP. It describes the key inputs to each step and expected key outputs. This section also describes how the intelligence preparation of the battlefield (IPB), targeting, composite risk management (CRM), and ISR synchronization are integrated throughout the MDMP.

RECEIPT OF MISSION

B-15. Commanders initiate the MDMP upon receipt or in anticipation of a mission. The purpose of this step is to alert all participants of the pending planning requirements, determine the amount of time available for planning and preparation, and decide on a planning approach, including guidance on design and how to abbreviate the MDMP, if required. When a new mission is identified, commanders and staffs perform the actions and produce the outputs as described in paragraphs B-16 through B-24.

Alert the Staff and Other Key Participants

B-16. ±As soon as a unit receives a new mission (or when the commander directs), the current operations integration cell alerts the staff of the pending planning requirement. Unit standard operating procedures (SOPs) should identify members of the planning staff who participate in mission analysis. In addition, the current operations integration cell also notifies other military, civilian, and host-nation organizations of pending planning events as required.

Gather the Tools

B-17. Once notified of the new planning requirement, the staff prepares for mission analysis by gathering the tools needed to perform it. These tools include, but are not limited to—

- Appropriate field manuals, including FM 5-0 and FM 1-02.
- All documents related to the mission and area of operations (AO), including the higher headquarters' OPLAN and OPORD, maps and terrain products, and operational graphics.
- Higher headquarters' and other organizations' intelligence and assessment products.
- Estimates and products of other military and civilian agencies and organizations.
- Both their own and the higher headquarters' SOPs.
- Current running estimates.
- Any design products, including the design concept.

B-18. The gathering of knowledge products continues throughout the MDMP. Staff officers carefully review the reference sections (located before paragraph **1. Situation**) of the higher headquarters' OPLANs and OPORDs to identify documents (such as theater policies and memoranda) related to the upcoming operation. If the MDMP occurs while in the process of replacing another unit, the staff begins collecting relevant documents—such as the current OPORD, branch plans, current assessments, operations and intelligence summaries, and SOPs—from that unit.

Update Running Estimates

B-19. While gathering the necessary tools for planning, each staff section begins updating its running estimate—especially the status of friendly units and resources and key civil considerations that affect each functional area. Running estimates not only compile critical facts and assumptions from the perspective of each staff section, but also include information from other staff sections and other military and civilian organizations. While this task is listed at the beginning of the MDMP, developing and updating running estimates continues throughout the MDMP and the operations process. (See appendix G.)

Conduct Initial Assessment

B-20. During receipt of mission, the commander and staff conduct an initial assessment of time and resources available to plan, prepare, and begin execution of an operation. This initial assessment helps commanders determine—

- The time needed to plan and prepare for the mission for both the headquarters and subordinate units.
- Guidance on design and abbreviating the MDMP, if required.
- Which outside agencies and organizations to contact and incorporate into the planning process.
- The staff's experience, cohesiveness, and level of rest or stress.

B-21. A key product of this assessment is an initial allocation of available time. The commander and staff balance the desire for detailed planning against the need for immediate action. The commander provides guidance to subordinate units as early as possible to allow subordinates the maximum time for their own planning and preparation of operations. As a rule, the commander allocates a minimum of two-thirds of available time for subordinate units to conduct their planning and preparation. This leaves one-third of the time for commanders and their staff to do their planning. They use the other two-thirds for their own preparation. Time, more than any other factor, determines the detail to which the commander and staff can plan.

B-22. Based on the commander's initial allocation of time, the COS (XO) develops a staff planning timeline that outlines how long the headquarters can spend on each step of the MDMP. The staff planning timeline indicates what products are due, who is responsible for them, and who receives them. It includes times and locations for meetings and briefings. It serves as a benchmark for the commander and staff throughout the MDMP.

Issue the Commander's Initial Guidance

B-23. Once time is allocated, the commander determines whether to initiate design, conduct design and MDMP in parallel, or proceed directly into the MDMP without the benefits of formal design activities. In time-sensitive situations where commanders decide to proceed directly into the MDMP, they may also issue guidance on how to abbreviate the process. Having determined the time available together with the scope and scale of the planning effort, commanders issue initial planning guidance. Although brief, the initial guidance includes—

- Initial time allocations.
- A decision to initiate design or go straight into the MDMP.
- How to abbreviate the MDMP, if required.
- Necessary coordination to perform, including liaison officers to exchange.
- Authorized movements and any reconnaissance and surveillance to initiate.
- Collaborative planning times and locations.
- Initial information requirements (IRs).
- Additional staff tasks.

Issue the Initial Warning Order

B-24. The last task in receipt of mission is to issue a WARNO to subordinate and supporting units. This order includes at a minimum the type of operation, the general location of the operation, the initial timeline, and any movement or reconnaissance to initiate.

MISSION ANALYSIS

B-25. The MDMP continues with an assessment of the situation called mission analysis. Commanders (supported by their staffs and informed by subordinate and adjacent commanders and by other partners) gather, analyze, and synthesize information to orient themselves on the current conditions of the operational environment. The commander and staff conduct mission analysis to better understand the situation and problem, and identify *what* the command must accomplish, *when* and *where* it must be done, and most importantly *why*—the purpose of the operation.

B-26. Since no amount of subsequent planning can solve a problem insufficiently understood, mission analysis is the most important step in the MDMP. This understanding of the situation and the problem allows commanders to visualize and describe how the operation may unfold in their initial commander's intent and planning guidance. During mission analysis, the commander and staff perform the process actions and produce the outputs shown in figure B-2. See FM 6-0 for specific areas of responsibility for each staff section.

Key inputs	Process	Key outputs
• Higher headquarters' plan or order • Higher headquarters' intelligence and knowledge products • Knowledge products from other organizations • Updated running estimates • Initial commander's guidance • COA evaluation criteria • Design concept (if design precedes mission analysis)	• Analyze the higher headquarters' plan or order • Perform initial IPB • Determine specified, implied, and essential tasks • Review available assets and identify resource shortfalls • Determine constraints • Identify critical facts and develop assumptions • Begin composite risk management • Develop initial CCIRs and EEFIs • Develop initial ISR synchronization tools • Develop initial ISR plan • Update plan for the use of available time • Develop initial themes and messages • Develop a proposed mission statement • Present the mission analysis briefing • Develop and issue initial commander's intent • Develop and issue initial planning guidance • Develop COA evaluation criteria • Issue a warning order	• Approved problem statement • Approved mission statement • Initial commander's intent • Initial CCIRs and EEFIs • Initial commander's planning guidance • Information themes and messages • Updated IPB products • Updated running estimates • Assumptions • Resource shortfalls • Updated operational timeline • COA evaluation criteria Warning Order

CCIR	commander's critical information requirement	IPB	intelligence preparation of the battlefield
COA	course of action	ISR	intelligence, surveillance, and reconnaissance
EEFI	essential element of friendly information		

±Figure B-2. Mission analysis

Analyze the Higher Headquarters' Plan or Order

B-27. Commanders and staffs thoroughly analyze the higher headquarters' plan or order. They aim to determine how their unit—by task and purpose—contributes to the mission, commander's intent, and concept of operations of the higher headquarters. The commander and staff seek to completely understand—

- The higher headquarters'—
    - Commander's intent.
    - Mission.
    - Concept of operations.
    - Available assets.
    - Timeline.
- The missions of adjacent, supporting, and supported units and their relationships to the higher headquarters' plan.
- The missions of interagency, intergovernmental, and nongovernmental organizations that work in the operational areas.
- Their assigned area of operations.

B-28. If the commander misinterprets the higher headquarters' plan, time is wasted. Additionally, when analyzing the higher order, the commander and staff may identify difficulties and contradictions in the higher order. Therefore, if confused by the higher headquarters' order or guidance, commanders seek clarification immediately. Liaison officers familiar with the higher headquarters' plan can help clarify issues. Collaborative planning with the higher headquarters also facilitates this task. Staffs also use requests for information (RFIs) to clarify or obtain additional information from the higher headquarters.

Perform Initial Intelligence Preparation of the Battlefield

B-29. IPB and the products it produces help the commander and staff understand situations. IPB is a systematic, continuous process of analyzing the threat and operational environment in a specific geographic area. Led by the intelligence officer, the entire staff participates in IPB to develop and maintain an understanding of the enemy, terrain and weather, and key civil considerations. (See FM 2-01.3 for a more detailed discussion of IPB.)

B-30. IPB begins in mission analysis and continues throughout the operations process. Results of the initial IPB include terrain products and weather products (to include the modified combined obstacle overlay), likely enemy COAs, high-value target lists, and explanations of how key civil considerations affect the operation. Additionally, the initial IPB identifies gaps in information that the commander uses to establish initial priority information requirements (PIRs) and RFIs.

Determine Specified, Implied, and Essential Tasks

B-31. The staff analyzes the higher headquarters' order and the higher commander's guidance to determine their specified and implied tasks. In the context of operations, a task is a clearly defined and measurable activity accomplished by Soldiers, units, and organizations that may support or be supported by other tasks. The "what" of a mission statement is always a task. From the list of specified and implied tasks, the staff determines essential tasks for inclusion in the recommended mission statement.

B-32. A *specified task* is a task specifically assigned to a unit by its higher headquarters. Paragraphs 2 and 3 of the higher headquarters' order or plan state specified tasks. Some tasks may be in paragraphs 4 and 5. Specified tasks may be listed in annexes and overlays. They may also be assigned verbally during collaborative planning sessions or in directives from the higher commander.

B-33. An *implied task* is a task that must be performed to accomplish a specified task or mission but is not stated in the higher headquarters' order. Implied tasks are derived from a detailed analysis of the higher headquarters' order, the enemy situation, the terrain, and civil considerations. Additionally, analysis of doctrinal requirements for each specified task might disclose implied tasks.

B-34. ±When analyzing the higher order for specified and implied tasks, the staff also identifies any be-prepared or on-order mission. **A *be-prepared mission* is a mission assigned to a unit that might be executed.** It is generally a contingency mission that units will execute because something planned has or has not been successful. In planning priorities, units plan a be-prepared mission after any on-order mission. **An *on-order mission* is a mission to be executed at an unspecified time.** A unit with an on-order mission is a committed force. Commanders envisions task execution in the concept of operations; however, they may not know the exact time or place of execution. Subordinate commanders develop plans and orders and allocate resources, task-organize, and position forces for execution.

B-35. Units with an assigned AO are responsible for ensuring that essential stability tasks are conducted for the population in areas they control. While some stability tasks will be specified, commanders consider the primary stability tasks found in FM 3-07 as sources for implied tasks. By analyzing these primary stability tasks and their associated subtasks, commanders and staffs develop implied tasks. These implied tasks, at a minimum, provide for civil security, restoration of essential services, and civil control for civil populations in their AO that they control. Based on this analysis, the staff determines if there are other agencies, civil or military, that can provide these tasks. If not, the unit plans to provide these tasks using available assets. If the unit determines that it does not have the assets, it informs its higher headquarters. The higher headquarters then either provide the assets or assigns the task to another unit.

B-36. Once staff members have identified specified and implied tasks, they ensure they understand each task's requirements and purpose. Any task that must be successfully completed for the commanders to accomplish their purpose is an essential task. **An *essential task* is a specified or implied task that must be executed to accomplish the mission**. Essential tasks are always included in the unit's mission statement.

Review Available Assets and Identify Resource Shortfalls

B-37. The commander and staff examine additions to and deletions from the current task organization, command and support relationships, and status (current capabilities and limitations) of all units. This analysis also includes the capabilities of civilian and military organizations (joint, special operations, and multinational) that operate within the unit's AO. They consider relationships among specified, implied, and essential tasks, and between them and available assets. From this analysis, staffs determine if they have the assets needed to accomplish all tasks. If shortages occur, they identify additional resources needed for mission success to the higher headquarters. Staffs also identify any deviations from the normal task organization and provide them to the commander to consider when developing the planning guidance. A more detailed analysis of available assets occurs during COA development.

Determine Constraints

B-38. The commander and staff identify any constraints placed on their command. **A *constraint* is a restriction placed on the command by a higher command. A constraint dictates an action or inaction, thus restricting the freedom of action of a subordinate commander**. Constraints are found in paragraph 3 in the OPLAN or OPORD. Annexes to the order may also include constraints. The operation overlay, for example, may contain a restrictive fire line or a no fire area. Constraints may also be issued verbally, in WARNOs, or in policy memoranda.

Note: Joint doctrine uses the term operational limitation that includes the terms constraints and restrictions that differ from Army doctrine. An *operational limitation* is an action required or prohibited by higher authority, such as a constraint or a restraint, and other restrictions that limit the commander's freedom of action, such as diplomatic agreements, rules of engagement, political and economic conditions in affected countries, and host nation issues (JP 5-0). In the context of joint operation planning, a *constraint* is requirement placed on the command by a higher command that dictates an action, thus restricting freedom of action (JP 5-0). In the context of joint operation planning, a *restraint* requirement placed on the command by a higher command that prohibits an action, thus restricting freedom of action (JP 5-0).

Identify Critical Facts and Develop Assumptions

B-39. Plans and orders are based on facts and assumptions. Commanders and staffs gather facts and develop assumptions as they build their plan. A fact is a statement of truth or a statement thought to be true at the time. Facts concerning the operational and mission variables serve as the basis for developing situational understanding, for continued planning, and when assessing progress during preparation and execution.

B-40. In the absence of facts, the commander and staff consider assumptions from their higher headquarters and develop their own assumptions necessary for continued planning. An *assumption* is a supposition on the current situation or a presupposition on the future course of events, either or both assumed to be true in the absence of positive proof, necessary to enable the commander in the process of planning to complete an estimate of the situation and make a decision on the course of action (JP 1-02).

B-41. Having assumptions requires commanders and staffs to continually attempt to replace those assumptions with facts. The commander and staff should list and review the key assumptions on which fundamental judgments rest throughout the MDMP. Rechecking assumptions is valuable at any time during the operations process prior to rendering judgments and making decisions. (See chapter 2 for a detailed discussion on verifying assumptions.)

Begin Composite Risk Management

B-42. CRM is the Army's primary process for identifying hazards and controlling risks during operations. CRM is the process of identifying, assessing, and controlling risks arising from operational factors and of making decisions that balance risk costs with mission benefits. (See FM 5-19 for a detailed discussion on CRM.)

B-43. The chief of protection (or S-3 in units without a protection cell) in coordination with the safety officer integrates CRM into the MDMP. All staff sections integrate CRM for hazards within their functional areas. The first four steps of CRM are conducted in the MDMP. The details for conducting CRM, including products of each step, are addressed in FM 5-19.

Develop Initial Commander's Critical Information Requirements and Essential Elements of Friendly Information

B-44. Mission analysis identifies gaps in information required for further planning and decisionmaking during preparation and execution. During mission analysis, the staff develops IRs. *Information requirements* are all information elements the commander and staff require to successfully conduct operations; that is, all elements necessary to address the factors of METT-TC (FM 6-0). Some IRs are of such importance to the commander that they are nominated to the commander to become a commander's critical information requirement (CCIR). The two types of CCIRs are friendly force information requirements and PIRs. (See chapter 2.)

B-45. Commanders determine their CCIRs and consider the nominations of the staff. CCIRs are situation-dependent and specified by the commander for each operation. Commanders continuously review the CCIRs during the planning process and adjust them as situations change. The initial CCIRs developed during mission analysis normally focus on decisions the commander needs to make to focus planning. Once the commander selects a COA, the CCIRs shift to information the commander needs in order to make decisions during preparation and execution. Commanders designate CCIRs to let the staff and subordinates know what information they deem essential for making decisions. The fewer the CCIRs, the better the staff can focus its efforts and allocate sufficient resources for collecting them.

B-46. In addition to nominating CCIRs to the commander, the staff also identifies and nominates essential elements of friendly information (EEFIs). Although EEFIs are not CCIRs, they have the same priority as CCIRs and require approval by the commander. An EEFI establishes an element of information to protect rather than one to collect. EEFIs identify those elements of friendly force information that, if compromised, would jeopardize mission success. Like CCIRs, EEFIs change as the operation progresses.

B-47. Depending on the situation, the commander and selected staff meet prior to the mission analysis brief to approve the initial CCIRs and EEFIs. This is especially important if the commander intends to conduct reconnaissance and intelligence collection early in the planning process. The approval of the initial CCIRs early in planning assist the staff in developing the initial ISR synchronization tools and the subsequent ISR plan. Approval of the EEFI allows the staff to begin planning and implementing measures to protect friendly force information, such as deception and operations security.

±Develop Initial ISR Synchronization Tools

B-48. Several activities conducted during mission analysis (such as IPB, developing running estimates, and developing requirements for targeting) create numerous IRs. ISR synchronization is a key integrating process that helps the commander and staff prioritize, manage, and develop a plan to collect on those IRs. ISR synchronization ensures all available information concerning the enemy, terrain and weather, and civil considerations is obtained through intelligence reach, RFIs, and reconnaissance and surveillance tasks. The results are successful reporting, production, and dissemination of relevant information and intelligence to support decisionmaking.

B-49. ISR synchronization accomplishes the following:
- Identifies requirements and intelligence gaps.
- Evaluates available assets (internal and external) to collect information.
- Determines gaps in the use of those assets.
- Recommends those ISR assets controlled by the organization to collect on the IRs.
- Submits RFIs for adjacent and higher collection support.
- The G-2 (S-2) submits information gathered during ISR synchronization to the G-3 (S-3) for integration and development of the ISR plan.

B-50. During mission analysis, the staff identifies IRs to support situational understanding and continued planning. Based on the commander's guidance, the staff, led by the G-2 (S-2), determines the best way of satisfying those requirements. In some instances, the G-2 (S-2) recommends that internal reconnaissance or surveillance assets are used to collect information. In other instances, the G-2 (S-2) recommends an RFI to the higher headquarters.

B-51. In many instances, a staff section within the headquarters can satisfy IRs by researching open sources. Open sources include books, magazines, encyclopedias, Web sites, and tourist maps. Academic sources, such as articles and university personnel, can also provide critical information. Many IRs concerning civil considerations, such as culture, language, history, current events, and actions of governments, are available through open sources. Teams of anthropologists and other social scientists attached to headquarters rely heavily on open sources to satisfy IRs. The knowledge management staff section can also assist them in accessing specific data.

B-52. The results of ISR synchronization conducted during mission analysis leads to the creation of initial intelligence synchronization tools. The intelligence staff section continues to refine the ISR synchronization tools throughout the MDMP for inclusion in Annex L (Intelligence, Surveillance, and Reconnaissance) of the OPLAN and OPORD.

Develop Initial Intelligence, Surveillance, and Reconnaissance Plan

B-53. ISR integration follows ISR synchronization. The G-3 (S-3) leads the staff through ISR integration to task available reconnaissance and surveillance assets to satisfy IRs identified in the initial ISR synchronization matrix. ISR integration consists of the following tasks:
- Develop the ISR plan by developing—
  - The ISR scheme of support.
  - The ISR tasking matrix.
  - The ISR overlay.
- Issue order (warning, operation, or fragmentary order).

B-54. The initial ISR plan is crucial to begin or adjust the collection effort to help answer IRs identified during ISR synchronization. ISR assets are tasked or dispatched as soon as possible. The initial ISR plan sets surveillance and reconnaissance in motion. It may be issued as part of a WARNO, a fragmentary order, or an OPORD. Upon the completion of planning, the initial ISR plan becomes annex L (Intelligence, Surveillance, and Reconnaissance) of the OPLAN and OPORD.

Update Plan for the Use of Available Time

B-55. As more information becomes available, the commander and staff refine their initial plan for the use of available time. They compare the time needed to accomplish tasks to the higher headquarters' timeline to ensure mission accomplishment is possible in the allotted time. They also compare the timeline to the assumed enemy timeline or the projected timelines within the civil sector with regard as to how conditions are anticipated to unfold. From this, they determine windows of opportunity for exploitation, times when the unit will be at risk for enemy activity, or when action to arrest deterioration in the civil sector is required.

B-56. The commander and COS (XO) also refine the staff planning timeline. The refined timeline includes the—

- Subject, time, and location of briefings the commander requires.
- Times of collaborative planning sessions and the medium over which they will take place.
- Times, locations, and forms of rehearsals.

±Develop a Proposed Problem Statement

B-57. A problem is an issue or obstacle that makes it difficult to achieve a desired goal or objective. (See chapter 1.) As such, a problem statement is the description of the primary issue or issues that may impede commanders from achieving their desired end state.

> *Note:* The problem statement is developed by the commander, staff, and other partners as part of design (see chapter 3). During mission analysis, the commander and staff review the problem statement and revise it as necessary based on the increased understanding of the situation. If design activities do not precede mission analysis, then the commander and staff develop a problem statement prior to moving to COA development.

B-58. How the problem is formulated leads to particular solutions. As such, it is important that commanders dedicate the time in identifying the right problem to solve and describe it clearly in a problem statement. Ideally, the commander and members of the staff meet to share their analysis of the situation. They dialog among each other to synthesize the results of the current mission analysis and determine the problem. If the commander is not available, the staff dialogs among themselves and prepares a proposed problem statement to be discussed and approved by the commander at the mission analysis brief.

B-59. To help identify and understand the problem, the staff—

- Compares the current situation to the desired end state.
- Brainstorms and lists issues or obstacles that are impeding the command from achieving the desired end state.
- Determines the primary obstacles that will impede the command from achieving the desired end state.

Based on this analysis, the staff develops a proposed problem statement—a statement of the problem to be solved—for the commander's approval.

Develop Initial Themes and Messages

B-60. ±Faced with the many different actors (individuals, organizations, and publics) that are connected with the operation, commanders identify and engage those actors that matter to their operational success. These actors have behaviors that can help solve or complicate the friendly forces' challenges as they strive to accomplish their missions. Gaining and maintaining the trust of key actors is an important aspect of operations.

B-61. Commanders and their units must coordinate what they do, say, and portray. Fundamental to that process is the development of information themes and messages in support of an operation and military action. An information theme is a unifying or dominant idea or image that expresses the purpose for military action. Information themes are tied to objectives, lines of effort, and end state conditions. Information themes are overarching and apply to the components and enablers of inform and influence activities, such as public affairs, military information support operations, and Soldier and leader engagements. A message is a verbal, written, or electronic communications that supports an information theme focused on a specific actor and in support of a specific action (task). Information themes and messages are transmitted to those actors whose perceptions, attitudes, beliefs, and behaviors matter to the success of an operation.

B-62. To assist in developing initial information themes and messages for the command, the G-7 (S-7) with support from the entire staff, reviews the higher headquarters' information themes and messages. If available, they also review internal design products (see chapter 3), including the initial commander's intent, mission narrative, and planning guidance. Information themes and messages are refined throughout the MDMP as commanders refine their commander's intent and planning guidance and COAs are developed, evaluated, and decided upon.

Develop a Proposed Mission Statement

B-63. The COS (XO) or operations officer prepares a proposed mission statement for the unit based on the mission analysis. This officer presents the unit's mission statement to the commander for approval normally during the mission analysis brief. A *mission statement* is a short sentence or paragraph that describes the organization's essential task (or tasks) and purpose—a clear statement of the action to be taken and the reason for doing so. The mission statement contains the elements of who, what, when, where, and why, but seldom specifies how (JP 5-0). The five elements of a mission statement answer the questions:

- Who will execute the operation (unit or organization)?
- What is the unit's essential task (tactical mission task)?
- When will the operation begin (by time or event) or what is the duration of the operation?
- Where will the operation occur (AO, objective, grid coordinates)?
- Why will the force conduct the operations (for what purpose)?

Example 1. Not later than 220400 Aug 09 (**when**), 1st Brigade (**who**) secures ROUTE SOUTH DAKOTA (**what/task**) in AO JACKRABBIT (**where**) to enable the movement of humanitarian assistance materials (**why/purpose**).

Example 2. 1-505th Parachute Infantry Regiment (**who**) seizes (**what/task**) JACKSON INTERNATIONAL AIRPORT (**where**) not later than D-day, H+3 (**when**) to allow follow-on forces to air-land into AO SPARTAN (**why/purpose**).

B-64. The mission statement may have more than one essential task. The following example shows a mission statement for a phased operation with a different essential task for each phase:

Example. 1-509th Parachute Infantry Regiment (**who**) seizes (**what/task**) JACKSON INTERNATIONAL AIRPORT (**where**) not later than D-day, H+3 (**when**) to allow follow-on forces to air-land into AO SPARTAN (**why/purpose**). On order (**when**), secure (**what/task**) OBJECTIVE GOLD (**where**) to prevent the 2d Pandor Guards Brigade from crossing the BLUE RIVER and disrupting operations in AO SPARTAN (**why/purpose**).

B-65. The *who, where,* and *when* of a mission statement are straightforward. The *what* and *why* are more challenging to write and can confuse subordinates if not stated clearly. The *what* is a task and expressed in terms of action verbs. These tasks are measurable and can be grouped as "actions by friendly forces" or "effects on enemy forces." The *why* puts the task into context by describing the reason for performing it.

The *why* provides the mission's purpose—the reason the unit is to perform the task. It is extremely important to mission command and mission orders.

B-66. Commanders should use tactical mission tasks or other doctrinally approved tasks contained in combined arms field manuals or mission training plans in mission statements. These tasks have specific military definitions that differ from dictionary definitions. A tactical mission task is the specific activity performed by a unit while executing a form of tactical operation or form of maneuver. FM 3-90, appendix B, describes each of the tactical tasks. FM 3-07 provides a list of primary stability tasks which military forces must be prepared to execute. Commanders and planners should carefully choose the task that best describes the commander's intent and planning guidance.

Present the Mission Analysis Briefing

B-67. The mission analysis briefing informs the commander of the results of the staff's analysis of the situation and helps the commander understand, visualize, and describe the operations. Throughout the mission analysis briefing, the commander, staff, and other partners discuss the various facts and assumptions about the situation. Staff officers present a summary of their running estimates from their specific functional area and how their findings impact or are impacted by other areas. This helps the commander and staff as a whole to focus on the interrelationships among the mission variables and to develop a deeper understanding of the situation. The commander issues guidance to the staff for continued planning based on situational understanding gained from the mission analysis briefing.

B-68. Ideally, the commander holds several informal meetings with key staff members before the mission analysis briefing, including meetings to assist the commander in developing CCIRs, the mission statement, and information themes and messages. These meetings are a forum for commanders to issue guidance for certain activities such as ISR operations and assist commanders with developing their initial commander's intent and planning guidance.

B-69. A comprehensive mission analysis briefing helps the commander, staff, subordinates, and other partners develop a shared understanding of the requirements of the upcoming operation. Time permitting, the staff briefs the commander on its mission analysis using the following outline:

- Mission and commander's intent of the headquarters two levels up.
- Mission, commander's intent, and concept of operations of the headquarters one level up.
- A proposed problem statement.
- A proposed mission statement.
- Review of the commander's initial guidance.
- Initial IPB products, including civil considerations that impact the conduct of operations.
- Specified, implied, and essential tasks.
- Pertinent facts and assumptions.
- Constraints.
- Forces available and resource shortfalls.
- Initial risk assessment.
- Proposed information themes and messages.
- Proposed CCIRs and EEFIs.
- Initial ISR plan.
- Recommended timeline.
- Recommended collaborative planning sessions.

B-70. During the mission analysis briefing or shortly thereafter, commanders approve the mission statement and CCIRs. They then develop and issue their initial commander's intent and planning guidance.

Develop and Issue Initial Commander's Intent

B-71. Based on their situational understanding, commanders summarize their visualization in their initial commander's intent statement. The initial commander's intent links the operation's purpose with conditions that define the desired end state. Commanders may change their intent statement as planning progresses and more information becomes available. It must be easy to remember and clearly understood two echelons down. The shorter the commander's intent, the better it serves these purposes. Typically, the commander's intent statement is three to five sentences long. (See chapter 2.)

Develop and Issue Initial Planning Guidance

B-72. Commanders provide planning guidance along with their initial commander's intent. Planning guidance conveys the essence of the commander's visualization. Guidance may be broad or detailed, depending on the situation. The initial planning guidance outlines an operational approach—the broad general actions that will produce the conditions that define the desired end state. The guidance should outline specific COAs the commander desires the staff to look at as well as rule out any COAs the commander will not accept. That kind of guidance allows the staff to develop several COAs without wasting effort on things that the commander will not consider. It reflects how the commander sees the operation unfolding. It broadly describes when, where, and how the commander intends to employ combat power to accomplish the mission within the higher commander's intent.

B-73. Commanders use their experience and judgment to add depth and clarity to their planning guidance. They ensure staffs understand the broad outline of their visualization while allowing the latitude necessary to explore different options. This guidance provides the basis for a detailed concept of operations without dictating the specifics of the final plan. As with their intent, commanders may modify planning guidance based on staff and subordinate input and changing conditions. (See appendix D for a detailed discussion of commander's planning guidance.)

Develop Course of Action Evaluation Criteria

B-74. Evaluation criteria are factors the commander and staff will later use to measure the relative effectiveness and efficiency of one COA relative to other COAs. Developing these criteria during mission analysis or as part of commander's planning guidance helps to eliminate a source of bias prior to COA analysis and comparison.

B-75. Evaluation criteria address factors that affect success and those that can cause failure. They change from mission to mission and must be clearly defined and understood by all staff members before starting the war game to test the proposed COAs. Normally, the COS (XO) initially determines each proposed criterion with weights based on the assessment of its relative importance and the commander's guidance. Commanders adjust criterion selection and weighting according to their own experience and vision. The staff member responsible for a functional area scores each COA using those criteria. The staff presents the draft evaluation criteria to the commander at the mission analysis brief for approval.

Issue a Warning Order

B-76. Immediately after the commander gives the planning guidance, the staff sends subordinate and supporting units a WARNO that contains, at a minimum—

- The approved mission statement.
- The commander's intent.
- Changes to task organization.
- The unit AO (sketch, overlay, or some other description).
- CCIRs and EEFIs.
- Risk guidance.
- Priorities by warfighting functions.
- Military deception guidance.
- Essential stability tasks.
- Specific priorities.

COURSE OF ACTION DEVELOPMENT

B-77. A COA is a broad potential solution to an identified problem. The COA development step generates options for follow-on analysis and comparison that satisfy the commander's intent and planning guidance. During COA development, planners use the problem statement, mission statement, commander's intent, planning guidance, and the various knowledge products developed during mission analysis to develop COAs.

B-78. Embedded in COA development is the application of operational and tactical art. Planners develop different COAs by varying combinations of the elements of operational art such as phasing, lines of effort, and tempo. (See FM 3-0.) The approved COA is converted into the concept of operations.

B-79. The commander's direct involvement in COA development greatly aids in producing comprehensive and flexible COAs within the available time. To save time, the commander may also limit the number of COAs to be developed or specify particular COAs not to explore. Each prospective COA is examined for validity using the following screening criteria:

- **Feasible**. The COA can accomplish the mission within the established time, space, and resource limitations.
- **Acceptable**. The COA must balance cost and risk with the advantage gained.
- **Suitable**. The COA can accomplish the mission within the commander's intent and planning guidance.
- **Distinguishable**. Each COA must differ significantly from the others (such as scheme or form of maneuver, lines of effort, phasing, day or night operations, use of the reserve, and task organization).
- **Complete**. A COA must incorporate—
  - How the decisive operation leads to mission accomplishment.
  - How shaping operations create and preserve conditions for success of the decisive operation or effort.
  - How sustaining operations enable shaping and decisive operations or efforts.
  - How offensive, defensive, and stability or civil support tasks are accounted for.
  - Tasks to be performed and conditions to be achieved.

B-80. A good COA positions the force for sequels and provides flexibility to meet unforeseen events during execution. It also gives subordinates the maximum latitude for initiative. During COA development, the commander and staff continue risk assessment, focus on identifying and assessing hazards to mission accomplishment, and incorporate proposed controls to mitigate them into COAs. The staff also continues to revise IPB products, emphasizing event templates. During COA development, commanders and staffs perform the process actions and produce the outputs shown in figure B-3, page B-16.

Note: If design precedes or is conducted in parallel with the MDMP, the updated design concept provides an overarching structure COA development.

Assess Relative Combat Power

B-81. *Combat power* is the total means of destructive, constructive, and information capabilities that a military unit/formation can apply at a given time. Army forces generate combat power by converting potential into effective action (FM 3-0). Combat power is the effect created by combining the elements of intelligence, movement and maneuver, fires, sustainment, protection, mission command, information and leadership. The goal is to generate overwhelming combat power to accomplish the mission at minimal cost.

B-82. To assess relative combat power, planners initially make a rough estimate of force ratios of maneuver units two levels down. For example, at division level, planners compare all types of maneuver battalions with enemy maneuver battalion equivalents. Planners then compare friendly strengths against enemy weaknesses, and vice versa, for each element of combat power. From these comparisons, they may deduce particular vulnerabilities for each force that may be exploited or may need protection. These comparisons provide planners insight into effective force employment.

Key inputs	Process	Key outputs

• Approved problem statement
• Approved mission statement
• Initial commander's intent and planning guidance
• Design concept (if developed)
• Specified and implied tasks
• Assumptions
• Updated running estimates and IPB products
• COA evaluation criteria
	• Assess relative combat power
	• Generate options
	• Array forces
	• Develop a broad concept
	• Assign headquarters
	• Develop COA statements and sketches
	• Conduct COA briefing
	• Select or modify COAs for continued analysis
		• Commander's selected COAs for war-gaming with COA statements and sketches
		• Commander's refined planning guidance to include:
		  - War-gaming guidance
		  - Evaluation criteria
		• Updated running estimates and IPB products
		• Updated assumptions

COA course of action	IPB intelligence preparation of the battlefield	

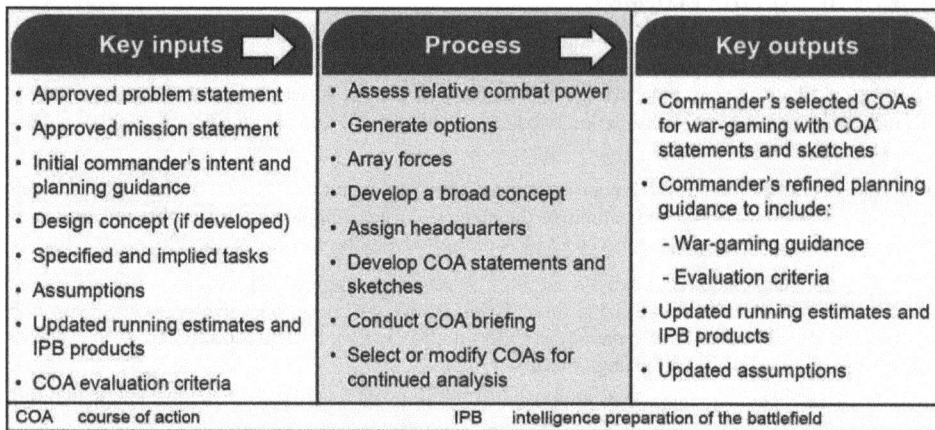

Figure B-3. COA development

B-83. For stability or civil support operations, staffs often determine relative combat power by comparing available resources to specified or implied stability or civil support tasks. This is known as troop-to-task analysis. This analysis provides insight as to what options are available and whether more resources are required. In such operations, the elements of sustainment, movement and maneuver, nonlethal effects, and information may dominate.

B-84. By analyzing force ratios and determining and comparing each force's strengths and weaknesses as a function of combat power, planners can gain insight into—

- Friendly capabilities that pertain to the operation.
- The types of operations possible from both friendly and enemy perspectives.
- How and where the enemy may be vulnerable.
- How and where friendly forces are vulnerable.
- Additional resources that may be required to execute the mission.
- How to allocate existing resources.

B-85. Planners must not develop and recommend COAs based solely on mathematical analysis of force ratios. Although some numerical relationships are used in the process, the estimate is largely subjective. Assessing combat power requires assessing both tangible and intangible factors, such as morale and levels of training. A relative combat power assessment identifies enemy weaknesses that can be exploited, identifies friendly weaknesses that require protection, and determines the combat power necessary to conduct essential stability or civil support tasks.

Generate Options

B-86. Based on the commander's guidance and the initial results of the relative combat power assessment, the staff generates options. A good COA can defeat all feasible enemy COAs while accounting for essential stability tasks. In an unconstrained environment, the goal is to develop several possible COAs. Time dependent, commanders may limit the options in the commander's guidance. Options focus on enemy COAs arranged in order of their probable adoption or on those stability tasks that are most essential to prevent the situation from deteriorating further.

B-87. Brainstorming is the preferred technique for generating options. It requires time, imagination, and creativity, but it produces the widest range of choices. The staff (and members of organizations outside the headquarters) must be unbiased and open-minded when developing proposed options.

B-88. In developing COAs, staff members determine the doctrinal requirements for each type of operation being considered, including doctrinal tasks for subordinate units. For example, a deliberate breach requires a breach force, a support force, and an assault force. Essential stability tasks require the ability to provide a level of civil security, civil control, and certain essential services. In addition, the staff considers the potential capabilities of attachments and other organizations and agencies outside military channels.

B-89. When generating options, the staff starts with the decisive operation identified in the commander's planning guidance. The staff checks that the decisive operation nests within the higher headquarters' concept of operations. The staff clarifies the decisive operation's purpose and considers ways to mass the effects (lethal and nonlethal) of overwhelming combat power to achieve it.

B-90. Next, the staff considers shaping operations. The staff establishes a purpose for each shaping operation tied to creating or preserving a condition for the decisive operation's success. Shaping operations may occur before, concurrently with, or after the decisive operation. A shaping operation may be designated as the main effort if executed before or after the decisive operation.

B-91. The staff then determines sustaining operations necessary to create and maintain the combat power required for the decisive operation and shaping operations. After developing the basic operational organization for a given COA, the staff then determines the essential tasks for each decisive, shaping, and sustaining operation.

B-92. Once staff members have explored possibilities for each COA, they examine each COA to determine if it satisfies the screening criteria stated in paragraph B-79. In doing so, they change, add, or eliminate COAs as appropriate. During this process, staffs must avoid the common pitfall of focusing on the development of one good COA among several throwaway COAs.

Array Forces

B-93. After determining the decisive and shaping operations and their related tasks and purposes, planners determine the relative combat power required to accomplish each task. To do this, planners may use minimum historical planning ratios shown in table B-1 as a starting point. For example, historically defenders have over a 50 percent probability of defeating an attacking force approximately three times their equivalent strength. Therefore, as a starting point, commanders may defend on each avenue of approach with roughly a 1:3 force ratio.

Table B-1. Historical minimum planning ratios

Friendly Mission	Position	Friendly: Enemy
Delay		1:6
Defend	Prepared or fortified	1:3
Defend	Hasty	1:2.5
Attack	Prepared or fortified	3:1
Attack	Hasty	2.5:1
Counterattack	Flank	1:1

B-94. Planners determine whether these and other intangibles increase the relative combat power of the unit assigned the task to the point that it exceeds the historical planning ratio for that task. If it does not, planners determine how to reinforce the unit. Combat power comparisons are provisional at best. Arraying forces is tricky, inexact work. It is affected by factors that are difficult to gauge, such as impact of past engagements, the quality of leaders, morale, maintenance of equipment, and time in position. It is also affected by levels of electronic warfare support, fire support, close air support, and civilian support, among many other factors.

B-95. In counterinsurgency operations, planners can develop force requirements by gauging troop density—the ratio of security forces (including host-nation military and police forces as well as foreign counterinsurgents) to inhabitants. Most density recommendations fall within a range of 20 to 25 counterinsurgents for every 1,000 residents in an AO. Twenty counterinsurgents per 1,000 residents are often considered the minimum troop density required for effective counterinsurgency operations; however, as with any fixed ratio, such calculations strongly depend on the situation. (See FM 3-24.)

B-96. Planners also determine relative combat power with regard to civilian requirements and conditions that require attention and then array forces and capabilities for stability tasks. For example, a COA may require a follow-on force to establish civil security, maintain civil control, and restore essential services in a densely populated urban area over an extended period. Planners conduct a troop-to-task analysis to determine the type of units and capabilities to accomplish these tasks.

B-97. Planners then proceed to initially array friendly forces starting with the decisive operation and continuing with all shaping and sustaining operations. Planners normally array ground forces two levels down. The initial array focuses on generic ground maneuver units without regard to specific type or task organization and then considers all appropriate intangible factors. For example, at corps level, planners array generic brigades. During this step, planners do not assign missions to specific units; they only consider which forces are necessary to accomplish its task. In this step, planners also array assets to accomplish essential stability tasks.

B-98. The initial array identifies the total number of units needed and identifies possible methods of dealing with the enemy and stability tasks. If the number arrayed is less than the number available, planners place additional units in a pool for use during the develop a concept step. If the number of units arrayed exceeds the number available and the difference cannot be compensated for with intangible factors, the staff determines whether the COA is feasible. Ways to make up the shortfall include requesting additional resources, accepting risk in that portion of the AO, or executing tasks required for the COA sequentially rather than simultaneously. Commanders should also consider requirements to minimize and relieve civilian suffering. Establishing civil security and providing essential services such as medical care, food and water, and shelter are implied tasks for commanders during any combat operation. See FM 3-07 for a full discussion on stability tasks.

Develop a Broad Concept

B-99. The broad concept describes how arrayed forces will accomplish the mission within the commander's intent. It concisely expresses the *how* of the commander's visualization and will eventually provide the framework for the concept of operations. The broad concept summarizes the contributions of all warfighting functions. The staff develops a broad concept for each COA that will be expressed in both narrative and graphic forms. A sound COA is more than the arraying of forces. It should present an overall combined arms idea that will accomplish the mission. The broad concept includes the following:

- The purpose of the operation.
- A statement of where the commander will accept risk.
- Identification of critical friendly events and transitions between phases (if the operation is phased).
- Designation of the decisive operation, along with its task and purpose, linked to how it supports the higher headquarters' concept.
- Designation of shaping operations, along with their tasks and purposes, linked to how they support the decisive operation.
- Designation of sustaining operations, along with their tasks and purposes, linked to how they support the decisive and shaping operations.
- Designation of the reserve, including its location and composition.
- Reconnaissance operations.
- Security operations.
- Essential stability tasks.
- Identification of maneuver options that may develop during an operation.
- Assignment of subordinate AOs.
- Scheme of fires.
- Information themes, messages, and means of delivery.
- Military deception operations.
- Key control measures.

B-100. Planners select control measures, including graphics, to control subordinate units during the operation. These establish responsibilities and limits that prevent subordinate units' actions from impeding one another. These measures also foster coordination and cooperation between forces without unnecessarily restricting freedom of action. Good control measures foster freedom of action, decisionmaking, and individual initiative. (See FM 3-90 for a discussion of control measures associated with offensive and defensive operations. See FM 1-02 for a listing of doctrinal control measures and rules for drawing control measures on overlays and maps.)

B-101. Planners may use both lines of operations and lines of effort to build their broad concept. Lines of operations portray the more traditional links among objectives, decisive points, and centers of gravity. A line of effort, however, helps planners link multiple tasks with goals, objectives, and end state conditions. Combining lines of operations and lines of efforts allows planners to include nonmilitary activities in their broad concept. This combination helps commanders incorporate stability or civil support tasks that, when accomplished, help set end state conditions of the operation.

B-102. Based on the commander's planning guidance (informed by the design concept if design preceded the MDMP), planners develop lines of effort by—
*   Confirming end state conditions from the initial commander's intent and planning guidance.
*   Determining and describing each line of effort.
*   Identifying objectives (intermediate goals) and determining tasks along each line of effort.

B-103. During COA development, lines of efforts are general and lack specifics, such as tasks to subordinate units associated to objectives along each line of effort. Lines of effort, to include specific tasks to subordinate units, are developed and refined during war-gaming. (See FM 3-0 and FM 3-07 for examples of operations depicted along lines of effort.)

B-104. As planning progresses, commanders may modify lines of effort and add details during war-gaming. Operations with other instruments of national power support a broader, comprehensive approach to stability operations. Each operation, however, differs. Commanders develop and modify lines of effort to focus operations on achieving the end state, even as the situation evolves.

Assign Headquarters

B-105. After determining the broad concept, planners create a task organization by assigning headquarters to groupings of forces. They consider the types of units to be assigned to a headquarters and the ability of that headquarters to control those units. Generally, a headquarters controls at least two subordinate maneuver units (but not more than five) for fast-paced offensive or defensive operations. The number and type of units assigned to a headquarters for stability operations will vary based on factors of METT-TC. If planners need additional headquarters, they note the shortage and resolve it later. Task organization takes into account the entire operational organization. It also accounts for the special mission command requirements for operations such as a passage of lines, gap crossing, or air assault.

Prepare Course of Action Statements and Sketches

B-106. The operations officer prepares a COA statement and supporting sketch for each COA. The COA statement clearly portrays how the unit will accomplish the mission. The COA statement should be a brief expression of how the combined arms concept will be conducted. The sketch provides a picture of the movement and maneuver aspects of the concept, including the positioning of forces. Together, the statement and sketch cover the who (generic task organization), what (tasks), when, where, and why (purpose) for each subordinate unit.

B-107. At a minimum, the COA sketch includes the array of generic forces and control measures, such as—
*   The unit and subordinate unit boundaries.
*   Unit movement formations (but not subordinate unit formations).
*   The line of departure, or line of contact and phase lines, if used.
*   Reconnaissance and security graphics.
*   Ground and air axes of advance.
*   Assembly areas, battle positions, strong points, engagement areas, and objectives.
*   Obstacle control measures and tactical mission graphics.
*   Fire support coordination and airspace control measures.

- Main effort.
- Location of command posts and critical information systems (INFOSYS) nodes.
- Enemy known or template locations.
- Population concentrations.

B-108. Planners can include identifying features (such as cities, rivers, and roads) to help orient users. The sketch may be on any medium. What it portrays is more important than its form. Figure B-4 provides a sample COA sketch and COA statement for a brigade combat team.

Conduct a Course of Action Briefing

B-109. After developing COAs, the staff briefs them to the commander. A collaborative session may facilitate subordinate planning. The COA briefing includes—

- An updated IPB.
- Possible enemy COAs.
- The approved problem statement and mission statement.
- The commander's and higher commander's intent.
- COA statements and sketches, including lines of effort if used.
- The rationale for each COA, including—
  - Considerations that might affect enemy COAs.
  - Critical events for each COA.
  - Deductions resulting from the relative combat power analysis.
  - The reason units are arrayed as shown on the sketch.
  - The reason the staff used the selected control measures.
  - The impact on civilians.
  - How it accounts for minimum essential stability tasks.
  - Updated facts and assumptions.
  - Refined COA evaluation criteria.

Select or Modify Courses of Action for Continued Analysis

B-110. After the COA briefing, the commander selects or modifies those COAs for continued analysis. The commander also issues planning guidance. If all COAs are rejected, the staff begins again. If one or more of the COAs are accepted, staff members begin COA analysis. The commander may create a new COA by incorporating elements of one or more COAs developed by the staff. The staff then prepares to war-game this new COA. The staff must incorporate those modifications and ensure all staff members understand the changed COA.

COURSE OF ACTION ANALYSIS AND WAR-GAMING

B-111. COA analysis enables commanders and staffs to identify difficulties or coordination problems as well as probable consequences of planned actions for each COA being considered. It helps them think through the tentative plan. COA analysis may require commanders and staffs to revisit parts of the COA as discrepancies arise. COA analysis not only appraises the quality of each COA but also uncovers potential execution problems, decisions, and contingencies. In addition, COA analysis influences how commanders and staffs understand the problem and may require the planning process to restart.

MISSION: On order, 3d HBCT clears remnants of the 72d Brigade in AO TIGER to establish security and enable the host-nation in reestablishing civil control and governance in the region.

INTENT: The purpose of this operation is to provide a safe and secure environment in AO TIGER that enables the host-nation and other civilian organization to reestablish civil control, restore essential services, and reestablish local governance within the area. At end state, the BCT has cleared remnant enemy forces in AO TIGER, secured population centers, and is prepared to transition responsibility for security to host-nation authority.

DECISIVE OPERATION: Combined Arms BN #1 (two armor/two mech) (ME) begins movement from ATK POS B, crosses LD at PD 1, and attacks along AXIS 1 to clear remnants of the 72d Brigade and secure the population in OBJ 1.

SHAPING OPERATIONS: Combined Arms BN #2 (-) (two armor/one mech) in the SOUTH follows Combined Arms BN #1 from ATK POS B, crosses LD at PD 2, and attacks along DIRECTION OF ATTACK 2 to clear OBJ 3 and provide security to dislocated civilian site vicinity EAST CITY. RECON squadron in the NORTH begins movement from ATK POS A, crosses LD at PD 3, and attacks along DIRECTION OF ATTACK 3 to clear hostile gang vic OBJ 2 and provide security to enable NGO delivery of humanitarian assistance to WEST CITY and DODGE CITY. 3rd HBCT Main CP moves and co-locates with RECON squadron.

The BCT reserve, Mech Company, locates with BSB vic AA DOG with priority of commitment: 1) OBJ 1 in support of Combined Arms BN #1; 2) MSR HONDA security; and 3) Security of supply/relief convoys.

3d HBCT TAC CP moves and co-locates with Combined Arms BN #1 in OBJ 1. HBCT main CP locates in ATK POS A. O/O moves and co-locates with RECON squadron in OBJ 2.

BCT FIRES will disrupt enemy mortars vic OBJ 1 and position to provide responsive precision fires to destroy remnant enemy forces in AO TIGER.

BCT ISR operations focus on: 1) Identifying the location and disposition of enemy forces vic. OBJ 1; 2) Observation of MSR HONDA between PL RED and PL BLUE; and 3) Observation of dislocated civilian traffic from CENTER CITY to EAST CITY.

SUSTAINING OPERATION: The BSB will establish LOGBASE DOG vic WEST CITY with MSR HONDA, ASR FORD, and ASR BUICK as the primary routes used to sustain operations. The BSB coordinates with humanitarian relief agencies to help rapidly restore essential services in AO TIGER.

TACTICAL RISK is assumed in the northeastern portion of AO TIGER by utilizing primarily ISR assets to maintain situational awareness of hostile elements that may use mountains to reconstitute forces.

AO	area of operations	HBCT	headquarters brigade combat team	NGO	nongovernmental organization
ASR	alternate supply route	ISR	intelligence, surveillance,	O/O	on order
ATK POS	attack position		and reconnaissance	OBJ	objective
BCT	brigade combat team	LC	line of contact	PD	point of departure
BN	battalion	LD	line of departure	PL	phase line
BSB	brigade support battalion	LOA	limit of advance	RECON	reconnaissance
CP	command post	MECH	mechanized	TAC	tactical
DC	displaced civilians	MSR	main supply route	vic	vicinity

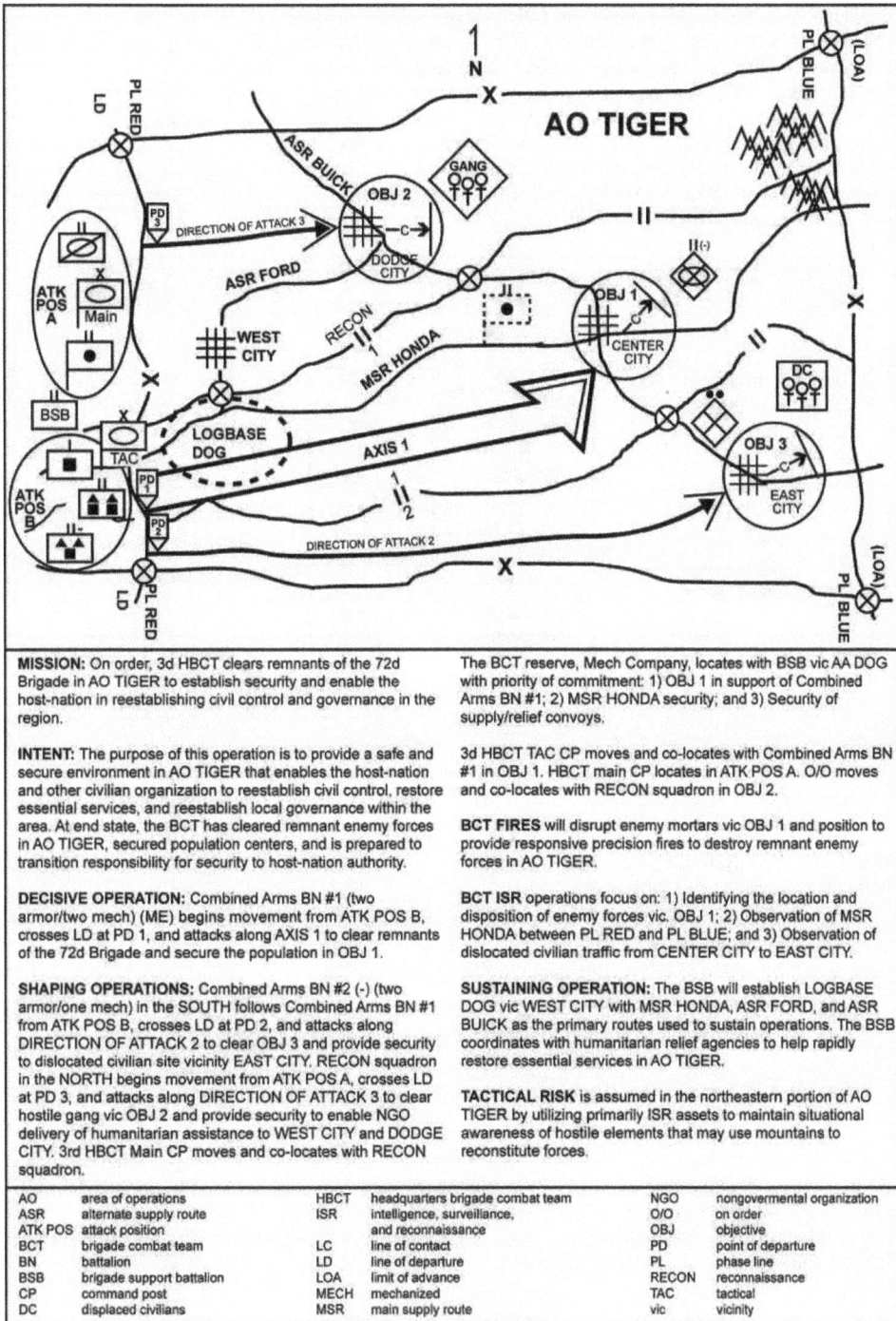

Figure B-4. Sample brigade COA sketch

B-112. War-gaming is a disciplined process, with rules and steps that attempt to visualize the flow of the operation, given the force's strengths and dispositions, enemy's capabilities and possible COAs, impact and requirements of civilians in the AO, and other aspects of the situation. The simplest form of war gaming is the manual method, often utilizing a tabletop approach with blowups of matrixes and templates. The most sophisticated form of war gaming is modern, computer-aided modeling and simulation. Regardless of the form used, each critical event within a proposed COA should be war-gamed using the action, reaction, and counteraction methods of friendly and enemy forces interaction. This basic war-gaming method (modified to fit the specific mission and environment) applies to offensive, defensive, and stability or civil support operations. When conducting COA analysis, commanders and staffs perform the process actions and produce the outputs shown in figure B-5.

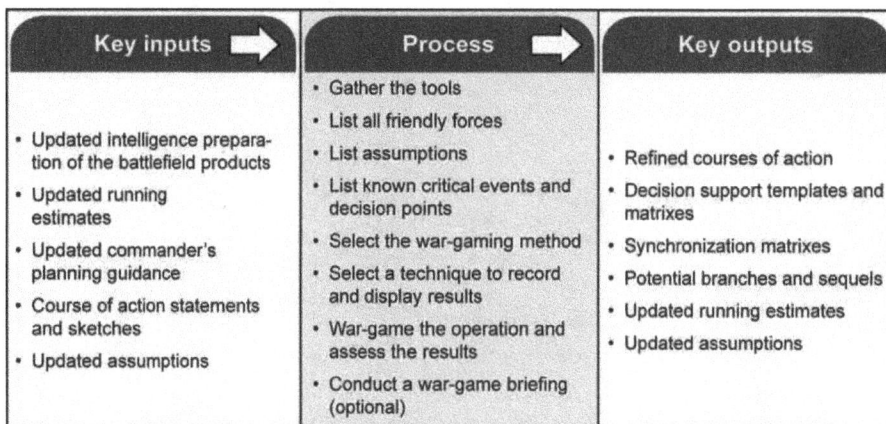

Key inputs	Process	Key outputs
• Updated intelligence preparation of the battlefield products • Updated running estimates • Updated commander's planning guidance • Course of action statements and sketches • Updated assumptions	• Gather the tools • List all friendly forces • List assumptions • List known critical events and decision points • Select the war-gaming method • Select a technique to record and display results • War-game the operation and assess the results • Conduct a war-game briefing (optional)	• Refined courses of action • Decision support templates and matrixes • Synchronization matrixes • Potential branches and sequels • Updated running estimates • Updated assumptions

Figure B-5. COA analysis and war-gaming

B-113. War-gaming results in refined COAs, a completed synchronization matrix, and decision support templates and matrixes for each COA. A synchronization matrix records the results of a war game. It depicts how friendly forces for a particular COA are synchronized in time, space, and purpose in relation to an enemy COA or other events in stability or civil support operations. The decision support template and matrix portray key decisions and potential actions that are likely to arise during the execution of each COA.

B-114. COA analysis allows the staff to synchronize the six warfighting functions for each COA. It also helps the commander and staff to—

- Determine how to maximize the effects of combat power while protecting friendly forces and minimizing collateral damage.
- Further develop a visualization of the operation.
- Anticipate operational events.
- Determine conditions and resources required for success.
- Determine when and where to apply force capabilities.
- Identify coordination needed to produce synchronized results.
- Determine the most flexible COA.

B-115. During the war game, the staff takes each COA and begins to develop a detailed plan while determining its strengths or weaknesses. War gaming tests and improves COAs. The commander, staff, and other available partners (and subordinate commanders and staffs if the war game is conducted collaboratively) may change an existing COA or develop a new COA after identifying unforeseen events, tasks, requirements, or problems.

General War-Gaming Rules

B-116. War gamers need to—

- Remain objective, not allowing personality or their sense of "what the commander wants" to influence them. They avoid defending a COA just because they personally developed it.
- Record advantages and disadvantages of each COA accurately as they emerge.
- Continually assess feasibility, acceptability, and suitability of each COA. If a COA fails any of these tests, they reject it.
- Avoid drawing premature conclusions and gathering facts to support such conclusions.
- Avoid comparing one COA with another during the war game. This occurs during COA comparison.

War-Gaming Responsibilities

B-117. This section provides the responsibilities of key staff members during the war game.

Chief of Staff (Executive Officer)

B-118. The COS (XO) coordinates actions of the staff during the war game. This officer is the unbiased controller of the process, ensuring the staff stays on a timeline and achieves the goals of the war-gaming session. In a time-constrained environment, this officer ensures that, at a minimum, the decisive operation is war-gamed.

Intelligence

B-119. The assistant chief of staff (ACOS), G-2 (S-2), intelligence, role-plays the enemy commander. This officer develops critical enemy decision points in relation to the friendly COAs, projects enemy reactions to friendly actions, and projects enemy losses. When additional intelligence staff members are available, the intelligence officer assigns different responsibilities to individual staff members within the section for war gaming (such as the enemy commander, friendly intelligence officer, and enemy recorder). The intelligence officer captures the results of each enemy action and counteraction as well as the corresponding friendly and enemy strengths and vulnerabilities. By trying to win the war game for the enemy, the intelligence officer ensures that the staff fully addresses friendly responses for each enemy COA. For the friendly force, the intelligence officer—

- Identifies IRs.
- Refines the situation and event templates, including named areas of interest that support decision points.
- Refines the event template with corresponding decision points, target areas of interest, and high-value targets.
- Participates in targeting to select high-payoff targets from high-value targets identified during IPB.
- Recommends PIRs that correspond to the decision points.

Movemenent and Maneuver

B-120. During the war game, the ACOS, G-3 (S-3), operations, and ACOS, G-5 (S-5), plans, are responsible for movement and maneuver.

B-121. The G-3 (S-3) normally selects the technique for the war game and role-plays the friendly maneuver commander. The G-3 (S-3) is assisted by various staff officers such as the aviation officer, engineer officer, and red team members. The G-3 (S-3) executes friendly maneuver as outlined in the COA sketch and COA statement.

B-122. The G-5 (S-5) assesses warfighting requirements, solutions, and concepts for each COA. This plans officer develops plans and orders and determines potential branches and sequels arising from the war-gaming of various COAs. The G-5 (S-5) coordinates and synchronizes warfighting functions in all plans and orders. The planning staff ensures that the war game of each COA covers every operational aspect of the mission. The members of the staff record each event's strengths and weaknesses and the rationale for each action. They complete the decision support template and matrix for each COA. The rationale for actions during the war game are annotated and used later with the commander's guidance to compare COAs.

Fires

B-123. The chief of fires (fire support officer) assesses the fire support feasibility of each COA. For each COA, the chief of fires develops the fire support execution matrix and evaluation criteria to measure the effectiveness of the fire support. This officer develops a proposed high-priority target list, target selection standards, and attack guidance matrix. The chief of fires identifies named and target areas of interest, high-value targets, high-priority targets, and additional events that may influence the positioning of fire support assets.

Protection

B-124. The provost marshal advises the commander regarding military police functions, security, force protection issues, and the employment of assigned or attached military police elements for each COA. The provost marshal assesses military police operations in support of freedom of movement, security for ground lines of communication, operational law enforcement, and operational internment and resettlement operations.

Sustainment

B-125. The following officers are responsible for sustainment:
- ACOS, G-1 (S-1), personnel.
- ACOS, G-4 (S-4), logistics.
- ACOS, G-8, financial management.
- Surgeon.

B-126. The G-1 (S-1) assesses the personnel aspect of building and maintaining the combat power of units. This officer identifies potential shortfalls and recommends COAs to ensure units maintain adequate manning to accomplish their mission. The personnel officer estimates potential personnel battle losses and assesses the adequacy of resources to provide human resources support for the operation.

B-127. The G-4 (S-4) assesses the logistics feasibility of each COA. This officer determines critical requirements for each logistics function (classes I through VII and IX) and identifies potential problems and deficiencies. The G-4 (S-4) assesses the status of all logistics functions required to support the COA, including potential support required to provide essential services to the civilians, and compares it to available assets. This officer identifies potential shortfalls and recommends actions to eliminate or reduce their effects. While improvising can contribute to responsiveness, only accurately predicting requirements for each logistics function can ensure continuous sustainment. The logistics officer ensures that available movement times and assets support each COA.

B-128. The G-8 assesses the commander's area of responsibility to determine the best COA for use of resources. This includes both core functions of financial management (resource management and finance operations). This officer determines partner relationships (joint, interagency, intergovernmental, and multinational), requirements for special funding, and support to the procurement process.

B-129. The surgeon section coordinates, monitors, and synchronizes the execution of the Army health system activities for the command for each COA to ensure a fit and healthy force. The surgeon provides advice for medically related matters and exercises technical supervision of all medical activities within the AO.

±Mission Command

B-130. The following officers are responsible for aspects of mission command:
- ACOS, G-6 (S-6), signal.
- ACOS, G-7 (S-7), inform and influence activities.

- ACOS, G-9 (S-9), civil affairs operations.
- Red team.
- Staff Judge Advocate.
- Operational research/systems analysis (ORSA).
- Recorders.

B-131. The G-6 (S-6) assesses network operations, electromagnetic spectrum operations, and electronic protection feasibility of each COA. The G-6 (S-6), determines communication systems requirements and compares them to available assets, identifies potential shortfalls, and recommends actions to eliminate or reduce their effects.

B-132. The G-7 (S-7) assesses how effectively the information themes and messages are reflected in operations. This officer assesses the effectiveness of the media. Lastly, this officer assesses how the information themes and messages impact various audiences of interest and populations in and outside the AO.

B-133. The G-9 (S-9) ensures each COA effectively integrates civil considerations (the "C" of METT-TC). The civil affairs operations officer considers not only tactical issues, but also sustainment issues. This officer assesses how operations affect civilians and estimates the requirements for essential stability tasks commanders might have to undertake based on the ability of the unified action. Host-nation support and care of dislocated civilians are of particular concern. The civil affairs operations officer's analysis considers how operations affect public order and safety, the potential for disaster relief requirements, noncombatant evacuation operations, emergency services, and the protection of culturally significant sites. This officer provides feedback on how the culture in the AO affects each COA. If the unit lacks an assigned civil affairs operations officer, the commander assigns these responsibilities to another staff member. The civil affairs operations officer represents the other actors' points of view if these agencies are not able to participate in the war game for security or other reasons.

B-134. The red team staff section provides the commander and G-2 with an independent capability to fully explore alternatives in plans, operations, concepts, organizations, and capabilities in the context of the operational environment from the perspectives of adversaries, partners, and others.

B-135. The Staff Judge Advocate advises the commander on all matters pertaining to law, policy, regulation, and good order and discipline for each COA. This officer provides legal advice across the spectrum of conflict on law of war, rules of engagement, international agreements, Geneva Conventions, treatment and disposition of noncombatants, and the legal aspects of lethal and nonlethal targeting.

B-136. The ORSA staff section provides analytic support to the commander for planning and assessment of operations. Specific responsibilities includes—

- Providing quantitative analytic support, including regression and trend analysis, to planning and assessment activities.
- Assisting other staff elements in developing customized analytical tools for specific requirements, providing a quality control capability, and conducting assessments to measure the effectiveness of operations.

B-137. The use of recorders is particularly important. Recorders are trained to capture coordinating instructions, subunit tasks and purposes, and information required to synchronize the operation. Doing this allows part of the order to be written before planning is complete. Automated INFOSYS simplify this process. These systems enable recorders to enter information into preformatted forms that represent either briefing charts or appendixes to orders. Each staff section keeps formats available to facilitate networked orders production.

Course of Action Process Actions

B-138. COA analysis consists of eight actions first shown in figure B-5 on page B-22.

Gather the Tools

B-139.   The first task for COA analysis is to gather the necessary tools to conduct the war game. The COS (XO) directs the staff to gather tools, materials, and data for the war game. Units war-game with maps, sand tables, computer simulations, or other tools that accurately reflect the terrain. The staff posts the COA on a map displaying the AO. Tools required include, but are not limited to—

- Running estimates.
- Event templates.
- A recording method.
- Completed COAs, including graphics.
- A means to post or display enemy and friendly unit symbols and other organizations.
- A map of the AO.

List All Friendly Forces

B-140.   The commander and staff consider all units that can be committed to the operation, paying special attention to support relationships and constraints. This list must include assets from all participants operating in the AO. The friendly forces list remains constant for all COAs.

List Assumptions

B-141.   The commander and staff review previous assumptions for continued validity and necessity.

List Known Critical Events and Decision Points

B-142.   Critical events are those that directly influence mission accomplishment. They include events that trigger significant actions or decisions (such as commitment of an enemy reserve), complicated actions requiring detailed study (such as a passage of lines), and essential tasks. The list of critical events includes major events from the unit's current position through mission accomplishment. It includes reactions by civilians that might affect operations or that will require allocation of significant assets to account for essential stability tasks.

B-143.   A *decision point* is a point in space and time when the commander or staff anticipates making a key decision concerning a specific course of action (JP 5-0). Decision points may also be associated with the friendly force and the status of ongoing operations. A decision point may be associated with CCIRs that describe what information the commander needs to make the anticipated decision. The PIR describes what must be known about the enemy or the operational environment and often is associated with a named area of interest. The friendly force information requirement describes friendly information the commander must protect from enemy disclosure, such as pending operations or locations of key nodes. A decision point requires a decision by the commander. It does not dictate what the decision is, only that the commander must make one, and when and where it should be made to maximally impact friendly or enemy COAs or the accomplishment of stability tasks.

Select the War-Gaming Method

B-144.   There are three recommended war-gaming methods: belt, avenue-in-depth, and box. Each considers the area of interest and all enemy forces that can affect the outcome of the operation. The methods can be used separately or in combination and modified for long-term operations dominated by stability.

B-145.   The belt method divides the AO into belts (areas) running the width of the AO. (See figure B-6.) The shape of each belt is based on the factors of METT-TC. The belt method works best when conducting offensive and defensive operations on terrain divided into well-defined cross-compartments, during phased operations (such as gap crossings, air assaults, or airborne operations), or when the enemy is deployed in clearly defined belts or echelons. Belts can be adjacent to or overlap each other.

B-146.   This war-gaming method is based on a sequential analysis of events in each belt. It is preferred because it focuses simultaneously on all forces affecting a particular event. A belt might include more than one critical event. Under time-constrained conditions, the commander can use a modified belt method. The modified belt method divides the AO into not more than three sequential belts. These belts are not necessarily adjacent or overlapping but focus on the critical actions throughout the depth of the AO.

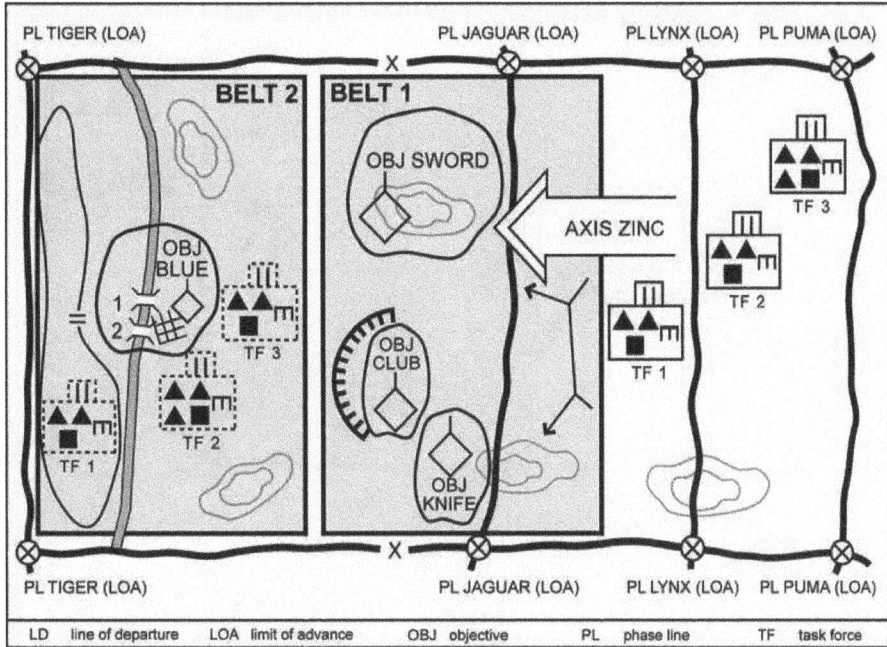

| LD | line of departure | LOA | limit of advance | OBJ | objective | PL | phase line | TF | task force |

Figure B-6. Sample belt method

B-147. In stability operations, the belt method can divide the COA by events, objectives (goals not geographic location), or events and objectives in a selected slice across all lines of effort. (See figure B-7.) It consists of war-gaming relationships among events or objectives on all lines of effort in the belt.

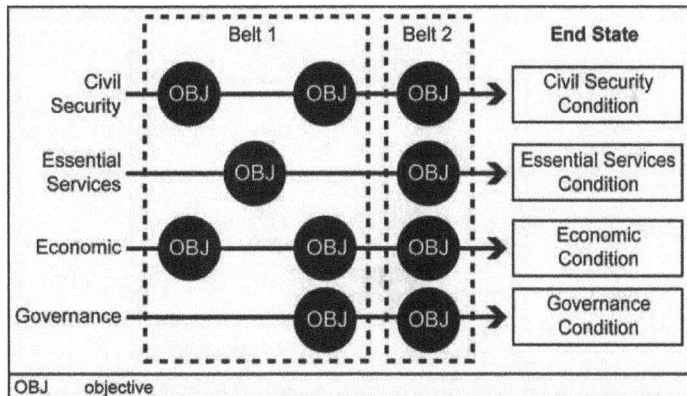

OBJ   objective

Figure B-7. Sample modified belt method using lines of effort

B-148. The avenue-in-depth method focuses on one avenue of approach at a time, beginning with the decisive operation. (See figure B-8, page B-28.) This method is good for offensive COAs or in the defense when canalizing terrain inhibits mutual support.

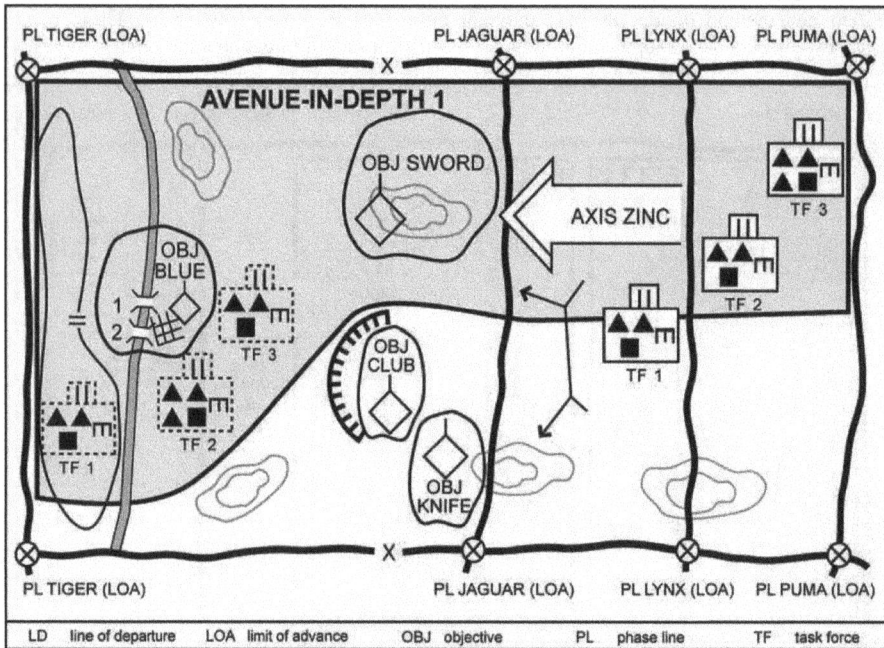

Figure B-8. Sample avenue-in-depth method

B-149. In stability operations, the avenue-in-depth method can be modified. Instead of focusing on a geographic avenue, the staff war-games a line of effort. This method focuses on one line of effort at a time, beginning with the decisive line. (See figure B-9.) It includes not only war-gaming events, objectives, or events and objectives in the selected line, but also war-gaming relationships among events or objectives on all lines of effort with respect to events in the selected line.

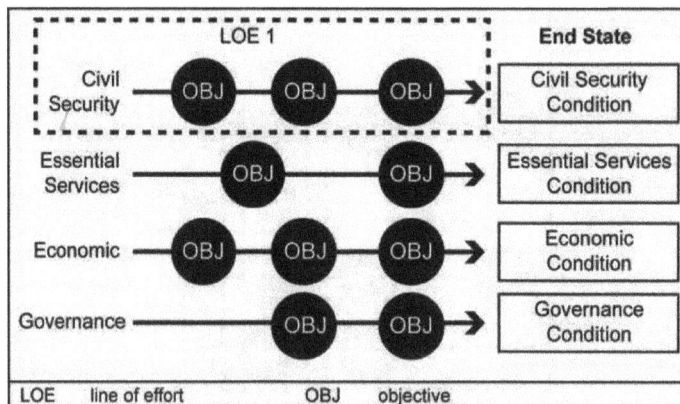

Figure B-9. Sample modified avenue-in-depth method using lines of effort

B-150. The box method is a detailed analysis of a critical area, such as an engagement area, a river-crossing site, or a landing zone. (See figure B-10.) It works best in a time-constrained environment, such as a hasty attack. It is particularly useful when planning operations in noncontiguous AOs. When using this method, the staff isolates the area and focuses on critical events in it. Staff members assume that friendly units can handle most situations in the AOs and focus their attention on essential tasks.

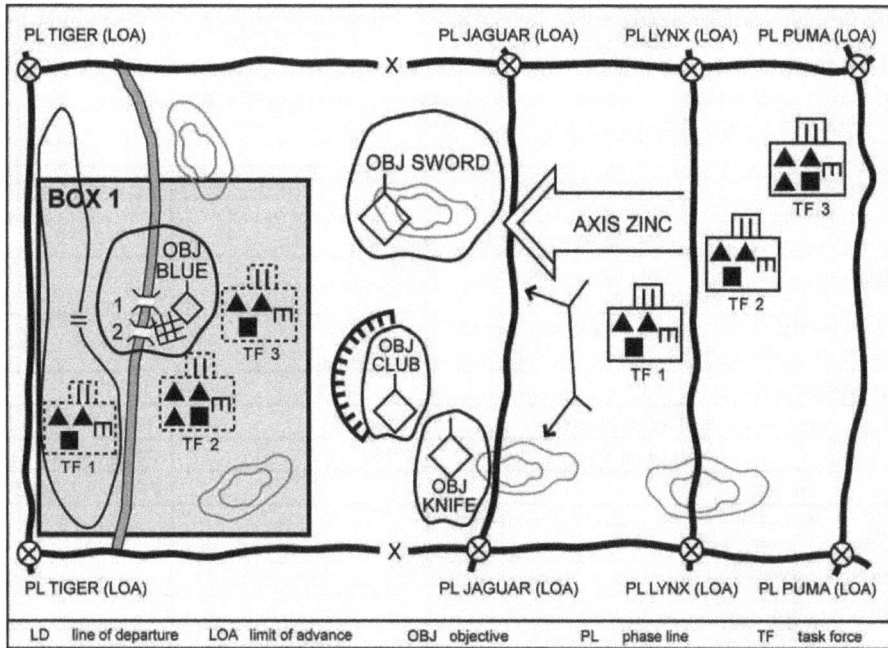

Figure B-10. Sample box method

B-151. In stability operations, the box method may focus analysis on a specific objective along a line of effort such as development of local security forces as part of improving civil security. (See figure B-11.)

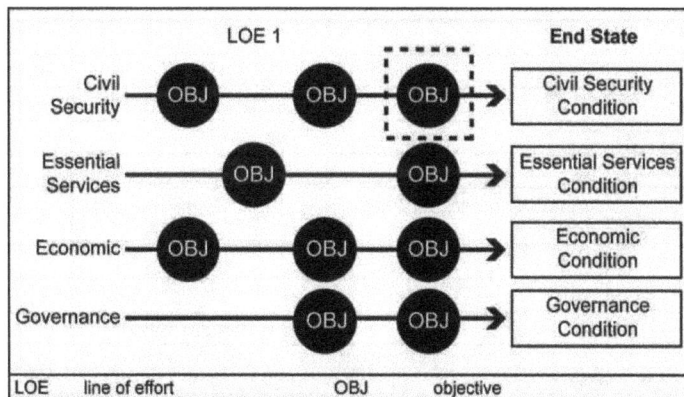

Figure B-11. Sample modified box method using lines of effort

Select a Technique to Record and Display Results

B-152. The war-game results provide a record from which to build task organizations, synchronize activities, develop decision support templates, confirm and refine event templates, prepare plans or orders, and compare COAs. Two techniques are commonly used to record and display results: the synchronization matrix technique and the sketch note technique. In both techniques, staff members record any remarks regarding the strengths and weaknesses they discover. The amount of detail depends on the time available. Unit SOPs address details and methods of recording and displaying war-gaming results.

B-153. The *synchronization matrix* is a tool the staff uses to record the results of war-gaming and helps them synchronize a course of action across time, space, and purpose in relationship to potential enemy and civil actions. (See figure B-12.) The first entry is time or phase of the operation. The second entry is the most likely enemy action. The third entry is the most likely civilian action. The fourth entry is the decision points for the friendly COA. The remainder of the matrix is developed around selected warfighting functions and their subordinate tasks and the unit's major subordinate commands.

Time/Event		H – 24 hours	H-hour	H + 24
Enemy or Adversary Action		Monitors movements	Defends from security zone	Commits reserve
Population		Orderly evacuation from area continues		
Decision Points		Conduct aviation attack of OBJ Irene		
Control Measures				
Movement and Maneuver	1st BCT	Move on Route Irish	Cross LD	Seize on OBJ Irene
	2d BCT	Move on Route Longstreet	Cross LD	Seize on OBJ Rose
	3d BCT			FPOL with 1st BCT
	Avn Bde	Attack enemy reserve on OBJ Irene		
	R&S			
Reserve				
Intelligence				
Fires		Prep fires initiated at H-5		
Protection	Engineer			
	PMO			
	AMD			
	CBRNE			
Sustainment				
Mission Command			Main CP with 1st BCT	
Close Air Support				
Electronic Warfare			Enemy network jammed	
Nonlethal		Surrender broadcasts and leaflets		
Host Nation				
Interagency				
NGOs			Begins refugee relief	
Note: The first column is representative only and can be modified to fit formation needs.				
AMD air and missile defense			FPOL forward passage of lines	
Avn Bde aviation brigade			LD line of departure	
BCT brigade combat team			NGO nongovernmental organization	
CBRNE chemical, biological, radiological, nuclear, and high-yield explosives			OBJ objective	
			PMO provost marshal office	
CP command post			R&S reconnaissance and surveillance	

±Figure B-12. Sample synchronization matrix technique

B-154. The sketch note technique uses brief notes concerning critical locations or tasks and purposes. (See figure B-13.) These notes refer to specific locations or relate to general considerations covering broad areas. The commander and staff mark locations on the map and on a separate war-game work sheet. Staff members use sequence numbers to link the notes to the corresponding locations on the map or overlay. Staff members also identify actions by placing them in sequential action groups, giving each subtask a separate number. They use the war-game work sheet to identify all pertinent data for a critical event. They assign each event a number and title and use the columns on the work sheet to identify and list in sequence—

- Units and assigned tasks.
- Expected enemy actions and reactions.
- Friendly counteractions and assets.
- Total assets needed for the task.
- Estimated time to accomplish the task.
- The decision point tied to executing the task.
- CCIRs.
- Control measures.
- Remarks.

Critical Event	Seize OBJ Sword
Sequence number	1
Action	TF 3 attacks to destroy enemy company on OBJ Sword
Reaction	Enemy company on OBJ Club counterattacks
Counteraction	TF 1 suppresses enemy company on OBJ Club
Assets	TF 3, TF 1, and 1-78 FA (155-SP)
Time	H+1 to H+4
Decision point	DP 3a and 3b
Commander's Critical information Requirements	Location of enemy armor reserve west of PL Jaguar
Control measures	Axis Zinc and support by fire position 1
Remarks	

Figure B-13. Sample sketch note technique

War-Game the Operation and Assess the Results

B-155. War-gaming is a conscious attempt to visualize the flow of operations given the friendly force's strengths and disposition, enemy's capabilities and possible COAs, and civilians. During the war game, the commander and staff try to foresee the actions, reactions, and counteractions of all participants to include civilians. The staff analyzes each selected event. They identify tasks that the force must accomplish one echelon down, using assets two echelons down. Identifying strengths and weaknesses of each COA allows the staff to adjust the COAs as necessary.

B-156. The war game focuses not so much on the tools used but on the people who participate. Staff members who participate in war-gaming should be the individuals deeply involved in developing COAs. Red team members (who can provide alternative points of view) provide insight on each COA. In stability operations, subject matter experts in areas such as economic or local governance can also help assess results of planned actions, including identifying possible unintended effects.

B-157. The war game follows an action-reaction-counteraction cycle. Actions are those events initiated by the side with the initiative. Reactions are the opposing side's actions in response. With regard to stability operations, the war game tests the effects of actions, including intended and unintended effects, as they stimulate anticipated responses from civilians and civil institutions. Counteractions are the first side's responses to reactions. This sequence of action-reaction-counteraction continues until the critical event is completed or until the commander decides to use another COA to accomplish the mission.

B-158. The staff considers all possible forces, including templated enemy forces outside the AO, which can influence the operation. The staff also considers the actions of civilians in the AO, the diverse kinds of coverage of unfolding events, and their consequences in the global media. The staff evaluates each friendly move to determine the assets and actions required to defeat the enemy at that point or to accomplish stability tasks. The staff continually considers branches to the plan that promote success against likely enemy counteractions or unexpected civilian reactions. Lastly, the staff lists assets used in the appropriate columns of the work sheet and lists the totals in the assets column (not considering any assets lower than two command levels down).

B-159. The commander and staff examine many areas during the war game. These include—
- All friendly capabilities.
- All enemy capabilities.
- Civilian reactions to all friendly actions.
- Global media responses to proposed actions.
- Movement considerations.
- Closure rates.
- Lengths of columns.
- Formation depths.
- Ranges and capabilities of weapon systems.
- Desired effects of fires.

B-160. The commander and staff consider how to create conditions for success, protect the force, and shape the operational environment. Experience, historical data, SOPs, and doctrinal literature provide much of the necessary information. During the war game, staff officers perform a risk assessment for their functional area for each COA. They then propose appropriate controls. They must continually assess the risk of adverse population and media reactions that result from actions taken by all sides in the operation. Staff officers develop ways to mitigate those risks.

B-161. The staff continually assesses the risk to friendly forces from catastrophic threats, seeking a balance between mass and dispersion. When assessing the risk of weapons of mass destruction to friendly forces, planners view the target that the force presents through the eyes of an enemy target analyst. They consider ways to reduce vulnerability and determine the appropriate level of mission-oriented protective posture consistent with mission accomplishment.

B-162. The staff identifies the required assets of the warfighting functions to support the concept of operations, including those needed to synchronize sustaining operations. If requirements exceed available assets, the staff recommends priorities based on the situation, commander's intent, and planning guidance. To maintain flexibility, the commander may decide to create a reserve to account for assets for unforeseen tasks or opportunities.

B-163. The commander can modify any COA based on how things develop during the war game. When doing this, the commander validates the composition and location of the decisive operation, shaping operations, and reserve forces. Control measures are adjusted as necessary. The commander may also identify situations, opportunities, or additional critical events that require more analysis. The staff performs this analysis quickly and incorporates the results into the war-gaming record.

B-164. An effective war game results in the commander and staff refining, identifying, analyzing, developing, and determining several effects.

B-165. An effective war game results in the commander and staff refining—
- Or modifying each COA, including identifying branches and sequels that become on-order or be-prepared missions.
- The locations and times of decisive points.
- The enemy event template and matrix.
- The task organization, including forces retained in general support.
- Control requirements, including control measures and updated operational graphics.
- CCIRs and IRs—including the last time information of value—and incorporating them into the ISR plan and information management plans.

B-166. An effective war game results in the commander and staff identifying—
- Key or decisive terrain and determining how to use it.
- Tasks the unit retains and tasks assigned to subordinates.

- Likely times and areas for enemy use of weapons of mass destruction and friendly chemical, biological, radiological, and nuclear defense requirements.
- Potential times or locations for committing the reserve.
- The most dangerous enemy COA.
- The most dangerous civilian reaction.
- Locations for the commander, command posts, and INFOSYS nodes.
- Critical events.
- Requirements for support of each warfighting function.
- Effects of friendly and enemy actions on civilians and infrastructure, and how these will affect military operations.
- Or confirming the locations of named areas of interest, target areas of interest, decision points, and IRs needed to support them.
- Analyzing, and evaluating strengths and weaknesses of each COA.
- Hazards, assessing their risk, developing controls for them, and determining residual risk.
- The coordination required for integrating and synchronizing interagency, host-nation, and nongovernmental organization involvement.

B-167. An effective war game results in the commander and staff analyzing—
- Potential civilian reactions to operations.
- Potential media reaction to operations.
- Potential impacts on civil security, civil control, and essential services in the AO.

B-168. An effective war game results in the commander and staff developing—
- Decision points.
- A synchronization matrix.
- A decision support template and matrix.
- Solutions to achieving minimum essential stability tasks in the AO.
- The ISR plan and graphics.
- Initial information themes and messages.
- Fires, protection, and sustainment plans and graphic control measures.

B-169. Lastly, an effective war game results in the commander and staff—
- Determining requirements for military deception and surprise.
- Determining the timing for concentrating forces and starting the attack or counterattack.
- Determining movement times and tables for critical assets, including INFOSYS nodes.
- Estimating the duration of the entire operation and each critical event.
- Projecting the percentage of enemy forces defeated in each critical event and overall.
- Projecting the percentage of minimum essential tasks that the unit can or must accomplish.
- Anticipating media coverage and impact on key audiences.
- Integrating targeting into the operation, to include identifying or confirming high-payoff targets and establishing attack guidance.
- Allocating assets to subordinate commanders to accomplish their missions.

Conduct a War-Game Briefing (Optional)

B-170. Time permitting, the staff delivers a briefing to all affected elements to ensure everyone understands the results of the war game. The staff uses the briefing for review and ensures that all relevant points of the war game are captured for presentation to the commander, COS (XO), or deputy or assistant commander in the COA decision briefing. In a collaborative environment, the briefing may include selected subordinate staffs. A war-game briefing format includes the following:
- Higher headquarters' mission, commander's intent, and military deception plan.
- Updated IPB.

- Friendly and enemy COAs that were war-gamed, including—
  - Critical events.
  - Possible enemy actions and reactions.
  - Possible impact on civilians.
  - Possible media impacts.
  - Modifications to the COAs.
  - Strengths and weaknesses.
  - Results of the war game.
- Assumptions.
- War-gaming technique used.

COURSE OF ACTION COMPARISON

B-171. COA comparison is an objective process to evaluate COAs independently of each other and against set evaluation criteria approved by the commander and staff. The goal to identify the strengths and weaknesses of COAs enable selecting a COA with the highest probability of success and further developing it in an OPLAN or OPORD. The commander and staff perform certain actions and processes that lead to the key outputs in figure B-14.

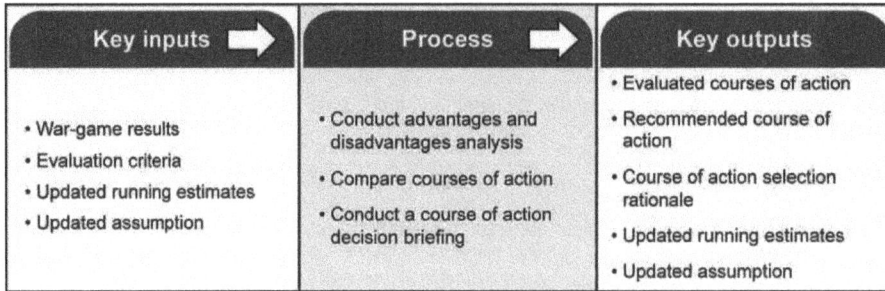

Key inputs	Process	Key outputs
• War-game results • Evaluation criteria • Updated running estimates • Updated assumption	• Conduct advantages and disadvantages analysis • Compare courses of action • Conduct a course of action decision briefing	• Evaluated courses of action • Recommended course of action • Course of action selection rationale • Updated running estimates • Updated assumption

Figure B-14. COA comparison

Conduct Advantages and Disadvantages Analysis

B-172. The COA comparison starts with all staff members analyzing and evaluating the advantages and disadvantages of each COA from their perspectives. (See figure B-15.) Staff members each present their findings for the others' consideration. Using the evaluation criteria developed before the war game, the staff outlines each COA, highlighting its advantages and disadvantages. Comparing the strengths and weaknesses of the COAs identifies their advantages and disadvantages with respect to each other.

Course of Action	Advantages	Disadvantages
COA 1	Decisive operation avoids major terrain obstacles. Adequate maneuver space available for units conducting the decisive operation and the reserve.	Units conducting the decisive operation face stronger resistance at the start of the operation. Limited resources available to establishing civil control to Town X.
COA 2	Shaping operations provide excellent flank protection of the decisive operations. Upon completion of decisive operations, units conducting shaping operations can quickly transition to establish civil control and provide civil security to the population in Town X.	Operation may require the early employment of the division's reserve.

Figure B-15. Sample advantages and disadvantages

Compare Courses of Action

B-173.   Comparison of COAs is critical. The staff may use any technique that facilitates developing those key outputs and recommendations and helping the commander making the best decision. A common technique is the decision matrix. This matrix uses evaluation criteria developed during mission analysis and refined during COA development to help assess the effectiveness and efficiency of each COA. (See figure B-16.)

Criteria[1]	Weight[2]	COA 1[3]	COA 2[3]
Simplicity	1	2 (2)	1 (1)
Maneuver	2	2 (4)	1 (2)
Fires	1	2 (2)	1 (1)
Civil control	1	1 (1)	2 (2)
Support mission narrative	2	1 (2)	2 (4)
Total (Min=Max) **Weighted TOTAL**		8 (11)	7 (10)

Notes:
[1] Criteria are those assigned in step 5 of COA analysis.
[2] The COS (XO) may emphasize one or more criteria by assigning weights to them based on a determination of their relative importance.
[3] COAs are those selected for war-gaming with values assigned to them based on comparison between them with regard to relative advantages and disadvantages of each, such as when compared for relative simplicity COA 2 is by comparison to COA 1 simpler and therefore is rated as 1 with COA 1 rated as 2.

Figure B-16. Sample decision matrix

B-174.   The decision matrix is a tool to compare and evaluate COAs in a thorough and logical manner. However, the process is based on highly subjective judgments that may change dramatically during the course of evaluation as it draws out and shapes critical thought from the commander and staff. In the example above, values reflect the relative advantages or disadvantages of each criterion for each COA as initially estimated by a COS (XO) during mission analysis. At the same time, the COS (XO) determines weights for each criterion based on a subjective determination of their relative value. The lower values signify a more favorable advantage, such as the lower the number, the more favorable the score. After comparing COAs and assigning values, the unweighted assigned scores in each column are added vertically under each COA and a total for each COA is noted. The same values are then multiplied by the weighted score associated with each criterion, and the product is noted in parenthesis in each appropriate box. These weighted products are then added vertically and noted in parenthesis in the space for "Weighted TOTAL" below each COA column. The totals are then compared to determine the "best" (lowest number) COA based on both criteria alone and then on weighted scores. Upon review and consideration, the commander—based on personal judgment—may elect to change either the value for the basic criterion or the weighted value. Although the lowest value denotes a "best" solution, the process for estimating relative values assigned to criterion and weighting is highly subjective. One result may be that the "best" COA may not be supportable without additional resources. This would enable the decisionmaker to decide whether to pursue additional support, alter the COA in some way, or determine that it is not feasible.

B-175. The decision matrix is one highly structured and effective method used to compare COAs against criteria that, when met, suggest a great likelihood of producing success. Specific broad categories of COA characteristics are given a basic numerical value based on evaluation criteria. Weights are assigned based on subjective judgment regarding their relative importance to existing circumstances. Basic values are then multiplied by the weight to yield a given criterion's final score. The staff member then totals all scores so to compare COAs.

B-176. However, the results of such a decision matrix alone do not provide a total basis for decision solutions. During the decision matrix process, planners use special care to avoid reaching conclusions from mainly subjective judgments as the result of purely quantifiable analysis. Comparing and evaluating COAs by category of criterion is probably more useful than merely comparing total scores. Often judgments change with regard to relative weighting of criterion of importance during close analysis of COAs, which would change matrix scoring.

B-177. The staff compares feasible COAs to identify the one with the highest probability of success against the most likely enemy COA, the most dangerous enemy COA, the most important stability task, or the most damaging environmental impact. The selected COA should also—

- Pose the minimum risk to the force and mission accomplishment.
- Place the force in the best posture for future operations.
- Provide maximum latitude for initiative by subordinates.
- Provide the most flexibility to meet unexpected threats and opportunities.
- Provide the most secure and stable environment for civilians in the AO.
- Best facilitate initial information themes and messages.

B-178. Staff officers may each use their own matrix to compare COAs with respect to their functional areas. Matrixes use the evaluation criteria developed before the war game. Decision matrixes alone cannot provide decision solutions. Their greatest value is providing a method to compare COAs against criteria that, when met, produce operational success. Staff officers use these analytical tools to prepare recommendations. Commanders provide the solution by applying their judgment to staff recommendations and making a decision.

Conduct a Course of Action Decision Briefing

B-179. After completing its analysis and comparison, the staff identifies its preferred COA and makes a recommendation. If the staff cannot reach a decision, the COS (XO) decides which COA to recommend. The staff then delivers a decision briefing to the commander. The COS (XO) highlights any changes to each COA resulting from the war game. The decision briefing includes—

- The commander's intent of the higher and next higher commanders.
- The status of the force and its components.

- The current IPB.
- The COAs considered, including—
  - Assumptions used.
  - Results of running estimates.
  - A summary of the war game for each COA, including critical events, modifications to any COA, and war-game results.
  - Advantages and disadvantages (including risk) of each COA.
  - The recommended COA. If a significant disagreement exists, then the staff should inform the commander and, if necessary, discuss the disagreement.

COURSE OF ACTION APPROVAL

B-180. After the decision briefing, the commander selects the COA to best accomplish the mission. If the commander rejects all COAs, the staff starts COA development again. If the commander modifies a proposed COA or gives the staff an entirely different one, the staff war-games the new COA and presents the results to the commander with a recommendation.

B-181. After selecting a COA, the commander issues the final planning guidance. The final planning guidance includes a refined commander's intent (if necessary) and new CCIRs to support execution. It also includes any additional guidance on priorities for the warfighting functions, orders preparation, rehearsal, and preparation. This guidance includes priorities for resources needed to preserve freedom of action and ensure continuous sustainment.

B-182. Commanders include risk they are willing to accept in the final planning guidance. If there is time, commanders use a video-teleconference (VTC) to discuss acceptable risk with adjacent, subordinate, and senior commanders. However, a commander must obtain the higher commander's approval to accept any risk that might imperil accomplishing the higher commander's mission.

B-183. Based on the commander's decision and final planning guidance, the staff issues a WARNO to subordinate headquarters. This WARNO contains the information subordinate units need to refine their plans. It confirms guidance issued in person or by VTC and expands on details not covered by the commander personally. The WARNO issued after COA approval normally contains—

- Mission.
- Commander's intent.
- Updated CCIRs and EEFIs.
- Concept of operations.
- The AO.
- Principal tasks assigned to subordinate units.
- Preparation and rehearsal instructions not included in the SOPs.
- A final timeline for the operations.

ORDERS PRODUCTION

B-184. The staff prepares the order or plan by turning the selected COA into a clear, concise concept of operations and required supporting information. The COA statement becomes the concept of operations for the plan. The COA sketch becomes the basis for the operation overlay. If time permits, the staff may conduct a more detailed war game of the selected COA to more fully synchronize the operation and complete the plan. The staff writes the OPLAN and OPORD using the Army's operation order format. See Annex E, (Protection).

B-185. Commanders review and approve orders before the staff reproduces and disseminates them unless they have delegated that authority. Subordinates immediately acknowledge receipt of the higher order. If possible, the order is briefed to subordinate commanders face-to-face by the higher commander and staff. The commander and staff conduct confirmation briefings with subordinates immediately afterwards. Confirmation briefings can be done collaboratively with several commanders at the same time or with single commanders. These briefings may be performed face-to-face or by VTC. (See appendix E for formats for plans and orders.)

PLANNING IN A TIME-CONSTRAINED ENVIRONMENT

B-186. The focus of any planning processes should aim to quickly develop a flexible, sound, and fully integrated and synchronized plan. However, any operation may "outrun" the initial plan. The most detailed estimates cannot anticipate every possible branch or sequel, enemy action, unexpected opportunity, or change in mission directed from higher headquarters. Fleeting opportunities or unexpected enemy action may require a quick decision to implement a new or modified plan. When this occurs, units often find themselves pressed for time in developing a new plan.

B-187. While the MDMP seeks the optimal solution, the rapid decisionmaking and synchronization process (RDSP) seeks a timely and effective solution within the commander's intent, mission, and concept of operations. Using the RDSP lets leaders avoid the time-consuming requirements of developing decision criteria and comparing COAs. (See chapter 5 for more information on RDSP.)

B-188. Before a unit can effectively conduct planning in a time-constrained environment, it must master the steps in the full MDMP. A unit can only shorten the process if it fully understands the role of each and every step of the process and the requirements to produce the necessary products. Training on these steps must be thorough and result in a series of staff battle drills that can be tailored to the time available.

B-189. Staffs must be able to produce simple, flexible, and tactically sound plans in a time-constrained environment. Any METT-TC factor, but especially limited time, may make it difficult to complete every step of the MDMP in detail. Applying an inflexible process to all situations will not work. Anticipation, organization, and prior preparation are the keys to successful planning under time-constrained conditions.

B-190. The time saved on any step of the MDMP can be used to—
- Refine the plan more thoroughly.
- Conduct a more deliberate and detailed war game.
- Consider potential branches and sequels in detail.
- Focus more on rehearsing and preparing the plan.
- Allow subordinate units more planning and preparation time.

THE COMMANDER'S ROLE

B-191. The commander decides how to adjust the MDMP, giving specific guidance to the staff to focus on the process and save time. Commanders (who have access to only a small portion of the staff or none at all) rely even more than normal on their own expertise, intuition, and creativity as well as on their understanding of the environment and of the art and science of warfare. They may have to select a COA, mentally war-game it, and confirm their decision to the staff in a relatively short time. If so, the decision is based more on experience than on a formal, integrated staff process.

B-192. Commanders should avoid changing their guidance unless a significantly changed situation requires major revisions. Frequent minor changes to the guidance can easily result in lost time as the staff constantly adjusts the plan with an adverse ripple effect throughout overall planning.

B-193. Commanders consult with subordinate commanders before making a decision, if possible. Subordinate commanders are closer to the operation and can more accurately describe the enemy, friendly, and civilian situations. Additionally, consulting with subordinates gives commanders insight into the upcoming operation and allows parallel planning. White boards and collaborative digital means of communicating greatly enhance parallel planning.

B-194. In situations where commanders must decide quickly, they advise their higher headquarters of the selected COA, if time is available. However, commanders do not let an opportunity pass just because they cannot report their actions.

THE STAFF'S ROLE

B-195. Staff members keep their running estimates current. When planning time is limited, they can provide accurate, up-to-date assessments quickly and move directly into COA development. Under time-constrained conditions, commanders and staffs use as much of the previously analyzed information and products as possible. The importance of running estimates increases as time decreases. Decisionmaking in a time-constrained environment almost always occurs after a unit has entered the AO and begun operations. This means that the IPB, an updated common operational picture, and some portion of running estimates should already exist. Civilian and military joint and multinational organizations operating in the AO should have well-developed plans and information to add insights to the operational environment. Detailed planning provides the basis for information that the commander and staff need to make decisions during execution.

B-196. Commanders shorten the MDMP when they lack time to perform each step in detail. The most significant factor to consider is time. It is the only nonrenewable, and often the most critical, resource.

TIME-SAVING TECHNIQUES

B-197. Several time-saving techniques can speed up the planning process. These techniques include the following:

- Increase commander's involvement.
- Limit the number of COAs to develop.
- Maximize parallel planning.
- Increase collaborative planning.
- Use liaison officers.

Increase Commander's Involvement

B-198. While commanders cannot spend all their time with the planning staff, the greater the commander's involvement in planning, the faster the staff can plan. In time-constrained conditions, commanders who participate in the planning process can make decisions (such as COA selection) without waiting for a detailed briefing from the staff. The first time-saving technique is to increase the commander's involvement. This technique allows commanders to make decisions during the MDMP without waiting for detailed briefings after each step.

Limit the Number of Courses of Action to Develop

B-199. Limiting the number of COAs developed and war-gamed can save planning time. If time is extremely short, the commander can direct development of only one COA. In this case, the goal is an acceptable COA that meets mission requirements in the time available. This technique saves the most time. The fastest way to develop a plan is for the commander to direct development of one COA with branches against the most likely enemy COA or most damaging civil situation or condition. However, this technique should be used only when time is severely limited. In such cases, this choice of COA is often intuitive, relying on the commander's experience and judgment. The commander determines which staff officers are essential to assist in COA development depending on the type of operation being planned. The minimum is normally the intelligence officer, operations officer, plans officer, chief of fires (fire support officer), engineer coordinator, civil affairs operations officer, inform and influence officer, and COS (XO). The commander may also include subordinate commanders, if available, either in person or by VTC. This team quickly develops a flexible COA that it feels will accomplish the mission. The commander mentally war-games this COA and gives it to the staff to refine.

Maximize Parallel Planning

B-200. Although parallel planning is the norm, maximizing its use in time-constrained environments is critical. In a time-constrained environment, the importance of WARNOs increases as available time decreases. A verbal WARNO now followed by a written order later saves more time than a written order one hour from now. The same WARNOs used in the full MDMP should be issued when abbreviating the process. In addition to WARNOs, units must share all available information with subordinates, especially IPB products, as early as possible. The staff uses every opportunity to perform parallel planning with the higher headquarters and to share information with subordinates.

Increase Collaborative Planning

B-201. Planning in real time with higher headquarters and subordinates improves the overall planning effort of the organization. Modern INFOSYS and a common operational picture shared electronically allow collaboration with subordinates from distant locations, can increase information sharing, and can improve the commander's visualization. Additionally, taking advantage of subordinate input and knowledge of the situation in their AOs often results in developing better COAs faster.

Use Liaison Officers

B-202. Liaison officers posted to higher headquarters allow the commander to have representation in their higher headquarters' planning session. These officers assist in passing timely information to their parent headquarters and can speed up the planning effort by transmitting timely information directly to the commander. Effective liaison officers have the commander's full confidence and the necessary rank and experience for the mission. Commanders may elect to use a single individual or a liaison team. Since liaison officers represent the commander, they must—

- Understand how their commander thinks and be able to interpret the commander's verbal and written guidance.
- Convey their commander's intent, planning guidance, mission, and concept of operations.
- Represent their commander's position.
- Know the unit's mission; tactics, techniques, and procedures; organization; capabilities; and communications equipment.
- Observe the established channels of command and staff functions.
- Be trained in their functional responsibilities.
- Be tactful.
- Possess the necessary language expertise.

Appendix C

Troop Leading Procedures

Troop leading procedures (TLP) provide small-unit leaders with a framework for planning and preparing for operations. Leaders of company and smaller units use TLP to develop plans and orders. This appendix describes the eight steps of TLP and their relationship to the military decisionmaking process (MDMP). While TLP are explained in this chapter from a ground-maneuver perspective, it applies to all types of small units. Formats for plans and orders are located in appendix E.

BACKGROUND AND COMPARISON TO THE MDMP

C-1.   Troop leading procedures extend the MDMP to the small-unit level. The MDMP and TLP are similar but not identical. They are both linked by the basic Army problem solving methodology explained in chapter 1. Commanders with a coordinating staff use the MDMP as their primary planning process. Company-level and smaller units lack formal staffs and use TLP to plan and prepare for operations. This places the responsibility for planning primarily on the commander or small-unit leader.

C-2.   *Troop leading procedures* **are a dynamic process used by small-unit leaders to analyze a mission, develop a plan, and prepare for an operation**. These procedures enable leaders to maximize available planning time while developing effective plans and preparing their units for an operation. TLP consist of eight steps. TLP are also supported by composite risk management. (See FM 5-19.) The sequence of the steps of TLP is not rigid. Leaders modify the sequence to meet the mission, situation, and available time. Some steps are done concurrently while others may go on continuously throughout the operation:

- Step 1 – Receive the mission.
- Step 2 – Issue a warning order.
- Step 3 – Make a tentative plan.
- Step 4 – Initiate movement.
- Step 5 – Conduct reconnaissance.
- Step 6 – Complete the plan.
- Step 7 – Issue the order.
- Step 8 – Supervise and refine.

C-3.   Leaders use TLP when working alone or with a small group to solve tactical problems. For example, a company commander may use the executive officer, first sergeant, fire support officer, supply sergeant, and communications sergeant to assist during TLP.

C-4.   The type, amount, and timeliness of information passed from higher to lower headquarters directly impact the lower unit leader's TLP. Figure C-1 on page C-2 illustrates the parallel sequences of the MDMP of a battalion with the TLP of a company and a platoon. The solid arrows depict when a higher headquarters' planning event could start TLP of a subordinate unit. However, events do not always occur in the order shown. For example, TLP may start with receipt of a warning order (WARNO), or they may not start until the higher headquarters has completed the MDMP and issued an operation order (OPORD). WARNOs from higher headquarters may arrive at any time during TLP. Leaders remain flexible. They adapt TLP to fit the situation rather than try to alter the situation to fit a preconceived idea of how events should flow.

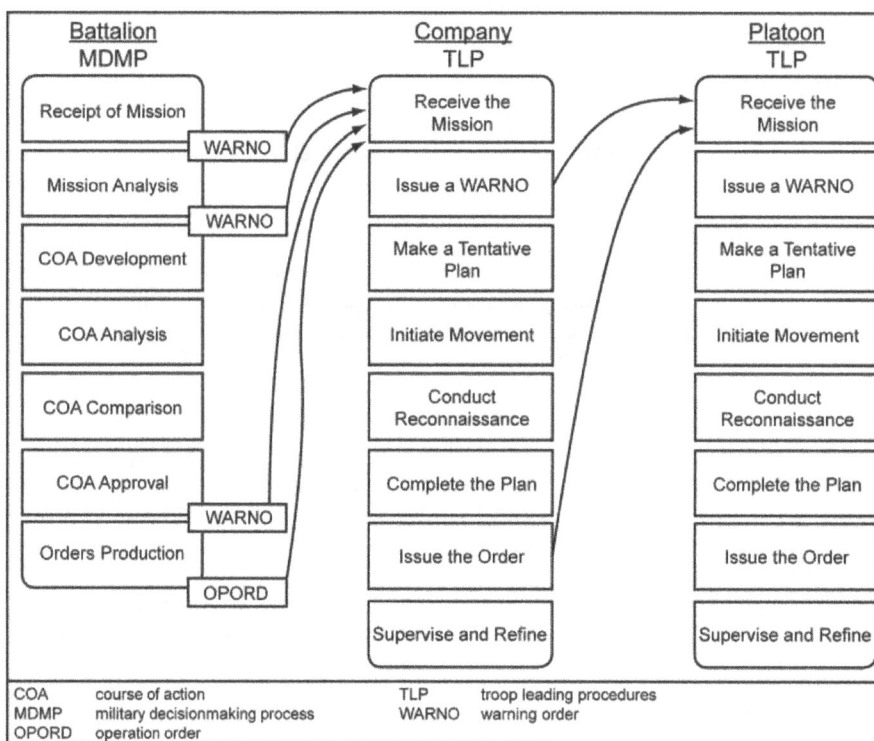

Figure C-1. Parallel planning

C-5. Normally, the first three steps (receive the mission, issue a WARNO, and make a tentative plan) of TLP occur in order. However, the sequence of subsequent steps is based on the situation. The tasks involved in some steps (for example, initiate movement and conduct reconnaissance) may occur several times. The last step, supervise and refine, occurs throughout.

C-6. A tension exists between executing current operations and planning for future operations. The small-unit leader must balance both. If engaged in a current operation, there is less time for TLP. If in a lull, transition, or an assembly area, leaders have more time to use TLP thoroughly. In some situations, time constraints or other factors may prevent leaders from performing each step of TLP as thoroughly as they would like. For example, during the step, make a tentative plan; small-unit leaders often develop only one acceptable course of action (COA) vice multiple COAs. If time permits, leaders may develop, compare, and analyze several COAs before arriving at a decision on which one to execute.

C-7. Ideally, a battalion headquarters issues at least three WARNOs to subordinates when conducting the MDMP as depicted in figure C-1. WARNOs are issued upon receipt of mission, completion of mission analysis, and when the commander approves a COA. However, the number of WARNOs is not fixed. WARNOs serve a function in planning similar to that of fragmentary orders (FRAGOs) during execution. Commanders may issue a WARNO whenever they need to disseminate additional planning information or initiate necessary preparatory action, such as movement or reconnaissance. (See appendix E for a detailed discussion on WARNOs.)

C-8. Leaders begin TLP when they receive the initial WARNO or receive a new mission. As each subsequent order arrives, leaders modify their assessments, update tentative plans, and continue to supervise and assess preparations. In some situations, the higher headquarters may not issue the full sequence of WARNOs; security considerations or tempo may make it impractical. Commanders carefully consider decisions to eliminate WARNOs. Subordinate units always need to have enough information to plan and prepare for the operation. In other cases, leaders may initiate TLP before receiving a WARNO based on existing plans and orders (contingency plans or be-prepared missions) and on their understanding of the situation.

C-9. Parallel planning hinges on distributing information as it is received or developed. (See chapter 2.) Leaders cannot complete their plans until they receive their unit mission. If each successive WARNO contains enough information, the higher headquarters' final order will confirm what subordinate leaders have already analyzed and put into their tentative plans. In other cases, the higher headquarters' order may change or modify the subordinate's tasks enough that additional planning and reconnaissance are required.

STEPS OF TROOP LEADING PROCEDURES

C-10. TLP provide small-unit leaders a framework for planning and preparing for operations. Figure C-2 depicts TLP along with key planning tasks. The box on the left shows the steps of TLP. The box in the middle (METT-TC for mission, enemy, terrain and weather, troops and support available, time available, civil considerations) represents the initial METT-TC analysis that leaders conduct to develop an initial assessment. This occurs in steps 1 and 2 of TLP and is refined in plan development. The box on the right depicts plan development tasks. Plan development occurs in step 3 and is completed in 6 of TLP. These tasks are similar to the steps of the MDMP. (See appendix B.)

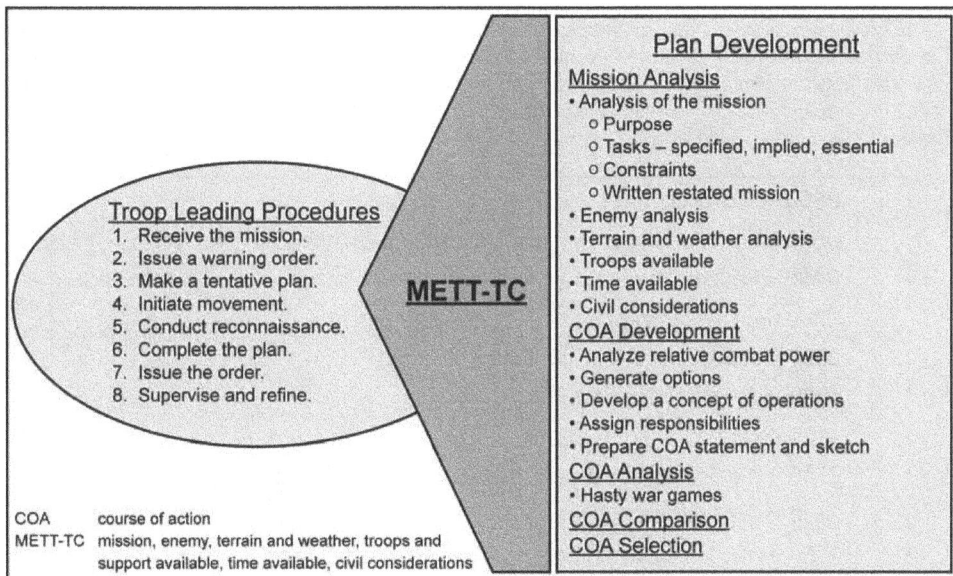

Figure C-2. Planning at company and below

RECEIVE THE MISSION

C-11. Receive the mission may occur in several ways. It may begin with the initial WARNO or OPORD from higher headquarters or when a leader anticipates a new mission. Frequently, leaders receive a mission in a FRAGO over the radio. Ideally, they receive a series of WARNOs, the OPORD, and a briefing from their commander. Normally after receiving an OPORD, leaders give a confirmation brief to their higher commander to ensure they understand the higher commander's intent and concept of operations. The leader obtains clarification on any portions of the higher headquarters plan as required.

C-12. When they receive the mission, leaders perform an initial assessment of the situation (mission analysis) and allocate the time available for planning and preparation. (Preparation includes rehearsals and movement.) This initial assessment and time allocation forms the basis of their initial WARNOs.

C-13. The initial assessment addresses the factors of METT-TC. The order and detail in which leaders analyze the factors of METT-TC is flexible. It depends on the amount of information available and the relative importance of each factor. For example, leaders may concentrate on the mission, enemy, and terrain, leaving weather and civil considerations until they receive more detailed information.

C-14. Often, leaders do not receive their final unit mission until the WARNO is disseminated after COA approval or after the OPORD. Effective leaders do not wait until their higher headquarters complete planning to begin their planning. Using all information available, leaders develop their unit mission as completely as they can. They focus on the mission, commander's intent, and concept of operations of their higher and next higher headquarters. They pick out the major tasks their unit will probably be assigned and develop a mission statement based on information they have received. At this stage, the mission may be incomplete. For example, an initial mission statement could be, "First platoon conducts an ambush in the next 24 hours." While not complete, this information allows subordinates to start preparations. Leaders complete a formal mission statement during TLP step 3 (make a tentative plan) and step 6 (complete the plan).

C-15. Based on what they know, leaders estimate the time available to plan and prepare for the mission. They begin by identifying the times at which major planning and preparation events, including rehearsals, must be complete. Reverse planning helps them do this. Leaders identify the critical times specified by higher headquarters and work back from them, estimating how much time each event will consume. Critical times might include times to load aircraft, the line of departure, or the start point for movement.

C-16. Leaders ensure that all subordinate echelons have sufficient time for their own planning and preparation needs. A general rule of thumb for leaders at all levels is to use no more than one-third of the available time for planning and issuing the OPORD. Leaders allocate the remaining two-thirds of it to subordinates. Figure C-3 is a sample time schedule for an infantry company. The company adjusts the tentative schedule as TLP progress.

```
0600 -Eecute mission.

0530 -finalize or adjust the plan     based on leader's reconnaissance.

0400 -Etablish the objective rallying po     int;begin leader reconnaissance.

0200 -Begin movement.

2100 -Conduct platoon inspections.

1900 -Conduct rehearsals.

1800 -Et meals.

1745 -Hold backbriefs (squad leaders to platoon leaders).

1630 -Issue platoon OPOBs.

1500 -Hold backbriefs (platoon  leaders to company commander).

1330 -Issue company OPOB.

1045 -Conduct reconnaissance.

1030 -Update company WARNO.

1000 -Bceive battalion OPOB.

0900 -Bceive battalion WARNO;issue company WARNO.
```

Figure C-3. Sample schedule

ISSUE A WARNING ORDER

C-17. As soon as leaders finish their initial assessment of the situation and available time, they issue a WARNO. Leaders do not wait for more information. They issue the best WARNO possible with the information at hand and update it as needed with additional WARNOs.

C-18. The WARNO contains as much detail as possible. It informs subordinates of the unit mission and gives them the leader's timeline. Leaders may also pass on any other instructions or information they think will help subordinates prepare for the new mission. This includes information on the enemy, the nature of the higher headquarters' plan, and any specific instructions for preparing their units. The most important thing is that leaders not delay in issuing the initial WARNO. As more information becomes available, leaders can—and should—issue additional WARNOs. By issuing the initial WARNO as quickly as possible, leaders enable their subordinates to begin their own planning and preparation.

C-19. WARNOs follow the five-paragraph OPORD format. (See appendix E.) Normally an initial WARNO issued below battalion level includes—

- The mission or nature of the operation.
- The time and place for issuing the OPORD.
- Units or elements participating in the operation.
- Specific tasks not addressed by unit standing operating procedures (SOPs).
- The timeline for the operation.

MAKE A TENTATIVE PLAN

C-20. Once they have issued the initial WARNO, leaders develop a tentative plan. This step combines the MDMP steps 2 through 6: mission analysis, COA development, COA analysis, COA comparison, and COA approval. At levels below battalion, these steps are less structured than for units with staffs. Often, leaders perform them mentally. They may include their principal subordinates—especially during COA development, analysis, and comparison. However, leaders, not their subordinates, select the COA on which to base the tentative plan.

Mission Analysis

C-21. To frame the tentative plan, leaders perform mission analysis. This mission analysis follows the METT-TC format, continuing the initial assessment performed in TLP step 1. FM 6-0 discusses the factors of METT-TC.

Mission

C-22. Leaders analyze the higher headquarters' WARNO or OPORD to determine how their unit contributes to the higher headquarters' mission. They examine the following information that affects their mission:

- Higher headquarters' mission and commander's intent.
- Higher headquarters' concept of operations.
- Specified, implied, and essential tasks.
- Constraints.

C-23. Leaders determine the mission and commander's intent of their higher and next higher headquarters. When these are unavailable, leaders infer them based on the information they have. When they receive the actual mission and commander's intent, they revise their plan, if necessary.

C-24. Leaders examine their higher headquarters' concept of operations to determine how their unit's mission and tasks contribute to the higher mission's success. They determine details that will affect their operations, such as control measures and execution times.

C-25. From WARNOs and the OPORD, leaders extract the specified and implied tasks assigned to their unit. They determine why each task was assigned to their unit so to understand how it fits within the commander's intent and concept of operations. From the specified and implied tasks, leaders identify essential tasks. These tasks must be completed to accomplish the mission. Failure to complete an essential task results in mission failure.

C-26. Leaders also identify any constraints placed on their unit. Constraints can take the form of a requirement (for example, maintain a reserve of one platoon) or a prohibition on action (for example, no reconnaissance forward of Line Bravo before H-hour).

C-27. The product of this part of the mission analysis is the restated mission. The restated mission is a simple, concise expression of the essential tasks the unit must accomplish and the purpose to be achieved. The mission statement states who (the unit), what (the task), when (either the critical time or on order), where (location), and why (the purpose of the operation). (See appendix B for a discussion of developing the unit's mission statement.)

Enemy

C-28. With the restated mission as the focus, leaders continue the analysis with the enemy. For small-unit operations, leaders need to know about the enemy's composition, disposition, strengths, recent activities, ability to reinforce, and possible COAs. Much of this information comes from higher headquarters. Additional information comes from adjacent units and other leaders. Some information comes from the leader's experience. Leaders determine how the available information applies to their operation. They also determine what they do not know about the enemy but should know. To obtain the necessary information, they identify these intelligence gaps to their higher headquarters or take action (such as sending out reconnaissance patrols).

Terrain and Weather

C-29. This aspect of mission analysis addresses the military aspects of terrain: observation and fields of fire, avenue of approach, key terrain, obstacles, and cover and concealment (known as OAKOC).

C-30. *Observation* is the condition of weather and terrain that permits a force to see the friendly, enemy, and neutral personnel and systems, and key aspects of the environment (FM 6-0). A *field of fire* is the area which a weapon or a group of weapons may cover effectively with fire from a given position (JP 1-02). Observation and fields of fire apply to both enemy and friendly weapons. Leaders consider direct-fire weapons and the ability of observers to mass and adjust indirect fire.

C-31. An *avenue of approach* is an air or ground route of an attacking force of a given size leading to its objective or to key terrain in its path (JP 2-01.3). Avenues of approach include overland, air, and underground avenues. Underground avenues are particularly important in urban operations.

C-32. *Key terrain* is any locality, or area, the seizure or retention of which affords a marked advantage to either combatant (JP 2-01.3). Terrain adjacent to the area of operations (AO) may be key if its control is necessary to accomplish the mission.

C-33. An *obstacle* is any obstruction designed or employed to disrupt, fix, turn, or block the movement of an opposing force, and to impose additional losses in personnel, time, and equipment on the opposing force. Obstacles can exist naturally or can be man-made, or can be a combination of both (JP 3-15). Obstacles include military reinforcing obstacles, such as minefields.

C-34. *Cover* is protection from the effects of fires (FM 6-0). *Concealment* is protection from observation and surveillance (JP 1-02). Terrain that offers cover and concealment limits fields of fire. Leaders consider friendly and enemy perspectives. Although remembered as separate elements, leaders consider the military aspects of terrain together.

C-35. There are five military aspects of weather: visibility, winds, precipitation, cloud cover, and temperature and humidity. (See FM 2-01.3.) The consideration of their effects is an important part of the mission analysis. Leaders review the forecasts and considerations available from Army and Air Force weather forecast models and develop COAs based on the effects of weather on the mission. The analysis considers the effects on Soldiers, equipment, and supporting forces, such as air and artillery support. Leaders identify the aspects of weather that can affect the mission. They focus on factors whose effects they can mitigate. For example, leaders may modify the SOPs for uniforms and carrying loads based on the temperature. Small-unit leaders include instructions on mitigating weather effects in their tentative plan. They check for compliance during preparation, especially during rehearsals.

Troops and Support Available

C-36. Perhaps the most important aspect of mission analysis is determining the combat potential of one's own force. Leaders know the status of their Soldiers' morale, their experience and training, and the strengths and weaknesses of subordinate leaders. They realistically determine all available resources. This includes troops attached to, or in direct support of, the unit. The assessment includes knowing the strength and status of their equipment. It also includes understanding the full array of assets in support of the unit. Leaders know, for example, how much indirect fire will become available, and when it is available, they will know the type. They consider any new limitations based on the level of training or recent fighting.

Time Available

C-37. Leaders not only appreciate how much time is available, they understand the time-space aspects of preparing, moving, fighting, and sustaining. They view their own tasks and enemy actions in relation to time. They know how long it takes under such conditions to prepare for certain tasks (such as orders production, rehearsals, and subordinate element preparations). Most important, leaders monitor the time available. As events occur, they assess their impact on the unit timeline and update previous timelines for their subordinates. Timelines list all events that affect the unit and its subordinate elements.

Civil Considerations

C-38. *Civil considerations* are the influence of manmade infrastructure, civilian institutions, and attitudes and activities of the civilian leaders, populations, and organizations within an AO on the conduct of military operations (FM 6-0). Rarely are military operations conducted in uninhabited areas. Most of the time, units are surrounded by noncombatants. These noncombatants include residents of the AO, local officials, and governmental and nongovernmental organizations. Based on information from higher headquarters and their own knowledge and judgment, leaders identify civil considerations that affect their mission. (See FM 6-0 and FM 3-05.401.) Civil considerations are analyzed in terms of six factors known by the memory aid ASCOPE:

- Areas.
- Structures.
- Capabilities.
- Organizations.
- People.
- Events.

Course of Action Development

C-39. Mission analysis provides information needed to develop COAs. The purpose of COA development is simple: to determine one or more ways to accomplish the mission. At lower echelons, the mission may be a single task. Most missions and tasks can be accomplished in more than one way. However, in a time-constrained environment, leaders may develop only one COA. Normally, they develop two or more. Leaders do not wait for a complete order before beginning COA development. They develop COAs as soon as they have enough information to do so. Usable COAs are suitable, feasible, acceptable, distinguishable, and complete. (See appendix B.) To develop them, leaders focus on the actions the unit takes at the objective and conduct a reverse plan to the starting point.

±Analyze Relative Combat Power

C-40. During COA development, leaders determine whether the unit has enough combat power to defeat the force (or accomplish a task in stability or civil support operations) against which it is arrayed by comparing the combat power of friendly and enemy forces. Leaders seek to determine where, when, and how friendly combat power (the elements of intelligence, movement and maneuver, fires, sustainment, protection, and mission command) can overwhelm the enemy. It is a particularly difficult process if the unit is fighting a dissimilar unit (for example, if the unit is attacking or defending against an enemy mechanized force as opposed to a similarly equipped light infantry force). Below battalion level, relative combat power comparisons are rough and generally rely on professional judgment instead of numerical analysis. When an enemy is not the object of a particular mission or tasks, leaders conduct a troop-to-task analysis to determine if they have enough combat power to accomplish the tasks. For example, a company commander assigned the task "establish civil control in town X" would need to determine if they had enough Soldiers and equipment (to include vehicles and barrier materials) to establish the necessary check points and security stations within the town to control the population in town X.

Generate Options

C-41. During this step, leaders brainstorm different ways to accomplish the mission. They determine the doctrinal requirements for the operation, including the tactical tasks normally assigned to subordinates. Doctrinal requirements give leaders a framework from which to develop COAs.

C-42. Next, leaders identify where and when the unit can mass overwhelming combat power to achieve specific results (with respect to enemy, terrain, time, or civil considerations) that accomplish the mission. Offensive and defensive operations focus on the destructive effects of combat power. Stability operations, on the other hand, emphasize constructive effects. Leaders identify the decisive point or points. Leaders determine what result they must achieve at the decisive points to accomplish the mission. This helps leaders determine the amount of combat power to apply at the decisive point and the required tasks.

C-43. After identifying the tasks, leaders next determine the purpose for each task. There is normally one primary task for each mission. The unit assigned this task is the main effort. The purpose of the other tasks should support the accomplishment of the primary task.

Develop a Concept of Operations

C-44. The concept of operations describes how the leader envisions the operation unfolding from its start to its conclusion or end state. It determines how accomplishing each task leads to executing the next. It identifies the best ways to use available terrain and to employ unit strengths against enemy weaknesses. Fire support considerations make up an important part of the concept of operations. Essential stability tasks are also identified. Leaders develop the graphic control measures necessary to convey and enhance the understanding of the concept of operations, prevent fratricide, and clarify the task and purpose of the main effort.

Assign Responsibilities

C-45. Leaders assign responsibility for each task to a subordinate. Whenever possible, they depend on the existing chain of command. They avoid fracturing unit integrity unless the number of simultaneous tasks exceeds the number of available elements. Different command and support arrangements may be the distinguishing feature among COAs.

Prepare a Course of Action Statement and Sketch

C-46. Leaders base the COA statement on the concept of operations for that COA. The COA statement focuses on all significant actions, from the start of the COA to its finish. Whenever possible, leaders prepare a sketch showing each COA. Another useful technique is to show the time it takes to achieve each movement and task in the COA sketch. Doing this helps subordinate leaders gain an appreciation for how much time will pass as each task of the COA is executed. The COA contains the following information:

- Form of movement or defense to be used.
- Designation of the main effort.
- Tasks and purposes of subordinate units.
- Necessary sustaining operations.
- Desired end state.

C-47. Figure C-4 provides a sample mission statement and course of action statement for an infantry company in the defense.

Mission Statement:	C Co/2-67 IN (L) defends NLT 281700(Z) AUG 2005 to destroy enemy forces from GL 375652 to GL 389650 to GL 394660 to GL 373665 to prevent the envelopment of A Co, the battalion main effort.
COA Statement:	The company defends with two platoons (PLTs) forward and one PLT in depth from PLT battle positions. The northern PLT (2 squads) destroys enemy forces to prevent enemy bypass of the main effort PLT on Hill 657. The southern PLT (3 squads, 2 Javelins) destroys enemy forces to prevent an organized company attack against the Co main effort on Hill 657. The main effort PLT (3 squads, 2 TOWS) retains Hill 657 (vic GL378659) to prevent the envelopment of Co A (BN main effort) from the south. The anti-armor section (1 squad, 4 Javelins) establishes ambush positions at the road junction (vic GL 377653) to destroy enemy recon to deny observation of friendly defensive position and to prevent a concentration of combat power against the main effort PLT. The company mortars establish a mortar firing point vic GL 377664 to suppress enemy forces to protect the main effort platoon.

Figure C-4. Sample mission and COA statements

Analyze Courses of Action (War Game)

C-48. For each COA, leaders think through the operation from start to finish. They compare each COA with the enemy's most probable COA. At the small-unit level, the enemy's most probable COA is what the enemy is most likely to do given what friendly forces are doing at that instant. The leader visualizes a set of actions and reactions. The object is to determine what can go wrong and what decision the leader will likely have to make as a result.

Course of Action Comparison and Selection

C-49. Leaders compare COAs by weighing the advantages, disadvantages, strengths, and weaknesses of each, as noted during the war game. They decide which COA to execute based on this comparison and on their professional judgment. They take into account—
- Mission accomplishment.
- Time available to execute the operation.
- Risks.
- Results from unit reconnaissance.
- Subordinate unit tasks and purposes.
- Casualties incurred.
- Posturing of the force for future operations.

INITIATE MOVEMENT

C-50. Leaders conduct any movement directed by higher headquarters or deemed necessary to continue mission preparation or position the unit for execution. They do this as soon as they have enough information to do so or the unit is required to move to position itself for a task. This is also essential when time is short. Movements may be to an assembly area, a battle position, a new AO, or an attack position. They may include movement of reconnaissance elements, guides, or quartering parties.

CONDUCT RECONNAISSANCE

C-51. Whenever time and circumstances allow, or as directed by higher headquarters, leaders personally observe the AO for the mission prior to execution. No amount of intelligence preparation of the battlefield can substitute for firsthand assessment of METT-TC from within the AO. Unfortunately, many factors can keep leaders from performing a personal reconnaissance. The minimum action necessary is a thorough map reconnaissance supplemented by imagery and intelligence products. As directed, subordinates or other elements (such as scouts) may perform the reconnaissance for the leader while the leader completes other TLP steps.

C-52. ±Leaders use results of the war game to identify information requirements. Reconnaissance operations seek to confirm or deny information that supports the tentative plan. They focus first on information gaps identified during mission analysis. Leaders ensure their leader's reconnaissance complements the higher headquarters' ISR plan. The unit may conduct additional reconnaissance operations as the situation allows. This step may also precede making a tentative plan if commanders lack enough information to begin planning. Reconnaissance may be the only way to develop the information required for planning.

±COMPLETE THE PLAN

C-53. During this step, leaders incorporate the results of reconnaissance into their selected COA to complete the plan or order. This includes preparing overlays, refining the indirect fire target list, coordinating sustainment with signal requirements, and updating the tentative plan because of the reconnaissance. At lower levels, this step may entail only confirming or updating information contained in the tentative plan. If time allows, leaders make final coordination with adjacent units and higher headquarters before issuing the order.

ISSUE THE ORDER

C-54. Small-unit orders are normally issued verbally and supplemented by graphics and other control measures. The order follows the standard five-paragraph OPORD format. (See appendix E.) Typically, leaders below company level do not issue a commander's intent. They reiterate the intent of their higher and next higher commanders.

C-55. The ideal location for issuing the order is a point in the AO with a view of the objective and other aspects of the terrain. The leader may perform a leader's reconnaissance, complete the order, and then summon subordinates to a specified location to receive it. Sometimes security or other constraints make it infeasible to issue the order on the terrain. Then leaders use a sand table, detailed sketch, maps, and other products to depict the AO and situation.

SUPERVISE AND REFINE

C-56. Throughout TLP, leaders monitor mission preparations, refine the plan, coordinate with adjacent units, and supervise and assess preparations. Normally, unit SOPs state individual responsibilities and the sequence of preparation activities. To ensure the unit is ready for the mission, leaders supervise subordinates and inspect their personnel and equipment.

C-57. A crucial component of preparation is the rehearsal. Rehearsals allow leaders to assess their subordinates' preparations. They may identify areas that require more supervision. Leaders conduct rehearsals to—

- Practice essential tasks.
- Identify weaknesses or problems in the plan.
- Coordinate subordinate element actions.
- Improve Soldier understanding of the concept of operations.
- Foster confidence among Soldiers.

C-58. Company and smaller sized units use four types of rehearsals discussed in appendix I:

- Backbrief.
- Combined arms rehearsal.
- Support rehearsal.
- Battle drill or SOP rehearsal.

Appendix D

Guidelines for Commander's Planning Guidance

This appendix provides guidelines to assist commanders in developing planning guidance within the military decisionmaking process (MDMP). (Appendix B defines and describes the MDMP.) The content of the planning guidance varies depending on the situation and the echelon. This appendix does not account for all possible situations. It is a generic list of information commanders consider as they develop planning guidance.

PLANNING GUIDANCE WITHIN THE MILITARY DECISIONMAKING PROCESS

D-1. Commanders develop planning guidance based on their understanding and visualization of the operation. Planning guidance may be broad or detailed, as circumstances require. Combined with the restated mission and commander's intent, planning guidance conveys the essence of the commander's visualization. Commanders use their experience and judgment to add depth and clarity to their planning guidance. Effective planning guidance gives the staff a broad outline of the commander's visualization while still allowing them latitude to explore different options.

D-2. Commanders issue planning guidance when conducting design (see chapter 3) and at specific points during the MDMP:

- Upon receipt of or anticipation of a mission (initial planning guidance).
- Following mission analysis (planning guidance for course of action [COA] development).
- Following COA development (revised planning guidance for COA improvements).
- COA approval (revised planning guidance to complete the plan).

D-3. ±Commanders use elements of operational art appropriate to their situation and echelon to help them formulate their guidance. See FM 3-0 for a full discussion on each element of operational art. The elements of operational art are—

- End state and conditions.
- Centers of gravity.
- Direct or indirect approach.
- Decisive points.
- Lines of operations and lines of effort.
- Operational reach.
- Tempo.
- Simultaneity and depth.
- Phasing and transitions.
- Culmination.
- Risk.

D-4. The level of detail in the planning guidance depends on situational understanding, time available, staff proficiency, and the latitude the next higher commander allows. Broad and general guidance allows a proficient staff to develop flexible and effective options. Time-constrained conditions require more specific guidance. The more detailed the planning guidance, the more quickly the staff can complete the plan. However, detailed guidance incurs the risk of overlooking or insufficiently examining things that might affect mission execution.

PLANNING GUIDANCE BY WARFIGHTING FUNCTIONS

D-5. The lists in paragraphs D-7 through D-12 are not intended to meet the needs of all situations. Commanders are neither required nor desired to address every item. Planning guidance is tailored to meet specific needs based on the situation. Commanders issue guidance on only those items appropriate to a particular mission.

D-6. As commanders formulate their planning guidance, they may want to address assumptions, specifically, those that their staff prepares and those that higher headquarters provides. Considerable effort should be made to validate those assumptions. Commanders should also be thinking through transitions—those that their formations will create and those that will be imposed by others outside the command. Finally, commanders may wish to give guidance regarding their unit's role in enabling other organizations and activities (joint, interagency, intergovernmental, and multinational) as appropriate.

INTELLIGENCE

D-7. For the intelligence warfighting function, planning guidance may include—
- Guidance on intelligence, surveillance, and reconnaissance.
- Gaps in knowledge required to understand the situation.
- Enemy COAs to consider during COA development and COA analysis. At a minimum, these may be the enemy's most probable COA, most dangerous COA, or a combination of the two. These COAs may include the—
  - Enemy commander's mission.
  - Enemy commander's concept of operations.
  - Enemy's critical decision points and vulnerabilities.
- Priority intelligence requirements.
- High-value targets.
- Desired enemy perception of friendly forces.
- Intelligence focus for each phase of the operation.
- Specific terrain (including identification of key terrain) and weather factors.
- Identification of key aspects of the environment, including civil considerations.
- Guidance on counterintelligence.
- Request for intelligence support from nonorganic resources and special collection requests.

MOVEMENT AND MANEUVER

D-8. For movement and maneuver, planning guidance may include—
- Initial commander's intent.
- COA development guidance consisting of—
  - Number of friendly COAs to consider.
  - COAs to consider or not to consider.
  - Critical events.
  - Elements of operational art.
  - Decisive, shaping, and sustaining operations.
  - Task organization.
  - Task and purpose of subordinate units.
  - Forms of maneuver.
  - Reserve guidance (composition, mission, priorities, and control measures).
  - Security and counterreconnaissance guidance.
  - Friendly decision points.
  - Possible branches and sequels.

- Intelligence, surveillance, and reconnaissance integration and priorities.
- Military deception.
- Risk—
  - To friendly forces.
  - Of collateral damage or civilian casualties.
  - Of any condition affecting mission accomplishment or achievement of desired end state.

FIRES

D-9. For fires, planning guidance may include—
- Synchronization and focus of fires with maneuver.
- Priority of fires.
- High-payoff targets to include—
  - Methods of engagement.
  - Desired effects.
- An observer plan.
- Requirements, restrictions, and priorities for special munitions.
- Task and purpose of fires.
- Counterfire.
- Target acquisition radar zones consisting of—
  - Critical friendly zones.
  - Call for fire zones.
  - Artillery target intelligence zones.
  - Sensor zones.
- Suppression of enemy air defenses.
- Fire support coordination measures.
- Attack guidance.
- A no-strike list, including cultural, religious, historical, and high-density civilian areas.
- Restricted target list.

PROTECTION

D-10. For protection, planning guidance may include—
- Protection priorities.
- Work priorities for survivability assets.
- Guidance on air and missile defense positioning.
- Specific terrain and weather factors.
- Intelligence focus and limitations for security efforts.
- Areas or events where risk is acceptable.
- Protected targets and areas.
- Vehicle and equipment safety or security constraints.
- Guidance on environmental considerations.
- Guidance on unexploded explosive ordnance.
- Operational security risk tolerance.
- Rules of engagement, standing rules for the use of force, and rules of interaction.
- Guidance on escalation of force and nonlethal weapons.

SUSTAINMENT

D-11. For sustainment, planning guidance may include—

- Priorities in terms of tactical sustainment functions (manning, fueling, fixing, arming, and moving the force, and sustaining Soldiers and their systems).
- Army health system support.
- Anticipated requirements and prestockage of class III, IV, and V supplies.
- Controlled supply rates.
- Guidance on construction and provision of facilities and installations.
- Guidance on the movement of detainees and the sustainment of internment and resettlement activities.

±MISSION COMMAND

D-12. For mission command, planning guidance may include—

- Friendly forces information requirements.
- Rules of engagement.
- Position of the command post.
- Position of the commander.
- Liaison officer guidance.
- Timeline guidance, including timeline for planning and the operational timeline.
- Type of order and rehearsal.
- Specific communications guidance.
- Succession of command.
- Initial themes and messages.
- Civil affairs operations that consist of—
  - Establishing a civil-military operations center.
  - Establishing liaison with host-nation, interagency, and governmental and nongovernmental organizations.
  - Providing resources for humanitarian assistance.
  - Prioritizing allocated funds dedicated to civil affairs operations.
  - Building a relationship between the command and civilian population.

Appendix E

Army Operation Plan and Order Format

This appendix provides instructions for preparing plans and orders for Army units. For guidance on preparing joint operation plans and orders, refer to JP 5-0.

±CHARACTERISTICS

E-1. Commanders direct operations and communicate their visualization, commander's intent, and decisions through plans and orders. Effective plans synchronize subordinate activities in time, space, and purpose to achieve objectives and accomplish missions. Plans and orders not only direct subordinate units but provide information to facilitate coordination among organizations outside the command. Effective plans and orders account for those military and civilian organizations involved in the operation.

E-2. The amount of detail provided in a plan or order depends on several factors, including the cohesion and experience of subordinate units and complexity of the operation. Effective plans and orders encourage subordinate's initiative by providing the what and why of tasks to subordinate units, and leave the how to perform the tasks to subordinates. (Paragraphs **Error! Reference source not found.** through **Error! Reference source not found.** discuss mission orders in detail.) To maintain clarity and simplicity, the base plan or order is kept as short and concise as possible. Detailed information and instructions are addressed in attachments as required.

E-3. Good operation plans (OPLANs) and operation orders (OPORDs)—
- Possess simplicity.
- Possess authoritative expression.
- Possess positive expression.
- Avoid qualified directives.
- Possess brevity.
- Possess clarity.
- Contain assumptions.
- Incorporate flexibility.
- Exercise timeliness.

E-4. Plans and orders are simple and direct to reduce misunderstanding and confusion. Simple plans executed on time are better than detailed plans executed late. Commanders at all echelons weigh potential benefits of a complex concept of operations against the risk that subordinates will fail to understand it. Multinational operations mandate simplicity due to the differences in language, doctrine, and culture.

E-5. Authoritative expression through the commander's intent is reflected in plans and orders. As such, their language is direct. Effective plans and orders unmistakably state what the commander wants the unit and its subordinate units to do and why.

E-6. Instructions in plans and orders are stated in the affirmative. For example, "Combat trains will remain in the assembly area" instead of "The combat trains will not accompany the unit."

E-7. Plans and orders avoid meaningless expressions, such as "as soon as possible (ASAP)." Indecisive, vague, and ambiguous language leads to uncertainty and lack of confidence.

E-8. Effective plans and orders are brief, clear, and concise. They use short words, sentences, and paragraphs. Use acronyms unless clarity is hindered. Do not include material covered in standard operating procedures (SOPs). Refer to those SOPs instead.

E-9. Plans and orders possess clarity. They use doctrinally correct terms and symbols, avoid jargon, and eliminate every opportunity for misunderstanding the commander's exact, intended meaning.

E-10. Effective plans and orders contain assumptions. This helps subordinates and others to better understand the logic behind a plan or order and facilitates the preparation of branches and sequels.

E-11. Plans and orders incorporate flexibility. They leave room to adapt and make adjustments to counter unexpected challenges and seize opportunities. Effective plans and orders identify decision points and proposed options at those decision points to build flexibility.

E-12. Plans and orders exercise timeliness. Plans and orders sent to subordinates in time allow subordinates to collaborate, plan, and prepare their own actions.

TYPES OF PLANS

E-13. ±A plan is a design for a future or anticipated operation. Plans come in many forms and vary in scope, complexity, and length of planning horizons. There are several types of plans:
- Campaign plan.
- Operation plan.
- Supporting plan.
- Concept plan.
- Branch.
- Sequel.

E-14. A campaign plan is a joint operation plan aimed at achieving strategic or operational objectives within a given time and space. Developing and issuing a campaign plan is appropriate when the contemplated simultaneous or sequential military operations exceed the scope of single major operation. Only joint force commanders develop campaign plans.

E-15. An *operation plan* is any plan for the conduct of military operations prepared in response to actual and potential contingencies (JP 5-0). An OPLAN may address an extended period connecting a series of objectives and operations, or it may be developed for a single part or phase of a long-term operation. An OPLAN becomes an OPORD when the commander sets an execution time or designates an event that triggers the operation.

E-16. A *supporting plan* is an operation plan prepared by a supporting commander, a subordinate commander, or an agency to satisfy the requests or requirements of the supported commander's plan (JP 5-0). For example, the ARFOR commander develops a supporting plan as to how Army forces will support the joint force commander's campaign plan or OPLAN.

E-17. A concept plan is an OPLAN in an abbreviated format that requires considerable expansion or alteration to convert it into a complete operation plan or operation order. Often branches and sequels are written in the form of concept plans. (See chapter 2 for a discussion on branches and sequels.) As time and the potential allow for executing a particular branch or sequel, these concept plans are developed in detail into OPLANs.

TYPES OF ORDERS

E-18. An *order* is a communication, written, oral, or by signal, which conveys instructions from a superior to a subordinate (JP 1-02). (See figures E-2 through E-5 for OPORD formats.) There are three types of orders:
- Operation order.
- Fragmentary order (FRAGO).
- Warning order (WARNO).

E-19. An *operation order* is a directive issued by a commander to subordinate commanders for the purpose of effecting the coordinated execution of an operation (JP 5-0). Commanders issue OPORDs to direct the execution of long-term operations as well as the execution of discrete short-term operations within the framework of a long-range OPORD.

E-20. A *fragmentary order* is an abbreviated form of an operation order issued as needed after an operation order to change or modify that order or to execute a branch or sequel to that order (JP 5-0). FRAGOs include all five OPORD paragraph headings and differ from OPORDs only in the degree of detail provided. After each paragraph heading, it provides either new information or states "no change." This ensures that recipients know they have received the entire FRAGO. FRAGOs provide brief and specific instructions. They address only those parts of the original OPORD that have changed. The higher headquarters issues a new OPORD when the situation changes completely or when many changes make the current order ineffective.

E-21. FRAGOs may be issued as overlay orders. An overlay order is a technique used to issue an order that has abbreviated instructions written on an overlay. Commanders may issue an overlay order when planning and preparation time is severely constrained and they must get the order to subordinate commanders as soon as possible. Commanders verbally issue the order using the standard five-paragraph outline. When giving a verbal briefing, the briefer discusses only the items in the order that have changed from an original order and focuses attention to key events and tasks, the main effort, priority of support, and control measures and graphics. The overlay order accompanies this verbal briefing and may be presented by any suitable graphic presentation. (See figure E-6 on page E-23 for a sample overlay order.)

E-22. A *warning order* is a preliminary notice of an order or action that is to follow (JP 3-33). WARNOs help subordinate units and staffs prepare for new missions by describing the situation, providing initial planning guidance, and directing preparation activities. WARNOs increase subordinates' planning time, provide details of the impending operation, and list events that accompany preparation and execution. The amount of detail a WARNO includes depends on the information and time available when it is issued and the information subordinate commanders need for planning and preparation. Unless specifically stated, a WARNO does not authorize execution other than planning and the words warning order precede the message text. (See figure E-4 on page E-20 for a WARNO formats.)

E-23. Commanders issue orders verbally or in writing. The five-paragraph format (situation, mission, execution, sustainment, and command and signal) remains the standard for issuing orders. The technique used to issue orders is at the discretion of the commander; each method is time and situation dependent.

VERBAL ORDERS

E-24. Commanders use verbal orders when operating in an extremely time-constrained environment. These orders offer the advantage of being passed quickly but risk important information being overlooked or misunderstood. Verbal orders are usually followed by written FRAGOs.

WRITTEN ORDERS

E-25. Commanders issue written plans and orders that contain both text and graphics. Graphics convey information and instructions through military symbols. (See FM 1-02.) They complement the written portion of a plan or an order and promote clarity, accuracy, and brevity. Written orders are often generated and disseminated by electronic means to shorten the time needed to gather and brief the orders group. Orders are easily edited and modified when electronically produced. The same order can be sent to multiple recipients simultaneously. Using computer programs to develop and disseminate precise corresponding graphics adds to the efficiency and clarity of the orders process.

E-26. Electronic editing makes importing text and graphics into orders very easy. Unfortunately, such ease can result in orders becoming unnecessarily large without added operational value. Commanders need to ensure that orders contain only that information needed to facilitate effective execution. Orders should not be a regurgitation of unit SOPs. They should be clear, concise, and relevant to the mission.

ADMINISTRATIVE INSTRUCTIONS

E-27. The following information pertains to administrative instructions for preparing all plans and orders. Unless otherwise stated, the term order refers to both plans and orders. The term base order refers to the main body of a plan or order without annexes.

E-28. Regardless of echelon, all orders adhere to the same guidance. Show all paragraph headings on written orders. A paragraph heading with no text will state "None" or "See [attachment type] [attachment letter or number]." In this context, attachment is a collective term for annex, appendix, tab, and exhibit.

E-29. The base order and all attachments follow a specific template for the paragraph layout. Every order follows the five-paragraph format. Title case, underline, and bold the titles of these five paragraphs—Situation, Mission, Execution, Sustainment, and Command and Signal. The paragraph title begins with a capital letter and is bold and underlined. For example, "situation" is **Situation**. All subparagraphs and subtitles begin with capital letters and are underlined. For example, "concept of operations" is Concept of Operations.

E-30. When a paragraph is subdivided, it must have at least two subdivisions. The tabs are 0.25 inches and the space is double between paragraphs. Subsequent lines of text for each paragraph may be flush left or equally indented at the option of the chief of staff or executive officer, as long as consistency is maintained throughout the order. (See figure E-1.)

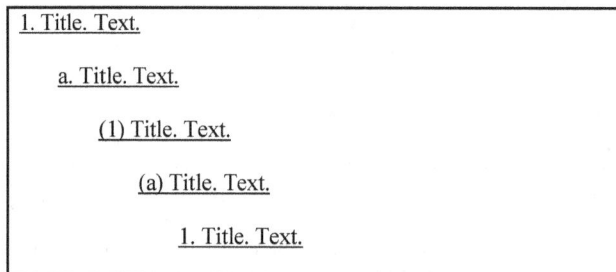

1. Title. Text.

    a. Title. Text.

       (1) Title. Text.

          (a) Title. Text.

             1. Title. Text.

Figure E-1. Paragraph layout for plans and orders

ACRONYMS AND ABBREVIATIONS

E-31. Use acronyms and abbreviations to save time and space if they do not cause confusion. Do not sacrifice clarity for brevity. Keep acronyms and abbreviations consistent throughout the order and its attachments. Do not use acronyms and abbreviations not found in FM 1-02 or JP 1-02. Spell out the entire acronym or abbreviation and place the acronym or abbreviation between parentheses at first use in the document. After this first use, use the acronym or abbreviation throughout the document.

PLACE AND DIRECTION DESIGNATIONS

E-32. Describe locations or points on the ground by—
- Providing the map datum used throughout the order.
- Referring to military grid reference system (MGRS) coordinates.
- Referring to longitude and latitude if available maps do not have the MGRS.

E-33. ±Designate directions in one of two ways:
- By using two locations or places. For example, direction ECKENTAL 18PV6690–PEGNITZ 18PV6851.
- As a magnetic, grid, or true bearing, stating the unit of measure. For example, 85 degrees (magnetic).

E-34. When first mentioning a place or feature on a map, print the name in capital letters exactly as spelled on the map and show its complete grid coordinates (grid zone designator, 100-kilometer grid square, and four-, six-, eight-, or ten-digit grid coordinates) in parentheses after it. When first using a control measure (such as a contact point), print the name or designation of the point followed by its complete grid coordinates in parentheses. Thereafter, repeat the coordinates only for clarity; use names, planning names, or codes.

E-35. Describe areas by naming the northernmost (12 o'clock) point first and the remaining points in clockwise order. Describe positions from left to right and from front to rear, facing the enemy. To avoid confusion, identify flanks by compass points, rather than right or left of the friendly force.

E-36. If the possibility of confusion exists when describing a route, add compass points for clarity. For example, "The route is northwest along the road LAPRAIRIE–DELSON." If a particular route already has a planning name, such as main supply route SPARTAN, refer to the route using only that designator.

E-37. Designate trails, roads, and railroads by the names of places along them or with grid coordinates. Precede place names with trail, road, or railroad. For example, "road GRANT–CODY." Designate the route for a movement by listing a sequence of grids from the start point to the release point. Otherwise, list the sequence of points from left to right or front to rear, facing the enemy.

E-38. Identify riverbanks as north, south, east, or west. In gap-crossing operations, identify riverbanks as either near or far.

E-39. Describe boundaries and phase lines by terrain features easily distinguishable from the ground or air or on a map. When designating boundaries between units, state which unit has responsibility and authority for the place, feature, or location to which the description refers. State each location along a boundary as either inclusive or exclusive to a unit. For example, "1st Brigade, exclusive crossroad 18PV621352." List boundaries and phase lines from left to right or front to rear, facing the enemy.

NAMING CONVENTIONS

E-40. Unit SOPs normally designate naming conventions for graphics. Otherwise, planners select them. For clarity, avoid multiword names, such as "Junction City." Simple names are better than complex ones. To ensure operations security, avoid assigning names that could reveal unit identities, such as the commander's name or the unit's home station. Do not name sequential phase lines and objectives in alphabetical order. For memory aids, use sets of names designated by the type of control measure or subordinate unit. For example, the division might use colors for objective names and minerals for phase line names.

±CLASSIFICATION MARKINGS

E-41. AR 380-5 contains a detailed description of marking, transmitting procedures, and other classification instructions. Each page and portions of the text on that page will be marked with the appropriate abbreviation ("TS" for TOP SECRET, "S" for SECRET, "C" for CONFIDENTIAL or "U for UNCLASSIFIED). Place classification markings at the top and bottom of each page. All paragraphs must have the appropriate classification marking immediately following the alphanumeric designation of the paragraph (preceding the first word if the paragraph is not numbered). The abbreviation "FOUO" will be used in place of "U" when a portion is UNCLASSIFIED but contains "For Official Use Only" information. AR 25-55 contains the definition and policy application of FOUO markings.

EXPRESSING UNNAMED DATES AND HOURS

E-42. Use specific letters to designate unnamed dates and times in plans and orders. (These definitions come from JP 1-02 unless noted otherwise.) See table E-1 on page E-4.

E-43. C-, D-, and M-days end at 2400 hours, Universal Time (ZULU time). They are assumed to be 24-hours long for planning. Plans and orders state the letters used and their meanings. If a plan mentions more than one event, refer to the secondary event in terms of the time of the primary event. Refer to days preceding or following C-, D-, or M-day by using a plus or minus sign and an Arabic number after the letter. For example, D − 3 is three days before D-day; D + 7 is seven days after D-day. When using a time element other than days, spell it out. For example, D + 3 months.

E-44. Refer to hours preceding or following (H- or L-hour) by a plus or minus sign and an Arabic number after the letter. For example, H − 3 is three hours before H-hour; H + 7 is seven hours after H-hour. When using a time element other than hours, spell it out. For example, H + 30 minutes.

E-45. Where it is necessary to identify a particular operation or exercise, place a nickname or code words before the letter, such as BALD EAGLE (D-day) or ANVIL EXPRESS (M-day).

±Table E-1. Designated letters for dates and times

Term	Definition
C-day	The unnamed day on which a deployment operation commences or is to commence. The deployment may be movement of troops, cargo, weapon systems, or a combination of these elements using any or all types of transport. The letter "C" will be the only one used to denote the above. The highest command or headquarters responsible for coordinating the planning will specify the exact meaning of C-day within the aforementioned definition. The command or headquarters directly responsible for the execution of the operation, if other than the one coordinating the planning, will do so in light of the meaning specified by the highest command or headquarters coordinating the planning.
D-day	The unnamed day on which a particular operation commences or is to commence. (JP 3-02)
F-hour	The effective time of announcement by the Secretary of Defense to the Military Departments of a decision to mobilize Reserve units.
H-hour	The specific hour on D-day at which a particular operation commences.
H-hour (amphibious operations)	For amphibious operations, the time the first assault elements are scheduled to touch down on the beach, or a landing zone, and in some cases the commencement of countermine breaching operations. (JP 3-02)
L-hour	The specific hour on C-day at which a deployment operation commences or is to commence.
L-hour (amphibious operations)	In amphibious operations, the time at which the first helicopter of the helicopter-borne assault wave touches down in the landing zone. (JP 3-02)
M-day	The term used to designate the unnamed day on which full mobilization commences or is due to commence.
N-day	The unnamed day an active duty unit is notified for deployment or redeployment.
P-hour (airborne operations)	In airborne operations, the specific hour on D-day at which a parachute assault commences with the exit of the first Soldier from an aircraft over a designated drop zone. (FM 5-0)
R-day	Redeployment day. The day on which redeployment of major combat, combat support, and combat service support forces begins in an operation.
S-day	The day the President authorizes Selective Reserve callup (not more than 200,000).
T-day	The effective day coincident with Presidential declaration of national emergency and authorization of partial mobilization (not more than 1,000,000 personnel exclusive of the 200,000 callup).
W-day	Declared by the President, W-day is associated with an adversary decision to prepare for war (unambiguous strategic warning). (JP 3-02.1)

EXPRESSING TIME

E-46. The effective time for implementing the plan or order is the same as the date-time group of the order. Express the date and time as a six-digit date-time group. The first two digits indicate the day of the month; the last four digits indicate the time. The letter at the end of the time indicates the time zone. Add the month or the month and year to the date-time group when necessary to avoid confusion. For example, a complete date-time group appears as 060140Z August 20XX.

E-47. If the effective time of any portion of the order differs from that of the order, identify those portions at the beginning of the coordinating instructions (in paragraph 3). For example, "Effective only for planning on receipt" or "Task organization effective 261300Z May 20XX."

E-48. Express all times in a plan or order in terms of one time zone, for example ZULU (Z) or LOCAL. (*Note:* Do not abbreviate local time as [L]. The abbreviation for the LIMA time is L.) Include the appropriate time zone indicator in the heading data and mission statement. For example, the time zone indicator for Central Standard Time in the continental United States is SIERRA. When daylight savings time is in effect, the time zone indicator for Central Standard Time is ROMEO. The relationship of local time to ZULU time, not the geographic location, determines the time zone indicator to use.

E-49. Express dates in the sequence day, month, and year (6 August 20XX). When using inclusive dates, express them by stating both dates separated by an en dash (6–9 August 20XX or 6 August–6 September 20XX). Express times in the 24-hour clock system by means of four-digit Arabic numbers. Include the time zone indicator.

IDENTIFYING PAGES

E-50. Identify pages following the first page of plans and orders with a short title identification heading. Include the number (or letter) designation of the plan or order and the issuing headquarters. For example, OPLAN 09-15—23d AD (base plan identification) or Annex B (Intelligence) to OPLAN 09-15—23d AD (annex identification).

NUMBERING PAGES

E-51. Use the following convention to indicate page numbers:
- Number the pages of the base order and each attachment separately beginning on the first page of each attachment. Use a combination of alphanumeric designations to identify each attachment.
- Use Arabic numbers only to indicate page numbers. Place page numbers after the alphanumeric designation that identifies the attachment. (Use Arabic numbers without any proceeding alphanumeric designation for base order page numbers.) For example, the designation of the third page to Annex C is C-3. Assign each attachment either a letter or Arabic number that corresponds to the letter or number in the attachment's short title. Assign letters to annexes, Arabic numbers to appendixes, letters to tabs, and Arabic numbers to exhibit. For example, the designation of the third page to Appendix 5 to Annex C is C-5-3.
- Separate elements of the alphanumeric designation with hyphens. For example, the designation of the third page of exhibit 2 to Tab B to Appendix 5 to Annex C is C-5-B-2-3.

ATTACHMENTS (ANNEXES, APPENDIXES, TABS, AND EXHIBITS)

E-52. Attachments (annexes, appendixes, tabs, and exhibits) are an information management tool. They simplify orders by providing a structure for organizing information. The staff member with responsibility for the functional area addressed in the attachment prepares it.

E-53. Attachments are part of an order. Using them increases the base order's clarity and usefulness by keeping it short. Attachments include information (such as sustainment), administrative support details, and instructions that expand upon the base order.

E-54. The number and type of attachments depend on the commander, level of command, and complexity or needs of the particular operation. Minimizing the number of attachments keeps the order consistent with completeness and clarity. If the information relating to an attachment's subject is brief, place that information in the base order, and omit the attachment. Avoid creating attachments below the level of exhibit.

E-55. List attachments under an appropriate heading at the end of the document they expand. For example, list annexes at the end of the base order, appendixes at the end of annexes, and so forth. Paragraph E-57 shows the required sequence of attachments.

E-56. When an attachment required by doctrine or an SOP is unnecessary, indicate this by stating, "[Type of attachment and its alphanumeric identifier] not used." For example, "Annex R not used."

E-57. Refer to attachments by letter or number and title. Use the following convention:

- **Annexes**. Designate annexes with capital letters. For example, Annex D (Fires) to OPORD 09-06—1 ID.
- **Appendixes**. Designate appendixes with Arabic numbers. For example, Appendix 1 (Intelligence Estimate) to Annex B (Intelligence) to OPORD 09-06—1 ID.
- **Tabs**. Designate tabs with capital letters. For example, Tab B (Target Synchronization Matrix) to Appendix 3 (Targeting) to Annex D (Fires) to OPORD 09-06—1 ID.
- **Exhibits**. Designate exhibits with Arabic numbers; for example, Exhibit 1 (Traffic Circulation and Control) to Tab C (Transportation) to Appendix 1 (Logistics) to Annex F (Sustainment) to OPORD 09-06—1 ID.

E-58. If an attachment has wider distribution than the base order or is issued separately, the attachment requires a complete heading and acknowledgment instructions. When attachments are distributed with the base order, these elements are not required.

EXAMPLES AND PROCEDURES FOR CREATING PLANS, ORDERS, AND ANNEXES

E-59. Some attachments do not follow the five-paragraph format. Attachments that are specified as a matrix, table, overlay, or list do not adhere to the five paragraph format. In addition, Annex A (Task Organization), Annex R (Reports), Annex Z (Distribution), and Appendix 1 (Design Concept) to Annex C (Operations) do not follow the five-paragraph format due to their content requirements.

[CLASSIFICATION]

Place the classification at the top and bottom of every page of the OPLAN/OPORD. Place the classification marking (TS), (S), (C), or (U) at the front of each paragraph and subparagraph in parentheses. Refer to AR 380-5 for classification and release marking instructions.

**Copy ## of ## copies
Issuing headquarters
Place of issue
Date-time group of signature
Message reference number**

The first line of the heading is the copy number assigned by the issuing headquarters. A log is maintained of specific copies issued to addressees. The second line is the official designation of the issuing headquarters (for example, 1st Infantry Division). The third line is the place of issue. It may be a code name, postal designation, or geographic location. The fourth line is the date or date-time group that the plan or order was signed or issued and becomes effective unless specified otherwise in the coordinating instructions. The fifth line is a headquarters internal control number assigned to all plans and orders in accordance with unit standing operating procedures (SOPs).

OPERATION PLAN/ORDER [number] [(code name)] [(classification of title)]

Number plans and orders consecutively by calendar year. Include code name, if any.

(U) References: *List documents essential to understanding the OPLAN/OPORD. List references concerning a specific function in the appropriate attachments.*

(a) List maps and charts first. Map entries include series number, country, sheet names, or numbers, edition, and scale.

(b) List other references in subparagraphs labeled as shown.

(U) Time Zone Used Throughout the OPLAN/OPORD: *State the time zone used in the area of operations during execution. When the OPLAN/OPORD applies to units in different time zones, use Greenwich Mean (ZULU) Time.*

(U) Task Organization: *Describe the organization of forces available to the issuing headquarters and their command and support relationships. Refer to Annex A (Task Organization) if long or complicated.*

1. (U) **Situation**. *The situation paragraph describes the conditions of the operational environment that impact operations in the following subparagraphs:*

a. (U) Area of Interest. *Describe the area of interest. Refer to Annex B (Intelligence) as required.*

b. (U) Area of Operations. *Describe the area of operations (AO). Refer to the appropriate map by its subparagraph under references, for example, "Map, reference (b)." Refer to the Appendix 2 (Operation Overlay) to Annex C (Operations).*

(1) (U) Terrain. *Describe the aspects of terrain that impact operations. Refer to Annex B (Intelligence) as required.*

(2) (U) Weather. *Describe the aspects of weather that impact operations. Refer to Annex B (Intelligence) as required.*

[page number]

[CLASSIFICATION]

Figure E-2. Annotated Army OPLAN/OPORD format

[CLASSIFICATION]

OPLAN/OPORD [number] [(code name)]—[issuing headquarters] [(classification of title)]

Place the classification and title of the OPLAN/OPORD and the issuing headquarters at the top of the second and any subsequent pages of the base plan or order.

    c. (U) <u>Enemy Forces</u>. *Identify enemy forces and appraise their general capabilities. Describe the enemy's disposition, location, strength, and probable courses of action. Identify known or potential terrorist threats and adversaries within the AO. Refer to Annex B (Intelligence) as required.*

    d. (U) <u>Friendly Forces</u>. *Briefly identify the missions of friendly forces and the objectives, goals, and missions of civilian organizations that impact the issuing headquarters in following subparagraphs:*

    (1) (U) <u>Higher Headquarters' Mission and Intent</u>. *Identify and state the mission and commander's intent for headquarters two levels up and one level up from the issuing headquarters.*

    (a) (U) [<u>Higher Headquarters Two Levels Up</u>]. *Identify the higher headquarters two levels up the paragraph heading (for example,* Joint Task Force-18*)*.

    1 (U) <u>Mission</u>.

    2 (U) <u>Commander's Intent</u>.

    (b) (U) [<u>Higher Headquarters</u>]. *Identify the higher headquarters one level up in the paragraph heading (for example,* 1st (U.S.) Armored Division*)*.

    1 (U) <u>Mission</u>.

    2 (U) <u>Commander's Intent</u>.

    (2) (U) <u>Missions of Adjacent Units</u>. *Identify and state the missions of adjacent units and other units whose actions have a significant impact on the issuing headquarters.*

    e. (U) <u>Interagency, Intergovernmental, and Nongovernmental Organizations</u>. *Identify and state the objective or goals and primary tasks of those non-Department of Defense organizations that have a significant role within the AO. Refer to Annex V (Interagency Coordination) as required.*

    f. (U) <u>Civil Considerations</u>. *Describe the critical aspects of the civil situation that impact operations. Refer to Appendix 1 (Intelligence Estimate) to Annex B (Intelligence) as required.*

    g. (U) <u>Attachments and Detachments</u>. *List units attached to or detached from the issuing headquarters. State when each attachment or detachment is effective (for example, on order, on commitment of the reserve) if different from the effective time of the OPLAN/OPORD. Do not repeat information already listed in Annex A (Task Organization).*

    h. (U) <u>Assumptions</u>. *List assumptions used in the development of the OPLAN/OPORD.*

2. (U) <u>Mission</u>. *State the unit's mission—a short description of the who, what (task), when, where, and why (purpose) that clearly indicates the action to be taken and the reason for doing so.*

3. (U) <u>Execution</u>. *Describe how the commander intends to accomplish the mission in terms of the commander's intent, an overarching concept of operations, schemes of employment for each warfighting function, assessment, specified tasks to subordinate units, and key coordinating instructions in the subparagraphs below.*

[page number]

[CLASSIFICATION]

Figure E-2. Annotated Army OPLAN/OPORD format (continued)

[CLASSIFICATION]

OPLAN/OPORD [number] [(code name)]—[issuing headquarters] [(classification of title)]

a. (U) <u>Commander's Intent</u>. *Commanders develop their intent statement personally. The commander's intent is a clear, concise statement of what the force must do and the conditions the force must establish with respect to the enemy, terrain, and civil considerations that represent the desired end state. It succinctly describes what constitutes the success of an operation and provides the purpose and conditions that define that desired end state. The commander's intent must be easy to remember and clearly understood two echelons down.*

b. (U) <u>Concept of Operations</u>. *The concept of operations is a statement that directs the manner in which subordinate units cooperate to accomplish the mission and establishes the sequence of actions the force will use to achieve the end state. It is normally expressed in terms of decisive, shaping, and sustaining operations. It states the principal tasks required, the responsible subordinate units, and how the principal tasks complement one another. Normally, the concept of operations projects the status of the force at the end of the operation. If the mission dictates a significant change in tasks during the operation, the commander may phase the operation. The concept of operations may be a single paragraph, divided into two or more subparagraphs, or if unusually lengthy, summarized here with details located in Annex C (Operations). If the concept of operations is phased, describe each phase in a subparagraph. Label these subparagraphs as "Phase" followed by the appropriate Roman numeral, for example, "Phase I." If the operation is phased, all paragraphs and subparagraphs of the base order and all annexes must mirror the phasing established in the concept of operations. The operation overlay and graphic depictions of lines of effort help portray the concept of operations and are located in Annex C (Operations).*

c. (U) <u>Scheme of Movement and Maneuver</u>. *Describe the employment of maneuver units in accordance with the concept of operations. Provide the primary tasks of maneuver units conducting the decisive operation and the purpose of each. Next, state the primary tasks of maneuver units conducting shaping operations, including security operations, and the purpose of each. For offensive operations, identify the form of maneuver. For defensive operations, identify the type of defense. For stability operations, describe the role of maneuver units by primary stability tasks. If the operation is phased, identify the main effort by phase. Identify and include priorities for the reserve. Refer to Annex C (Operations) as required.*

(1) (U) <u>Scheme of Mobility/Countermobility</u>. *State the scheme of mobility/countermobility including priorities by unit or area. Refer to Annex G (Engineer) as required.*

(2) (U) <u>Scheme of Battlefield Obscuration</u>. *State the scheme of battlefield obscuration, including priorities by unit or area. Refer to Appendix 9 (Battlefield Obscuration) to Annex C (Operations) as required.*

(3) (U) <u>Scheme of Intelligence, Surveillance, and Reconnaissance</u>. *Describe how the commander intends to use <u>intelligence, surveillance, and reconnaissance</u> (ISR) to support the concept of operations. Include the primary reconnaissance objectives. Refer to Annex L (<u>Intelligence, Surveillance, and Reconnaissance</u>) as required.*

*(**Note:** Army forces do not conduct ISR within the United States and its territories. For domestic operations, this paragraph is titled "Information Awareness and Assessment" and the contents of this paragraph comply with Executive Order 12333.)*

[page number]

[CLASSIFICATION]

Figure E-2. Annotated Army OPLAN/OPORD format (continued)

[CLASSIFICATION]

OPLAN/OPORD [number] [(code name)]—[issuing headquarters] [(classification of title)]

d. (U) <u>Scheme of Intelligence</u>. *Describe how the commander envisions intelligence supporting the concept of operations. Include the priority of effort to situation development, targeting, and assessment. State the priority of intelligence support to units and areas. Refer to Annex B (Intelligence) as required.*

e. (U) <u>Scheme of Fires</u>. *Describe how the commander intends to use fires to support the concept of operations with emphasis on the scheme of maneuver. State the fire support tasks and the purpose of each task. State the priorities for, allocation of, and restrictions on fires. Refer to Annex D (Fires) as required. If Annex D is not used, use subparagraphs for fires categories (for example, field artillery or cyber/electromagnetic activities) based on the situation.*

f. (U) <u>Scheme of Protection</u>. *Describe how the commander envisions protection supporting the concept of operations. Include the priorities of protection by unit and area. Include survivability. Address the scheme of operational area security, including security for routes, bases, and critical infrastructure. Identify tactical combat forces and other reaction forces. Use subparagraphs for protection categories (for example, air and missile defense and explosive ordnance disposal) based on the situation. Refer to Annex E (Protection) as required.*

g. (U) <u>Stability Operations</u>. *Describe how the commander envisions the conduct of stability operations in coordination with other organizations through the primary stability tasks. (See FM 3-07.) If other organizations or the host nation are unable to provide for civil security, restoration of essential services, and civil control, then commanders with an assigned AO must do so with available resources, request additional resources, or request relief from these requirements from higher headquarters. Commanders assign specific responsibilities for stability tasks to subordinate units in paragraph 3.i (Tasks to Subordinate Units) and paragraph 3.j (Coordinating Instructions). Refer to Annex C (Operations) and Annex K (Civil Affairs Operations) as required.*

h. (U) <u>Assessment</u>. *Describe the priorities for assessment and identify the measures of effectiveness used to assess end state conditions and objectives. Refer to Annex M (Assessment) as required.*

i. (U) <u>Tasks to Subordinate Units</u>. *State the task assigned to each unit that reports directly to the headquarters issuing the order. Each task must include who (the subordinate unit assigned the task), what (the task itself), when, where, and why (purpose). Use a separate subparagraph for each unit. List units in task organization sequence. Place tasks that affect two or more units in paragraph 3.j (Coordinating Instructions).*

j. (U) <u>Coordinating Instructions</u>. *List only instructions and tasks applicable to two or more units not covered in unit SOPs.*

(1) (U) <u>Timing</u>. *State the <u>time or condition when the OPORD becomes effective and list the operational timeline.</u>*

(2) (U) <u>Commander's Critical Information Requirements</u>. *List commander's critical information requirements (CCIRs) here.*

(3) (U) <u>Essential Elements of Friendly Information</u>. *List essential elements of friendly information (EEFIs) here.*

(4) (U) <u>Fire Support Coordination Measures</u>. *List critical fire support coordination or control measures.*

[page number]

[CLASSIFICATION]

±Figure E-2. Annotated Army OPLAN/OPORD format (continued)

[CLASSIFICATION]

OPLAN/OPORD [number] [(code name)]—[issuing headquarters] [(classification of title)]

(5) (U) <u>Airspace Coordinating Measures</u>. *List critical airspace coordinating or control measures.*

(6) (U) <u>Rules of Engagement</u>. *List rules of engagement here. Refer to Appendix 12 (Rules of Engagement) to Annex C (Operations) as required.*

*(**Note:** For operations within the United States and its territories, title this paragraph "Rules for the Use of Force").*

(7) (U) <u>Risk Reduction Control Measures</u>. *State measures specific to this operation not included in unit SOPs. They may include mission-oriented protective posture, operational exposure guidance, troop-safety criteria, and fratricide prevention measures. Refer to Annex E (Protection) as required.*

(8) (U) <u>Personnel Recovery Coordination Measures</u>. *Refer to Appendix 2 (Personnel Recovery) to Annex E (Protection) as required.*

(9) (U) <u>Environmental Considerations</u>. *Refer to Appendix 6 (Environmental Considerations) to Annex G (Engineer) as required.*

(10) (U) <u>Themes and Messages</u>. *List themes and messages.*

(11) (U) <u>Other Coordinating Instructions</u>. *List additional coordinating instructions and tasks that apply to two or more units as subparagraphs at this level as required.*

4. (U) <u>Sustainment</u>. *Describe the concept of sustainment, including priorities of sustainment by unit or area. Include instructions for administrative movements, deployments, and transportation—or references to applicable appendixes—if appropriate. Use the following subparagraphs to provide the broad concept of support for logistics, personnel, and Army health system support. Provide detailed instructions for each sustainment subfunction in the appendixes to Annex F (Sustainment) listed in table E-2.*

a. (U) <u>Logistics</u>. *Refer to Appendix 1 (Logistics) to Annex F (Sustainment) as required.*

b. (U) <u>Personnel</u>. *Refer to Appendix 2 (Personnel Services Support) to Annex F (Sustainment) as required.*

c. (U) <u>Health System Support</u>. *Refer to Appendix 3 (Army Health System Support) to Annex F (Sustainment) as required.*

5. (U) <u>Command and Signal</u>.

a. (U) <u>Command</u>.

(1) (U) <u>Location of Commander</u>. *State where the commander intends to be during the operation, by phase if the operation is phased.*

(2) (U) <u>Succession of Command</u>. *State the succession of command if not covered in the unit's SOPs.*

(3) (U) <u>Liaison Requirements</u>. *State liaison requirements not covered in the unit's SOPs.*

[page number]

[CLASSIFICATION]

±Figure E-2. Annotated Army OPLAN/OPORD format (continued)

[CLASSIFICATION]

OPLAN/OPORD [number] [(code name)]—[issuing headquarters] [(classification of title)]

b. (U) <u>Control</u>.

(1) (U) <u>Command Posts</u>. *Describe the employment of command posts (CPs), including the location of each CP and its time of opening and closing, as appropriate. State the primary controlling CP for specific tasks or phases of the operation (for example, "Division tactical command post will control the air assault").*

(2) (U) <u>Reports</u>. *List reports not covered in SOPs. Refer to Annex R (Reports) as required.*

c. (U) <u>Signal</u>. *Describe the concept of signal support, including location and movement of key signal nodes and critical electromagnetic spectrum considerations throughout the operation. Refer to Annex H (Signal) as required.*

ACKNOWLEDGE: *Include instructions for the acknowledgement of the OPLAN/OPORD by addressees. The word "acknowledge" may suffice. Refer to the message reference number if necessary. Acknowledgement of a plan or order means that it has been received and understood.*

[Commander's last name]
[Commander's rank]

The commander or authorized representative signs the original copy. If the representative signs the original, add the phrase "For the Commander." The signed copy is the historical copy and remains in the headquarters' files.

OFFICIAL:

[Authenticator's name]
[Authenticator's position]

Use only if the commander does not sign the original order. If the commander signs the original, no further authentication is required. If the commander does not sign, the signature of the preparing staff officer requires authentication and only the last name and rank of the commander appear in the signature block.

ANNEXES: *List annexes by letter and title. If a particular annex is not used, place "not used" beside that annex letter.*

A – Task Organization
B – Intelligence
C – Operations
D – Fires
E – Protection
F – Sustainment
G – Engineer
H – Signal
I – not used
J – Inform and Influence Activities
K – Civil Affairs Operations
L – Intelligence, Surveillance, and Reconnaissance

[page number]

[CLASSIFICATION]

Figure E-2. Annotated Army OPLAN/OPORD Format (continued)

[CLASSIFICATION]

OPLAN/OPORD [number] [(code name)]—[issuing headquarters] [(classification of title)]

M – Assessment
N – Space Operations
O – not used
P – Host-Nation Support
Q – spare
R – Reports
S – Special Technical Operations
T – spared
U – Inspector General
V – Interagency Coordination
W– spare
X – spare
Y – spare
Z – Distribution

DISTRIBUTION: *Furnish distribution copies either for action or for information. List in detail those who are to receive the plan or order. Refer to Annex Z (Distribution) if lengthy.*

[page number]

[CLASSIFICATION]

Figure E-2. Annotated Army OPLAN/OPORD format (continued)

E-60. Table E-2 lists the annexes and their associated appendices as well as the staff officers responsible for developing each attachment.

±Table E-2. List of attachments and responsible staff officers

ANNEX A – TASK ORGANIZATION (G-5 or G-3 [S-3])
ANNEX B – INTELLIGENCE (G-2 [S-2])
Appendix 1 – Intelligence Estimate
Appendix 2 – Intelligence, Surveillance, and Reconnaissance Synchronization Matrix
Appendix 3 – Counterintelligence
Appendix 4 – Signals Intelligence
Appendix 5– Human Intelligence
Appendix 6 – Geospatial Intelligence
Appendix 7 – Measurement and Signature Intelligence
Appendix 8 – Open Source Intelligence
ANNEX C – OPERATIONS (G-5 or G-3 [S-3])
Appendix 1 – Design Concept
Appendix 2 – Operation Overlay
Appendix 3 – Decision Support Products
Appendix 4 – Gap Crossing Operations
Appendix 5 – Air Assault Operations
Appendix 6 – Airborne Operations
Appendix 7 – Amphibious Operations
Appendix 8 – Special Operations (G-3 [S-3])
Appendix 9 – Battlefield Obscuration (CBRN Officer)
Appendix 10 – Airspace Command and Control (G-3 [S-3] or Airspace Command and Control Officer)
Appendix 11 – Rules of Engagement (Staff Judge Advocate)
Appendix 12 – Law and Order Operations (Provost Marshal)
Appendix 13 – Internment and Resettlement Operations (Provost Marshal)
ANNEX D – FIRES (Chief of Fires/Fire Support Officer)
Appendix 1 – Fire Support Overlay
Appendix 2 – Fire Support Execution Matrix
Appendix 3 – Targeting
Appendix 4 – Field Artillery Support
Appendix 5 – Air Support
Appendix 6 – Naval Fire Support
Appendix 7 – Cyber/Electromagnetic Activities (Electronic Warfare Officer)
ANNEX E – PROTECTION (Chief of Protection/Protection Coordinator as designated by the commander)
Appendix 1 – Air and Missile Defense (Air and Missile Defense Coordinator)
Appendix 2 – Personnel Recovery (Personnel Recovery Coordinator)
Appendix 3 – Fratricide Prevention
Appendix 4 – Operational Area Security (Provost Marshal)
Appendix 5 – Antiterrorism (Antiterrorism Officer)
Appendix 6 – Chemical, Biological, Radiological, and Nuclear Defense (CBRN Officer)
Appendix 7 – Safety (Safety Officer)
Appendix 8 – Operations Security (Operations Security Officer)
Appendix 9 – Explosive Ordnance Disposal (Explosive Ordnance Disposal Officer)
Appendix 10 – Force Health Protection (Surgeon)

Table E-2. List of attachments and responsible staff officers (continued)

ANNEX F – SUSTAINMENT (Chief of Sustainment [S-4])

Appendix 1 – Logistics (G-4 [S-4])
    Appendix 2 – Personnel Services Support
    Appendix 3 – Army Heath System Support (Surgeon)

ANNEX G – Engineer

Appendix 1 – Mobility/Countermobility
    Appendix 2 – Survivability (Engineer Officer)
    Appendix 3 – General Engineering
    Appendix 4 – Geospatial Engineering
    Appendix 5 – Engineer Task Organization and Execution Matrix
    Appendix 6 – Environmental Considerations

ANNEX H – SIGNAL (G-6 [S-6])

Appendix 1 – Information Assurance
    Appendix 2 – Voice and Data Network Diagrams
    Appendix 3 – Satellite Communications
    Appendix 4 – Foreign Data Exchanges
    Appendix 5 – Electromagnetic Spectrum Operations

ANNEX I – Not Used
ANNEX J – INFORM AND INFLUENCE ACTIVITIES (G-7 [S-7])

Appendix 1 – Public Affairs
    Appendix 2 – Military Deception
    Appendix 3 – Military Information Support Operations
    Appendix 4 – Soldier and Leader Engagement

ANNEX K – CIVIL AFFAIRS OPERATIONS (G-9 [S-9])
ANNEX L – INTELLIGENCE, SURVEILLANCE, AND RECONNAISSANCE (G-3 [S-3])
Appendix 1 – Intelligence, Surveillance, and Reconnaissance Overlay   Appendix 2 – Intelligence, Surveillance, and Reconnaissance Tasking Matrix
ANNEX M – ASSESSMENT (G-5 [S-5] or G-3 [S-3])
ANNEX N – SPACE OPERATIONS (Space Operations Officer)
ANNEX O – Not Used
ANNEX P – HOST-NATION SUPPORT (G-4 [S-4])
ANNEX Q – Spare
ANNEX R – REPORTS (G-3 [S-3])
ANNEX S – SPECIAL TECHNICAL OPERATIONS
ANNEX T – Spare
ANNEX U – INSPECTOR GENERAL
ANNEX V – INTERAGENCY COORDINATION (G-3 [S-3])
ANNEX W – Spare
ANNEX X – Spare
ANNEX Y – Spare
ANNEX Z – DISTRIBUTION (G-3 [S-3])

E-61. Figure E-3 is an example of an annotated attachment format. Figure E-4, page E-20, illustrates a sample WARNO. Figure E-5, page E-22, illustrates a sample FRAGO.

[CLASSIFICATION]

(Change from verbal orders, if any)

> Copy ## of ## copies
> Issuing headquarters
> Place of issue
> Date-time group of signature
> Message reference number

Include heading if attachment is distributed separately from the base order or higher-level attachment.

[Attachment type and number/letter] [(attachment title)] TO [higher-level attachment type and number/letter, if applicable] [(higher-level attachment title, if applicable)] TO OPERATION PLAN/ORDER [number] [(code name)] [(classification of title)]

References:

Time Zone Used Throughout the Order:

1. (U) <u>Situation</u>. *Include information affecting the functional area that paragraph 1 of the OPLAN/OPORD does not cover or that needs to be expanded.*

    a. (U) <u>Area of Interest</u>. *Refer to Annex B (Intelligence) as required.*

    b. (U) <u>Area of Operations</u>. *Refer to Appendix 2 (Operation Overlay) to Annex C (Operations).*

       (1) (U) <u>Terrain</u>. *List all critical terrain aspects that impact functional area operations. Refer to Tab A (Terrain) to Appendix 1 (Intelligence Estimate) to Annex B (Intelligence) as required.*

       (2) (U) <u>Weather</u>. *List all critical weather aspects that impact functional area operations. Refer to Tab B (Weather) to Appendix 1 (Intelligence Estimate) to Annex B (Intelligence) as required.*

    c. (U) <u>Enemy Forces</u>. *List known and templated locations and activities of enemy functional area units for one echelon up and two echelons down. List enemy maneuver and other area capabilities that will impact friendly operations. State expected enemy courses of action and employment of enemy functional area assets. Refer to Annex B (Intelligence) as required.*

    d. (U) <u>Friendly Forces</u>. *Outline the higher headquarters' plan as it pertains to the functional area. List designation, location, and outline of plan of higher, adjacent, and other functional area assets that support or impact the issuing headquarters or require coordination and additional support.*

    e. (U) <u>Interagency, Intergovernmental, and Nongovernmental Organizations</u>. *Identify and describe other organizations in the area of operations that may impact the conduct of functional area operations or implementation of functional area-specific equipment and tactics.*

    f. (U) <u>Civil Considerations</u>. *Refer to Annex K (Civil Affairs Operations) as required.*

    g. (U) <u>Attachments and Detachments</u>. *List units attached or detached only as necessary to clarify task organization.*

    h. (U) <u>Assumptions</u>. *List any functional area-specific assumptions that support the annex development.*

[page number]

[CLASSIFICATION]

±Figure E-3. Annotated attachment format (general)

[CLASSIFICATION]

[Attachment type and number/letter] [(attachment title)] TO [higher-level attachment type and number/letter, if applicable] [(higher-level attachment title, if applicable)] TO OPERATION PLAN/ORDER [number] [(code name)]—[issuing headquarters] [(classification of title)]

2. (U) <u>Mission</u>. *State the mission of the functional area in support of the base plan or order.*

3. (U) <u>Execution</u>.

   a. (U) <u>Scheme of Support</u>. *Describe how the functional area supports the commander's intent and concept of operations. Establish the priorities of support to units for each phase of the operation. Refer to Annex C (Operations) as required.*

   b. (U) <u>Tasks to Subordinate Units</u>. *List functional area tasks assigned to specific subordinate units not contained in the base order.*

   c. (U) <u>Coordinating Instructions</u>. *List only instructions applicable to two or more subordinate units not covered in the base order.*

4. (U) <u>Sustainment</u>. *Identify priorities of sustainment for functional area key tasks and specify additional instructions as required. Refer to Annex F (Sustainment) as required.*

5. (U) <u>Command and Signal</u>.

   a. (U) <u>Command</u>. *State the location of key functional area leaders.*

   b. (U) <u>Control</u>. *State the functional area liaison requirements not covered in the base order.*

   c. (U) <u>Signal</u>. *Address any functional area-specific communications requirements or reports. Refer to Annex H (Signal) as required.*

ACKNOWLEDGE: *Include only if attachment is distributed separately from the base order.*

OFFICIAL:

[Authenticator's name]
[Authenticator's position]

Either the commander or coordinating staff officer responsible for the functional area may sign attachments.

ATTACHMENT: *List lower level attachments.*

DISTRIBUTION: *Show only if distributed separately from the base order or higher-level attachments.*

[page number]

[CLASSIFICATION]

Figure E-3. Annotated attachment format (general) (continued)

[CLASSIFICATION]

(Change from verbal orders, if any) (Optional)

[Heading data is the same as for OPLAN/OPORD]

WARNING ORDER [number]

(U) References: *Refer to higher headquarters' OPLAN/OPORD and identify map sheets for operation (Optional).*

(U) Time Zone Used Throughout the OPLAN/OPORD: *(Optional).*

(U) Task Organization: *(Optional).*

1. **(U) Situation**. *The situation paragraph describes the conditions and circumstances of the operational environment that impact operations in the following subparagraphs:*

    a. (U) Area of Interest.

    b. (U) Area of Operations.

    c. (U) Enemy Forces.

    d. (U) Friendly Forces.

    e. (U) Interagency, Intergovernmental, and Nongovernmental Organizations.

    f. (U) Civil Considerations.

    g. (U) Attachments and Detachments. *Provide initial task organization.*

    h. (U) Assumptions. *List any significant assumptions for order development.*

2. **(U) Mission**. *State the issuing headquarters' mission.*

3. **(U) Execution**.

    a. (U) Initial Commander's Intent. *Provide brief commander's intent statement.*

    b. (U) Concept of Operations. *This may be "to be determined" for an initial WARNO.*

    c. (U) Tasks to Subordinate Units. *Include any known tasks at time of issuance of WARNO.*

    d. (U) Coordinating Instructions.

4. **(U) Sustainment**. *Include any known logistics, personnel, or Army health system preparation tasks.*

5. **(U) Command and Signal**. *Include any changes to the existing order or state "no change."*

[page number]

[CLASSIFICATION]

±Figure E-4. Annotated WARNO format

[CLASSIFICATION]

(Change from verbal orders, if any) (Optional)

[Heading data is the same as for OPLAN/OPORD]

WARNING ORDER [number]

ACKNOWLEDGE:

[Commander's last name]
[Commander's rank]

OFFICIAL:

[Authenticator's name]
[Authenticator's position]

ANNEXES:

DISTRIBUTION:

[page number]

[CLASSIFICATION]

Figure E-4. Annotated WARNO format (continued)

[CLASSIFICATION]

(Change from verbal orders, if any) (Optional)

Copy ## of ## copies
Issuing headquarters
Place of issue
Date-time group of signature
Message reference number

FRAGMENTARY ORDER [number]

(U) References: *Refer to higher the order being modified.*

(U) Time Zone Used Throughout the OPLAN/OPORD:

(U) Task Organization: *List changes to the task organization.*

1. (U) <u>Situation</u>. *Include any changes to the existing order or state "No change." For example, "No change to OPORD 03-XX."*

2. (U) <u>**Mission**</u>. *State "No change."*

3. (U) <u>**Execution**</u>. *Include any changes or state "No change."*

    a. (U) <u>Commander's Intent</u>. *Include any changes or state "No change."*

    b. (U) <u>Concept of Operations</u>. *Include any changes or state "No change."*

    c. (U) <u>Scheme Movement and Maneuver</u>. *Include any changes or state "No change."*

    d. (U) <u>Scheme of Intelligence</u>. *Include any changes or state "No change."*

    e. (U) <u>Scheme of Fires</u>. *Include any changes or state "No change."*

    f. (U) <u>Scheme of Protection</u>. *Include any changes or state "No change."*

    g. (U) <u>Stability Operations</u>. *Include any changes or state "No change."*

    h. (U) <u>Assessment</u>. *Include any changes or state "No change."*

    i. (U) <u>Tasks to Subordinate Units</u>. *Include any changes or state "No change."*

    j. (U) <u>Coordinating Instructions</u>. *Include any changes or state "No Change."*

4. (U) <u>**Sustainment**</u>. *Include any changes or state "No change."*

5. (U) <u>**Command and Signal**</u>. *Include any changes or state "No change."*

ACKNOWLEDGE:

                        [Commander's last name]

                        [Commander's rank]

OFFICIAL:

[Authenticator's name]

[Authenticator's position]

ANNEXES:

DISTRIBUTION:

               [page number]

[CLASSIFICATION]

±Figure E-5. Annotated sample FRAGO

E-62. ±Figure E-6 is a sample overlay order graphic with text.

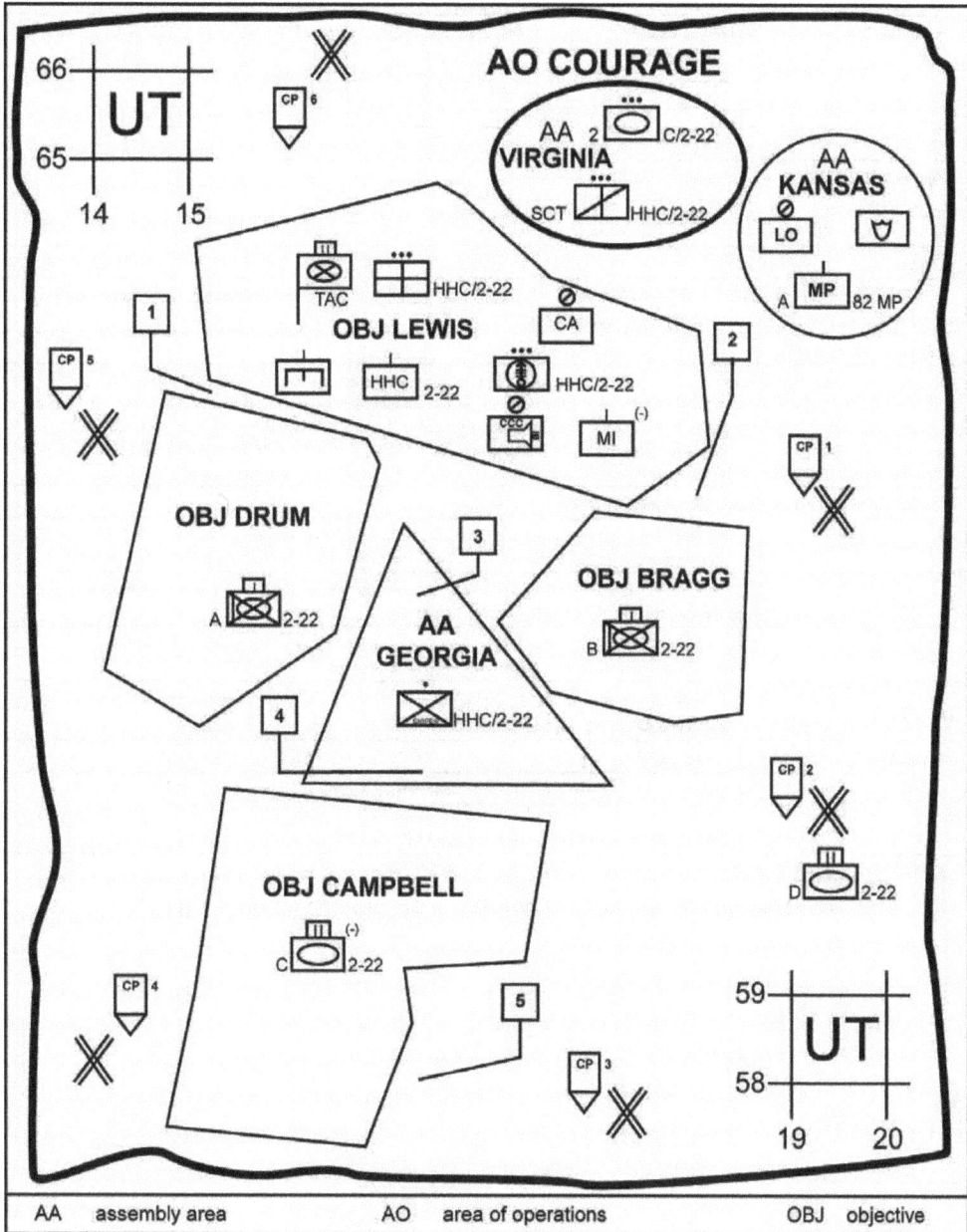

±Figure E-6. Example of overlay order graphic

TASK ORGANIZATION				
TF Control	A/2-22 IN	B/2-22 IN	C/2-22 AR	D/2-22 AR
Sniper Sqd/HHC/2-22	1/A/2-22 IN 2/A/2-22 IN 3/C/2-22 AR	1/B/2-22 IN 2/B/2-22 IN 3/D/2-22 AR	1/C/2-22 AR 2/C/2-22 AR 3/A/2-22 IN	1/D/2-22 AR 2/D/2-22 AR 3/B/2-22 IN

HHC	HN Civil Authorities (DIRLAUTH)
Scout PLT/2-22 IN Mortars/HHC/2-22 Medical/HHC/2-22	None

MISSION:

TF 2-22 conducts a cordon and search in AO COURAGE NLT 120900ZJAN07 to capture anti-coalition forces (ACF) and seize weapons caches in order to limit the attacks on coalition forces

COMMANDER'S INTENT:

Simultaneous occupation of outer cordon checkpoints (CKPs) to isolate search objectives and prevent ACF exfiltration or infiltration Lead with information dissemination of information themes and messages Exercise patience discipline and respect for host-nation population and property while conducting thorough searches Immediate evacuation of ACF personnel to BCT Detainee Collection Point for processing and evacuation End state is OBJ's LEWIS DRUM BRAGG and CAMPBELL free of ACF and companies postured for future operations

EXECUTION – TASKS TO SUBORDINATE UNITS:

A/2-22 IN	**TF Decisive Operation:** Secure OBJ DRUM (inner cordon) and conduct search to capture ACF and seize weapons caches in order to limit the attacks on coalition forces
B/2-22 IN	Secure OBJ BRAGG (inner cordon) and conduct search to capture ACF and seize weapons caches in order to limit the attacks on coalition forces
C/2-22 AR	1 Secure OBJ CAMPBELL (inner cordon) and conduct search to capture ACF and seize weapons caches in order to limit the attacks on coalition forces
D/2-22 AR	1 Secure the outer cordon at CKPs 1-6 2 Secure AA KANSAS for HNCA occupation
HHC (-)/2-22	1 Secure TF tactical command post and TF Forward Aid Station in OBJ LEWIS
Sniper/HHC/2-22	1 Occupy AA GEORGIA and provide observation and surveillance of OBJs DRUM BRAGG and CAMPBELL 2 O/O deliver precision fires to destroy ACF

Acknowledge: A/2-22 IN B/2-22 IN C/2-22 AR D/2-22 AR HHC/2-22 Sniper/2-22 IN

‡Figure E-6. Example of overlay order graphic (continued)

Task Organization

This appendix discusses the fundamentals of task organization, including command and support relationships. It provides instructions, formats and examples for listing task organization, and unit listing sequence. See JP 1 for doctrine on joint command and control relationships.

FUNDAMENTAL CONSIDERATIONS

F-1. A *task organization* is a temporary grouping of forces designed to accomplish a particular mission (FM 3-0). *Task-organizing* is the act of designing an operating force, support staff, or logistic package of specific size and composition to meet a unique task or mission. Characteristics to examine when task-organizing the force include, but are not limited to: training, experience, equipage, sustainability, operating environment, enemy threat, and mobility. For Army forces, it includes allocating available assets to subordinate commanders and establishing their command and support relationships (FM 3-0). Command and support relationships provide the basis for unity of command in operations.

> *Note:* Army command relationships are similar but not identical to joint command authorities and relationships. (See FM 3-0.) Differences stem from the way Army forces task-organize internally and the need for a system of support relationships between Army forces. Another important difference is the requirement for Army commanders to handle the administrative control requirements.

F-2. ±Military units consist of organic components. Organic parts of a unit are those forming an essential part of the unit and are listed in its table of organization and equipment. Commanders can alter organizations' organic unit relationships to better allocate assets to subordinate commanders. They also can establish temporary command and support relationships to facilitate exercising mission command.

F-3. Establishing clear command and support relationships is fundamental to organizing for any operation. These relationships establish clear responsibilities and authorities between subordinate and supporting units. Some command and support relationships (for example, tactical control) limit the commander's authority to prescribe additional relationships. Knowing the inherent responsibilities of each command and support relationship allows commanders to effectively organize their forces and helps supporting commanders to understand their unit's role in the organizational structure.

F-4. Commanders designate command and support relationships to weight the decisive operation and support the concept of operations. Task organization also helps subordinate and supporting commanders support the commander's intent. These relationships carry with them varying responsibilities to the subordinate unit by the parent and gaining units as listed in table F-1 and table F-2, pages F-3 and F-4 respectively. Commanders consider two organizational principles when task-organizing forces:

- Maintain cohesive mission teams.
- Do not exceed subordinates' span of control capabilities.

F-5. When possible, commanders maintain cohesive mission teams. They organize forces based on standing headquarters, their assigned forces, and habitual associations when possible. When not feasible and ad hoc organizations are created, commanders arrange time for training and establishing functional working relationships and procedures. Once commanders have organized and committed a force, they keep its task organization unless the benefits of a change clearly outweigh the disadvantages. Reorganizations may result in a loss of time, effort, and tempo. Sustainment considerations may also preclude quick reorganization.

F-6. ±Commanders carefully avoid exceeding the span of control capabilities of subordinates. Span of control refers to the number of subordinate units under a single commander. This number is situation dependent and may vary. As a rule, commanders can effectively command two to six subordinate units. Allocating subordinate commanders more units gives them greater flexibility and increases options and combinations. However, increasing the number of subordinate units increases the number of decisions to be made in a timely fashion.

F-7. Running estimates and course of action (COA) analysis of the military decisionmaking process provide information that help commanders determine the best task organization. An effective task organization—

- Facilitates the commander's intent and concept of operations.
- Retains flexibility within the concept of operations.
- Adapts to conditions imposed by mission variables.
- Accounts for the requirements to conduct essential stability tasks for populations within an area of operation.
- Creates effective combined arms teams.
- Provides mutual support among units.
- Ensures flexibility to meet unforeseen events and support future operations.
- Allocates resources with minimum restrictions on their employment.
- Promotes unity of command.
- Offsets limitations and maximizes the potential of all forces available.
- Exploits enemy vulnerabilities.

F-8. Creating an appropriate task organization requires understanding—

- The mission, including the higher commander's intent and concept of operations.
- The fundamentals of full spectrum operations (see FM 3-0), basic tactical concepts (see FM 3-90), and the fundamentals of stability (see FM 3-07).
- The roles and relationships among the warfighting functions.
- The status of available forces, including morale, training, and equipment capabilities.
- Specific unit capabilities, limitations, strengths, and weaknesses.
- The risks inherent in the plan.

F-9. During COA analysis, commanders identify what resources they need, and where, when, and how frequently they will need them. Formal task organization and the change from generic to specific units begin after COA analysis when commanders assign tasks to subordinate commanders. Staffs assign tasks to subordinate headquarters and determine if subordinate headquarters have enough combat power, reallocating combat power as necessary. They then refine command and support relationships for subordinate units and decide the priorities of support. Commanders approve or modify the staff's recommended task organization based on their evaluation of the factors (listed in paragraphs F-7 and F-8) and information from running estimates and COA analysis. (Appendix B defines and describes the military decisionmaking process.)

F-10. In allocating assets, the commander and staff consider the—

- Task organization for the ongoing operation.
- Potential adverse effects of breaking up cohesive teams by changing the task organization.
- Time necessary to realign the organization after receipt of the task organization.
- Limits on control over supporting units provided by higher headquarters.

ARMY COMMAND AND SUPPORT RELATIONSHIPS

F-11. Army commanders build combined arms organizations using command and support relationships. Command relationships define command responsibility and authority. Support relationships define the purpose, scope, and effect desired when one capability supports another.

ARMY COMMAND RELATIONSHIPS

F-12. Table F-1 lists the Army command relationships. Command relationships define superior and subordinate relationships between unit commanders. By specifying a chain of command, command relationships unify effort and enable commanders to use subordinate forces with maximum flexibility. Army command relationships identify the degree of control of the gaining Army commander. The type of command relationship often relates to the expected longevity of the relationship between the headquarters involved and quickly identifies the degree of support that the gaining and losing Army commanders provide. (See FM 3-0 for additional discussion on command relationships.)

Table F-1. Army command relationships

If relation-ship is:	Then inherent responsibilities:							
	Have command relation-ship with:	May be task organized by:[1]	Unless modified, ADCON have responsi-bility through:	Are assigned position or AO by:	Provide liaison to:	Establish/maintain communi-cations with:	Have priorities establish-ed by:	Can impose on gaining unit further command or support relation-ship of:
Organic	All organic forces organized with the HQ	Organic HQ	Army HQ specified in organizing document	Organic HQ	N/A	N/A	Organic HQ	Attached; OPCON; TACON; GS; GSR; R; DS
Assigned	Combatant command	Gaining HQ	Gaining Army HQ	OPCON chain of command	As required by OPCON	As required by OPCON	ASCC or Service-assigned HQ	As required by OPCON HQ
Attached	Gaining unit	Gaining unit	Gaining Army HQ	Gaining unit	As required by gaining unit	Unit to which attached	Gaining unit	Attached; OPCON; TACON; GS; GSR; R; DS
OPCON	Gaining unit	Parent unit and gaining unit; gaining unit may pass OPCON to lower HQ[1]	Parent unit	Gaining unit	As required by gaining unit	As required by gaining unit and parent unit	Gaining unit	OPCON; TACON; GS; GSR; R; DS
TACON	Gaining unit	Parent unit	Parent unit	Gaining unit	As required by gaining unit	As required by gaining unit and parent unit	Gaining unit	TACON; GS GSR; R; DS

Note: [1] In NATO, the gaining unit may not task organize a multinational force. (See TACON.)

ADCON	administrative control	HQ	headquarters
AO	area of operations	N/A	not applicable
ASCC	Army Service component command	NATO	North Atlantic Treaty Organization
DS	direct support	OPCON	operational control
GS	general support	R	reinforcing
GSR	general support–reinforcing	TACON	tactical control

ARMY SUPPORT RELATIONSHIPS

F-13. Table F-2 on page F-4 lists Army support relationships. Army support relationships are not a command authority and are more specific than the joint support relationships. Commanders establish support relationships when subordination of one unit to another is inappropriate. They assign a supportrelationship when—

- The support is more effective if a commander with the requisite technical and tactical expertise controls the supporting unit rather than the supported commander.
- The echelon of the supporting unit is the same as or higher than that of the supported unit. For example, the supporting unit may be a brigade, and the supported unit may be a battalion. It would be inappropriate for the brigade to be subordinated to the battalion; hence, the echelon uses an Army support relationship.
- The supporting unit supports several units simultaneously. The requirement to set support priorities to allocate resources to supported units exists. Assigning support relationships is one aspect of mission command.

Table F-2. Army support relationships

If relation-ship is:	Then inherent responsibilities:							
	Have command relation-ship with:	May be task organized by:	Receive sustain-ment from:	Are assigned position or an area of operations by:	Provide liaison to:	Establish/ maintain communi-cations with:	Have priorities established by:	Can impose on gaining unit further command or support relation-ship by:
Direct support[1]	Parent unit	Parent unit	Parent unit	Supported unit	Supported unit	Parent unit; supported unit	Supported unit	See note[1]
Reinforc-ing	Parent unit	Parent unit	Parent unit	Reinforced unit	Reinforced unit	Parent unit; reinforced unit	Reinforced unit; then parent unit	Not applicable
General support–reinforc-ing	Parent unit	Parent unit	Parent unit	Parent unit	Reinforced unit and as required by parent unit	Reinforced unit and as required by parent unit	Parent unit; then reinforced unit	Not applicable
General support	Parent unit	Parent unit	Parent unit	Parent unit	As required by parent unit	As required by parent unit	Parent unit	Not applicable

Note: [1] Commanders of units in direct support may further assign support relationships between their subordinate units and elements of the supported unit after coordination with the supported commander.

F-14. Army support relationships allow supporting commanders to employ their units' capabilities to achieve results required by supported commanders. Support relationships are graduated from an exclusive supported and supporting relationship between two units—as in direct support—to a broad level of support extended to all units under the control of the higher headquarters—as in general support. Support relationships do not alter administrative control. Commanders specify and change support relationships through task organization.

TASK ORGANIZATION FORMAT

F-15. Task organization is typically displayed in an outline format in Annex A of the operation plan or order. Units are listed under the headquarters to which they are allocated or that they support. (See figure F-1.) This format is recognized and understood by the other Services and multinational forces and should be used during joint and multinational operations.

2/52 HBCT
- 1-77 IN (-)
- 1-30 AR (-)
- 1-20 CAV
- A/4-52 CAV (ARS) (DS)
- 2-606 FA (2x8)
  - TACP/52 ASOS (USAF)
- 521 BSB
  - 2/2/311 QM CO (MA)
  - 1/B/2-52 AV (GSAB) (TACON)
  - 2/577 MED CO (GRD AMB) (attached)
  - 842 FST
- 2 BSTB
  - 31 EN CO (MRBC) (DS)
  - 63 EOD
  - 2/244 EN CO (RTE CL) (DS)
  - 1/2/1/55 SIG CO (COMCAM)
- 2D MP PLT
  - RTS TM 1/A/52 BSTB
  - RTS TM 2/A/52 BSTB
  - RTS TM 3/A/52 BSTB
  - RTS TM 4/A/52 BSTB

2/54 HBCT
- 4-77 IN
- 2-30 AR
- 3-20 CAV
- 2/C/4-52 CAV (ARS) (DS)
- 2-607 FA
  - TACP/52 ASOS (USAF)
- 105 BSB
  - 3/2/311 QM CO (MA)
  - 2/B/2-52 AV (GSAB) (TACON)
  - 843 FST
  - 3/577 MED CO (GRD AMB)
- 3 BSTB
  - A 388 CA BN
  - 1/244 EN CO (RTE CL) (DS)
  - 763 EOD
  - 2/2/1/55 SIG CO (COMCAM)
- 3D MP PLT

116 HBCT (+)
- 3-116 AR
- 1-163 IN
- 2-116 AR
- 1-148 FA
- 145 BSB
  - 4/B/2-52 AV (GSAB) (TACON)
  - 4/2/311 QM CO (MA)
  - 4/577 MED CO (GRD AMB)
  - 844 FST
- 116 BSTB
  - 366 EN CO (SAPPER) (DS)
  - 1/401 EN CO (ESC) (DS)
  - 2/244 EN CO (RTE CL) (DS)
  - 52 EOD
  - 1/301 MP CO
  - 1/3/1/55 SIG CO (COMCAM)
  - 1/467 CM CO (MX) (S)
  - C/388 CA BN
- 116 MP PLT

87 IBCT
- 1-80 IN
- 2-80 IN
- 3-13 CAV
- A/3-52 AV (ASLT) (DS)
- B/1-52 AV (ARB) (DS)
- C/4-52 CAV (ARS) (-) (DS)
- 2-636 FA
  - A/3-52 FA (+)
  - TACP/52 ASOS (USAF)
  - Q37 52 FA BDE (GS)
- 99 BSB
  - 845 FST
  - 1/577 MED CO (GRD AMB)
  - 3/B/2-52 AV (GSAB) (TACON)
  - 1/2/311 QM CO (MA)
- 87 BSTB
  - 53 EOD
  - 3/2/1/55 SIG CO (COMCAM)
  - B/420 CA BN
  - 2 HCT/3/B/52 BSTB
  - 745 EN CO (MAC) (DS)
  - 1/1/52 CM CO (R/D) (R)
  - 2/467 CM CO (MX) (S)
  - 1/1102 MP CO (CS) (DS)

52 CAB AASLT
- HHC/52 CAB
  - 1/B/1-77 IN (DIV QRF) (OPCON)
- 1-52 AV (ARB) (-)
- 4-52 CAV (ARS) (-)
- 3-52 AV (ASLT) (-)
- 2-52 AV (GSAB)
- 1 (TUAS)/B/52 BSTB (-) (GS)
- 2/694 EN CO (HORIZ) (DS)

52 FIRES BDE
- HHB
- TAB (-)
- 1-52 FA (MLRS)
- 3-52 FA (-) (M109A6)
- 1/694 EN CO (HORIZ) (DS)

17 MEB 52 ID
- 25 CM BN (-)
- 700 MP BN
- 7 EN BN
- 2/2/1/55 SIG CO (COMCAM)
- 11 ASOS (USAF)

52 SUST BDE
- 52 BTB
- 520 CSSB
- 521 CSSB
- 10 CSH
  - 168 MMB

52 HHB
- A/1-30 AR (DIV RES)
- 35 SIG CO (-) (DS)
- 154 LTF
- 2/1/55 SIG CO (-)
- 14 PAD
- 388 CA BN (-) (DS)

±Figure F-1. Sample outline format for a task organization (52d Infantry Division)

AASLT	air assault	EOD	explosive ordnance disposal	MLRS	multiple launch rocket
AR	armor	ESC	expeditionary sustainment		system
ARB	attack reconnaissance		command	MMB	multifunctional medical
	battalion	FA	field artillery		battalion
ARS	attack reconnaissance	FST	forward surgical team	MP	military police
	squadron	GRD AMB	ground ambulance	MRBC	multi-role bridge company
ASLT	assault	GS	general support	MX	mechanized
ASOS	air support operations	GSAB	general support aviation	OPCON	operational control
	squadron		battalion	PAD	public affairs detachment
AV	aviation	HBCT	heavy brigade combat team	PLT	platoon
BDE	brigade	HCT	human intelligence	QM	quartermaster
BN	battalion		collection team	QRF	quick reaction force
BSB	brigade support battalion	HHB	headquarters and	R	reinforcing
BSTB	brigade special troops		headquarters battalion	R/D	reconnaissance/
	battalion	HHC	headquarters and		decontamination
BTB	brigade troop battalion		headquarters company	RES	reserve
CA	civil affairs	HORIZ	horizontal	RTE CL	route clearance
CAB	combat aviation brigade	IBCT	infantry brigade combat	RTS	retransmission
CAV	cavalry		team	S	smoke
CM	chemical	ID	infantry division	SIG	signal
CO	company	IN	infantry	SUST	sustainment
COMCAM	combat camera	LTF	logistics task force	TAB	target acquisition battery
CS	combat support	MA	mortuary affairs	TACON	tactical control
CSH	combat support hospital	MAC	mobility augmentation	TACP	tactical air control party
CSSB	combat sustainment support		company	TM	team
	battalion	MEB	maneuver enhancement	TUAS	tactical unmanned aircraft
DIV	division		brigade		system
DS	direct support	MED	medical	USAF	United States Air Force
EN	engineer				

Figure F-1. Sample outline format for a task organization (52d Infantry Division) (continued)

F-16. ±List subordinate units under the headquarters to which they are assigned, attached, or in support. Place direct support (DS) units below the units they support. Indent subordinate and supporting units two spaces. Identify relationships other than attached with parenthetical terms—for example, general support (GS) or (DS).

±UNIT LISTING SEQUENCE

F-17. List major subordinate control headquarters in the sequence shown in table F-3. If applicable, list task organizations according to the phases of the operation during which it applies.

F-18. Group units by controlling headquarters. List major subordinate maneuver units first (for example, 2d HBCT; 1-77th IN; A/4-52d CAV). Place them in alphabetical or numerical order. List brigade combat teams ahead of brigades, combined arms battalions before battalions, and company teams before companies. Follow maneuver headquarters with the field artillery (for example, fires brigade after maneuver brigades), intelligence units, maneuver enhancement units, and the sustainment units. The last listing should be any special troops units under the control of the force headquarters.

F-19. Use a plus (+) symbol when attaching one or more subelements of a similar function to a headquarters. Use a minus symbol (–) when deleting one or more subelements of a similar function to a headquarters. Always show the symbols in parenthesis. Do not use a plus symbol when the receiving headquarters is a combined arms task force or company team. Do not use plus and minus symbols together (as when a headquarters detaches one element and receives attachment of another); use the symbol that portrays the element's combat power with respect to other similar elements. Do not use either symbol when two units swap subelements and their combat power is unchanged. Here are some examples:

- C Company loses one platoon to A Company; the battalion task organization will show A Co. (+) and C Co. (–).
- 4-77th Infantry receives a tank company from 1-30 Armor; the brigade task organization will show TF 4-77 IN (+) and 1-30 AR (–).

±Table F-3. Order for listing units in a task organization

	Corps	Division	Brigade	Battalion	Company
Movement and Maneuver	Divisions Separate maneuver brigades or battalions Combat aviation brigades or battalions Special operations forces • Ranger • Special forces	Brigade-size ground units • Infantry • Heavy • Stryker • Brigades in numerical order Battalion TF • Named TFs in alphabetical order • Numbered TFs in numerical order Combat aviation brigade	Battalion TFs Battalions • Combined arms • Infantry • Reconnaissance Company teams Companies Air cavalry squadron	Company teams • Named teams in order • Letter designated teams in alphabetical order Companies • Rifle • Mechanized infantry • Armor	Organic platoons Attached platoons
Fires	Fires brigade	Fires brigade	Fires battalion	Mortar platoon	
Intelligence	Battlefield surveillance brigade	Battlefield surveillance brigade	RSTA squadron	Scout platoon	
Protection	MEB Air defense CBRN Engineer Military police EOD	MEB Air defense CBRN Engineer Military police EOD	Air defense CBRN Engineer Military police	Air defense CBRN Engineer	
Sustainment	Sustainment brigade Medical brigade	Sustainment brigade Medical brigade	BSB	FSC	
Mission Command	Signal Public affairs Civil affairs MISO Space	Signal Public affairs Civil affairs MISO Space	Signal Public affairs Civil affairs MISO		

BSB	brigade support battalion		MISO	military information support operations
CBRN	chemical, biological, radiological, and nuclear		RSTA	reconnaissance, surveillance, and target acquisition
EOD	explosive ordnance disposal			
FSC	forward support company		TF	task force
MEB	maneuver enhancement brigade			

F-20. When the effective attachment time of a nonorganic unit to another unit differs from the effective time of the plan or order, add the effective attachment time in parentheses after the attached unit—for example, 1-80 IN (OPCON 2 HBCT Ph II). List this information either in the task organization in the base order or in Annex A (Task Organization). For clarity, list subsequent command or support relationships under the task organization in parentheses following the affected unit—for example, "..on order, OPCON to 2 HBCT" is written (O/O OPCON 2 HBCT).

F-21. During multinational operations, insert the country code between the numeric designation and the unit name—for example, show 3rd Panzer Division as 3d (GE) Panzer Division. (FM 1-02 contains authorized country codes.)

F-22. Use abbreviated designations for organic units. Use the full designation for nonorganic units—for example, 1-52 FA (MLRS) (GS) rather than 1-52 FA. Specify a unit's command or support relationship only if it differs from that of its higher headquarters.

F-23. Designate task forces with the last name of the task force commander (for example, TF WILLIAMS), a code name (for example, TF WARRIOR), or a number (for example, TF 47 or TF 1-77 IN).

F-24. For unit designation at theater army level, list major subordinate maneuver units first, placing them in alphabetical or numerical order, followed by fires, intelligence, maneuver enhancement, sustainment, and any units under the control of the force headquarters. For each function following maneuver, list headquarters in the order of commands, groups, brigades, squadrons, and detachments.

Appendix G

Running Estimates

This appendix defines the running estimate and describes how the commander and members of the staff build and maintain their running estimates throughout the operations process. This appendix provides a generic running estimate format modified by the commander and each staff section to fit their functional area. See JP 5-0 for information on joint estimates.

TYPES OF RUNNING ESTIMATES

G-1. **A *running estimate* is the continuous assessment of the current situation used to determine if the current operation is proceeding according to the commander's intent and if planned future operations are supportable**. The commander and each staff section maintain a running estimate. In their running estimates, the commander and each staff section continuously consider the effects of new information and update the following:

- Facts.
- Assumptions.
- Friendly force status.
- Enemy activities and capabilities.
- Civil considerations.
- Conclusions and recommendations.

G-2. Commanders maintain their running estimates to consolidate their understanding and visualization of an operation. The commander's running estimate includes a summary of the problem and integrates information and knowledge of the staff's and subordinate commanders' running estimates.

G-3. ±Building and maintaining running estimates is a primary task of each staff section. The running estimate helps the staff to track and record pertinent information as well as to provide recommendations to commanders. Running estimates represent the analysis and expert opinion of each staff section by functional area. Running estimates are maintained throughout the operations process to assist commanders and staffs in the exercise of mission command.

G-4. Each staff section and command post functional cell maintains a running estimate focused on how their specific areas of expertise are postured to support future operations. Because an estimate may be needed at any time, running estimates must be developed, revised, updated, and maintained continuously while in garrison and during operations. While in garrison, staffs must maintain a running estimate on friendly capabilities.

ESSENTIAL QUALITIES OF RUNNING ESTIMATES

G-5. A comprehensive running estimate addresses all aspects of operations and contains both facts and assumptions based on the staff's experience within a specific area of expertise. Figure G-1 on page G-2 provides the base format for a running estimate that parallels the planning process. Each staff section modifies it to account for their specific functional areas. All running estimates cover essential facts and assumptions including a summary of the current situation by the mission variables, conclusions, and recommendations. Once they complete the plan, commanders and staff sections continuously update their estimates.

---

1. **SITUATION AND CONSIDERATIONS.**
   a.   **Area of Interest.** Identify and describe those factors of the area of interest that affect functional area considerations.
   b.   **Characteristics of the Area of Operations.**
       (1) Terrain. State how terrain affects staff functional area's capabilities.
       (2) Weather. State how weather affects staff functional area's capabilities.
       (3) Enemy Forces. Describe enemy disposition, composition, strength, and systems within a functional area as well as enemy capabilities and possible courses of action (COAs) with respect to their effects on a functional area.
       (4) Friendly Forces. List current functional area resources in terms of equipment, personnel, and systems. Identify additional resources available for the functional area located at higher, adjacent, or other units. List those capabilities from other military and civilian partners that may be available to provide support within the functional area. Compare requirements to current capabilities and suggest solutions for satisfying discrepancies.
       (5) Civilian Considerations. Describe civil considerations that may affect the functional area to include possible support needed by civil authorities from the functional area as well as possible interference from civil aspects.
   c.   **Assumptions.** List all assumptions that affect the functional area.
2. **MISSION.** Show the restated mission resulting from mission analysis.
3. **COURSES OF ACTION.**
   a.   List friendly COAs that were war-gamed.
   b.   List enemy actions or COAs that were templated that impact the functional area.
   c.   List the evaluation criteria identified during COA analysis. All staff use the same criteria.
4. **ANALYSIS.** Analyze each COA using the evaluation criteria from COA analysis. Review enemy actions that impact the functional area as they relate to COAs. Identify issues, risks, and deficiencies these enemy actions may create with respect to the functional area.
5. **COMPARISON.** Compare COAs. Rank order COAs for each key consideration. Use a decision matrix to aid the comparison process.
6. **RECOMMENDATIONS AND CONCLUSIONS.**
   a.   Recommend the most supportable COAs from the perspective of the functional area.
   b.   Prioritize and list issues, deficiencies, and risks and make recommendations on how to mitigate them.

Figure G-1. Generic base running estimate format

G-6.   The base running estimate addresses information unique to each functional area. It serves as the staff section's initial assessment of the current readiness of equipment and personnel and of how the factors considered in the running estimate affect the staff's ability to accomplish the mission. Each staff section identifies functional area friendly and enemy strengths, systems, training, morale, leadership, and weather and terrain effects, and how all these factors impact both the operational environment and area of operations. Because the running estimate is a picture relative to time, facts, and assumptions, each staff section constantly updates the estimate as new information arises, as assumptions become facts or are invalidated, when the mission changes, or when the commander requires additional input. Running estimates can be presented verbally or in writing.

RUNNING ESTIMATES IN THE OPERATIONS PROCESS

G-7.   Commanders and staff sections immediately begin updating their running estimates upon receipt of mission. They continue to build and maintain their running estimates throughout out the operations process in planning, preparation, execution, and assessment as discussed in paragraphs G-8 through **Error! Reference source not found.**.

RUNNING ESTIMATES IN PLANNING

G-8.   During planning, running estimates are key sources of information during mission analysis. Following mission analysis, commanders and staff sections update their running estimates throughout the rest of the military decisionmaking process. Based on the mission and the initial commander's intent, the staff develops one or more proposed courses of action (COAs) and continually refines its running estimates to account for the mission variables. The updated running estimates then support COA analysis (wargaming) in which the strengths and weaknesses of each COA are identified. The staff relies on its updated running estimate to provide input to the war game. Following COA analysis, the staff compares the proposed COAs against each other and recommends one of them to the commander for approval. During all these activities, each staff section continues to update and refine its running estimate to give commanders the best possible information available at the time to support their decisions. The selected COA provides each staff section an additional focus for its estimates and the key information it will need during orders production. Key information recorded in the running estimate is included in orders, particularly in the functional annexes.

RUNNING ESTIMATES IN PREPARATION

G-9. The commander and staff transition from planning to execution. As they transition, they use running estimates to identify the current readiness of the unit in relationship to its mission. The commander and staff also use running estimates to develop, then track, mission readiness goals and additional requirements.

RUNNING ESTIMATES IN EXECUTION

G-10. During execution, the commander and staff incorporate information included in running estimates into the common operational picture. This enables the commander and staff to depict key information from each functional area or warfighting function as they impact current and future operations. This information directly supports the commander's visualization and rapid decisionmaking during operations.

RUNNING ESTIMATES IN ASSESSMENT

G-11. Each staff section continuously analyzes new information during operations to create knowledge and understand if operations are progressing according to plan. Staffs use their running estimates to develop measures of effectiveness and measures of performance to support their analyses. The assessment of current operations also supports validation or rejection of additional information that will help update the estimates and support further planning. At a minimum, a staff section's running estimate assesses the following:

- Friendly force capabilities with respect to ongoing and planned operations.
- Enemy capabilities as they affect the staff section's area of expertise for current operations and plans for future operations.
- Civil considerations as they affect the staff section's area of expertise for current operations and plans for future operations.

This page intentionally left blank.

Appendix H
Formal Assessment Plans

This appendix provides guidelines to assist commanders and their staffs in developing formal assessment plans. See chapter 6 for a discussion of the fundamentals of assessment.

ASSESSMENT PLAN DEVELOPMENT

H-1. Units with staffs develop formal assessment plans when appropriate. A critical element of the commander's planning guidance is determining which formal assessment plans to develop. An assessment plan focused on the end state often works well. It is also possible, and may be desirable, to develop an entire formal assessment plan for an intermediate objective, a named operation subordinate to the base operation plan, or a named operation focused solely on a single line of operations or geographic area. The time, resources, and added complexity involved in generating a formal assessment plan strictly limit the number of such efforts.

ASSESSMENT STEPS

H-2. Commanders and staffs develop assessment plans during planning using six steps:
- Step 1 – Gather tools and assessment data.
- Step 2 – Understand current and desired conditions.
- Step 3 – Develop assessment measures and potential indicators.
- Step 4 – Develop the collection plan.
- Step 5 – Assign responsibilities for conducting analysis and generating recommendations.
- Step 6 – Identify feedback mechanisms.

Once commanders and their staffs develop the assessment plan, they apply the assessment process of monitor, evaluate, and recommend or direct continuously throughout preparation and execution.

STEP 1 – GATHER TOOLS AND ASSESSMENT DATA

H-3. Planning begins with receipt of mission. The receipt of mission alerts the staffs who begin updating their running estimates and gather the tools necessary for mission analysis and continued planning. Specific tools and information gathered regarding assessment include, but are not limited to—
- The higher headquarters' plan or order, including the assessment annex if available.
- If replacing a unit, any current assessments and assessment products.
- Relevant assessment products (classified or open-source) produced by civilian and military organizations.
- The identification of potential data sources, including academic institutions and civilian subject matter experts.

STEP 2 – UNDERSTAND CURRENT AND DESIRED CONDITIONS

H-4. Fundamentally, assessment is about measuring progress toward the desired end state. Staffs compare current conditions in the area of operations against the desired conditions. Mission analysis and intelligence preparation of the battlefield help develop an understanding of the current situation. The commander and staff identify the desired conditions and key underlying assumptions for an operation during design and the military decisionmaking process.

H-5. Understanding current and desired conditions requires explicitly acknowledging the underlying assumptions. Assumptions identified during planning are continually challenged during the evaluation phase of the assessment process. If the assumptions are subsequently disproven, then reframing the problem may be appropriate.

H-6. Following mission analysis, commanders issue their initial commander's intent, planning guidance, and commander's critical information requirements. The end state in the initial commander's intent describes the desired conditions the commander wants to achieve. The staff section charged with responsibility for the assessment plan identifies each specific desired condition mentioned in the commander's intent. These individual desired conditions focus the overall assessment of the operation. Monitoring focuses on the corresponding conditions in the current situation. If the conditions that define the end state change during the planning process, the staff updates these changes for the assessment plan.

H-7. To measure progress effectively, the staff identifies both the current situation and the desired end state. For example, the commander provides the end state condition "Essential services restored to prehostility levels." The staff develops a plan to obtain indicators of this condition. These indicators also identify the current and prehostility levels of essential services across the area of operations. By taking these two actions, the staff establishes a mechanism to assess progress toward this condition.

STEP 3 – DEVELOP ASSESSMENT MEASURES AND POTENTIAL INDICATORS

H-8. A formal assessment plan has a hierarchical structure—known as the assessment framework—that begins with end state conditions, followed by measures of effectiveness (MOEs), and finally indicators. Commanders broadly describe the operation's end state in their commander's intent. Specific desired conditions are then identified from the commander's intent. Each condition is measured by MOEs. The MOEs are in turn informed by indicators.

H-9. A formal assessment plan focuses on measuring changes in the situation and whether desired conditions are being attained while continually monitoring and evaluating assumptions to validate or invalidate them. MOEs are the measures used to do this. Normally, measures of performance (MOPs) are not part of formal assessment plans. MOPs are developed and tracked by the current operations integration cell and in individual staff sections' running estimates. However, occasionally specific tasks are assessed as part of the assessment plan using the following hierarchical structure: tasks, MOPs, and indicators. Formal, detailed assessments of task completion tend to be the exception rather than the rule.

H-10. Developing assessment measures and potential indicators involves—

- Selecting and writing MOEs.
- Selecting and writing indicators.
- Building the assessment framework.

Selecting and Writing Measures of Effectiveness

H-11. Guidelines for selecting and writing MOEs consist of the following:

- Select only MOEs that measure the degree to which the desired outcome is achieved.
- Choose distinct MOEs.
- Include MOEs from different causal chains.
- Use the same MOE to measure more than one condition when appropriate.
- Avoid additional reporting requirements for subordinates.
- Structure MOEs so that they have measurable, collectable, and relevant indicators.
- Write MOEs as statements not questions.
- Maximize clarity.

H-12. Commanders select only MOEs that measure the degree to which the desired outcome is achieved. A good basis must exist for the theory that this MOE is expected to change if the condition is being achieved.

H-13. Commanders choose MOEs for each condition as distinct from each other as possible. Using similar MOEs can skew the assessment by containing virtually the same MOE twice.

H-14. Commanders include MOEs from differing relevant causal chains for each condition whenever possible. When MOEs have a cause and effect relationship with each other, either directly or indirectly, it decreases their value in measuring a particular condition. Measuring progress towards a desired condition by multiple means adds rigor to the assessment. For example, in figure H-1 under condition 1, MOE 1 and MOE 3 have no apparent cause and effect relationship with each other although both are valid measures of the condition. This adds rigor and validity to the measurement of that condition. MOE 2 does have a cause and effect relationship with MOE 1 and MOE 3 but is a worthwhile addition because of the direct relevancy and mathematical rigor of that particular source of data.

Condition 1: Enemy Division X forces prevented from interfering with corps decisive operation.

MOE 1: Enemy Division X forces west of phase line blue are defeated.
- **Indicator 1**: Friendly forces occupy OBJ Slam (Yes/No).
- **Indicator 2**: Number of reports of squad-sized or larger enemy forces in the division area of operations in the past 24 hours.
- **Indicator 3**: Current G-2 assessment of number of enemy Division X battalions west of phase line blue.

MOE 2: Enemy Division X forces indirect fire systems neutralized.
- **Indicator 1**: Number of indirect fires originating from enemy Division X's integrated fires command in the past 24 hours.
- **Indicator 2**: Current G-2 assessment of number of operational 240mm rocket launchers within enemy Division X's integrated fires command.

MOE 3: Enemy Division X communications systems disrupted.
- **Indicator 1**: Number of electronic transmissions from enemy Division X detected in the past 24 hours.
- **Indicator 2**: Number of enemy Division X battalion and higher command posts destroyed.

Figure H-1. Sample of end state conditions for defensive operations

H-15. Commanders use the same MOE to measure more than one condition when appropriate. This sort of duplication in the assessment framework does not introduce significant bias unless carried to the extreme. The MOE duplication to be concerned about is among MOEs measuring the same condition.

H-16. Commanders avoid or minimize additional reporting requirements for subordinate units. In many cases, commanders use information requirements generated by other staff sections as MOEs and indicators in the assessment plan. With careful consideration, commanders and staffs can often find viable alternative MOEs without creating new reporting requirements. Excessive reporting requirements can render an otherwise valid assessment plan onerous and untenable.

H-17. Commanders structure MOEs so that measurable, collectable, and relevant indicators exist for them. A MOE is of no use if the staff cannot actually measure it.

H-18. Commanders write MOEs as statements not questions. MOEs can be expressed as a number. They are answers to questions rather than the questions themselves. (See figures H-1 and H-2 on page H-4 for examples.)

H-19. Commanders maximize clarity. A MOE should describe the sought information precisely, including specifics on time, information, geography, or unit, if needed. Any staff member should be able to read the MOE and understand exactly what information it describes.

Condition 1: Enemy defeated in the brigade area of operations.

MOE 1: Enemy kidnapping activity in the brigade area of operations disrupted.

- **Indicator 1**: Monthly reported dollars in ransom paid as a result of kidnapping operations.

- **Indicator 2**: Monthly number of reported attempted kidnappings.

- **Indicator 3**: Monthly poll question #23: "Have any kidnappings occurred in your neighborhood in the past 30 days?" Results for provinces ABC only.

MOE 2: Public perception of security in the brigade area of operations improved.

- **Indicator 1**: Monthly poll question #34: "Have you changed your normal activities in the past month because of concerns about your safety and that of your family?" Results for provinces ABC only.

- **Indicator 2**: Monthly K through12 school attendance in provinces ABC as reported by the host-nation ministry of education.

- **Indicator 3**: Monthly number of tips from local nationals reported to the brigade terrorism tips hotline.

MOE 3: Sniper events in the brigade area of operations disrupted.

- **Indicator 1**: Monthly decrease in reported sniper events in the brigade area of operations. (*Note:* It is acceptable to have only one indicator that directly answers a given MOE. Avoid complicating the assessment needlessly when a simple construct suffices.)

Condition 2: Role 1 medical care available to the population in city X.

MOE 1: Public perception of medical care availability improved in city X.

- **Indicator 1**: Monthly poll question #42: "Are you and your family able to visit the hospital when you need to?" Results for provinces ABC only.

- **Indicator 2**: Monthly poll question #8: "Do you and your family have important health needs that are not being met?" Results for provinces ABC only.

- **Indicator 3**: Monthly decrease in number of requests for medical care received from local nationals by the brigade.

MOE 2: Battalion commander estimated monthly host-nation medical care availability in battalion area of operations.

- **Indicator 1**: Monthly average of reported battalion commander's estimates (scale of 1 to 5) of host-nation medical care availability in the battalion area of operation.

Figure H-2. Sample of end state conditions for stability operations

Selecting and Writing Indicators

H-20. Indicators are developed that provide insights into MOEs. Indicators must be—

- Measurable.
- Collectable.
- Relevant.

H-21. A measurable indicator can be gauged either quantitatively or qualitatively. This is sometimes a problem with imprecisely defined indicators. For example, the indicator "Number of local nationals shopping" is not measurable. The information lacks clear parameters in time or geography. The revised indicator "Average daily number of local nationals visiting main street market in city X this month" is measurable. Additionally, the indicator should be designed to minimize bias. This is particularly true when only qualitative indicators are available for a given MOE. Many qualitative measures are easily biased, and Soldiers must use safeguards to protect objectivity in the assessment process.

H-22. An indicator is collectable if the data associated with the indicator can be reasonably obtained. In some cases, the data may not exist or the data may be prohibitively difficult to collect. For example, the indicator "Average daily number of local nationals visiting main street market in city X this month" is likely not collectable. This number exists, but unless a trusted source is tracking and reporting it, there is no way to collect it. The revised indicator "Battalion commander's monthly estimate of market activity in city X on a scale of 1 to 5" is collectable. In this case, a quantitative indicator was not available, so a qualitative indicator was substituted.

H-23. An indicator is relevant if it provides insight into a supported MOE or MOP. Commanders must ask pertinent questions. They might include the following: Does a change in this indicator actually indicate a change in the MOE? (Which is the cause and which is the effect is not the point here; what matters is that a correlation exists.) What factors unrelated to the MOE could cause this indicator to change? How reliable is the correlation between the indicator and the MOE? For example, the indicator "Decrease in monthly weapons caches found and cleared in the division area of operations" is not relevant to the MOE "Decrease in enemy activity in the division area of operations." This indicator could plausibly increase or decrease with a decrease in enemy activity. An increase in friendly patrols, particularly in areas not previously patrolled on a regular basis, could result in greater numbers of caches found and cleared. It may also be difficult to determine when the enemy left the weapons, raising the question of when the enemy activity actually occurred. These factors, unrelated to enemy activity, could artificially inflate the indicator, creating a false impression of increased enemy activity within the assessment framework. In this example, enemy activity levels can be reliably measured without considering weapons caches, and the indicator should not be used for this MOE.

Building the Assessment Framework

H-24. An assessment framework is a hierarchy used in formal assessments that numerically describes progress toward achieving desired conditions. It typically quantifies end state conditions, MOEs, and indicators. In some cases, it may include an objective rather than the end state or MOPs rather than MOEs.

H-25. A formal assessment framework is simply a tool to assist commanders with estimating progress. Using a formal assessment framework does not imply that the outcomes of military operations are mathematically deterministic. Commanders and staff officers apply judgment to mathematical assessment results to assess the progress holistically.

H-26. For example, commanders in an enduring operation may receive a monthly formal assessment briefing from their staff. This briefing includes both the products of the formal assessment process as well as the expert opinions of members of the staff, subordinate commanders, and other partners. In this way, the commander receives both a mathematically rigorous analysis as well as expert opinions. Commanders combine what they find useful in those two viewpoints with their personal assessment of the operations, considering recommendations and directing action as needed.

H-27. A significant amount of human judgment goes into designing an assessment framework. Choosing MOEs and indicators that accurately measure progress toward each desired condition is an art. Processing elements of the assessment framework requires establishing weights and thresholds for each MOE and indicator. Setting proper weights and thresholds requires operational expertise and judgment. Input from the relevant staff sections and subject matter experts is critical. The logic of why each MOE and indicator is chosen should be recorded. This facilitates personnel turnover as well as understanding the assessment plan among all staff sections.

H-28. Each component of the assessment framework is standardized, assigned a weight, and given thresholds. They are combined mathematically starting at the indicator's level and worked up through MOEs and conditions to the end state. (See figure H-3 on page H-6.)

H-29. Standardization means that each component is expressed as a number on a common scale such as 1 to 5 or 1 to 10. Setting a common scale aids understanding and comparing as well as running the mathematical model. For example, Indicator 1 for MOE 1 for Condition 1 in figure H-3 could be monthly reported dollars in ransom paid as a result of kidnapping operations. For the month of June, that number is $250,000. That number is normalized to a scale of 1 to 10, with 1 being bad and 10 being good. The value of that indicator within the framework is 6.8.

H-30. A weight is a number that expresses relative significance. Some indicators may be more significant than others for informing a given MOE. They count for more in the real world and should literally count for more in the mathematical assessment framework. Weights are used as multipliers for MOEs and indicators. The standard weight of 1.0 implies equal significance. A weight of 2.0 for an MOE (or indicator) implies that MOE carries twice the significance.

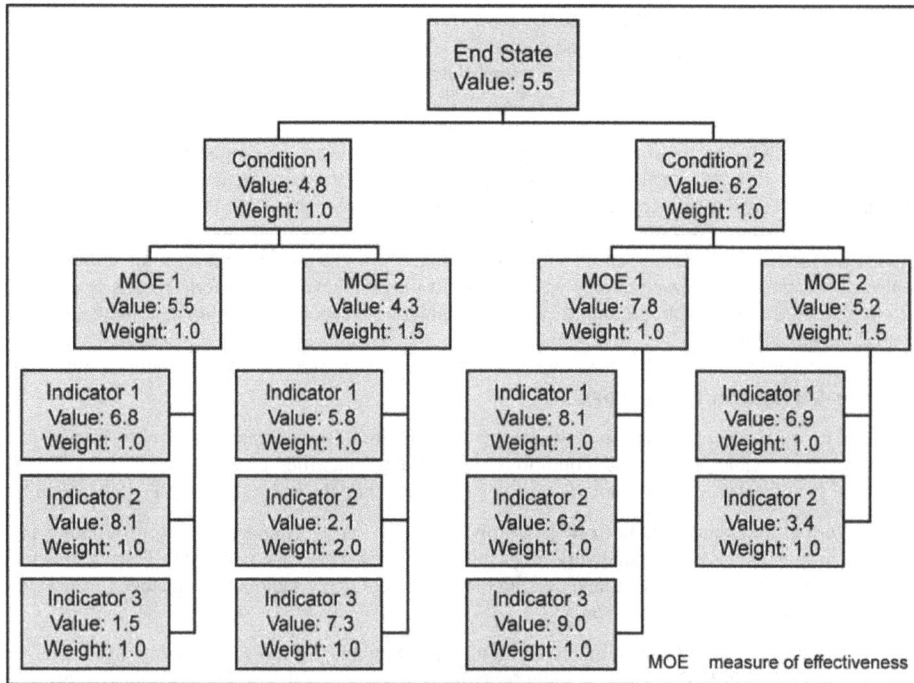

Figure H-3. Sample assessment framework

H-31. A threshold is a value above which one category is in effect and below which another category is in effect. Thresholds answer the question for a given indicator or MOE of what good and bad is. The categories can be whatever the commander finds useful, such as colors or numbers. A commonly used color example is red, amber, yellow, and green. Mathematical thresholds are often set at plus or minus one standard deviation. Whatever category commanders use, they must define it in the assessment plan. They also must weigh the value of insight against the risk of bias.

H-32. Establishing a baseline for comparison is often useful in a formal assessment plan. A baseline is a time in the past against which the present is compared. The word baseline is a statistical term. In the context of assessment, do not use it to mean starting point. Often commanders choose the baseline from a time when conditions are similar to their desired conditions. However, the baseline must be recent enough to be relevant. In protracted operations, the baseline may represent conditions from which commanders are trying to move away. Baselines provide a focus for the commander and staff in comparing data across different blocks of time. Baselines are particularly useful when using standard deviations to establish thresholds. The standard deviation is calculated over the baseline, and multiples of those values are used to set thresholds.

STEP 4 – DEVELOP THE COLLECTION PLAN

H-33. Each indicator represents an information requirement. In some instances, these information requirements are fed into the intelligence, surveillance, and reconnaissance (ISR) synchronization process and tasked to ISR assets. In other instances, reports in the unit standing operating procedures may suffice. If not, the unit may develop a new report. The information requirement may be collected from organizations external to the unit. For example, a host nation's central bank may publish a consumer price index for that nation. The source for each indicator is identified in the assessment plan along with the staff member who collects that information. Assessment information requirements compete with other information requirements for resources. When an information requirement is not resourced, staffs cannot collect the associated indicator and must remove it from the plan. Adjustments are then made to the assessment framework to ensure that the MOE or MOP is properly worded.

STEP 5 – ASSIGN RESPONSIBILITIES FOR CONDUCTING ANALYSIS AND GENERATING RECOMMENDATIONS

H-34. In addition to assigning responsibility for collection, members of the staff are assigned responsibility for analyzing assessment data and developing recommendations. For example, the intelligence officer leads the assessment of enemy forces. The engineer leads the effort on assessing infrastructure development. The civil affairs operations officer leads assessment concerning the progress of local and provincial governments. The chief of staff aggressively requires staff principals and subject matter experts to participate in processing the formal assessment and in generating smart, actionable recommendations.

STEP 6 – IDENTIFY FEEDBACK MECHANISMS

H-35. A formal assessment with meaningful recommendations never heard by the appropriate decisionmaker wastes time and energy. The assessment plan identifies the who, what, when, where, and why of that presentation. Feedback leading up to and following that presentation is discussed as well. Feedback might include which assessment working groups are required and how to act and follow up on recommendations.

H-36. In units with an assessment cell, both the assessment cell and the appropriate staff principal present their findings to the commander. The assessment cell presents the assessment framework with current values and discusses key trends observed. Any relevant insights from the statistical analysis of the information are presented. Then the staff principal either agrees or disagrees with the values provided in the formal model and discusses relevant insights and factors not considered or not explicit in the model. The staff principal then provides meaningful, actionable recommendations based on the assessment.

This page intentionally left blank.

Appendix I

Rehearsals

Rehearsing key actions before execution allows Soldiers to become familiar with the operation and translate the abstract ideas of the written plan into concrete actions. This appendix describes rehearsal types and techniques. It lists the responsibilities of those involved. It also contains guidelines for conducting rehearsals.

REHEARSAL OVERVIEW

I-1.   Rehearsals allow leaders and their Soldiers to practice executing key aspects of the concept of operations. These actions help Soldiers orient themselves to their environment and other units before executing the operation. Rehearsals help Soldiers to build a lasting mental picture of the sequence of key actions within the operation.

I-2.   Rehearsals are the commander's tool to ensure staffs and subordinates understand the commander's intent and the concept of operations. They allow commanders and staffs to identify shortcomings (errors or omissions) in the plan not previously recognized. Rehearsals also contribute to external and internal coordination as additional coordinating requirements are identified.

I-3.   Effective and efficient units habitually rehearse during training. Commanders at every level routinely train and practice various rehearsal types and techniques. Local standing operating procedures (SOPs) identify appropriate rehearsal types, techniques, and standards for their execution. All leaders conduct periodic after action reviews to ensure their units conduct rehearsals to standard and correct substandard performances. After action reviews also enable leaders to incorporate lessons learned into existing plans and orders or into subsequent rehearsals.

I-4.   Adequate time is essential when conducting rehearsals. The time required varies with the complexity of the mission, the type and technique of rehearsal, and the level of participation. Rehearsals are conducted at the lowest possible level, using the most thorough technique possible, given the time available. Under time-constrained conditions, leaders conduct abbreviated rehearsals, focusing on critical events determined by reverse planning. Each unit will have different critical events based on the mission, unit readiness, and the commander's assessment.

I-5.   Whenever possible, rehearsals are based on a completed operation order. However, a unit may rehearse a contingency plan to prepare for an anticipated deployment. The rehearsal is a coordination event, not an analysis. It does not replace war-gaming. Commanders war-game during the military decisionmaking process to analyze different courses of action to determine the optimal one. Rehearsals practice that selected course of action. Commanders avoid making major changes to operation orders during rehearsals. They make only those changes essential to mission success and risk mitigation.

REHEARSAL TYPES

I-6.   Each rehearsal type achieves a different result and has a specific place in the preparation timeline. The four types of rehearsals are—
- Backbrief.
- Combined arms rehearsal.
- Support rehearsal.
- Battle drill or SOP rehearsal.

BACKBRIEF

I-7. **A *backbrief* is a briefing by subordinates to the commander to review how subordinates intend to accomplish their mission**. Normally, subordinates perform backbriefs throughout preparation. These briefs allow commanders to clarify the commander's intent early in subordinate planning. Commanders use the backbrief to identify any problems in the concept of operations.

I-8. The backbrief differs from the confirmation brief (a briefing subordinates give their higher commander immediately following receipt of an order) in that subordinate leaders are given time to complete their plan. Backbriefs require the fewest resources and are often the only option under time-constrained conditions. Subordinate leaders explain their actions from start to finish of the mission. Backbriefs are performed sequentially, with all leaders reviewing their tasks. When time is available, backbriefs can be combined with other types of rehearsals. Doing this lets all subordinate leaders coordinate their plans before performing more elaborate drills.

COMBINED ARMS REHEARSAL

I-9. A combined arms rehearsal is a rehearsal in which subordinate units synchronize their plans with each other. A maneuver unit headquarters normally executes a combined arms rehearsal after subordinate units issue their operation order. This rehearsal type helps ensure that subordinate commanders' plans achieve the higher commander's intent.

SUPPORT REHEARSAL

I-10. The support rehearsal helps synchronize each warfighting function with the overall operation. This rehearsal supports the operation so units can accomplish their missions. Throughout preparation, units conduct support rehearsals within the framework of a single or limited number of warfighting functions. These rehearsals typically involve coordination and procedure drills for aviation, fires, engineer support, or casualty evacuation. Support rehearsals and combined arms rehearsals complement preparations for the operation. They may be conducted separately and then combined into full-dress rehearsals. Although these rehearsals differ slightly by warfighting function, they achieve the same result.

BATTLE DRILL OR STANDING OPERATING PROCEDURE REHEARSAL

I-11. A battle drill is a collective action rapidly executed without applying a deliberate decisionmaking process. A battle drill or SOP rehearsal ensures that all participants understand a technique or a specific set of procedures. Throughout preparation, units and staffs rehearse battle drills and SOPs. These rehearsals do not need a completed order from higher headquarters. Leaders place priority on those drills or actions they anticipate occurring during the operation. For example, a transportation platoon may rehearse a battle drill on reacting to an ambush while awaiting to begin movement.

I-12. All echelons use these rehearsal types; however, they are most common for platoons, squads, and sections. They are conducted throughout preparation and are not limited to published battle drills. They can rehearse such actions as a command post shift change, an obstacle breach lane-marking SOP, or a refuel-on-the-move site operation.

REHEARSAL TECHNIQUES

I-13. Techniques for conducting rehearsals are limited only by the commander's imagination and available resources. Generally, six techniques are used. (See figure I-1.) Resources required for each technique range from broad to narrow. As listed, each successive technique takes less time and fewer resources. Each rehearsal technique also imparts a different level of understanding to participants.

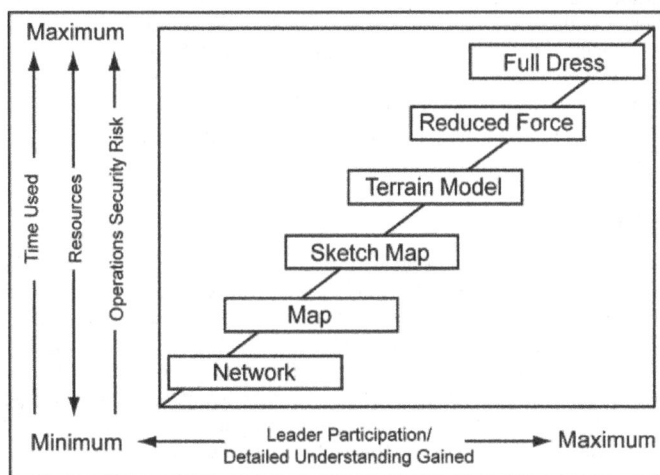

Figure I-1. Rehearsal techniques

I-14. Paragraphs I-15 through I-30 address these considerations:
- **Time**–the amount of time required to conduct (plan, prepare, execute, and assess) the rehearsal.
- **Echelons involved**–the number of echelons that can participate in the rehearsal.
- **Operations security risk**–the ease by which adversary can exploit friendly actions from the rehearsal.
- **Terrain**–the amount of space needed for the rehearsal.

FULL-DRESS REHEARSAL

I-15. A full-dress rehearsal produces the most detailed understanding of the operation. It includes every participating Soldier and system. Leaders rehearse their subordinates on terrain similar to the AO, initially under good light conditions, and then in limited visibility. Small-unit actions are repeated until executed to standard. Full-dress rehearsals help Soldiers to clearly understand what is expected of them. It helps them gain confidence in their ability to accomplish the mission. Supporting elements, such as aviation crews, meet with Soldiers and rehearse with them to synchronize the operation.

I-16. The unit may conduct full-dress rehearsals. They also may be conducted and supported by the higher headquarters. The full-dress rehearsal is the most difficult to accomplish at higher echelons. At those levels, commanders may develop an alternate rehearsal plan that mirrors the actual plan but fits the terrain available for the rehearsal.

I-17. Full-dress rehearsals have the following implications:
- **Time**. Full-dress rehearsals consume more time than any other rehearsal type. For companies and smaller units, full-dress rehearsals most effectively ensure all units in the operation understand their roles. However, brigade and task force commanders consider how much time their subordinates need to plan and prepare when deciding whether to conduct a full-dress rehearsal.
- **Echelons involved**. All echelons involved in the operation participate in the full-dress rehearsal.

- **Operations security risk**. Moving a large part of the force may attract unwanted enemy attention. Commanders develop a plan to protect the rehearsal from enemy surveillance and reconnaissance. One method is to develop an alternate plan, including graphics and radio frequencies, which rehearses selected actions without compromising the actual operation order. Commanders take care not to confuse subordinates when doing this.
- **Terrain**. Terrain management for a full-dress rehearsal can be difficult. The rehearsal area must be identified, secured, cleared, and maintained throughout the rehearsal.

REDUCED-FORCE REHEARSAL

I-18. Circumstances may prohibit a rehearsal with all members of the unit. A reduced-force rehearsal involves only key leaders of the organization and its subordinate units. It normally takes fewer resources than a full-dress rehearsal. Terrain requirements can be the same as a full-dress rehearsal, even though there are fewer participants. The commander first decides the level of leader involvement. Then the selected leaders rehearse the plan while traversing the actual or similar terrain. Often commanders use this technique to rehearse fire control measures for an engagement area during defensive operations. A reduced-force rehearsal may be used to prepare key leaders for a full-dress rehearsal. It may require developing a rehearsal plan that mirrors the actual plan but fits the terrain of the rehearsal.

I-19. Often, smaller scale replicas of terrain or buildings substitute for the actual AO. Leaders not only explain their plans, but also walk through their actions or move replicas across the rehearsal area or sand table. This is called a rock drill. It reinforces the backbrief given by subordinates since everyone can see the concept of operations and sequence of tasks.

I-20. Reduced-force rehearsals have the following implications:

- **Time**. A reduced-force rehearsal normally requires less time than a full-dress rehearsal. Commanders consider how much time their subordinates need to plan and prepare when deciding whether to conduct a reduced-force rehearsal.
- **Echelons involved**. A small unit can perform a full-dress rehearsal as part of a larger organization's reduced-force rehearsal.
- **Operations security risk**. A reduced-force rehearsal is less likely to present operations security vulnerabilities than a full-dress rehearsal because it has fewer participants. However, the number of radio transmissions required is the same as for a full-dress rehearsal and must be considered.
- **Terrain**. Terrain management for the reduced-force rehearsal can be as difficult as for the full-dress rehearsal. The rehearsal area must be identified, secured, cleared, and maintained throughout the rehearsal.

TERRAIN-MODEL REHEARSAL

I-21. The terrain-model rehearsal is the most popular rehearsal technique. It takes less time and fewer resources than a full-dress or reduced-force rehearsal. (A terrain-model rehearsal takes a proficient brigade between one to two hours to execute to standard.) An accurately constructed terrain model helps subordinate leaders visualize the commander's intent and concept of operations. When possible, commanders place the terrain model where it overlooks the actual terrain of the AO. However, if the situation requires more security, they place the terrain model on a reverse slope within walking distance of a point overlooking the AO. The model's orientation coincides with that of the terrain. The size of the terrain model can vary from small (using markers to represent units) to large (on which the participants can walk). A large model helps reinforce the participants' perception of unit positions on the terrain.

I-22. Terrain-model rehearsals have the following implications:

- **Time**. Often, constructing the terrain model is the most time-consuming part of this technique. Units require a clear SOP that states how to build the model so it is accurate, large, and detailed enough to conduct the rehearsal. A good SOP also establishes staff responsibility for building the terrain model and a timeline for its completion.
- **Echelons involved**. Because a terrain model is geared to the echelon conducting the rehearsal, multiechelon rehearsals using this technique are difficult.

- **Operations security risk**. This rehearsal can present operations security vulnerabilities if the area around the rehearsal site is not secured. Assembled commanders and their vehicles can draw enemy attention. Units must sanitize the terrain model after completing the rehearsal.
- **Terrain**. Terrain management is less difficult than with the previous techniques. A good site is easy for participants to find yet concealed from the enemy. An optimal location overlooks the terrain where the unit will execute the operation.

I-23. With today's digital capabilities, users can construct terrain models in virtual space. Units drape high resolution imagery over elevation data thereby creating a fly-through or walk-through. Holographic imagery produces the view in three dimensions. Often, graphics, detailed information, unmanned aircraft systems, and ground imagery are hot linked to key points in the model providing more insight into the plan. Digital terrain models reduce the operations security risk because real terrain is not used. The unit geospatial engineers or imagery analysts can assist in digital model creation. Detailed city models already exist for many world cities.

I-24. Digital terrain-model rehearsals have the following implications:

- **Time**. The time it takes to create the three-dimensional model depends on the amount of available data on the terrain being modeled.
- **Echelons involved**. This type of rehearsal best suits small units, although with a good local area network, a wider audience can view the graphics. All echelons may be provided copies of the digital model to take back to their headquarters for a more detailed examination.
- **Operations security risk**. If not placed on a computer network, there is limited security risk because no site is secured and the rehearsal can be conducted under cover. However, if placed on a computer network, digital terrain models can be subject to enemy exploitation due to inherent vulnerabilities of networks.
- **Terrain**. This space requires the least space of all rehearsals. Using tents or enclosed areas conceal the rehearsal from the enemy.

SKETCH-MAP REHEARSAL

I-25. Commanders can use the sketch-map technique almost anywhere, day or night. The procedures are the same as for a terrain-model rehearsal except the commander uses a sketch map in place of a terrain model. Effective sketches are large enough for all participants to see as each participant walks through execution of the operation. Participants move markers on the sketch to represent unit locations and maneuvers.

I-26. Sketch-map rehearsals have the following implications:

- **Time**. Sketch-map rehearsals take less time than terrain-model rehearsals and more time than map rehearsals.
- **Echelons involved**. Because a sketch map is geared to the echelon conducting the rehearsal, multiechelon rehearsals using this technique are difficult.
- **Operations security risk**. This rehearsal can present operations security vulnerabilities if the area around the rehearsal site is not secured. Assembled commanders and their vehicles can draw enemy attention. Units must sanitize, secure, or destroy the sketch map after use.
- **Terrain**. This technique requires less space than a terrain-model rehearsal. A good site is easy for participants to find yet concealed from the enemy. An optimal location overlooks the terrain where the unit will execute the operation.

MAP REHEARSAL

I-27. A map rehearsal is similar to a sketch-map rehearsal except the commander uses a map and operation overlay of the same scale used to plan the operation.

I-28. Map rehearsals have the following implications:

- **Time**. The most time-consuming part is the rehearsal itself. A map rehearsal is normally the easiest technique to set up since it requires only maps and graphics for current operations.
- **Echelons involved**. Because the operation overlay is geared to the echelon conducting the rehearsal, multiechelon rehearsals using this technique are difficult.
- **Operations security risk**. This rehearsal can present operations security vulnerabilities if the area around the rehearsal site is not secured. Assembled commanders and their vehicles can draw enemy attention.
- **Terrain**. This technique requires the least space of all rehearsals. A good site is one that is easy for participants to find yet concealed from the enemy. An optimal location overlooks the terrain where the unit will execute the operation.

NETWORK REHEARSAL

I-29. Network rehearsals are conducted over wide-area networks or local area networks. Commanders and staffs practice these rehearsals by talking through critical portions of the operation over communications networks in a sequence the commander establishes. The organization rehearses only the critical parts of the operation. These rehearsals require all information systems needed to execute that portion of the operation. All participants require working information systems, the operation order, and overlays. Command posts can rehearse battle tracking during network rehearsals.

I-30. Network rehearsals have the following implications:

- **Time**. This technique can be time efficient if SOPs are clear. However, if the organization has unclear SOPs, has units not operating on the network, or has units without working communications, this technique can be time-consuming.
- **Echelons involved**. This technique lends itself to multiechelon rehearsals. Participation is limited only by the commander's intent and the capabilities of the command's information systems.
- **Operations security risk**. If a network rehearsal is executed from current unit locations, the risk may be higher. The enemy may monitor the increased volume of transmissions and potentially compromise information. The organization should use different frequencies from those planned for the operation. Using wire systems is an option but does not exercise the network systems, which is the strong point of this technique.
- **Terrain**. If a network rehearsal is executed from unit locations, terrain considerations are minimal. If a separate rehearsal area is required, considerations are similar to those of a reduced-force rehearsal.

REHEARSAL RESPONSIBILITIES

I-31. This discussion addresses responsibilities for conducting rehearsals. It is based on the combined arms rehearsal. Responsibilities are the same for support rehearsals.

PLANNING

I-32. Commanders and chiefs of staff (executive officers at lower echelons) plan rehearsals.

Commander

I-33. Commanders provide certain information as part of the commander's guidance during the initial mission analysis. They may revise the following information when they select a course of action:

- Rehearsal type.
- Rehearsal technique.
- Location.
- Attendees.
- Enemy course of action to be portrayed.

Chief of Staff (Executive Officer)

I-34. The chief of staff or executive officer ensures all rehearsals are included in the organization's time-management SOP. The chief of staff or executive officer responsibilities include—

- Publishing the rehearsal time and location in the operation order or warning order.
- Conducting staff rehearsals.
- Determining rehearsal products, based on type, technique, and mission variables.
- Coordinating liaison officer attendance from adjacent units.

PREPARATION

I-35. Everyone involved in executing or supporting the rehearsal has responsibilities during preparation.

Commander

I-36. Commanders prepare to rehearse operations with events phased in proper order, from start to finish. Under time-constrained conditions, this often proves difficult. Commanders—

- Identify and prioritize key events to rehearse.
- Allocate time for each event.
- Perform personal preparation, including reviews of—
  - Task organization completeness.
  - Personnel and materiel readiness.
  - Organizational level of preparation.

Chief of Staff (Executive Officer)

I-37. The chief of staff or executive officer, through war-gaming and coordination with the commander—

- Prepares to serve as the rehearsal director.
- Coordinates time for key events requiring rehearsal.
- Establishes rehearsal time limits per the commander's guidance and mission variables.
- Verifies rehearsal site preparation. A separate rehearsal site may be required for some events, such as a possible obstacle site. A good rehearsal site includes—
  - Appropriate markings and associated training aids.
  - Parking areas.
  - Local security.
- Determines the method for controlling the rehearsal and ensuring its logical flow, such as a script. (See paragraphs I-57 through I-64.)

Subordinate Leaders

I-38. Subordinate leaders complete their planning. This planning includes—

- Completing unit operation orders.
- Identifying issues derived from the higher headquarters' operation order.
- Providing a copy of their unit operation order with graphics to the higher headquarters.
- Performing personal preparation similar to that of the commander.
- Ensuring they and their subordinates bring all necessary equipment.

Conducting Headquarters Staff

I-39. Conducting headquarters staff members—

- Develop an operation order with necessary overlays.
- Deconflict all subordinate unit graphics. Composite overlays are the first step for leaders to visualize the organization's overall plan.
- Publish composite overlays at the rehearsal including, at a minimum—
  - Movement and maneuver.
  - Intelligence.
  - Fires.
  - Sustainment.
  - Command and control, including signal operations.
  - Protection.

EXECUTION

I-40. During execution, the commander, chief of staff, assistants, subordinate leaders, recorder, and staff from the conducting headquarters all have specific responsibilities.

Commander

I-41. Commanders command the rehearsal just as they will command the operation. They maintain the focus and level of intensity, allowing no potential for subordinate confusion. Although the staff refines the operation order, it belongs to the commander. The commander uses the order to conduct operations. An effective rehearsal is not a commander's brief to subordinates. It validates synchronization—the what, when, and where—of tasks that subordinate units will perform to execute the operation and achieve the commander's intent.

Chief of Staff (Executive Officer)

I-42. Normally, the chief of staff or executive officer serves as the rehearsal director. This officer ensures each unit will accomplish its tasks at the right time and cues the commander to upcoming decisions. The chief of staff's or executive officer's script is the execution matrix and the decision support template. The rehearsal director—

- Starts the rehearsal on time.
- Has a formal roll call.
- Ensures everyone brings the necessary equipment. This equipment includes organizational graphics and previously issued orders.
- Validates the task organization. Linkups must be complete or on schedule, and required materiel and personnel must be on hand. The importance of this simple check cannot be overemphasized.
- Ensures sustaining operations are synchronized with shaping operations and the decisive operation.
- Rehearses the synchronization of combat power from flank and higher organizations. These organizations are often beyond communication range of the commander and G-3 (S-3) when away from the command post.
- Synchronizes the timing and contribution of each warfighting function by ensuring the rehearsal of operations against the decisive points by time or event that connect to a decision.
- For each decisive point, defines conditions required to—
  - Commit the reserve or striking forces.
  - Move a unit.
  - Close or emplace an obstacle.
  - Fire at planned targets.
  - Move a medical unit, change a supply route, and alert specific observation posts.

- Disciplines leader movements, enforces brevity, and ensures completeness. The operation order, decision support template, and execution matrix are the chief of staff's tools.
- Keeps within time constraints.
- Ensures that the most important events receive the most attention.
- Ensures that absentees and flank units receive changes to the operation order. Transmits changes to them as soon as practical.
- Communicates the key civil considerations of the operation.

Assistant Chief of Staff, G-3 (S-3)

I-43. The G-3 (S-3) assists the commander with the rehearsal. The G-3 (S-3)—

- Portrays the friendly scheme of maneuver.
- Ensures subordinate unit actions comply with the commander's intent.
- Normally provides the recorder.

Assistant Chief of Staff, G-2 (S-2)

I-44. The G-2 (S-2) portrays the adversary forces and other variables of the operational environment during rehearsals. The G-2 (S-2) bases actions on the enemy course of action that the commander selected during the military decisionmaking process. The G-2 (S-2)—

- Provides participants with current intelligence.
- Portrays the best possible assessment of the enemy course of action.
- Communicates the adversary's presumed concept of operations, desired effects, and end state.
- Explains other factors of the operational environment that may hinder or complicate friendly actions.
- Communicates the key civil considerations of the operation.

Subordinate Leaders

I-45. Subordinate unit leaders, using an established format—

- Effectively articulate their units' actions and responsibilities.
- Record changes on their copies of the graphics or operation order.

Recorder

I-46. The recorder is normally the G-3 (S-3) or a representative from the operations cell. During the rehearsal, the recorder—

- Captures all coordination made during execution.
- Notes unresolved problems.

I-47. At the end of the rehearsal, the recorder—

- Presents any unresolved problems to the commander for resolution.
- Restates any changes, coordination, or clarifications directed by the commander.
- Estimates when a written fragmentary order codifying the changes will follow.

Conducting Headquarters Staff

I-48. The staff updates the operation order, decision support template, and execution matrix based on the decisions of the commander.

ASSESSMENT

I-49. The commander establishes the standard for a successful rehearsal. A properly executed rehearsal validates each leader's role and how each unit contributes to the overall operation—what is done, when it is done relative to times and events, and where it is done to achieve desired effects. An effective rehearsal ensures commanders have a common vision of the enemy, their own forces, the terrain, and the relationship among them. It identifies specific actions requiring immediate staff resolution and informs the higher commander of critical issues or locations that the commander, chief of staff (executive officer), or G-3 (S-3) must personally oversee.

I-50. The commander (or rehearsal director in the commander's absence) assesses and critiques all parts of the rehearsal. Critiques center on how well the operation achieves the commander's intent and on the coordination necessary to accomplish that end. Usually, the internal execution of tasks within the rehearsal is left to the subordinate unit commander's judgment and discretion.

CONDUCTING A REHEARSAL

I-51. All participants have responsibilities before, during, and after a rehearsal. Before a rehearsal, the rehearsal director states the commander's expectations and orients the other participants on details of the rehearsal as necessary. During a rehearsal, all participants rehearse their roles in the operation. They make sure they understand how their actions support the overall operation and note any additional coordination required. After a rehearsal, participants ensure they understand any changes to the operation order and coordination requirements, and they receive all updated staff products.

I-52. Commanders do not normally address small problems that arise during rehearsals. Instead, these are recorded. This ensures the rehearsal's flow is not interrupted. If the problem remains at the end of the rehearsal, the commander resolves it then. However, if the problem can wait until the end of the rehearsal, it may not have been a real problem. If the problem jeopardizes mission accomplishment, the staff accomplishes the coordination necessary to resolve it before the participants disperse. Identifying and solving such problems is a major reason for conducting rehearsals. If corrections are not made while participants are assembled, the opportunity to do so may be lost. Coordinating among dispersed participants and disseminating changes to them is more difficult than accomplishing these actions in person.

BEFORE THE REHEARSAL

I-53. Before the rehearsal, the rehearsal director calls the roll and briefs participants on information needed for execution. The briefing begins with an introduction, overview, and orientation. It includes a discussion of the rehearsal script and ground rules. The detail of this discussion is based on participants' familiarity with the rehearsal SOP.

I-54. Before the rehearsal, the staff develops an operation order with at least the basic five paragraphs and necessary overlays. Annexes may not be published; however, the responsible staff officers should know their content.

Introduction and Overview

I-55. Before the rehearsal, the rehearsal director introduces all participants as needed. Then, the director gives an overview of the briefing topics, rehearsal subjects and sequence, and timeline, specifying the no-later-than ending time. The rehearsal director explains after action reviews, describes how and when they occur, and discusses how to incorporate changes into the operation order. The director explains any constraints, such as pyrotechnics use, light discipline, weapons firing, or radio silence. For safety, the rehearsal director ensures all participants understand safety precautions and enforces their use. Last, the director emphasizes results and states the commander's standard for a successful rehearsal. Subordinate leaders state any results of planning or preparation (including rehearsals) they have already conducted. If a subordinate recommends a change to the operation order, the rehearsal director acts on the recommendation before the rehearsal begins, if possible. If not, the commander resolves the recommendation with a decision before the rehearsal ends.

Orientation

I-56. The rehearsal director orients the participants to the terrain or rehearsal medium. Orientation is identified using magnetic north on the rehearsal medium and symbols representing actual terrain features.

The director explains any graphic control measures, obstacles, and targets and then issues supplemental materials, if needed.

Rehearsal Script

I-57. An effective technique for controlling rehearsals is to use a script. It keeps the rehearsal on track. The script provides a checklist so the organization addresses all warfighting functions and outstanding issues. It has two major parts: the agenda and the response sequence.

Agenda

I-58. An effective rehearsal follows a prescribed agenda that everyone knows and understands. An effective rehearsal includes—

- Roll call.
- Participant orientation to the terrain.
- Location of local civilians.
- Enemy situation brief.
- Friendly situation brief.
- Description of expected adversary actions.
- Discussion of friendly unit actions.
- A review of notes made by the recorder.

I-59. The execution matrix, decision support template, and operation order outline the rehearsal agenda. These tools, especially the execution matrix, both drive and focus the rehearsal. The commander and staff use them to control the operation's execution. Any templates, matrixes, or tools developed within each of the warfighting functions (for example an intelligence synchronization matrix or fires execution matrix) should tie directly to the supported unit's execution matrix and decision support template.

I-60. An effective rehearsal requires the enemy force and other variables of the operational environment to be portrayed realistically and quickly without distracting from the rehearsal. One technique for doing this has the G-2 (S-2) preparing an actions checklist. It lists a sequence of events much like the one for friendly units but from the enemy or civilian perspective.

Response Sequence

I-61. Participants respond in a logical sequence: either by warfighting function or by unit as the organization is deployed, from front to rear. The commander determines the sequence before the rehearsal. It is posted at the rehearsal site, and the rehearsal director may restate it.

I-62. Effective rehearsals allow participants to visualize and synchronize the concept of operations. As the rehearsal proceeds, participants talk through the concept of operations. They focus on key events and the synchronization required to achieve the desired effects. The commander leads the rehearsal. The commander gives orders during the operation. Subordinate commanders enter and leave the discussion at the time they expect to begin and end their tasks or activities during the operation. This practice helps the commander assess the adequacy of synchronization. They do not "re-war-game" unless absolutely necessary to ensure subordinate unit commanders understand the plan.

I-63. The rehearsal director emphasizes integrating fires, events that trigger different branch actions, and actions on contact. The chief of fires (fire support officer) or fires unit commander states when fires are initiated, who is firing, from where the firing comes, the ammunition available, and the desired target effect. Subordinate commanders state when they initiate fires per their fire support plans. The rehearsal director speaks for any absent staff section and ensures all actions on the synchronization matrix and decision support template are addressed at the proper time or event.

I-64. The rehearsal director ensures that key sustainment and protection actions are included in the rehearsal at the times they are executed. (See table I-1 on page I-12.) Failure to do so reduces the value of the rehearsal as a coordination tool. The staff officer with coordinating staff responsibility inserts these items into the rehearsal at appropriate times. Special staff officers should brief by exception when a friendly or enemy event occurs within their area of expertise. Summarizing these actions at the end of the rehearsal can reinforce coordination requirements identified during the rehearsal. The staff updates the decision support template and gives a copy to each participant. Under time-constrained conditions, the conducting headquarters staff may provide copies before the rehearsal and rely on participants to update them with pen-and-ink changes.

Table I-1. Example sustainment and protection actions for rehearsals

• Casualty evacuation routes	• Support area displacement times and locations
• Ambulance exchange point locations	• Enemy prisoner of war collection points
• Refuel-on-the-move points	• Aviation support
• Class IV and class V resupply points	• Military police actions
• Logistics release points	

Ground Rules

I-65. After discussing the rehearsal script, the rehearsal director—

- States the standard (what the commander will accept) for a successful rehearsal.
- Ensures everyone understands the parts of the operation order to rehearse. If the entire operation will not be rehearsed, the rehearsal director states the events to be rehearsed.
- Quickly reviews the rehearsal SOP if all participants are not familiar with it. An effective rehearsal SOP states—
    - Who controls the rehearsal.
    - Who approves the rehearsal venue and its construction.
    - When special staff officers brief the commander.
    - The relationship between how the execution matrix portrays events and how units rehearse events.
- Establishes the timeline; it designates the rehearsal starting time in relation to H-hour. For example, begin the rehearsal by depicting the anticipated situation one hour before H-hour. One event executed before rehearsing the first event is deployment of forces.
- Establishes the time interval to begin and track the rehearsal. For example, specify a ten-minute interval equates to one hour of actual time.
- Updates friendly and adversary activities as necessary, for example, any ongoing reconnaissance.

The rehearsal director concludes the orientation with a call for questions.

DURING THE REHEARSAL

I-66. After the rehearsal director finishes discussing the ground rules and answering questions, the G-3 (S-3) reads the mission statement, the commander reads the commander's intent, and the G-3 (S-3) establishes the current friendly situation. The rehearsal then begins, following the rehearsal script.

I-67. Paragraphs I-68 through I-80 outline a generic set of rehearsal steps developed for combined arms rehearsals. However, with a few modifications, these steps support any rehearsal technique. The products depend on the rehearsal type.

Step 1 – Enemy Forces Deployed

I-68. The G-2 (S-2) briefs the current enemy situation and operational environment and places markers on the map or terrain board (as applicable) indicating where enemy forces and other operationally significant groups or activities would be before the first rehearsal event. The G-2 (S-2) then briefs the most likely enemy course of action and operational context. The G-2 (S-2) also briefs the status of reconnaissance and surveillance operations (for example, citing any patrols still out or any observation post positions).

Step 2 – Friendly Forces Deployed

I-69. The G-3 (S-3) briefs friendly maneuver unit dispositions, including security forces, of the rehearsal starting time. Subordinate commanders and other staff officers brief their unit positions at the starting time and any particular points of emphasis. For example, the chemical, biological, radiological, and nuclear officer states the mission-oriented protective posture level, and the chief of fires (fire support officer) or fires unit commander states the range of friendly and enemy artillery. Other participants place markers for friendly forces, including adjacent units, at the positions they will occupy at the rehearsal starting time. As participants place markers, they state their task and purpose, task organization, and strength.

I-70. Sustainment and protection units brief positions, plans, and actions at the starting time and at points of emphasis the rehearsal director designates. Subordinate units may include forward arming and refueling points, refuel-on-the-move points, communications checkpoints, security points, or operations security procedures that differ for that period. The rehearsal director restates the commander's intent, if necessary.

Step 3 – Initiate Action

I-71. The rehearsal director states the first event on the execution matrix. Normally this involves the G-2 (S-2) moving enemy markers according to the most likely course of action at the point on the execution matrix being rehearsed. The depiction must tie enemy actions to specific terrain or to friendly unit actions. The G-2 (S-2) portrays enemy actions based on the situational template developed for staff war-gaming. The enemy is portrayed as uncooperative but not invincible.

I-72. As the rehearsal proceeds, the G-2 (S-2) portrays the enemy and other operational factors and walks through the most likely enemy course of action (per the situational template). The G-2 (S-2) stresses reconnaissance routes, objectives, security force composition and locations, initial contact, initial fires (artillery, air, and attack helicopters), probable main force objectives or engagement areas, and likely commitment of reserve forces. The G-2 (S-2) is specific, tying enemy actions to specific terrain or friendly unit actions. The walk through should accurately portray the event template.

Step 4 – Decision Point

I-73. When the enemy movement and operational context is complete, the commander assesses the situation to determine if a decision point has been reached. Decision points are taken directly from the decision support template. The commander determines if the organization is—

- **Not at a decision point**. If the organization is not at a decision point and not at the end state, the rehearsal director continues the rehearsal by stating the next event on the execution matrix. Participants use the response sequence (see paragraphs I-61 through I-64) and continue to act out and describe their units' actions.
- **At a decision point**. When conditions that establish a decision point are reached, the commander decides whether to continue with the current course of action or by selecting a branch. If electing the current course of action, the commander states the next event from the execution matrix and directs movement of friendly units. If selecting a branch, the commander states why that branch, states the first event of that branch, and continues the rehearsal until the organization has rehearsed all events of that branch. As the unit reaches decisive points, the rehearsal director states the conditions required for success.

I-74. If units in the reserve force participate, they rehearse all their branches beginning with the most likely.

I-75. When it becomes obvious that the operation requires additional coordination to ensure success, participants immediately begin coordinating. This is one of the key reasons for rehearsals. The rehearsal director ensures that the recorder captures and all participants understand the coordination.

Step 5 – End State Reached

I-76. Achieving the desired end state completes that phase of the rehearsal. In an attack, this will usually be when the unit is on the objective and has finished consolidation and casualty evacuation. In the defense, this will usually be after the decisive action (such as committing the reserve or striking force), the final destruction or withdrawal of the enemy, and casualty evacuation is complete. In a stability operation, this is usually when targeted progress within a designated line of effort is achieved.

Step 6 – Reset

I-77. At this point, the commander states the next branch to rehearse. The rehearsal director resets the situation to the decision point where that branch begins and states the criteria for a decision to execute that branch. Participants assume those criteria have been met and then refight the operation along that branch until they attain the desired end state. They complete any coordination needed to ensure all participants understand and can meet any requirements. The recorder records any changes to the branch.

I-78. The commander then states the next branch to rehearse. The rehearsal director again resets the situation to the decision point where that branch begins, and participants repeat the process. This continues until all decision points and branches the commander wants to rehearse have been addressed.

I-79. If the standard is not met and time permits, the commander directs participants to repeat the rehearsal. The rehearsal continues until participants are prepared or until the time available expires. (Commanders may allocate more time for a rehearsal but must assess the effects on subordinate commanders' preparation time.) Successive rehearsals, if conducted, should be more complex and realistic.

I-80. At the end of the rehearsal, the recorder restates any changes, coordination, or clarifications the commander directed and estimates how long it will take to codify changes in a written fragmentary order.

AFTER THE REHEARSAL

I-81. After the rehearsal, the commander leads an after action review. The commander reviews lessons learned and makes the minimum required modifications to the existing plan. (Normally, a fragmentary order effects these changes.) Changes should be refinements to the operation order; they should not be radical or significant. Changes not critical to the operation's execution may confuse subordinates and hinder the synchronization of the plan. The commander issues any last minute instructions or reminders and reiterates the commander's intent.

I-82. Based on the commander's instructions, the staff makes any necessary changes to the operation order, decision support template, and execution matrix based on the rehearsal results. Subordinate commanders incorporate these changes into their units' operation orders. The chief of staff (executive officer) ensures the changes are briefed to all leaders or liaison officers who did not participate in the rehearsal.

I-83. A rehearsal is the final opportunity for subordinates to identify and fix unresolved issues. An effective staff ensures that all participants understand any changes to the operation order and that the recorder captures all coordination done at the rehearsal. All changes to the published operation order are, in effect, verbal fragmentary orders. As soon as possible, the staff publishes these verbal fragmentary orders as a written fragmentary order that changes the operation order.

Appendix J

Military Briefings

This appendix describes the four types of military briefings presented to commanders, staffs, or other audiences. It also describes steps of the military briefings.

TYPES OF MILITARY BRIEFINGS

J-1.   The Army uses four types of briefings: information, decision, mission, and staff.

INFORMATION BRIEFING

J-2.   An information briefing presents facts in a form the audience can easily understand. It does not include conclusions or recommendations nor does it result in decisions. (See figure J-1.)

---

1. Introduction
- **Greeting**. Address the audience. Identify yourself and your organization.
- **Type and Classification of Briefing**. Identify the type and classification of the briefing. For example, "This is an information briefing. It is classified SECRET."
- **Purpose and Scope**. Describe complex subjects from general to specific.
- **Outline or Procedure**. Briefly summarize the key points and general approach. Explain any special procedures (such as demonstrations, displays, or tours). For example, "During my briefing, I will discuss the six phases of our plan. I will refer to maps of our area of operations. Then my assistant will bring out a sand table to show you the expected flow of battle." The key points may be placed on a chart that remains visible throughout the briefing.

2. Main Body
- Arrange the main ideas in a logical sequence.
- Use visual aids to emphasize main points.
- Plan effective transitions from one main point to the next.
- Be prepared to answer questions at any time.

3. Closing
- Ask for questions.
- Briefly recap main ideas and make a concluding statement.

Figure J-1. Information briefing format

J-3.   Briefers begin an information briefing by greeting the audience, identifying themselves and their organization, and then providing the classification of the briefing. The briefer states that the purpose of the briefing is to inform the audience and that no decision is required. The briefer then introduces the subject, orients the audience to any visual aids, and presents the information. Examples of appropriate topics for information briefings include—

- High-priority information requiring immediate attention.
- Complex information such as complicated plans, systems, statistics or charts, or other items that require detailed explanations.
- Controversial information requiring elaboration and explanation.

DECISION BRIEFING

J-4.   A decision briefing obtains the answer to a question or a decision on a course of action. The briefer presents recommended solutions from the analysis or study of a problem or problem area. (Chapter 2 discusses Army problem solving.) Decision briefings vary in formality and level of detail depending on the commander's or decisionmaker's knowledge on the subject.

J-5.   If the decisionmaker is unfamiliar with the problem, the briefing format adheres to the decision briefing format. (See figure J-2.) Decision briefings should include all facts and assumptions relevant to the problem, a discussion of alternatives, analysis-based conclusions, and any coordination required.

---

1. Introduction
- **Greeting**. Address the decisionmaker. Identify yourself and your organization.
- **Type and Classification of Briefing**. Identify the type and classification of the briefing. For example, "This is a decision briefing. It is UNCLASSIFIED."
- **Problem Statement**. State the problem.
- **Recommendation**. State the recommendation.

2. Body
- **Facts**. Provide an objective presentation of both positive and negative facts bearing upon the problem.
- **Assumptions**. Identify necessary assumptions made to bridge any gaps in factual data.
- **Solutions**. Discuss the various options that can solve the problem.
- **Analysis**. List the criteria by which the briefer will evaluate how to solve the problem (screening and evaluation). Discuss relative advantages and disadvantages for each course of action.
- **Comparison**. Show how the courses of action rate against the evaluation criteria.
- **Conclusion**. Describe why the recommended solution is best.

3. Closing
- Ask for questions.
- Briefly recap main ideas and restate the recommendation.
- Request a decision.

Figure J-2. Decision briefing format

J-6.   When the decisionmaker is familiar with the subject or problem, the briefing format often resembles that of a decision paper: problem statement, essential background information, impacts, and recommended solution. In addition to this format, briefers must be prepared to present assumptions, facts, alternative solutions, reasons for recommendations, and any additional coordination required.

J-7.   The briefer begins by stating, "This is a decision briefing." If no decision is provided upon conclusion of the decision briefing, the briefer will ask for one. The briefer ensures all participants clearly understand the decision and asks for clarification if necessary.

J-8.   Recommendations presented during decision briefings should be clearly stated and precisely worded to prevent ambiguity and to be easily translated into a decision statement. If the decision requires an implementation document, briefers present that document at the time of the briefing for the decisionmaker to sign. If the chief of staff or executive officer is absent, the briefer should inform the secretary of the general staff or designated authority of the decision upon conclusion of the briefing.

MISSION BRIEFING

J-9.   Mission briefings are informal briefings that occur during operations or training. Briefers may be commanders, staffs, or special representatives. (See appendix B for a discussion of a mission briefing within the military decisionmaking process.)

J-10. Mission briefings serve to convey critical mission information not provided in the plan or order to individuals or smaller units. Mission briefings—
- Issue or enforce an order.
- Provide more detailed instructions or requirements.
- Instill a general appreciation for the mission.

- Review key points for an operation.
- Ensure participants know the mission objective, their contribution to the operation, problems that may be confronted, and ways to overcome them.

J-11. The mission briefing format is determined by the nature and content of the information being provided. The common approach for a mission briefing is to use the same format as the operation plan or order being briefed. (See appendix E for types of plans and orders.)

STAFF BRIEFING

J-12. Staff briefings are used to inform the commander and staff of the current situation to coordinate and synchronize efforts within the unit. The individual convening the staff briefing sets the briefing agenda. Each staff element presents relevant information from their functional areas. Staff briefings facilitate information exchange, announce decisions, issue directives, or provide guidance. The staff briefing format may include characteristics of the information briefing, decision briefing, and mission briefing.

J-13. Staff briefings commonly include the commander; deputies or assistants; chiefs of staff or executive officers; and coordinating, personal, and special staff officers. Representatives from major subordinate commands may also be present. The chief of staff or executive officer often presides over the briefing. The commander may take an active role during the briefing and normally concludes the briefing.

STEPS OF MILITARY BRIEFING

J-14. These four steps correspond to the operations process and lay the foundation for an effective briefing:

- **Plan**—analyze the situation and prepare a briefing outline.
- **Prepare**—collect information and construct the briefing.
- **Execute**—deliver the briefing.
- **Assess**—follow up as required.

ANALYZE THE SITUATION AND PREPARE A BRIEFING OUTLINE

J-15. Upon receipt of the task to conduct a briefing, the briefer analyzes the situation and determines the—

- Audience.
- Purpose and type.
- Subject.
- Classification.
- Physical facilities and support needed.
- Preparation timeline and schedule.

J-16. Based on the analysis, the briefer assembles a briefing outline. The briefing outline is the plan for the preparation, execution, and follow-up for the briefing. The briefer uses the timeline as a tool to manage preparations for the briefing and refine the briefing as new information becomes available.

J-17. Briefers consider many factors during planning (see figure J-3), including—

- Audience preferences for decision briefings, such as how the decisionmaker wants to see information presented.
- Time available.
- Facilities and briefing aids available.

Analyze the Situation and Prepare a Briefing Outline

1. Audience.
   - What is the size and composition? Single Service or joint? Civilians? Foreign nationals?
   - Who are the ranking members and their official duty positions?
   - How well do they know the subject?
   - Are they generalists or specialists?
   - What are their interests?
   - What is the anticipated reaction?
2. Purpose and Type.
   - Is it an information briefing (to inform)?
   - Is it a decision briefing (to obtain decision)?
   - Is it a mission briefing (to review important details)?
   - Is it a staff briefing (to exchange information)?
3. Subject.
   - What is the specific subject?
   - What is the desired depth of coverage?
   - How much time is allocated?
4. Classification.
   - What is the security classification?
   - Do all attendees meet this classification?
5. Physical Facilities and Support Needed.
   - Where is the briefing to be presented?
   - What support is needed?
6. Preparation Timeline and Schedule.
   - Prepare preliminary outline.
   - Determine requirements for training aids, assistants, and recorders.
   - Schedule rehearsals, facilities, and critiques.
   - Arrange for final review by responsible authority.

Figure J-3. Considerations during planning

J-18. The briefer then estimates suspense times for each task and schedules the preparation effort accordingly. The briefer alerts support personnel and any assistants as soon as possible.

COLLECT INFORMATION AND CONSTRUCT THE BRIEFING

J-19. The briefing construction varies with type and purpose. (See figure J-4.) The analysis of the briefing determines the basis for this. Briefers follow these key steps to prepare a briefing:
- Collect materials needed.
- Prepare first draft.
- Revise first draft and edit.
- Plan use of visual aids.
- Practice.

Collect Information and Construct the Briefing

1. Collect materials needed.
    - Use the Seven-Step Army Problem Solving Method.
    - Research.
    - Become familiar with the subject.
    - Collect authoritative opinions and facts.
2. Prepare First Draft.
    - Prepare draft outline.
    - Include visual aids.
    - Review with appropriate authority.
3. Revise First Draft and Edit.
    - Verify facts, including those that are important and necessary.
    - Include answers to anticipated questions.
    - Refine materials.
4. Plan Use of Visual Aids.
    - Check for simplicity and readability.
5. Practice.
    - Rehearse (with assistants and visual aids).
    - Refine.
    - Isolate key points.
    - Memorize outline.
    - Develop transitions.
    - Anticipate and prepare for possible questions.

Figure J-4. Considerations during preparation

DELIVER THE BRIEFING

J-20. The success of a briefing often depends on how well it is presented. A confident, relaxed, and forceful delivery that is clearly enunciated helps convince the audience. Conciseness, objectivity, and accuracy also characterize good delivery. The briefer should remain aware of the following:

- The basic purpose is to present the subject as directed and ensure the audience understands it.
- Brevity precludes a lengthy introduction or summary.
- Conclusions and recommendations must flow logically from facts and assumptions.

J-21. Interruptions and questions may occur at any point. If and when they occur, briefers answer each question before continuing or indicate that the question will be answered later in the briefing. When briefers answer question later in the briefing, they make specific reference to the earlier question when they introduce material. They anticipate possible questions and are prepared to answer them.

FOLLOW UP AS REQUIRED

J-22. When the briefing is over, the briefer must follow up as required. To ensure understanding, the briefer prepares a memorandum for record (MFR). This MFR records the subject, date, time, and location of the briefing as well as the ranks, names, and positions of audience members. The briefing's content is concisely recorded to help ensure understanding. The briefer records the decision. Recommendations and their approval, disapproval, or approval with modification are recorded as well as instructions or directed actions. Recommendations can include who is to take action. When a decision is involved and any ambiguity exists about the commander's intent, the briefer submits a draft of the MFR for correction before preparing the final document. Lastly, the briefer informs proper authorities. The briefer distributes the final MFR to staff sections and agencies required to act on the decisions or instructions, or whose plans or operations may be affected.

This page intentionally left blank.

Glossary

The glossary lists acronyms and terms with Army or joint definitions, and other selected terms. Where Army and joint definitions are different, *(Army)* follows the term. Terms for which FM 5-0 is the proponent manual (the authority) are marked with an asterisk (*). The proponent manual for other terms is listed in parentheses after the definition.

SECTION I – ACRONYMS

AAR	after action review
ACOS	assistant chief of staff
AO	area of operations
ARFOR	*See* ARFOR under terms.
CCIR	commander's critical information requirement
COA	course of action
COS	chief of staff
CP	command post
CRM	composite risk management
DA	Department of the Army
DS	direct support
EEFI	essential element of friendly information
FM	field manual
FMI	field manual–interim
FRAGO	fragmentary order
G-1	assistant chief of staff, personnel
G-2	assistant chief of staff, intelligence
G-3	assistant chief of staff, operations
G-4	assistant chief of staff, logistics
G-5	assistant chief of staff, plans
G-6	assistant chief of staff, signal
±G-7	assistant chief of staff, inform and influence activities
G-8	assistant chief of staff, financial management
G-9	assistant chief of staff, civil affairs operations
GS	general support
INFOSYS	information systems
IPB	intelligence preparation of the battlefield
IR	information requirement
ISR	intelligence, surveillance, and reconnaissance
MCWP	Marine Corps warfighting publication

MDMP	military decisionmaking process
METT-TC	*See* METT-TC under terms.
MFR	memorandum for record
MGRS	military grid reference system
MOE	measure of effectiveness
MOP	measure of performance
OPLAN	operation plan
OPORD	operation order
ORSA	operations research/systems analysis
PIR	priority information requirements
RDSP	rapid decisionmaking and synchronization process
RFI	request for information
S-1	personnel staff officer
S-2	intelligence staff officer
S-3	operations staff officer
S-4	logistics staff officer
S-5	plans staff officer
S-6	signal staff officer
±S-7	inform and influence activities staff officer
S-9	civil affairs operations staff officer
SOP	standard operating procedure
TLP	troop leading procedures
U.S.	United States
VTC	video-teleconference
WARNO	warning order
XO	executive officer

SECTION II – TERMS

ARFOR

The Army Service component headquarters for a joint task force or a joint and multinational force.

assessment

(Army) The continuous monitoring and evaluation of the current situation, particularly the enemy, and progress of an operation. (FM 3-0)

assumption

(joint) A supposition on the current situation or a presupposition on the future course of events, either or both assumed to be true in the absence of positive proof, necessary to enable the commander in the process of planning to complete an estimate of the situation and make a decision on the course of action. (JP 1-02)

avenue of approach

(joint) An air or ground route of an attacking force of a given size leading to its objective or to key terrain in its path. (JP 2-01.3)

*backbrief

A briefing by subordinates to the commander to review how subordinates intend to accomplish their mission.

battle rhythm

(joint) A deliberate daily cycle of command, staff, and unit activities intended to synchronize current and future operations. (JP 3-33)

±*be-prepared mission

A mission assigned to a unit that might be executed.

*board

(Army) A grouping of predetermined staff representatives with delegated decision authority for a particular purpose or function.

branch

(joint) The contingency options built into the base plan. A branch is used for changing the mission, orientation, or direction of movement of a force to aid success of the operation based on anticipated events, opportunities, or disruptions caused by enemy actions and reactions. (JP 5-0)

campaign plan

(joint) A joint operation plan for a series of related major operations aimed at achieving strategic or operational objectives within a given time and space. (JP 5-0)

civil considerations

The influence of manmade infrastructure, civilian institutions, and attitudes and activities of the civilian leaders, populations, and organizations within an AO on the conduct of military operations. (FM 6-0)

*collaborative planning

Commanders, subordinate commanders, staffs, and other partners sharing information, knowledge, perceptions, ideas, and concepts regardless of physical location throughout the planning process.

combat power

(Army) The total means of destructive, constructive, and information capabilities that a military unit/formation can apply at a given time. Army forces generate combat power by converting potential into effective action. (FM 3-0)

±*command group

The commander and selected staff members who assist the commander in controlling operations away from a command post.

*command post

(Army) A unit headquarters where the commander and staff perform their activities.

*command post cell

A grouping of personnel and equipment organized by warfighting function or by planning horizon to facilitate the exercise of mission command.

commander's intent

(Army) A clear, concise statement of what the force must do and the conditions the force must establish with respect to the enemy, terrain, and civil considerations that represent the desired end state. (FM 3-0)

commander's visualization

The mental process of developing situational understanding, determining a desired end state, and envisioning the broad sequence of events by which the force will achieve that end state. (FM 3-0)

concealment

(joint) Protection from observation and surveillance. (JP 1-02)

concept of operations

(Army) A statement that directs the manner in which subordinate units cooperate to accomplish the mission and establishes the sequence of actions the force will use to achieve the end state. It is normally expressed in terms of decisive, shaping, and sustaining operations. (FM 3-0)

*constraint

(Army) A restriction placed on the command by a higher command. A constraint dictates an action or inaction, thus restricting the freedom of action of a subordinate commander. (joint) A requirement placed on the command by a higher command that dictates an action, thus restricting freedom of action. (JP 5-0)

control measure

A means of regulating forces or warfighting functions. (FM 3-0)

cover

(Army) Protection from the effects of fires. (FM 6-0)

decision point

(joint) A point in space and time when the commander or staff anticipates making a key decision concerning a specific course of action. (JP 5-0)

*decision support matrix

A written record of a war-gamed course of action that describes decision points and associated actions at those decision points.

decision support template

(joint) A combined intelligence and operations graphic based on the results of wargaming. The decision support template depicts decision points, timelines associated with movement of forces and the flow of the operation, and other key items of information required to execute a specific friendly course of action. (JP 2-01.3)

decisive point

(joint) A geographic place, specific key event, critical factor, or function that, when acted upon, allows commanders to gain a marked advantage over an adversary or contribute materially to achieving success. (JP 3-0)

*design

A methodology for applying critical and creative thinking to understand, visualize, and describe complex, ill-structured problems and develop approaches to solve them.

±*early-entry command post

A lead element of a headquarters designed to control operations until the remaining portions of the headquarters are deployed and operational.

*essential task

(Army) A specified or implied task that must be executed to accomplish the mission.

*evaluating

Using criteria to judge progress toward desired conditions and determining why the current degree of progress exists.

exceptional information

Information that would have answered one of the commander's critical information requirements if the requirement for it had been foreseen and stated as one of the commander's critical information requirements. (FM 6-0)

execution

Putting a plan into action by applying combat power to accomplish the mission and using situational understanding to assess progress and make execution and adjustment decisions. (FM 3-0)

*execution matrix

A visual and sequential representation of the critical tasks and responsible organizations by time.

field of fire

The area which a weapon or a group of weapons may cover effectively with fire from a given position. (JP 1-02)

fragmentary order

(joint) An abbreviated form of an operation order issued as needed after an operation order to change or modify that order or to execute a branch or sequel to that order. (JP 5-0)

full spectrum operations

Army forces combine offensive, defensive, and stability or civil support operations simultaneously as part of an interdependent joint force to seize, retain, and exploit the initiative, accepting prudent risk to create opportunities to achieve decisive results. They employ synchronized action—lethal and nonlethal—proportional to the mission and informed by a thorough understanding of all variables of the operational environment. Mission command that conveys intent and an appreciation of all aspects of the situation guides the adaptive use of Army forces. (FM 3-0)

*implied task

(Army) A task that must be performed to accomplish a specified task or mission but is not stated in the higher headquarters' order.

*indicator

(Army) In the context of assessment, an item of information that provides insight into a measure of effectiveness or measure of performance.

information requirements

(Army) All information elements the commander and staff require to successfully conduct operations; that is, all elements necessary to address the factors of METT-TC. (FM 6-0)

key terrain

(joint) Any locality, or area, the seizure or retention of which affords a marked advantage to either combatant. (JP 2-01.3)

leadership

The process of influencing people by providing purpose, direction, and motivation, while operating to accomplish the mission and improving the organization. (FM 6-22)

±*main command post

A facility containing the majority of the staff designed to control current operations, conduct detailed analysis, and plan future operations.

main effort

The designated subordinate unit whose mission at a given point in time is most critical to overall mission success. It is usually weighted with the preponderance of combat power. (FM 3-0)

measure of effectiveness

(joint) A criterion used to assess changes in system behavior, capability, or operational environment that is tied to measuring the attainment of an end state, achievement of an objective, or creation of an effect. (JP 3-0)

measure of performance

(joint) A criterion used to assess friendly actions that is tied to measuring task accomplishment. (JP 3-0)

METT-TC

A memory aid used in two contexts: 1. In the context of information management, the major subject categories into which relevant information is grouped for military operations: mission, enemy, terrain and weather, troops and support available, time available, civil considerations. (FM 6-0) 2. In the context of tactics, major variables considered during mission analysis (mission variables). (FM 3-90)

*military decisionmaking process

An iterative planning methodology that integrates the activities of the commander, staff, subordinate headquarters, and other partners to understand the situation and mission; develop and compare courses of action; decide on a course of action that best accomplishes the mission; and produce an operation plan or order for execution.

mission

(joint) The task, together with the purpose, that clearly indicates the action to be taken and the reason therefore. (JP 1-02)

±mission command

The exercise of authority and direction by the commander using mission orders to enable disciplined initiative within the commander's intent to empower agile and adaptive leaders in the conduct of full spectrum operations. It is commander-led and blends the art of command and the science of control to integrate the warfighting functions to accomplish the mission. (FM 3-0)

±mission command networks and systems

The coordinated application of personnel, networks, procedures, equipment and facilities, knowledge management, and information management systems essential for the commander to conduct operations. (FM 3-0)

*mission narrative

The expression of the operational approach for a specified mission.

mission orders

A technique for developing orders that emphasizes to subordinates the results to be attained, not how they are to achieve them. It provides maximum freedom of action in determining how to best accomplish assigned missions. (FM 3-0)

mission statement

(joint) A short sentence or paragraph that describes the organization's essential task (or tasks) and purpose—a clear statement of the action to be taken and the reason for doing so. The mission statement contains the elements of who, what, when, where, and why, but seldom specifies how. (JP 5-0)

*monitoring

(Army) Continuous observation of those conditions relevant to the current operation.

*nested concepts

A planning technique to achieve unity of purpose whereby each succeeding echelon's concept of operations is aligned by purpose with the higher echelons' concept of operations.

objective

(Army) A location on the ground used to orient operations, phase operations, facilitate changes of direction, and provide for unity of effort. (FM 3-90)

observation

The condition of weather and terrain that permits a force to see the friendly, enemy, and neutral personnel and systems, and key aspects of the environment. (FM 6-0)

obstacle

Any obstruction designed or employed to disrupt, fix, turn, or block the movement of an opposing force, and to impose additional losses in personnel, time, and equipment on the opposing force. Obstacles can exist naturally or can be man-made, or can be a combination of both. (JP 3-15)

±*on-order mission

A mission to be executed at an unspecified time.

operation order

(joint) A directive issued by a commander to subordinate commanders for the purpose of effecting the coordinated execution of an operation. (JP 5-0)

operation plan

(joint) Any plan for the conduct of military operations prepared in response to actual and potential contingencies. (JP 5-0)

operational approach

A broad conceptualization of the general actions that will produce the conditions that define the desired end state.

operational art

(joint) The application of creative imagination by commanders and staffs—supported by their skill, knowledge, and experience—to design strategies, campaigns, and major operations and organize and employ military forces. Operational art integrates ends, ways, and means across the levels of war. (JP 3-0)

operational environment

(joint) A composite of the conditions, circumstances, and influences that affect the employment of capabilities and bear on the decisions of the commander. (JP 3-0)

operational initiative

The setting or dictating the terms of action throughout an operation. (FM 3-0)

operational limitation

(joint) An action required or prohibited by higher authority, such as a constraint or a restraint, and other restrictions that limit the commander's freedom of action, such as diplomatic agreements, rules of engagement, political and economic conditions in affected countries, and host nation issues. (JP 5-0)

operations process

The major mission command activities performed during operations: planning, preparing, executing, and continuously assessing the operation. The commander drives the operations process through leadership. (FM 3-0)

order

(joint) A communication, written, oral, or by signal, which conveys instructions from a superior to a subordinate. (JP 1-02)

*parallel planning

Two or more echelons planning for the same operation nearly simultaneously.

±persistent conflict

The protracted confrontation among state, nonstate, and individual actors that are increasingly willing to use violence to achieve their political and ideological ends. (FM 3-0)

phase

(Army) A planning and execution tool used to divide an operation in duration or activity. A change in phase usually involves a change of mission, task organization, or rules of engagement. Phasing helps in planning and controlling and may be indicated by time, distance, terrain, or an event. (FM 3-0)

±*P-hour (airborne operations)

In airborne operations, the specific hour on D-day at which a parachute assault commences with the exit of the first Soldier from an aircraft over a designated drop zone.

planning

The process by which commanders (and the staff, if available) translate the commander's visualization into a specific course of action for preparation and execution, focusing on the expected results. (FM 3-0)

*planning horizon

A point in time commanders use to focus the organization's planning efforts to shape future events.

preparation

> Activities performed by units to improve their ability to execute an operation. Preparation includes, but is not limited to, plan refinement; rehearsals; intelligence, surveillance, and reconnaissance; coordination; inspections; and movement. (FM 3-0)

*priority of support

> A priority set by the commander to ensure a subordinate unit has support in accordance with its relative importance to accomplish the mission.

*rehearsal

> A session in which a staff or unit practices expected actions to improve performance during execution.

restraint

> (joint) Requirement placed on the command by a higher command that prohibits an action, thus restricting freedom of action. (JP 5-0)

*running estimate

> The continuous assessment of the current situation used to determine if the current operation is proceeding according to the commander's intent and if planned future operations are supportable.

sequel

> (joint) A major operation that follows the current major operation. In a single major operation, a sequel is the next phase. Plans for a sequel are based on the possible outcomes (success, stalemate, or defeat) associated with the current operation. (JP 5-0)

situational understanding

> The product of applying analysis and judgment to relevant information to determine the relationships among the mission variables to facilitate decisionmaking. (FM 3-0)

*specified task

> (Army) A task specifically assigned to a unit by its higher headquarters.

*staff section

> A grouping of staff members by area of expertise under a coordinating, special, or personal staff officer.

supporting plan

> (joint) An operation plan prepared by a supporting commander, a subordinate commander, or an agency to satisfy the requests or requirements of the supported commander's plan. (JP 5-0)

*synchronization matrix

> A tool the staff uses to record the results of war-gaming and helps them synchronize a course of action across time, space, and purpose in relationship to potential enemy and civil actions.

±*tactical command post

> A facility containing a tailored portion of a unit headquarters designed to control portions of an operation for a limited time.

task

> A clearly defined and measurable activity accomplished by individuals and organizations. (FM 7-0)

task organization

> (Army) A temporary grouping of forces designed to accomplish a particular mission. (FM 3-0)

task-organizing

> (Army) The act of designing an operating force, support staff, or logistic package of specific size and composition to meet a unique task or mission. Characteristics to examine when task-organizing the force include, but are not limited to: training, experience, equipage, sustainability, operating environment, enemy threat, and mobility. For Army forces, it includes allocating available assets to subordinate commanders and establishing their command and support relationships. (FM 3-0)

*terrain management

The process of allocating terrain by establishing areas of operation, designating assembly areas, and specifying locations for units and activities to deconflict activities that might interfere with each other.

*troop leading procedures

A dynamic process used by small-unit leaders to analyze a mission, develop a plan, and prepare for an operation.

troop movement

The movement of troops from one place to another by any available means. (FM 3-90)

understanding

Knowledge that has been synthesized and had judgment applied to it in a specific situation to comprehend the situation's inner relationships. (FM 6-0)

unity of effort

(joint) Coordination and cooperation toward common objectives, even if the participants are not necessarily part of the same command or organization—the product of successful unified action. (JP 1)

variance

A difference between the actual situation during an operation and what the plan forecasted the situation would be at that time or event. (FM 6-0)

warning order

(joint) A preliminary notice of an order or action that is to follow. (JP 3-33)

*working group

(Army) A grouping of predetermined staff representatives who meet to provide analysis, coordinate, and provide recommendations for a particular purpose or function.

This page intentionally left blank.

References

Field manuals and selected joint publications are listed by new number followed by old number.

REQUIRED PUBLICATIONS

These documents must be available to intended users of this publication.

FM 1-02 (101-5-1). *Operational Terms and Graphics*. 21 September 2004.

JP 1-02. *Department of Defense Dictionary of Military and Associated Terms*. 12 April 2001.

RELATED PUBLICATIONS

These documents contain relevant supplemental information.

JOINT AND DEPARTMENT OF DEFENSE PUBLICATIONS

Most joint publications are available online: <http://www.dtic.mil/doctrine/new_pubs/jointpub.htm.>

JP 1. *Doctrine for the Armed Forces of the United States*. 02 May 2007.

JP 2-01.3. *Joint Intelligence Preparation of the Operational Environment*. 16 June 2009.

JP 3-0. *Joint Operations*. 17 September 2006.

JP 3-02. *Amphibious Operations*. 10 August 2009.

JP 3-08. *Interagency, Intergovernmental Organization, and Nongovernmental Organization Coordination During Joint Operations*. 17 March 2006.

JP 3-15. *Barriers, Obstacles, and Mine Warfare for Joint Operations*. 26 April 2007.

JP 3-28. *Civil Support*. 14 September 2007.

JP 3-31. *Command and Control for Joint Land Operations*. 23 March 2004.

JP 3-33. *Joint Task Force Headquarters*. 16 February 2007.

JP 5-0. *Joint Operation Planning*. 26 December 2006.

ARMY PUBLICATIONS

Most Army doctrinal publications are available online: <https://akocomm.us.army.mil/usapa/doctrine/Active_FM.html>. Army regulations are produced only in electronic media. Most are available online: < http://www.army.mil/usapa/index.html>.

±AR 25-55. *The Department of the Army Freedom of Information Act Program*. 1 November 1997.

AR 380-5. *Department of the Army Information Security Program*. 31 October 2000.

AR 380-10. *Foreign Disclosure and Contacts with Foreign Representatives*. 22 July 2005.

FM 2-0. *Intelligence*. 17 May 2004.

FM 2-01.3. *Intelligence Preparation of the Battlefield/Battlespace*. 15 October 2009.

±FM 3-0. *Operations*. 27 February 2008 (including Change 1).

FM 3-05.401. *Civil Affairs Tactics, Techniques, and Procedures*. 5 July 2007.

FM 3-07. *Stability Operations*. 6 October 2008.

FM 3-24. *Counterinsurgency*. 15 December 2006.

FM 3-37. *Protection*. 30 September 2009.

FM 3-52 (FM 100-103). *Army Airspace Command and Control in a Combat Zone*. 1 August 2002.

FM 3-60 (FM 6-20-10). *The Targeting Process*. 26 November 2010.

FM 3-90. *Tactics*. 4 July 2001.

FM 5-19. *Composite Risk Management*. 21 August 2006.

FM 6-0. *Mission Command: Command and Control of Army Forces*. 11 August 2003.

FM 6-01.1. *Knowledge Management Section*. 29 August 2008.

FM 6-22 (FM 22-100). *Army Leadership*. 12 October 2006.

FM 7-0. *Training for Full Spectrum Operations*. 12 December 2008.

FM 7-15. *The Army Universal Task List*. 27 February 2009.

±TC 2-01 (FMI 2-01). *Intelligence, Surveillance, and Reconnaissance Synchronization*. 22 September 2010.

OTHER PUBLICATIONS

MCWP 5-1. *Marine Corps Planning Process*. 5 January 2000.

RECOMMENDED PUBLICATIONS

This bibliography is a tool for Army leaders to help them increase their knowledge of the exercise of mission command. Reading what others have written provides a foundation that leaders can use to assess situations and make appropriate decisions. The books and articles that follow are not the only good ones on these subjects. The field is vast and rich. They are, however, some of the more useful readings for Soldiers.

WAR AND THE NATURE OF OPERATIONS

Ames, Roger T., trans. *Sun-tzu: The Art of Warfare*. New York: Ballantine Books, a division of Random House, Inc., 1993.

Arreguín-Toft, Ivan. *How the Weak Win Wars: A Theory of Asymmetric Conflict*. Cambridge: Cambridge University Press, 2005.

Biddle, Stephen. *Military Power: Explaining Victory and Defeat in Modern Battle*. Princeton: Princeton University Press, 2004.

Corbett, Julian. *Some Principles of Maritime Strategy*. Annapolis, MD: Naval Institute Press, 1988.

Joint Doctrine Note 1/09. The Significance of Culture to the Military. Shrivenham, England: The Development, Concepts and Doctrine Centre, 2009.

Kalyvas, Stathis N. *The Logic of Violence in Civil War*. Cambridge, MA: Cambridge University Press, 2006.

Kilcullen, David. *The Accidental Guerrilla: Fighting Small Wars in the Midst of a Big One*. Oxford: Oxford University Press, 2009.

Lawrence, T. E. *Seven Pillars of Wisdom: a Triumph*. London: Penguin Books, 1983.

Liddell Hart, Sir Basil. *Thoughts on War*. London: Faber & Faber, 1944.

Mao, Tse-tung. *Selected Military Writings of Mao Tse-tung*. Beijing: Foreign Language Press, 1967.

McFeely, Mary Drake, William S. McFeely, and Richard B. Russell, eds. *Ulysses S. Grant: Memoirs and Selected Letters: Personal Memoirs of U.S. Grant/Selected Letters 1839-1865*. New York: Library of America, 1990.

Naveh, Shimon. *In Pursuit of Military Excellence: The Evolution of Operational Theory*. London: Routledge, 1997.

Slim, Field Marshal Viscount. *Defeat into Victory: Battling Japan in Burma and India, 1942-1945*. London: Macmillan-PaperMac, 1986.

Spiller, Roger J. *Sharp Corners: Urban Operations at Century's End*. Fort Leavenworth, KS: U.S. Army Command and General Staff College Press, 2000.

von Clausewitz, Carl. *On War*. Michael Howard and Peter Paret, eds. and trans. New York: Alfred A. Knopf, 1993.

COMMAND

Allard, Kenneth. *Command, Control, and the Common Defense*, rev. ed. Washington, DC: National Defense University Press, 1996.

Coakley, Thomas. *Command and Control for War and Peace*. Washington, DC: National Defense University Press, 1992.

Cohen, Eliot A. and John Gooch. *Military Misfortunes: The Anatomy of Failure in War*. New York: Anchor, 1991.

Fuller, J. F. C. *Generalship: Its Diseases and Their Cure*. Harrisburg, PA: Military Service Publishing Co., 1936.

Heifetz, Ronald A. *Leadership Without Easy Answers*. Cambridge, MA: Harvard University Press, 1994.

McCann, Carol and Ross Pigeau, eds. *The Human in Command: Exploring the Modern Military Experience*. New York: Kluwer Academic Press, 2000.

Snyder, Frank M. *Command and Control: The Literature and Commentaries*. Washington, DC: National Defense University Press, 1993.

van Creveld, Martin. *Command in War*. Cambridge, MA: Harvard University Press, 1987.

DECISIONMAKING

Gilovich, Thomas, Dale Griffin and Daniel Kahneman, eds. *Heuristics and Biases: The Psychology of Intuitive Judgment*. New York: Cambridge University Press, 2002.

Greenfield, Kent Roberts, ed. *Command Decisions*. Washington, DC: Center of Military History, 2000.

Hart, Paul 't, Eric K. Stern, and Bengt Sundelius, eds. *Beyond Groupthink: Political Group Dynamics and Foreign Policy-making*. Ann Arbor, MI: University of Michigan, 1997.

Janis, Irving L. and Leon Mann. *Decision Making: A Psychological Analysis of Conflict, Choice, and Commitment*. New York: The Free Press, a division of Macmillan Publishing Company, 1977.

Kahneman, Daniel and Amos Tversky. "Part I: Introduction–Judgment Under Uncertainty: Heuristics and Biases." In *Judgment Under Uncertainty: Heuristics and Biases*, edited by Daniel Kahneman, Paul Slovic, and Amos Tversky. New York: Cambridge University Press, 1982.

Klein, Gary. *Sources of Power: How People Make Decisions*. Cambridge, MA: The MIT Press, 1998.

Leedom, Dr. Dennis K., James Murphy, Bill Killam, and Dr. Leonard Adelman. *Final Report: Cognitive Engineering of the Human-Computer Interface for ABCS*. Andover, MA: Dynamics Research Corporation, 1998.

Neustadt, Richard E. and Ernest R. May. *Thinking in Time: The Uses of History for Decision Makers*. New York: Free Press, 1986.

Simon, Herbert A. *Administrative Behavior: A Study of Decision-Making Processes in Administrative Organization*. New York: Free Press, 1997.

_____. *The Sciences of the Artificial, 3d ed*. Cambridge, MA: The MIT Press, 1996.

Turner, Marlene E. and Anthony R. Pratkanis. "Twenty-Five Years of Groupthink Theory and Research: Lessons from the Evaluation of a Theory." *Organizational Behavior and Human Decision Processes* 73 (February–March 1998): 105–115.

PLANNING AND PROBLEM SOLVING

Dörner, Dietrich. *The Logic of Failure: Why Things Go Wrong and What We Can Do to Make Them Right*. New York: Metropolitan Books, 1996.

Gole, Henry G. *The Road to Rainbow: Army Planning for Global War, 1934-1940*. Annapolis, MD: Naval Institute Press, 2003.

Kirkpatrick, Charles E. *An Unknown Future and a Doubtful Present: Writing the Victory Plan of 1941*. Washington, DC: Center of Military History, 1990.

Mintzberg, Henry. *The Rise and Fall of Strategic Planning*: *Reconceiving Roles for Planning, Plans, Planners*. New York: Free Press, 1994.

Rein, Martin and Donald A. Schön. "Frame-Reflective Policy Discourse." In *Social Sciences and Modern States: National Experiences and Theoretical Crossroads*, edited by Peter Wagner, Carol H. Weiss, Björn Wittrock, and Hellmut Wollmans. New York: Cambridge University Press, 1991.

Rittel, Horst W. J. "On the Planning Crisis: Systems Analysis of the 'First and Second Generations'." *Bedriftsøkonomen* 8 (1972): 390–396.

Rittel, Horst W. J. and Melvin M. Weber. "Dilemmas in a General Theory of Planning." *Policy Sciences* 4 (1973): 155–169.

DESIGN

Banach, Stefan J. "Educating by Design: Preparing Leaders for a Complex World." *Military Review* (March–April 2009): 96–104.

Banach, Stefan J. and Alex Ryan. "The Art of Design: A Design Methodology." *Military Review* (March–April 2009): 105–115.

Berger, Warren. *Glimmer: How Design Can Transform Your Life, and Maybe Even the World*. New York: Penguin Press, 2009.

Brown, Tim. *Change by Design: How Design Thinking Transforms Organizations and Inspires Innovation*. New York: Harper Business, 2009.

Checkland, Peter and John Poulter. *Learning for Action: A Short Definitive Account of Soft Systems Methodology and Its Use for Practitioner, Teachers and Students*. Hoboken, NJ: Wiley, 2006.

Cross, Nigel. "Forty Years of Design Research." *Design Research Quarterly* (January 2007): 3–5.

Denning, Stephen. *The Leader's Guide to Storytelling: Mastering the Art and Discipline of Business Narrative*. San Francisco: Jossey-Bass, a Wiley imprint, 2005.

Dodge, Jennifer, Sonia M. Ospina, and Erica Gabrielle Foldy. "Integrating Rigor and Relevance in Public Administration Scholarship: The Contribution of Narrative Inquiry." *Public Administration Review* (May/June 2005): 286–300.

Jones, J. Christopher. *Design Methods: Seeds of Human Futures*. New York: Wiley-Interscience, 1970.

Kem, Jack D. *Design: Tools of the Trade*. Fort Leavenworth, KS: U.S. Army Command and General Staff College, U.S. Army Combined Arms Center, 2009.

Lawson, Bryan. *How Designers Think: The Design Process Demystified*. Boston: Architectural Press, 1997.

Ospina, Sonia M. and Jennifer Dodge. "It's About Time: Catching Method Up to Meaning—The Usefulness of Narrative Inquiry in Public Administration Research." *Public Administration Review* (March 2005): 143–157.

Schön, Donald A. *The Reflective Practitioner: How Professionals Think in Action*. New York: Basic Books, 1983.

Schwarz, Roger, Anne Davidson, Peg Carlson, and Sue McKinney. *The Skilled Facilitator Fieldbook: Tips, Tools, and Tested Methods for Consultants, Facilitators, Managers, Trainers, and Coaches*. San Francisco: Jossey-Bass, 2005.

CRITICAL THINKING

Archer, Margaret, Roy Bhaskar, Andrew Collier, Tony Lawson, and Alan Norrie, eds. *Critical Realism: Essential Readings*. New York: Routledge, 1998.

Checkland, Peter. *Systems Thinking, Systems Practice*. New York: J. Wiley, 1981.

Gharajedaghi, Jamshid. *Systems Thinking: Managing Chaos and Complexity: A Platform for Designing Business Architecture*. Boston: Butterworth-Heinemann, 1999.

Paul, Richard and Linda Elder. *Critical Thinking: Tools for Taking Charge of Your Learning and Your Life*. Upper Saddle River, NJ: Prentice Hall, 2001.

Plato. *Theaetetus*, translated by Robin A. H. Waterfield. New York: Viking Penguin, 1987.

Vasquez, John A. "The Post-Positivist Debate: Reconstructing Scientific Enquiry and International Relations Theory After Enlightenment's Fall." In *International Relations Theory Today*, edited by Ken Booth and Steve Smith. University Park, PA: The Pennsylvania University Press, 1995.

White, Hayden. *The Content of the Form: Narrative Discourse and Historical Representation.* Baltimore, MD: Johns Hopkins University Press, 1987.

_____. *Tropics of Discourse: Essays in Cultural Criticism.* Baltimore, MD: Johns Hopkins University Press, 1978.

COMPLEXITY

Axelrod, Robert and Michael D. Cohen. *Harnessing Complexity: Organizational Implications of a Scientific Frontier.* New York: Free Press, 1999.

Bar-Yam, Yaneer. *Making Things Work: Solving Complex Problems in a Complex World.* Cambridge, MA: Knowledge Press, 2004.

Beyerchen, Alan. "Clausewitz, Nonlinearity and the Unpredictability of War." *International Security* (Winter 1992): 59–90.

DeLanda, Manuel. *A New Philosophy of Society: Assemblage Theory and Social Complexity.* New York: Continuum, 2006.

Holland, John H. *Hidden Order: How Adaptation Builds Complexity.* Reading, MA: Addison-Wesley Publishing Co., 1995.

Waldrop, M. Mitchell. *Complexity: The Emerging Science at the Edge of Order and Chaos.* New York: Simon and Schuster, 1992.

LEARNING ORGANIZATIONS

Hatch, Mary Jo. *Organization Theory: Modern, Symbolic, and Postmodern Perspectives.* New York: Oxford University Press, 1997.

Schön, Donald A. *Educating the Reflective Practitioner: Toward a New Design for Teaching and Learning in the Professions.* San Francisco: Jossey-Bass, 1987.

Senge, Peter M. *The Fifth Discipline: The Art and Practice of the Learning Organization.* New York: Currency Books, published by Doubleday, a division of Random House, 1990.

Weick, Karl E. *Making Sense of the Organization.* Malden, MA: Blackwell Publishing, 2001.

_____. *Sensemaking in Organizations.* Thousand Oaks, CA: Sage Publications, 1995.

ASSESSMENT

Fiss, Peer C. and Paul M. Hirsch. "The Discourse of Globalization: Framing and Sensemaking of an Emerging Concept." *American Sociological Review* (February 2005): 29–52.

Jullien, Francois. *A Treatise on Efficacy: Between Western and Chinese Thinking*, translated by Janet Lloyd. Honolulu: University of Hawai'i Press, 2004.

Kuhn, Thomas S. *The Structure of Scientific Revolutions, 3d ed.* Chicago: University of Chicago Press, 1996.

Pearl, Judea. "Epilogue: The Art and Science of Cause and Effect." In *Causality: Models, Reasoning, and Inference.* New York: Cambridge University Press, 2000.

Quade, E. S., ed. *Analysis for Military Decisions.* Chicago: Rand McNally, 1964.

Salmon, Wesley C. *Causality and Explanation.* New York: Oxford University Press, 1998.

Wendt, Alexander. *Social Theory of International Politics*: New York: Cambridge University Press, 1999.

SOURCES USED

This source is quoted in this publication.

Eisenhower, Dwight D. "Remarks at the National Defense Executive Reserve Conference,"
14 November 1957, edited by John T. Woolley and Gerhard Peters, *The American Presidency Project* [online]. Santa Barbara, CA. Available from World Wide Web:
<http://www.presidency.ucsb.edu/ws/?pid=10951> (accessed 26 February 2010).

PRESCRIBED FORMS

None

REFERENCED FORMS

DA forms are available on the APD website: <www.apd.army.mil>.

DA Form 2028. *Recommended Changes to Publications and Blank Forms.*

Index

Entries are by paragraph number.

Entries are by paragraph number.

Entries are by paragraph number.

Entries are by paragraph number.

Entries are by paragraph number.

Entries are by paragraph number.

Entries are by paragraph number.

Entries are by paragraph number.

Entries are by paragraph number.

Entries are by paragraph number.

No index entries found.

FM 5-0
26 March 2010

By order of the Secretary of the Army:

GEORGE W. CASEY, JR.
General, United States Army
Chief of Staff

Official:

JOYCE E. MORROW
Administrative Assistant to the
Secretary of the Army
1006104

DISTRIBUTION:

Active Army, the Army National Guard, and the United States Army Reserve: To be distributed in accordance with the initial distribution number 110412, requirements for FM 5-0.

www.ingramcontent.com/pod-product-compliance
Lightning Source LLC
Chambersburg PA
CBHW081407270326
41931CB00016B/3403